20.00

BS
2650.2
.48
1996

THEOLOGY AND ETHICS
IN PAUL AND HIS INTERPRETERS

Victor Paul Furnish

THEOLOGY AND ETHICS
IN PAUL AND HIS INTERPRETERS

Essays in Honor of Victor Paul Furnish

EDITED BY

EUGENE H. LOVERING, JR.
JERRY L. SUMNEY

Colorado Christian University
Library
180 S. Garrison
Lakewood, Colorado 80226

Abingdon Press
Nashville

THEOLOGY AND ETHICS
IN PAUL AND HIS INTERPRETERS

Copyright © 1996 by Abingdon Press

All Rights Reserved

No part of this work may be reproduced or transmitted in any form or by any means, electronic or mechanical, including photocopying and recording, or by means of any information storage or retrieval system, except as may be expressly permitted by the 1976 Copyright Act or in writing from the publisher. Requests for permission should be addressed in writing to Abingdon Press, 201 Eighth Avenue, South, Nashville, TN 37203, USA.

Library of Congress Cataloging in Publication Data

Theology and ethics in Paul and his interpreters : essays in honor of
  Victor Paul Furnish / edited by Eugene H. Lovering, Jr., Jerry L. Sumney.
       p.   cm
   Includes bibliographical references.
   ISBN 0-687-00767-4 (alk. paper)
    1. Bible. N.T. Epistles of Paul—Criticism, interpretation, etc.
2. Bible. N.T. Epistles of Paul—Criticism, interpretation, etc.—
History.   3. Paul, the Apostle, Saint.   I. Furnish, Victor Paul.
II. Lovering, Eugene H., 1952–   .   III. Sumney, Jerry L.
BS2650.2.T48   1996
241'.0412'092—dc20   96-31336
                                                                         CIP

Unless otherwise noted, all Scripture quotations are the authors' own or from the New Revised Standard Version Bible, Copyright © 1989 by the Division of Christian Education of the National Council of the Churches of Christ in the USA. Used by permission.

This book is printed on acid-free paper.
96 97 98 99 00 01 02 03 04 — 10 9 8 7 6 5 4 3 2 1
Manufactured in the United States of America

Contents

Contributors

Paul J. Achtemeier
Herbert Worth and Annie H. Jackson Professor of Biblical Interpretation, Union Theological Seminary in Virginia

Harold W. Attridge
Professor of New Testament and Christian Origins, and Dean of the College of Arts and Letters, University of Notre Dame

William Baird
Professor Emeritus of New Testament, Brite Divinity School, Texas Christian University

C. K. Barrett
Professor of Divinity, Emeritus, University of Durham

Jouette M. Bassler
Professor of New Testament, Perkins School of Theology, Southern Methodist University

C. Clifton Black
Associate Professor of New Testament, Perkins School of Theology, Southern Methodist University

James D. G. Dunn
Lightfoot Professor of Divinity, University of Durham

Beverly Roberts Gaventa
Helen H. P. Manson Professor of New Testament Literature and Exegesis, Princeton Theological Seminary

Richard B. Hays
Professor of New Testament, The Divinity School, Duke University

Morna D. Hooker
The Lady Margaret's Professor, The University of Cambridge

Leander E. Keck
Winkley Professor of Biblical Theology, Yale Divinity School

Andreas Lindemann
Professor of New Testament, Kirchliche Hochschule Bethel,
Bielefeld

Eduard Lohse
Landesbischof (retired), Göttingen

J. Louis Martyn
Edward Robinson Professor Emeritus of Biblical Theology, Union
Theological Seminary, New York

Wayne A. Meeks
Woolsey Professor of Biblical Studies, Yale University

Schubert M. Ogden
University Distinguished Professor of Theology Emeritus, Perkins
School of Theology, Southern Methodist University

J. Paul Sampley
Boston University

Robin Scroggs
Professor of New Testament, Union Theological Seminary, New York

D. Moody Smith
George Washington Ivey Professor of New Testament, The Divinity
School, Duke University

Wendell L. Willis
Associate Professor of Bible, Abilene Christian University

Preface

These essays, presented in honor of Victor Paul Furnish on the occasion of his sixty-fifth birthday, are intended to relate to two primary spheres of his professional life which he has purposefully and gracefully held together—the advancement of knowledge, particularly the understanding of Paul and his letters, and seminary education. Professor Furnish's work on Paul's ethics has influenced and shaped American thought in the field throughout the past three decades. His *Theology and Ethics in Paul*, whose title we now acknowledge in the title of this book, remained in print for a quarter century, sparking interest in Pauline ethics and serving as a touchstone for further studies. And his subsequent books and articles (such as *The Love Command in the New Testament* and *The Moral Teaching of Paul*) have been equally influential. Beyond Pauline ethics, Professor Furnish's exegetical acumen has produced what is widely regarded as the standard English-language commentary on 2 Corinthians for this generation. He has also given leadership to recent explorations of what it means to speak of Paul's theology and of what that theology might be. He has served as editor of the *Journal of Biblical Literature* and as President of the Society of Biblical Literature. And he has carried out all his duties with the kind of academic care and professional reserve which have earned him the highest respect among his peers.

While contributing in the above ways to the discipline of biblical studies, Professor Furnish has never forgotten his primary commitment to the education of pastors. His more than thirty-five years at Perkins School of Theology have been spent largely with seminary rather than graduate students. Although he was presented on various occasions with opportunities in which the balance between these two types of students would have changed, Professor Furnish chose to remain in the seminary to which he received his first teaching appointment. There, he has approached the task of preparing ministers to read Paul, interpret the gospel, and serve the needs of their congregations with the utmost seriousness. His teaching style is a lesson in both helping and prodding students to develop their capacities for interpreting the New Testament. His patient persistence with the less disciplined among his students and his challenge and encouragement to the more energetic are exemplary.

These comments would be woefully deficient if we neglected to mention Victor Furnish's service to the church in areas beyond the training of ministers. Himself an ordained United Methodist clergyperson, he has found time, throughout his career, to accept a wide range of speaking opportunities as well as positions—some of them uncomfortably controversial—on the church's official study groups and committees. In all cases, whether received eagerly or with suspicion (or even decided hostility), he has sought to walk a course of truth and openness, sharing the fruits of his scholarship and calling the church to faithfulness to the gospel as he understands it.

This volume of essays, then, seeks to honor Victor Furnish's commitments by advancing the knowledge of Paul's theology and ethics and by addressing questions of how the apostle's thought can properly be interpreted and received in the modern day. With these studies, Vic's colleagues, students, and friends, celebrate his sixty-fifth birthday and wish him—and the academy and church he serves—well.

A few words about format. The essays have been written to be accessible not only to scholars but also to seminary students, pastors, and general readers. Hence, for example, foreign-language materials have generally been translated into English even where, for accuracy, the original also appears. The abbreviations used in the footnotes are fairly standard and may be found in the common reference sources (including *The Chicago Manual of Style*, the *Journal of Biblical Literature* "Instructions for Contributors," and the *Theological Dictionary of the New Testament*). In many cases, contributors to this volume have rendered their own translations of biblical texts, but where a published version has been used, it has—unless otherwise indicated—been the *New Revised Standard Version Bible*.

Finally, the editors wish to express thanks to the publication team at Abingdon Press, and especially to Rex Matthews, Senior Academic Books Editor, for taking on this project and for assisting, patiently enduring, and carefully overseeing respective stages of the preparation process. Happily, the Press's Product Manager, Vickie E. Pittard, is another of Victor Furnish's former students, and we are grateful for her and her co-workers' care in pursuing the multitude of details connected with the book's final production. Abingdon has, over the years, played a part in several of Victor Furnish's publication projects, and we are pleased that they were able to "conspire" with us on this one as well.

Jerry L. Sumney
Eugene H. Lovering, Jr.

The Accountable Self

Leander E. Keck

Were Christian ethics, whether as a basic Christian concern or as a discipline, to allow itself to be instructed more deeply by Paul, its primary question might well not be, What must/ought/should/may I do? but rather, To whom am I accountable and for what?

The Apostle does not, to be sure, discuss accountability as a theme. He simply assumes that it is an inescapable aspect of human existence in general and of Christian existence in particular. He does not find it necessary to argue for it; instead, he can argue from it, appealing to some aspect of it in order to clarify and undergird something else. Apart from the possible exception of the letter to Philemon, some use of the accountability theme appears in each of the seven uncontested letters, though demonstrating this would exceed both the bounds of this essay and its purpose—to substantiate the thesis stated in the foregoing paragraph.

To do that, it is necessary to begin by doing what the Apostle did not do—clarify the concept itself (I). Then, after looking at key passages which reflect or express the concept (II), the essay will reflect on some differences between the deciding self and the accountable self for the Christian life (III). Venturing such reflections is appropriate for this essay, since Professor Furnish's own work has not eschewed relating Paul to the moral life of the Christian community.

I. Accountability

Nouns or pronouns that are modified by adjectives formed by adding the suffix "~able" to verbs (like teach) acquire the force of the verb. Thus a teachable student is one who is open to being taught. Similarly, to be accountable is to be expected legitimately to give an account, an explanation or a justification for a deed or attitude. Adding the suffix "~ity" to the adjective forms an abstract noun expressing the quality or state of the adjective, as in teachability or accountability.[1] The abstract noun allows us to discuss the concept as such.

---

[1] "Accountability" is not a New Testament term; the idea is there, expressed in various ways, such as giving an account (a *logos*, as in Rom 14:12; Heb 4:13; 13:17; 1 Pet 4:5). For

Accountability has much in common with "responsibility," and some-times we use them interchangeably, as in "accountable to/for" and "responsible to/for." They are not synonymous, however, for while we would say, "He is a responsible citizen" we would not say, "He is an accountable citizen." The subtle difference appears also in the fact that while we might urge someone to take responsibility for a project, we would not urge her to take accountability for it. Taking responsibility connotes a forward look to what is to be undertaken and so implies accountability; accountability, on the other hand, implies existing responsibility and so connotes a backward look to what has already been done. The responsible self, we assume, takes commitment seriously and acts judiciously; the accountable self is vulnerable to a verdict by someone authorized to render it.

Accountability implies, therefore, an acknowledged authority struc-ture in which the self knows that it owes an account and expects a response. This account-giving differs from reciprocal reporting of activities between equals (e.g., business partners). If the authority structure is accepted, accountability is deemed to be neither irrational, onerous nor intolerable. Some accountability structures are entered voluntarily, as when one enlists in the army; others are givens that are discovered, as when a child discovers that having parents entails being accountable to them for one's behavior.

Accountability toward a person differs from accountability oriented toward an impersonal system, law, ideal, or cause. The difference between them deserves thorough analysis, though obviously that cannot be undertaken here, where it must suffice to note that only the person to whom one is accountable can forgive failure and rehabilitate the failed person.

By no means have these terse paragraphs delineated adequately the in-built logic of accountability. Still, enough may have been sketched to provide a sense of what an examination of some Pauline passages will disclose, and to understand afresh the implicit theological rationale of what will be found. Indeed, each of the foregoing formal, abstractly stated aspects of accountability is expressed concretely or assumed in the Apostle's letters.

"accountable" (ὑπόδικος in Rom 3:19), Jas 2:10 uses ἔνοχος. In the Synoptics, the motif is expressed in the parables concerning the slave or steward who is called to account; see Matt 24:43–51 par.; Luke 16:1–9; Matt 25:14–30 par.

2

II. Accountability in Paul

Only once does Paul use the semi-technical, legal term ὑπόδικος, commonly rendered "accountable," namely in Rom 3:19 where he brings to a head his indictment of humanity by saying, "And we know that whatever the law says it says to those in the [jurisdiction of] the law, so that every mouth may be shut and the whole world become accountable to God" (my tr.). According to Paul, Gentiles lacking Moses are as accountable to God as Jews, because by doing "the things of the law" (of Moses) they show that "what the law requires is written in their hearts"; this is confirmed by the phenomenon of conscience which either condemns or defends them "on the day when . . . God . . . will judge the secret thoughts of all" (Rom 2:14–16). This will be the "day of wrath when God's righteous judgment will be revealed" (Rom 2:5).

In Rom 2:1–11, Paul writes repeatedly about God's judgment. Like his scripture, and especially the apocalyptic tradition in early Judaism, Paul assumes that God will be the judge (Rom 3:5–6; 12:19; 13:4–5), though he can also say that the judge will be Christ (2 Cor 5:10), or that God will act as judge through Christ (Rom 2:16; see also 1 Cor 4:5),[2] just as he can mention "the wrath" of judgment day without specifying it further (1 Thess 1:10; Rom 5:9; 12:19). So basic is the coming judgment that when Paul refers to the conversion of the Gentiles in Thessalonica, he mentions not only their turning from idolatry but also their expecting the Son to come from heaven, namely "Jesus who rescues us from the coming wrath" (1 Thess 1:9–10).[3] Paul shows no interest in describing what will happen on judgment day; what interests him is its inevitablility and its meaning: everyone will be held accountable.[4] The logical tension between viewing Christ as the judge and as the rescuer from the wrath does not suggest that Paul changed his mind; he was not in the business of providing instruction about the coming judgment, but of interpreting the human situation, especially that of the believers, in its light.[5] In short, accountability to God translates the import of the

---

[2] Paul's understanding of the roles of Christ and God in the coming judgment is the focus of L. Joseph Kreitzer's *Jesus and God in Paul's Eschatology* (JSNTSup 19; Sheffield: Academic Press, 1987); see esp. chap. 2.

[3] The likelihood that here Paul cites a piece of Christian tradition does not detract from the point's importance.

[4] See the honoree's perceptive, concise paragraph in *Theology and Ethics in Paul* (Nashville, TN: Abingdon, 1968) 120.

[5] So also Ernst Synofzik, who rightly observes that Paul's references to the judgment and recompense lack unity because he did not "thematize" them but relied on various traditional concepts to reinforce his immediate argument (*Die Gerichts- und Vergeltungsaussagen bei Paulus. Eine traditionsgeschichtliche Untersuchung* [Göttingen: Vandenhoeck & Ruprecht, 1977] 105).

coming judgment for Paul's anthropology (A) as well as for his ecclesiology (B).[6]

A. One reason Paul's letters are persistently concerned with the moral life of his readers is that he assumes that Christians are accountable to God for their behavior, because accountability is an *anthropological* given, inherent in the relation of the human creature to the Creator; it is not an option to be exercised but a given to be discerned and reckoned with. Moreover, this implies, among other things, that because God cares about human activity, accountability to God confers on the doer and on the doer's deeds moral significance beyond traceable consequences, for it affects one's relation to the Alpha and Omega, the Creator and the Judge of existence itself. Here Paul's anthropology, along with its obverse, theology, is 180 degrees from that of the Epicureans, who argued that the gods are indifferent to human deeds. It differs also from Aristotle's view that one should evaluate every deed in relation to the highest good whence it derives its real meaning. This emphasis on the right human construal differs from Paul's conviction that it is not his own view of his deeds that matters but God's (1 Cor 4:3–4; see below).[7] In other words, Paul does not see himself accountable to himself, nor is there any discernible place in his thought for "Unto thine own self be true."

Moreover, although the law specfies that for which one is accountable, it is not to the law that one is accountable but to the Lawgiver. The law brings knowledge of sin (Rom 3:20; 7:7), and by extension, so do moral principles, ideals or causes, because they too expose the doer's failure to achieve. Accordingly, Paul's moral reasoning is not at all oriented toward impersonal principles, ideals, virtues, or causes, but toward the person-like God whose will aims at the hallowing of the self through the presence of the Spirit, namely at sanctification (1 Thess

---

[6] To be sure, one can also explore the import of the coming judgment for Paul's soteriology, as did Karl Paul Donfried, "Justification and Last Judgment in Paul," *ZNW* 67 (1976) 90–110. Donfried rightly insists that Paul does not equate justification and salvation; see p. 100.

[7] J. Paul Sampley rightly calls attention to the role of self-assessment in Paul's letters (e.g., at the Supper, 1 Cor 11:28, 31): "Self-evaluation anticipates the eschatological judgment of God and permits the individual believer to make a mid-course correction" (*Walking Between the Times: Paul's Moral Reasoning* [Minneapolis, MN: Fortress, 1991] 52). However, when he says that "God's or Christ's end-time judgment is not a fearful prospect precisely because of the believer's capacity for self-assessment" (p. 69), he overlooks not only the point made above, but also the Apostle's explicit statement in 1 Cor 4:3–4, "I do not even judge myself. I am not aware of anything against myself, but I am not thereby acquitted. It is the Lord who judges me." More important, Paul's confidence as he thinks about God's judgment is not grounded in the self's capacity but in the character of the Christ event.

4:3). So too, when Paul mentions living "according to the Spirit" (Rom 8:5; Gal 5:16) or being "led by the Spirit" (Gal 5:18), he implies that one is accountable to the Spirit and its Giver.

For Paul, the erstwhile Pharisee, "God" was neither an optional synonym for the all-pervading, cosmos-governing Logos, nor a postulate like Aristotle's Unmoved Mover needed to avoid infinite regression, nor Anselm's being than whom nothing greater can be thought, but the personal Reality of which scripture speaks: the creator of all that is, the chooser of Israel and giver of the Law, and especially the sender of the Son as the way of keeping the promise to Abraham. The One to whom Paul is accountable is the living God with integrity (righteousness), will, and power, who had chosen Paul before·he was born and who had transformed him by revealing the Son to him (Gal 1:15). He knows himself accountable not to some awesome, distant deity, but to the God who is a sovereign, saving, succoring presence, despite Paul's conflicts, imprisonments and the "thorn in the flesh."

Given Paul's understanding of the intimate relation between God and Christ, comparable observations apply to his accountability to Christ, before whose judgment seat all will appear to be punished or rewarded (2 Cor 5:10). Lest one overlook the full force of this assertion, it is useful to reverse the subject and predicate in usual title-oriented christology: instead of saying simply that Christ is the judge, one should ponder the import of the judge being Christ, the one in whom Paul lives (ἐν Χριστῷ) and "who lives in me," and "who loved me and gave himself for me" (Gal 2:20); this Christ "redeemed us from the curse of the law" (Gal 3:13), and, having been seated at God's right hand, now "intercedes for us" (Rom 8:33–34). It is not surprising that the Apostle therefore gives neither hint of being resentful because he is accountable nor sign that he lives in anxious dread of that day when God will judge the heart's secrets, and whose fiery judgment will reveal the true character and quality of one's work (1 Cor 3:13).[8] It is not dread of the coming judgment that prompts him to urge the Philippians to "work out their salvation with fear and trembling" but the fact that God is at work in them "both to will and to work for his good pleasure" (Phil

---

[8] Donfried insists that 1 Cor 3:5–15 "has nothing to do with the sins of individual Christians nor with their consequent salvation in spite of their sins"; rather, it concerns the durability and quality of Paul's (and the Corinthians') ministry ("Justification and Last Judgment," 105–106). Some years before, Calvin Roetzel had insisted that "it is the building, i.e., the church, that will be tested and purged at the last judgment. Each man's reward or loss will stand in direct proportion to the quality of materials he places in the building" (*Judgement in the Community: A Study of the Relationship Between Eschatology and Ecclesiology in Paul* [Leiden: Brill, 1972] 164).

5

2:12–13). Knowing that God is at work in one's doing must not elicit hubris but deepen the meaning of being accountable.

The quotation from Philippians functions as a reminder: whoever wants to understand the anthropological import of Paul's construal of accountability must follow him in his dialectical thinking about human and divine action. According to Paul, the self is simultaneously an accountable doer and the place where Christ (or God, or the Spirit) is the real doer. How else would one account for that powerful paradox in Gal 2:19–20: "I have been crucified with Christ; and it is no longer I who live, but it is Christ who lives in me. And the life I now live in the flesh I live by faith in the Son of God"?

This claim is doubly fascinating because, as the expression of Christian existence in the domain of Christ, it is the obverse of non-Christian existence as a slave in the domain of Sin (according to Romans 7). Here, in the most penetrating analysis of the human condition apart from Christ, Paul reflects on what is implied in the fact that what he does is not the good (the law) that he wants to do but the exact opposite. [9] His inference is startling: "But in fact it is no longer I that do it, but sin that dwells within me" (Rom 7:17; repeated in v. 20). But if Sin is a resident power so strong that it compels the self to do the opposite of its intent and so is the real doer, why does Paul not conclude that the victimized self is not accountable? Because the law remains the expression of God's will, and the self, though victimized by Sin, remains an accountable creature. Precisely this creates the dilemma expressed as, "Wretched man that I am!" In this miserable situation, apart from Christ, one can only expect "wrath and fury" from the God who "will repay according to each one's deeds" (Rom 2:6–8). But instead of that future, Paul declares that there is now "no condemnation for those who are in Christ Jesus" because in them the indwelling Spirit has displaced resident Sin (Rom 8:1–9). [10] In other words, whether Paul has in view the pre-Christian self who acts because acted upon by Sin, or the Christian self who lives because Christ (or the

---

[9] The point made here does not require one to determine whether the "I" in Rom 7:7–25 is stylistic or autobiographical; on the other hand, that the "I" is "sold under sin" (v. 14) clearly indicates that Paul is analyzing pre-Christian experience.

[10] Paul's unequivocal declaration either calls into question Sampley's assertion, "In Paul's thought world, surviving the end-time judgment depends on the works the believer has to offer" (*Walking Between the Times*, 70) or requires one to infer that "no condemnation now" as well as the resident Spirit have little bearing on one's future salvation. That one can forfeit one's salvation is clear in 1 Cor 10:1–12, as Donfried sees ("Justification and Last Judgment," 194). Donfried also notes that the issue at the judgment is one's obedience to God's gift of justification and to the Spirit, "not how many good works man has performed—this is irrelevant since it is the Spirit which enables man to do those deeds of love" (102).

6

Spirit) lives in him, the self is a doer whose acts result from power exerted *on* it.[11] Accountability itself is never in question, even if the self is never truly autonomous but always an acting self who is acted upon.

B. To this point, the discussion of accountability, seen as the anthropological meaning of the coming judgment, has focused on the self, since Paul assumes—rightly—that in God's courtroom no proxy will be allowed: "all must carry their own loads" (Gal 6:5). One would sell his understanding short, however, by inferring that he thought only of individual eschatological accountability "on that day." In addressing problems in the small house churches, he reckons with current *ecclesial accountability* as well. He himself pointed this out when he corrected the Corinthians' misinterpretation of a letter, now lost, in which he had urged the readers not to associate with immoral people; now he explains that it was immoral insiders who were to be shunned, not outsiders, adding, "For what have I to do with judging those outside? Is it not those who are inside that you are to judge? God will judge those outside. Drive out the wicked man from among *you*" (1 Cor 5:12–13, citing Deut 17:7 LXX).

Paul insists on this intramural judging because, it appears, the Corinthians had not only tolerated one of their member's incestuous relations but had even been proud of him. The details of Paul's response (1 Cor 5:1–5) remain opaque, but what is of concern here is not: the church is currently accountable for its moral integrity,[12] and by ordering the expulsion of the offender Paul assumes that it is now accountable to him. Moreover, he takes responsibility for its moral well-being because he understands himself to be accountable to the Lord for the results of his apostleship. This is disclosed in the metaphors he uses for his role: father in Christ (1 Cor 4:15; see also 1 Thess 2:11); mother (Gal 4:19); nurse (1 Thess 2:7);[13] marriage broker (implied at 2 Cor 11:2); public servant or priest (λειτουργός, Rom 15:16). He takes this accountability seriously because at the judgment the believers' standing and his will be intertwined (2 Cor 1:14). If they are found "blameless" (Phil 1:10; 1 Thess 3:13; 5:23), they will be his "crown of boasting before our Lord Jesus at his coming" (1 Thess 2:19; Phil 2:14–16); if, on the other hand, they be found faithless, his labor

---

[11] This is clearly implied in Rom 6:15–23, where Paul develops the point that one is a slave of whatever one obeys, Sin or obedience (v. 16).

[12] Ernst Synofzig points out that 1 Cor 3:15 rejects current ecclesial judgment in view of God's future judgment on the Christian's *work*, but 1 Cor 5:5 calls for ecclesial judgment now on Christian *sin* (*Die Gerichts- und Vergeltungsaussagen*, 56).

[13] See A. J. Malherbe, "'Gentle as a Nurse': The Cynic Background to 1 Thess ii," *NovT* 12 (1970) 203–17.

will have been in vain (1 Cor 9:26–27; Gal 4:10–11; Phil 2:16; 1 Thess 3:5), however "meaningful" their experience in the church might have been. What he tells the Corinthians sums up his sense of accountability: he, Apollos and Cephas are "servants of Christ, stewards of the mysteries of God. Moreover, it is required of stewards that they be found trustworthy"—by God, he assumes. That is why he is not accountable even to himself, for "it is the Lord who judges me" (1 Cor 4:1–5).

That accountability implies a relationship in which the accountable self or group acknowledges a superior authority is confirmed by what Paul writes to the Roman believers in Rom 14:1–15:13.[14] Apparently, those who were scrupulous about observing matters pertaining to days[15] and diets were hectoring and passing judgment on those who were rather indifferent regarding such matters. Paul reprimands the former for acting as if the latter were accountable to them: "Who are you to pass judgment on the servants of another? It is before their own lord that they stand or fall" (Rom 14:4)—i.e., not before you. The scrupulous are not their superiors but their equals, for God has welcomed them both (14:3; in 15:7 it is Christ); moreover, Christ died for both (14:9). Since both groups are the Lord's servants, they are accountable to him (or to God) alone. They are not to issue verdicts about each other, since every one "shall give an account (λόγον δώσει) of himself to God" (14:12 RSV). To condemn each other is to preempt God's role (Rom 14:10; 1 Cor 4:5). Accordingly, Paul can rephrase accountability as living or dying "to the Lord" because either way "we are the Lord's" (14:8). Consequently, "we do not live to ourselves" (14:7; see also 2 Cor 10:15), or as he twice points out to the Corinthians, "You are not your own; you were bought with a price" (1 Cor 6:20; 7:23).

But the truly remarkable aspect of Paul's understanding of ecclesial accountability emerges—albeit between the lines—in what he goes on to say, beginning at Rom 14:13–15:1. Having implied clearly that the two groups are not accountable to each other because neither is the other's lord, Paul now tacitly proceeds to hold the "liberated"

---

[14] For a concise, perceptive discussion, see Wayne A. Meeks, "Judgment and the Brother: Romans 14:1–15:13," in *Tradition and Interpretation in the New Testament* (E. Earle Ellis FS; ed. G. F. Hawthorne and O. Betz; Grand Rapids, MI: Eerdmans; Tübingen: Mohr-Siebeck, 1987) 290–300. Meeks rightly refuses to equate "the weak" with Jewish Christians and "the strong" with Gentile believers, as is often done.

[15] Although interpreters often assume that the "day" (v.5) is the sabbath (so recently Herold Weiss, "Paul and the Judging of Days," *ZNW* 86 [1995] 137–53), Paul's argument does not require this identification; indeed, Meeks points out that "there were many reasons for a pagan to judge one day more auspicious or more dangerous than another" and that Paul's language would have been meaningful to both Jew and Gentile ("Judgment and the Brother" 292–93).

accountable to God for the continuing integrity of the faith of the scrupulous, writing with noticeable tact in doing so. (a) He insists that what is really at stake is whether "eating" will put a stumbling block in the way of the scrupulous. (b) While not saying explicitly that the scrupulous are wrong, he points out twice that those who eat are in fact right (vv. 14, 20). (c) At the same time, being right is not enough because the meat "is unclean for anyone who thinks it unclean." Even if this opinion is not correct, it is held "in honor of the Lord" (v. 6), as a conscientious expression of faith, and so it is to be respected since that makes for peace in the community (v. 19).[16] (d) Not until the end of the discussion does Paul openly side with those who eat, including himself in their self-designation ("we who are strong," ἡμεῖς οἱ δυνατοί) and using their language for the scrupulous ("the weak," ἀδύνατοι; literally, "the not strong"), which might be paraphrased as "we who are able [to eat]" and "those who are unable [to eat]" because of their faith-convictions. (e) Here he also discloses why the opinions of "the weak" are not errors to be corrected by "the strong"—they are "weaknesses" (τὰ ἀσθενήματα) to be borne. (f) Because both eating and not eating are done in faith, in honor of the Lord, those who are induced to eat while doubting that it is permissible are actually "condemned, if they eat, because they do not act from faith; for whatever does not proceed from faith is sin" (14:23). Whenever the strong create such a situation, they put a stumbling block in the way, injure the brother or sister, "cause the ruin of one for whom Christ died" (v. 15), "destroy the work of God" for the sake of food (v. 20). Were that to happen, the strong would be accountable for the destruction of their fellow believers and fellow beneficiaries of Christ's work.

Despite the uncertainties that surround the relation of Romans 14–15 to 1 Corinthians 8 and 10,[17] what matters for this discussion is clear enough: throughout, Paul manifests the same robust sense of being accountable for the integrity of all believers' faith,[18] even though he is

---

[16] The reference to intramural peace (Rom 14:19) suggests why Paul made "the strong" accountable should the faith of any of "the weak" be violated: on his expected arrival in Rome he did not want to find a community torn by dissent. He had already signalled his concern in 12:16.

[17] E.g., whether or not Paul's counsel in 1 Corinthians 8 differs from that in chap. 10, both are generated by the fact that Christians had to decide whether it was permissible to eat meat that had been offered to the gods before it was sold; there is no mention of this issue in Romans. Conversely, the problem of the "days" is absent from 1 Corinthians. See also the following note.

[18] Only in Romans does Paul explicitly refer to the believer's faith (14:22, 23), and only in Romans does he refer to the "weak in faith" (14:1) while in 1 Corinthians 8 it is the conscience that is "weak" (1 Cor 8:7, 11, 12; see also the role of conscience in 1 Cor 10:25–29). These differences should not be emphasized unduly because in both letters he

convinced that "food will not commend us to God," whether by actualizing freedom to eat meat which had been offered to the gods, or by scrupulous refusal to eat it. Indeed, rather than be the cause of a fellow believer's "falling," he is willing to become a vegetarian (1 Cor 8:13). Moreover, he clearly expects his stance to become that of his readers as well: "Be imitators of me, as I am of Christ" (1 Cor 11:1).

In sum, what Christians are answerable for is not the habits of their fellow believers but what makes them believers in the first place—their faith, their complete reliance on God. Accordingly, he urges his readers to seek not their own good but that of the neighbor (1 Cor 10:24), to build up each other (1 Cor 14:12; 1 Thess 5:11); this, indeed, is how he sees his role in the exercise of apostolic authority (2 Cor 10:8; 13:10).

Three generalizations will put into wider context the observations garnered from this brief examination of relevant Pauline texts. (a) Paul's understanding of accountability—his own and that of the newly Christianized readers—reflects his unique and unrepeatable situation: he writes with authority as a God-chosen apostle to small house churches which, apart from those in Rome, had come into existence in response to his message about the redemptive significance of the Christ-event, and in which the intimate face-to-face relationships created an atmosphere in which accountability had become a problem. As a sent-one he is accountable to the Sender not only for the integrity of his own word and life but also for that of these new communities. (b) Paul's understanding of accountability is woven so tightly into his theology as a whole that it cannot be abstracted from it without tearing the fabric. As Christ's slave, he is accountable to the Lord who died on his behalf, who is present as Spirit, and whose coming (and the judgment at which his accountability will be evident) is imminent. (c) Even though his theology was hammered out on the anvil of his pioneering and unrepeatable mission, Paul's understanding of what it means to be an accountable Christian self transcends the context in which it took shape. That is why it is possible for Christian ethics to be instructed by him today. Commenting on the difference between the accountable self and the deciding self can abet this process.

III. The Deciding Self and the Accountable Self

At issue is not whether care in decision-making is important. Indeed, the more clearly one sees oneself as accountable to God/Christ, the more careful one is likely to be in choosing a course of action. What is at issue is which self-understanding has priority—the deciding self or

refers to the scrupulous as "the weak" (Rom 15:1; 1 Cor 8:9).

the accountable self. This priority, moreover, is not one of logic but of "weight," because accountability to God/Christ can be an acknowledged theologoumenon without having a formative impact on the deciding self. To be instructed by Paul, however, is to appropriate into one's self-understanding those elements of his thinking that were not peculiar to his apostolic office but remain basic to Christian existence and its morality, because he insisted that his readers too were accountable.

Paul, of course, expected that he and his readers would soon render an account at the parousia and the coming judgment; for him, the chronological, mundane future was steadily growing shorter because "salvation is nearer to us now than when we became believers" (Rom 13:11). While some Christians would not hesitate to say the same today, those who do not expect an imminent "Second Coming" and Last Judgment (neither being Paul's terms) will develop other ways of understanding their accountability.

On the one hand, some may retain conceptually the link between accountability to God/Christ and the coming judgment, but marginalize both by regarding them as harmless mythological ideas with no particular relevance. The *dies irae* remains in the Catholic requiem mass, and "he shall come to judge the living and the dead" is repeated in the Apostles' Creed, but the content has long disappeared from most Protestant funerals and memorial services, lest such a negative note mar their eulogistic character.

On the other hand, some will marginalize the notion of the coming judgment but retain the sense of accountability by secularizing it, so that now one is accountable primarily to one's contemporaries and descendants, to "the verdict of history"—probably unaware that the latter makes them liable to a judgment that is merciless and unforgiving. Either one, each in its own way, leads to the primacy of the deciding self.

Paul's letters imply another alternative. His care for the churches implies that he recognizes that the coming judgment will manifest the accountability that already shapes his life. The *that* of his accountability is not tied to its *when*. Theologically, what is implicit in Paul can be made explicit today. In other words, instead of marginalizing one's accountability to God/Christ or secularizing it, one can emphasize the theological/anthropological meaning of the coming judgment as valid in its own right because of who we are in relation to God. Pursuing this option leads to the primacy of the accountable self.

Even though the accountable self also decides, the differences between the primacy of the one and that of the other are multiple as well as subtle, and affect the construal of God as well as of the self. The following bold strokes, like those of a cartoon, can outline these two overlapping yet quite distinct views of the moral self.

First, by definition, the deciding self's intense concern with "What must/ought/should/may I do?" puts a premium on the deed as the result of careful choice; the accountable self's central concern with "To whom am I accountable, and for what?" puts the emphasis on the doer's vulnerable relation to the sovereign Other. Second, the deciding self inevitably relies on the capacity to reason rightly by determining which principles apply and by judging whether they are applied properly. The deciding self tends to reason prudentially, with a keen eye for the consequences of possible alternative deeds. Because principles and rules can be applied, modified or countered with other principles and rules as one moves carefully through the labyrinthine reasoning process, the deciding self proceeds as a rational self accountable primarily to the canons of ethical reasoning. The constraints imposed by non-negotiable loyalties and commitments easily frustrate the tight reasoning based on principles and consequences. The more this reasoning follows the widely accepted norms of ethical logic, the less room there is for a significant reference to God's nature and will, thereby implying that for the deciding self God is a sponsor or observer, somewhat like the patient parent watching the young child work at getting the round block into the round hole instead of the square one.

For the accountable self, on the other hand, loyalty to God is the non-negotiable starting-point and guiding factor in deciding what is to be done or not done, because—for Paul at least—the One to whom one is accountable has already realigned the self's God-relation. This determines what is brought to bear on the accountable self's moral reasoning, so that the chosen act's impact on the fellow believer's relation to God can never be overlooked or minimized.

Third, whereas the acts chosen by the deciding self result from astute reasoning applied to each situation, those of the accountable self will, over time, reflect the persistent loyalty to God/Christ, and so flow from an emerging disposition or character. For the accountable self, there is always the possibility that one is constrained to do what is not the result of judicious reasoning but of an unshakable conviction that it must be done because loyalty to God requires it, irrational as it may appear.

Finally, while the accountable self too reasons carefully, in the last analysis he/she knows that one does not have to get it right (besides, who besides God determines *that*?), not only because "we see through a glass darkly," but also because he/she has learned to trust the God who "through Jesus Christ will judge the secret thoughts of all."

By itself, accountability is not the most important factor, either in Paul's ethics or in ours. Its importance escalates dramatically, however, when it is seen as the anthropological meaning of the coming judgment, which for Paul is an inherent, though yet future, part of what *is* decisive—the redemptive meaning of the Christ-*event*.[19] Indeed, it is just this linkage that makes recovering accountability an urgent task for Christian ethics today. Not only would this restoration ameliorate the preoccupation with the deciding self, but it would also make it clear that an ethics that intends to be Christian must be shaped by a defining event, the redemption wrought in Christ.

---

[19] Furnish implies the same when he faults Meeks's book, *The Origins of Christian Morality*, for emphasizing the role the coming judgment but neglecting the experience of God's grace "through the impact of Jesus' life and death" (Victor Paul Furnish, "Can Ethics be Christian?" *The Christian Century* [Oct. 26, 1994] 991, 993).

Paul and the Eschatological Body

Robin Scroggs

According to Philo the human being is composed of both "earthly nature (γεώδους οὐσίας) and divine spirit (πνεύματος θείου). . . . Hence it may with propriety be said that the [human] is the borderland between mortal (θνητῆς) and immortal (ἀθανάτου) nature, partaking of each so far as is needful, and that [it] was created at once mortal and immortal, mortal in respect of the body, but in respect of the mind immortal."[1] The person is thus composite, divided according to Greek sensibilities into material and immaterial realities. It is, of course, the νοῦς that can live after death. Its function in this life is so to control the material reality that the spiritual is worthy of eternal life.

Translated into Hebraic psychology, this split is known to the rabbis and is almost certainly a commonplace in early Jewish tradition. God created Adam "with four attributes of the higher beings (מלמעלה) and four attributes of the lower beings (מלמטן)." Like the ministering angels (מלאכי השרת) Adam stands upright, speaks, understands, and sees. Like the animals (בהמה) he eats and drinks, procreates, excretes, and dies.[2] Part of this tradition is found in Mark 12:25 in the argument between Jesus and the Sadducees. "When they rise from the dead they neither marry nor are given in marriage, but are like angels in heaven." Thus the general point of view is quite early. In and of itself there is nothing surprising in the statements of either Philo or the rabbis.[3]

Paul, it may fairly be judged, knows and accepts this point of view, whether or not he knew the logion as we find it in Philo and the rabbis. For Paul, corporeality belongs to this world, but it will not exist in the Kingdom of God. "Flesh and blood (σάρξ καὶ αἷμα) cannot inherit the kingdom of God, nor does the perishable inherit the imperishable" (1 Cor 15:50). A transformation will occur at the final moment, and at that time those who will live in the Kingdom will be given a "spiritual body."

---

[1] Philo *De opificio mundi* 135 (LCL 226 [modified]; London: W. Heinemann, 1962).

[2] *Gen. Rab.* 8.11. Attributed by "the rabbis" to R. Eleazar (a Tanna).

[3] E.g., a somewhat similar statement is made in the longer recension of *II Enoch* 30.10, but this may be quite late.

14

What this means to Paul is, of course, not entirely clear. But there can be no question that the spiritual body is non-corporeal.[4]

Paul differs from Philo and the rabbis, however, in that he thinks that in some real way the eschatological reality is present in believers, individually and corporately. "So if anyone is in Christ, there is a new creation: everything old has passed away; see, everything has become new" (2 Cor 5:17—the NRSV sounds a bit flowery for Paul's terse text, but nonetheless seems accurate). Believers should, whether they do or not, be able thus to live in the present world in a way that is consonant with life in the Kingdom of God.

Paul's conviction of the presence of the Kingdom *puts him squarely on the horns of a dilemma*, one that was not necessary for Philo and the rabbis. For them eschatological angelic reality was reserved entirely for the future. The body belonged to the "vestibule of the world to come," to this world, to the "old" creation. But if Paul claims believers live now in the "new" creation, what does this say about the body and its actions? To which world do bodily actions belong? Or do they straddle both? Does Paul see bodily expression as part of the reality of the new creation, or is it for him an unfortunate remnant which ties the believer necessarily to the old world? Does the Apostle view his instructions about bodily expression as descriptive of life in the new creation or does he see them as 'rear-guard' descriptions of how believers are to live in the midst of the old order?

Paul must have been conflicted by this dilemma—how could he not have been? The famous ὡς μή [as though not] passage in 1 Cor 7:29–31 suggests he is not willing to give up either horn; it is not accidental that the 'live in the world as if you are not living in it' perspective is given an eschatological grounding: "For the present form of this world is passing away" (v. 31).[5] With this in mind, it may be instructive to look once again at his ethical injunctions about the body, asking to which world these instructions belong. Paul is caught between two worlds, and I do not suppose he is single-minded about the issue, if he even thought about it in such terms. Our conclusions thus must be tentative.

Bultmann taught two generations of interpreters that Paul's view of the body was essentially neutral. He rescued σάρξ from the pejorative evaluation that earlier scholars had assigned it, on the assumption that Paul was influenced by Greek thought. Given this neutrality there is no

---

[4] See my *The Last Adam: A Study in Pauline Anthropology* (Philadelphia: Fortress, 1966) 59–74.

[5] Cf. the insightful monograph by V. Wimbush, *Paul the Worldly Ascetic: Response to the World and Self-Understanding according to 1 Corinthians 7* (Macon, GA: Mercer University Press, 1987).

reason why corporeality could not be a medium of a present reality of the Kingdom—at least to the same extent that any other self-expression could be. A recent, provocative book by Daniel Boyarin, however, reintroduces the possibility that Paul may have seen the body negatively, from a Platonic perspective.[6] If this should be the case, Paul's view of corporeality is that it is at best inferior and at worst evil. There would be no possibility of a bodily action which was part of the new creation, since the true world is spiritual not material. While I think Boyarin's claim cannot be sustained,[7] the issue of Paul's view of corporeality is not as settled as Bultmann's followers may have thought. By asking the question about the eschatology of Paul's ethics of corporeality, can we gain a different perspective which will help clarify Paul's evaluation of bodily expressions "in the Lord?"

To claim the possibility of a different perspective on Pauline ethics is perhaps presumptuous in a volume honoring a scholar who has devoted much of his career to issues of ethics, both in ancient texts and in the contemporary church. I know, however, from a friendship extending over the years, that Victor Furnish is gracious and caring and patient in listening. I dedicate this effort to a person whom I admire and respect and whose wise maturity I hold in a bit of awe.

Presuppositions

1. To find the right terms by which to delineate what I try to do here is virtually impossible. Any dualistic division of a person is foreign to many people today, including myself. All actions involve corporeality and all involve mental, emotional dimensions. We speak of a person as "embodied" and that means, I take it, that *all* expressions of any sort are bodily expressions. We use 'body language' to help us understand a person's speech, for example, and to evaluate the 'real' feelings of the speaker. At the same time what we traditionally think of as bodily, fleshly expressions are also expressive of a person's feelings and commitments, as sexual acts obviously are. Thus the category "ethics of the body" may no longer be meaningful for us today. Whether it was meaningful for Paul is also uncertain. If he held to the old Hebraic psychology, he may have tended to agree with our modern perspective. If, on the other hand, he held to some sort of division of the self, involving spirit and/or mind, and body—as it seems to me his letters

---

[6] D. Boyarin, *A Radical Jew: Paul and the Politics of Identity* (Berkeley: University of California Press, 1994). "For [Paul], sexuality per se is tainted with immorality" (172).

[7] I agree, rather, with Furnish who judges that "Paul does not subscribe to the Gnostic idea of the flesh as something sinful in and of itself" (V. P. Furnish, *Theology and Ethics in Paul* [Nashville, TN: Abingdon, 1968] 136).

occasionally suggest—he may have had a place in his thinking for an "ethics of the body." We cannot know.

What I will investigate here are actions which have traditionally been associated with the body: eating, ritual performance, and gender issues.[8] What I will try to show is that "in Christ" any of these bodily actions are expressions of the transformed *self.* The basic issue for Paul is how the 'new creature' is free to express her or his new reality through the 'old' forms of bodily activity. Thus whether or not the apostle held to some dualistic notion of the person, his view of bodily actions as eschatological in effect creates a unified self.

2. In no way will this brief essay be a word study of such key terms as σάρξ, σῶμα, καρδία, or συνείδησις [flesh, body, heart, or conscience]. Indeed, when one inspects carefully the passages which I deal with in this paper, the remarkable fact emerges that neither σάρξ nor σῶμα is frequently used, and when the terms do appear they have mostly ordinary, non-technical meanings. For example κατὰ σάρκα [according to the flesh] occurs only once, and that in a neutral sense.[9] Mostly Paul uses simply ἐγώ [I] or circumlocutions such as παλαιὸς ἄνθρωπος, ἔξω and ἔσω ἄνθρωπος [old person, outer and inner person] to point to the *person.* Thus this study will deal with 'body' in the sense of corporeal activity, regardless of the terms Paul uses.[10]

3. I will avoid as much as possible actions which are not 'bodily' in the sense described above and thus discussion of terms which are usually used to point to such actions. Particularly I will avoid the term πνεῦμα [spirit]. Paul and especially his interpreters are likely to ascribe everything the believer does which is 'right' to the Spirit as cause and even agent. In my judgment this only confuses the issue. To claim that a bodily action is caused by God's spirit may blunt the issue of the human agent's participation and blur the question of its eschatological reality.

4. I will not deal with the issue of νόμος [law] or any other appeal to external authority. In this paper I am not primarily interested in *how* Paul knows how the person should act in body. I *do* think, however— and this is important—that an identification of an action with a Torah rule does not exclude the act's possible eschatological significance. For

---

[8] The issue of the role of suffering in an eschatological body is also crucially important, but there is no space to deal with that issue in this paper.

[9] 1 Cor 10:18. Interestingly, nine of the fifteen Pauline occurrences of συνείδησις appear in 1 Cor 8:7–13 and 10:23–31, which deal with eating in connection with pagan worship. Did the Corinthians' questions to him about these matters use that term?

[10] I agree with a number of scholars who think Bultmann overstates his case with regard to σῶμα [body]. There are surely instances where that word refers to or points to corporeality. On the other hand, I still believe that σάρξ [flesh] has the 'neutral' meaning Bultmann argues for, except for the phrase κατὰ σάρκα [according to the flesh].

Paul the Torah *is* descriptive of God's will for humans (even if he is selective about his use of Torah). That believers obey a Torah description is a function not of its 'oughtness' but of the freedom and the eschatological power of the believer to perform.

5. What I *will* search out is the kind or quality of bodily action Paul envisages and ask whether this action is for him an expression of the 'new' creature and thus whether the body in some way is an authentic reality of the new creation in its present, partial manifestation.

The Transformed Person

Paul is clear that the believer is a transformed person who is thus enabled to perform 'right' actions.[11] Rom 12:1–2 is the key text:

> I exhort you then, fellow believers, through God's mercies, to present your bodies (σώματα)[12] as a holy, living sacrifice to God—this is your reasoning[13] service. And do not be conformed to this age, but be transformed by the making-new of your mind, that you may (accurately) test out[14] the will of God, the good and pleasing and perfect" (auth. tr.).

Victor Furnish has made it clear that Paul's claims about God's act in Christ and the appropriate human ethical response are all of a piece.[15] Behind the transformed person lies commitment to a theological perspective, whether it is justification by grace, or incorporation into Christ, or both. Rom 12:1–2 then shows the result of that commitment. The total self, including its corporeality, becomes transformed, and the restored intellectual insight enables accurate perception of God's will. The transformed person is then free for, and committed to, living out of that perception.[16]

---

[11] Cf. Furnish, *Theology and Ethics*, 214–27. The believer "has been given not just the *possibility* of a new life, but an actually and totally new existence" (225).

[12] Paul's use of the word σῶμα [body] seems clearly a double entendre. Bultmann is correct in arguing that it refers to one's total person—hence "selves" would be an appropriate translation. Yet Paul is using a sacrificial metaphor here, in which the body of the animal is presented to God on the altar.

[13] Λογικός is usually translated "spiritual," but this does not capture the intellective dimension in the word. "Rational," on the other hand, sounds too intellectual. Hence I prefer "reasoning," although this is still a bit awkward.

[14] Δοκιμάζω means to come to accurate judgment about a matter. It is, for Paul, the restoration of a faculty given in creation but lost in the fallen condition (Rom 1:28). Cf. my discussion in "New Being: Renewed Mind: New Perception. Paul's View of the Source of Ethical Insight," *The Text and the Times* (Minneapolis, MN: Fortress, 1993) 174–81.

[15] See, e.g., V. P. Furnish, *Theology and Ethics*, 112.

[16] This interpretation of Rom 12:1–2 obviously means that I cannot agree with interpreters who take Rom 7:7–25 to refer to a believer's "I." I follow Bultmann and

This transformed person, however, lives in the ordinary world in which ordinary activities and relationships must still be realized. For Paul transformation means transformed relationships, certainly inside the church and probably outside as well.[17] The transformed person lives out of the realities of freedom, joy, peace, love and upbuilding, and these "middle axioms" should determine the quality of relationships. *But the same situation pertains to what I am calling here "bodily activities."* Paul pays attention to these bodily activities *insofar as they appear to him to be relational,* i.e., things one does with one's body in relationship to others. The transformed relationship determines how one uses one's body. It is in this way that the body is an expression of eschatological reality. In this sense there *is* an "eschatological body."[18]

In what follows I can only be selective in topic and text; nor do I intend to try to shed new light on details within the passages. These materials have been subjected to much brilliant analysis by other scholars, not the least, of course, by the person this volume honors. And I limit myself in thinking about these texts to one question: given the ambiguity of the body in the present eschatological situation, does the body belong to the new or the old creation?

Eating

I will reflect here on four passages, one which speaks from a theoretical perspective, and three which concern particular situations.

Romans 14:1–23. In this very provocative section, Paul works with two faith convictions. The first is stated in verse 14a: "I know and am persuaded in the Lord Jesus that nothing is unclean in itself." The second occurs in 23b: "For whatever does not proceed from faith is sin." The first affirms an ethic of freedom about food. As a blanket statement it declares that Jewish kosher laws are not based on real distinctions of

---

Käsemann, among many others, who take the "I" in this passage to speak of Paul's post-call experience of what life under the Torah entailed. I further agree with Bultmann that the passage concerns life vs. death, not obedience vs. disobedience; see his "Romans 7 and the Anthropology of Paul," *Existence & Faith: Shorter Writings of Rudolf Bultmann* (ed. S. Ogden; Cleveland: Meridian, 1960) 147–57. For a recent, opposing view, see M. Winger, *By What Law? The Meaning of* Νόμος *in the Letters of Paul* (SBLDS 128; Atlanta: Scholars Press, 1992) 159–196.

[17] For outside relationships we do not have much explicitly said, except that Paul assumes such relationships continue (e.g., 1 Cor 5:9–12). But would Paul expect any less of a believer than the manifestation of eschatological actions? Cf. Rom 12:18.

[18] This view is also affirmed by Susanne Heine, *Leibhafter Glaube: Ein Beitrag zum Verständnis der theologischen Konzeption des Paulus* (Vienna: Herder, 1976). "Der Leib ist eben nicht nur natürliche Beschaffenheit des Menschen, sondern Ort der Verwirklichung von Glauben" (141; "The body is not merely a natural human condition but precisely the locus where faith is enacted").

divine ordinance, and it denies the claim made in some believing communities that eating meat sacrificed to other gods is prohibited (cf. the following passages in 1 Corinthians). Rom 14:23b on the other hand states that the ultimate grounds for an individual's decision about such matters is not what "really is the case" but what the individual *thinks* to be the case. On the one hand we have an ethic of complete freedom with regard to food and drink (objective); on the other, a basic concern for an individual's personal involvement in the issue (subjective).

If all thought what "really is the case" to be, in fact, the case, then there would be no issue. The fact that members of the communities are divided forces Paul to think through what the proper stand should be. He reveals certain priorities. Primary is the preservation of the faith of other believers, a loss of which means their ultimate destruction (v. 16). Secondary is the legitimate freedom to eat and drink anything. In the face of the conflict between these two realities, his decision about what gives way is inevitable. Preservation of a fellow believer takes precedence over the freedom to eat and drink. "It is good not to eat meat or drink wine or do anything that makes your brother or sister stumble" (v. 21).

Food belongs to this world and Paul's judgment about it stems from his particular view of creation. God created all things good (note his citation of Ps 24:1). But because food is of the created order, decisions about it are not significant (1 Cor 8:8). And for the same reason, food and the human digestion system will perish (1 Cor 6:13a). Thus food and eating are at the same time both good and irrelevant. One might say that choice of food and drink is an aesthetic not a moral judgment.

Salvation of a fellow believer is, to the contrary, of ultimate, eschatological significance. Thus the stance a believer should take about his or her eating is determined by the issue of the other's salvation, not by the legitimate freedom one is told one has. Paul's view can be stated in paradoxical form: what one does *in* the body is irrelevant but what one does *through* the body is of ultimate significance. For Paul, given the eschatological tension out of which he lives, the body can only be ambiguous. It belongs to this world, but it is only through the body that eschatological realities can be expressed in this world. Thus what one does through the body belongs to that eschatological world.

1 Corinthians 8:7–13; 10:23–31; 11:17–34a. Here Paul deals with concrete situations, and since, in my judgment, they all are specifications of the more theoretical judgments expressed in Romans 14, they can be dealt with in summary fashion.

1. 1 Cor 8:7–13 treats the case of a believer being seen eating at some event in a temple. The likelihood that this was specifically a temple ritual to the god or goddess perhaps strains the imagination of what even the Corinthian believers may have countenanced.[19] Since temples were used, however, for "secular" occasions as well, such as birthday parties, it may be more likely that a believer's participation in such eating belongs to this latter category. However that may be, Paul seems to judge that, on some theoretical level, there is nothing wrong with a believer eating food in that context. He knows, however, that other believers feel differently and speaks from their perspective. Eating is in itself permissible but unimportant. The damage such eating might cause to a believer's faith *is* important, indeed essential.

2. 1 Cor 10:23–31 explores the same tension, here at a private dinner party, presumably in someone's private space. Paul seems to feel more comfortable with this private setting and is stronger in his acceptance of the eating: "Eat whatever is sold in the meat market without raising any question" (v. 25). But the same tension rises and the same conclusion is made. Food is ultimately unimportant, but the conscience of the other believer *is* of significance and determines what one does in the body with regard to food.

3. In 1 Cor 11:17–34a Paul essentially makes the same point. The issue is not the eating and drinking in itself that he condemns but the fact that some eating and drinking destroys the community and its ritual and humiliates other believers. Here it is not the kind of food or drink (although Paul may know that the better-off have a higher quality of food and drink than others) but the way of eating which, in Paul's view, compromises both the community and the ritual.

In summary, food belongs to this world, but what one does in eating *through* the body belongs to eschatological reality. Food is of no importance but how one eats food is. Since this is the case, Paul is concerned about bodily actions. Through the body are expressed eschatological, ultimate realities. When a believer *does* express through the body those realities, then the body is truly an eschatological body.

Ritual Performance

Ritual performances involve the body. Paul mentions a number of such practices but these tend to be occasional statements, and it is not easy to draw a unified conclusion about Paul's understanding of

---

[19] Although this is usually assumed by commentators. See, e.g., H. Conzelmann, *An die Korinther. I/II* (HNT 9; Tübingen: Mohr-Siebeck, 1949) 39; C. K. Barrett, *The First Epistle to the Corinthians* (HNTC; New York: Harper, 1968) 196; G. D. Fee, *The First Epistle to the Corinthians* (NICNT; Grand Rapids, MI: Eerdmans, 1987) 379–80.

corporeal ritual actions. By going through these statements, however, it may be possible to make a judgment that has basic self-consistency as well as consonance with his attitudes toward other bodily activities.

Sacred Days. Embedded in the larger discussion about eating in Romans 14 is a brief comment on "days," an issue that Paul obviously includes because the issue fits under the same judgment he is making about eating. In terse, almost shorthand prose he says: "Some judge one day to be better than another, while others judge all days to be alike. Let all be fully convinced in their own minds. Those who observe the day, observe it in honor of the Lord" (vv. 5–6a). Presumably some (Roman?) believers observe the Sabbath, or perhaps Sunday, while others have no especial ritual appreciation of any particular day. It is impossible to say from this passage on which side Paul stood. He makes two judgments. One is that each believer should be "fully convinced" about his or her decision. The other is that no believer should pass judgment on someone who holds a different conviction (vv. 10–13). The implication might be, based on the larger issue about eating, that a believer should give up acting on his conviction if it troubled another believer. But Paul does not say this explicitly about the issue of day observance, and it is best not to import a statement about eating into the issue of days. What is clear is that the decision about days is not in itself important. What *is* important is avoidance of a judgmental attitude toward someone with a different point of view. Presumably *either* action, if taken with the confidence of faith, would be an eschatological action.

Circumcision. Paul makes it clear in Galatians that male Gentiles should not be circumcised *if* that means an act considered essential to salvation. He stakes his life on that premise and will even curse an angel who argues differently (Gal 1:8). In 1 Cor 7:18–19, in a section I have argued is part of a homily on the baptismal formula of Gal 3:26–28,[20] the Apostle puts the matter in a somewhat larger context. No male Jewish believer should try to hide his circumcision; no male Gentile believer should be circumcised. The general rubric under which this judgment is made is that one should remain in his or her social situation. But the specific warrant given for circumcision is more explicit: "Circumcision is nothing and uncircumcision is nothing; but obeying the commandments of God is everything" (v. 19).

Properly understood, says Paul, the external mark is irrelevant to the correct relationship with God. *How* one views this mark is, however, crucial. Paul makes it clear (1 Cor 9:19–23) that he is as willing to live inside a Jewish ritual framework as a Gentile (probably more easily, in

---

[20] See my "Paul and the Eschatological Woman," *The Text and the Times*, 82.

fact, given his upbringing). The external mark is something that pertains to one's cultural past, not to one's standing vis-à-vis God.[21] Paul, I would insist, *values* different cultures and respects them. Eschatological reality can be expressed equally through a "Gentile" body and a "Jewish" body.

Implicit in this stance is certainly the judgment Paul has made explicit elsewhere, that a believer should not judge negatively a different mark in another male believer. To *claim* superiority over another believer because one is or is not circumcised is to value the body falsely. What the body is, or has had done to it, is not important. How one acts through the body *is* crucial.

The Lord's Supper. We have already looked at 1 Cor 11:17–34a in connection with the issue of eating. Here there is little to add except to say that in Paul's judgment the social relationships created or damaged by eating determine whether the ritual is effective (whatever that might mean) or is rather a judgment on the church. Improper eating and interrelationship means that the church does not truly enact the ritual event (v. 20). Even more, it produces "condemnation" (κρίμα—vv. 33–34a). The ritual is thus not *opus operatum*, nor is it simply one's "intention" that is the criterion. Rather it is how one relates to others in the community through the body that determines whether the ritual act in fact does what it says it is doing.

The Worship Service. In 1 Corinthians 14 Paul makes various judgments about what should happen in worship. He accepts all kinds of activity, which the Corinthians have, presumably, been practicing—speaking in tongues, prophesying, singing, reading, interpretations. All of these acts in the body are legitimate, even tongues. Paul claims to have and use that gift (v. 18), and he specifically warns against denying tongues its place in worship (v. 39). His priorities are, however, clear. What

---

[21] It is at this point that Boyarin claims that Paul makes a judgment upon Judaism because the Apostle discards a view that would have been basic to all Jews *who did not believe in Christ* (see Boyarin, *A Radical Jew*, 136–57, and the statement on p. 152: "Paul has simply allegorized our difference quite out of existence"). Cf. also p. 10, where Boyarin argues that Jewish difference means recognizing "their 'right' to remain unconvinced by the gospel." Everything depends on what one means by "recognizing their 'right.'" If that means granting to a culture or religion a "truth" which conflicts with one's own conviction, this so relativizes truth or faith convictions that it is hard to imagine that any meaning could attach to the very faith one holds. Boyarin accepts the fact that Paul is tolerant, but then says that tolerance (in and of itself) is flawed (10). What Boyarin seems to expect, however, is such an extreme tolerance that it results in relativism. Paul certainly must have felt that Jewish ritual activity is an appropriate way of expressing faith in God. Indeed, to the often-raised question, would Paul as a believer in Christ have circumcised his own son, my judgment is that he would have.

upbuilds the community, what aids the community's understanding, what encourages the group—these are for Paul the aims of worship.[22] The acts of the body (within the parameters accepted by the Corinthians and Paul) are equally acceptable in and of themselves (cf. here 1 Cor 12). But the final determination is the value of those bodily acts in the upbuilding of the community. *What* the person does bodily is one thing. *How* the person relates in worship to the needs of the community is crucial (which, of course, does influence what is considered appropriate in the social context).

Worship of Other Gods. If an actual ritual involving Greco-Roman gods and goddesses is the issue in 1 Cor 10:14–22, as it seems to me almost certain, then it is not surprising that Paul shows no flexibility or tolerance to the possibility of participation. To perform such an act is to participate in the demonic world. Paul almost opens the door for a possible participation in v. 19 by seeming to claim that such worship is entirely sham; but he draws back by introducing the issue of demons. Paul will not admit any interior understanding that makes such participation possible for the believer. There are some bodily actions that cannot be expressions of eschatological reality.

Dress in worship. Paul's refusal to be flexible appears in one other passage, the issue of appropriate dress of worship leaders of the two sexes (1 Cor 11:2–16). In this case the reason for the inflexibility is unclear. Male leaders are *not* to cover their head; female leaders are. Much effort has gone into trying to imagine why Paul is so petulant and what is the underlying reason for his judgment.[23] The best hunch, it still seems to me, is that Paul is concerned, in the face of the legitimate abolishment of sexual differentiation in liturgical leadership, to keep clear symbolically (by a dress code) sexual distinctions in the life of the community. Ultimately, then, this belongs more appropriately in the following section. I would not want to conclude, however, that there is such a thing as "eschatological dress."

Conclusion. Paul's various judgments cannot be neatly collected under one overriding principle. Insofar, however, as one is dominant, it seems to be the determination that ritual acts should lead to the upbuilding of the community. Such acts are not to be seen as bodily

---

[22] Order and decency (v. 40) surely is not the primary aim of some overly-rigid Paul. He mentions this because the *primary* contributions of mutual upbuilding and learning cannot occur in ecstatic disorder.

[23] The literature is voluminous. See, e.g., my "Paul and the Eschatological Woman," 87–92, for an earlier summary of views. For a more recent compilation of references and a careful discussion of possibilities, cf. G. Fee, *The First Epistle to the Corinthians*, 491–530.

acts independently of *how* they work within the church as a gathered community. If one can speak of "eschatological worship," then such worship occurs when individuals through their bodily actions show acceptance of, and bestow insight and encouragement upon, other members. When this is done, ritual acts become not just bodily acts but truly eschatological acts. It is *how* one acts in the body that makes the liturgical act one which comes from an eschatological body.

Gender Issues

Paul's judgments that fit under this rubric are the most frequent and most complicated of any of the categories. In current scholarship they are also the most controverted and call forth the most urgent, even strident opinions.[24] Thus, it is no surprise that the literature in recent decades that has been devoted to this issue is immense. What I can do here is only to keep attention focused on the primary issue of this paper: when a believer through the body performs as Paul exhorts, is it an eschatological body, or does it simply belong to this world?

On the surface, Paul's judgments seem rather commonplace. He echoes values enunciated in the Torah and widespread in some of the ideals of Greco-Roman culture.[25] He avoids extremes. He does not reject the body as a sexual instrument in and of itself. He does not agree with an ascetic position based on denigration of corporeality. His preference for sexual abstinence has a social base, as we will see. On the other hand, he is no proponent of any sort of sexual license, although he may have been accused of this. He has provincial views of marriage, the necessity for fidelity in it, the legitimacy of sexuality only within the marriage relationship. He opposes homosexuality as he knew about it in the ancient world (although his comments about this are sparse and occur only in material stamped with traditional Jewish wisdom).[26] He is against prostitution.

To make this provincialism the final judgment upon Paul is, however, precarious. In the first place, it is not surprising that Paul should reflect Torah values. He *does* believe that God has revealed his description of authentic human life in its pages. True, he does not seem to have been impressed by the emphasis upon the begetting of children as

---

[24] This is not the place to list bibliography. One could compile resources by checking the relevant references in books such as E. Schüssler Fiorenza, *In Memory of Her* (New York: Crossroad, 1984), B. Witherington III, *Women in the Earliest Churches* (Cambridge: Cambridge University Press, 1988), G. Fee, *The First Epistle to the Corinthians*, and V. Furnish, *The Moral Teaching of Paul: Selected Issues* (2d ed.; Nashville, TN: Abingdon, 1985).

[25] As he appeals to in 1 Cor 5:1.

[26] See R. Scroggs, *The New Testament and Homosexuality* (Philadelphia: Fortress, 1983), where I argue that in substance what Paul opposes are certain forms of pederasty.

the basis of sexuality that one finds (implicitly) in the Torah and in early Judaism (Philo, for example). Similarly, his preference for the single state within the community of faith is not an echo of Torah. Thus Paul seems to be able to make judgments independently of Torah values. But it is important to emphasize that Paul's agreement with Torah *does not mean that his ethical thought is non-eschatological.* If Torah reveals God's will for authentic humanity, then it would be natural for the Apostle to find in it guidance for how humans in the present eschatological situation should conduct their relationships. Eschatological humanity is, after all, the fulfillment of God's promise for humankind. One is saved *into* humanity, not out of it, even though in God's ultimate kingdom there is no giving or receiving in marriage.[27]

In the second place, eschatological reality is found not in the structures themselves but in the quality of relationship exhibited within the structures. Paul can even acknowledge that accepted structures can be dissolved when the quality of relationship does not exhibit eschatological realities.[28] It is what happens within the structures that makes the structure *become* an eschatological reality itself.

In a remarkable statement in 1 Cor 7:7 Paul writes: "I wish everyone to be as I am [i.e., sexually celibate]; but each has his own gift (χάρισμα) from God, one of one sort, one of another" (auth. tr.). Two interpretations are possible here. In each interpretation, the ability to remain celibate is seen as an eschatological gift, because it means the concentration of energy toward the community of faith. But to what does the second gift refer? Does it refer to marriage conducted as an eschatological relationship or to some other gift of the Spirit which Paul will list in 1 Cor 12:7–11? Either interpretation is possible, but the immediate context favors the former. If that is the case, then Paul can accept either celibacy or marriage as an eschatological χάρισμα. Obviously it would not be just any celibacy or any marriage that is such a gift, but only those infused with the quality of relationship Paul knows as eschatological. Thus sexual structures, however common in this world, can become the vehicles of eschatological reality. To put it slightly differently, sexual bodies, by becoming vehicles of eschatological reality, become eschatological bodies.

---

[27] See R. Scroggs, *The Last Adam* (Philadelphia: Fortress, 1966) 59–72.

[28] In 1 Cor 7:15–16 Paul sanctions a mixed-marriage divorce if the impetus for separation stems from the unbelieving spouse. The difficult sentences lies in v. 15c, "For God has called you [or us] in peace." Does this give the rationale for the separation or for a continued attempt to make the marriage work? I think it is the former; if so, Paul is saying that if the eschatological reality of peace does not exist, due to the squabbling of the spouses, divorce is permissible. Paul's language is, however, difficult and judgment depends in part upon how one reads the questions in v. 16.

I have space for only two examples, one dealing with a person in marriage, one with a person in relation to the community of faith. In 1 Cor 7:1–7 Paul responds to a question in a letter addressed to him by the Corinthians concerning sexual relations within marriage.[29] Here Paul acknowledges the legitimacy of sexuality in marriage as over against a celibacy which is threatened by sexual desire. Within marriage sexuality should be a normal function, interrupted only by occasional mutual agreement.[30]

Within this discussion Paul makes what still seems to me a remarkable set of statements (not the least because made by a person who may never have experienced sexual union). In verses 3–4 he urges that each partner give his or her body to the other. Since nothing is said about procreation, it may be assumed that the purpose of this giving is the sexual pleasure of the other. Neither person has "authority" over his or her body—that authority belongs to the partner. Here we can see how Paul's emphasis on the "upbuilding" of the other finds a place in sexual ethics. In the marriage of faith the believer offers the body for the pleasure of the spouse. This is how one cares, loves, and upbuilds the other within marriage. Thus even within sexuality, the body can act eschatologically.

The second example is Paul's concern for the primacy of the community of faith over that of other, potentially competing relationships such as marriage. Paul obviously prefers that believers be unmarried and celibate. The question is why? Although Boyarin has recently proposed that Paul is close to considering sexuality as sin (reviving an old argument mostly discarded today),[31] I do not consider his argument successful. Most interpreters today are in agreement that for the apostle sex is not sin and not an inferior part of this world's reality.

Perhaps the usual reason given for Paul's preference toward celibacy is the "eschatological"—meaning his references in 1 Cor 7:29–31 to the brevity of time before the eschaton arrives. People should remain in their present social situation. Yet Paul has just said (v. 28) explicitly that marriage in the present is *not* wrong. Furthermore, in verses 29–31 he assumes that social relationships continue, including marriage. When he says that "even those who have wives [should] be as though they had none," he cannot be promoting sexual abstinence in marriage, since he

---

[29] I accept the now common judgment that v. 1 contains a judgment made in the letter which Paul counters in v. 2.

[30] I take the concession mentioned in v. 6 to refer to temporary sexual abstinence, not to marriage itself, a judgment consonant with that mentioned in the previous note, that v. 1 is not Paul's own view.

[31] Boyarin, *Radical Jew*, 158–79.

has explicitly counseled continual sexual relationships between spouses earlier in vv. 2–5. What he must mean in vv. 29–31 is an awareness that corporeal, earthly relationships are not to be given ultimate loyalty. Ultimate loyalty is rather to be reserved for "affairs of the Lord" (vv. 32–35).[32]

In my judgment the real reason why Paul prefers that the believer be celibate is found in vv. 32–35. Here the married person is shown to be in inevitable tension (anxiety) with the larger believing community (pointed to by the references to the "Lord"). The married man or woman cares (as should be the case) for the spouse and the emotional energy available to a person is thus split. A married person just cannot give undivided emotional and intellectual attention to the church. For Paul, of course, *the* eschatological reality insofar as it exists in the present is the church.[33] Marriage, however legitimate, cannot help but get in the way of the church, not because it is not expressive of eschatological reality but *precisely because* marriage is a place where the person of faith is called to give and to care.

This tension between two structures, both of which can exhibit eschatological realities, is what makes Paul ambiguous in his judgments. Marriage can be a χάρισμα [gift] when infused by eschatological realities; certainly the church community should exhibit such realities. In the face of that Paul prefers that one give attention to the primary structure but he cannot deny the legitimacy and efficacy of the other.

---

[32] V. Wimbush argues that vv. 29b–31 are of non-Pauline origin, though used here by Paul. What Paul is saying here is that "Christian existence is to be experienced in the world, but not on the world's terms. . . . He emphasizes, instead of the imminence of the End, the transience of the things of the world" (*Paul the Worldly Ascetic*, 47). I have argued that the section, 7:17–31, is an independent homily based on the baptismal formula in Gal 3:26–28 inserted into the present context (cf. n. 20 above, but I do not disagree with Wimbush's judgment about 29b–31). This different origin might help explain the apparently different nuance between 29b–31 and the earlier part of the chapter.

The hard issue here is whether marriage relationships can be considered eschatological relationships, as I have argued, when at the same time Paul encourages a certain reserve toward the ultimacy of those very relationships. Can a relationship exhibit eschatological reality when it is not the ultimate relationship? I think Paul would say 'yes' to that question, but the very way of putting the question shows Paul's inevitable ambivalence, highlighted at the beginning of this paper, between this corporeal world and the coming spiritual world. Yes, one can live a corporeal relationship in an eschatological manner, but one should not lose sight of the transience of that corporeal reality.

[33] Wimbush's comments are instructive. "The world itself is not evil, thus, no renunciation of it is required. But it does bring with it its own set of demands. It can be distracting. It makes claims, demands commitment . . . , the same kind of commitment the Lord requires" (*Worldly Ascetic*, 70).

Conclusion

Paul's dilemma is set by his view, inherited from a Jewish tradition, that the resurrected body is not corporeal, over against his faith that for the believer life now is already life in the new creation. Given this dilemma, it seems to me a bit surprising that Paul maintains as consistent a view as he does. His basic understanding is that corporeality belongs to this world and will be replaced for the believer with a spiritual, non-corporeal body in the kingdom of God. But—and this is an all-important qualifier—the believer's body is, or at least can and should be, an expression of eschatological reality. The corporeal body in and of itself is not important; what one *does* in that body is.

Thus Paul takes bodily actions with the utmost importance. Neither asceticism nor libertinism is acceptable, because these begin with a judgment on the body in and of itself. For the Apostle the body is part of the good world and I do not think it can be sustained that he takes a negative view of it. On the other hand, the body is a *communicator* of either the reality of this world (κατὰ σάρκα) or of God's new creation (κατὰ πνεῦμα). By the renewal of one's νοῦς [mind] the believer can come to know God's will and express this eschatological reality in and through the body. Corporeality is not in and of itself eschatological reality; but it can and should *become* an eschatological body when it is used to express that caring for others (and self) which Paul so neatly summarizes in Gal 5:22–23: "For the fruit of the Spirit is love, joy, peace, patience, kindness, generosity, faithfulness, gentleness, and self-control."

The Role of Scripture in Paul's Ethics

Richard B. Hays

I. The Problem

How does Scripture function in Paul's ethics? We might expect it to play a major role in his moral teaching, for he writes in Rom 15:4:

> For whatever was written in former days was written for our instruction (εἰς τὴν ἡμετέραν διδασκαλίαν), so that by steadfastness and by the encouragement of the scriptures (διὰ τῆς παρακλήσεως τῶν γραφῶν) we might have hope.

Here the biblical writings are portrayed as a fundamental source of instruction (διδασκαλία) and moral exhortation (παράκλησις). Such a view of the texts is hardly surprising for one who called himself a "Hebrew of Hebrews" (Phil 3:5) and distinguished himself among his contemporaries by his zeal for "the traditions of [his] ancestors" (Gal 1:14). The scriptures of Israel were imbedded deeply in his bones. Recent studies of Paul's thought have increasingly recognized the major role played by Scripture[1] in constituting his imaginative world.[2]

Yet when we consider Paul's actual use of Scripture in shaping his *ethical* arguments, the evidence appears to be remarkably slight; Paul's own practice of moral teaching does not self-evidently exemplify the didactic role ascribed to Scripture in the programmatic statement of

---

[1] Paul characteristically uses the term "Scripture" (ἡ γραφή) to refer to Israel's sacred texts. He never uses the expression "Old Testament." His single use of the term "old covenant" (ἡ παλαιὰ διαθήκη, 2 Cor 3:14) refers not to the canon of scripture as a whole but specifically to the Mosaic law. The term "Hebrew Bible," also never used by Paul, is confusing and inappropriate since Paul, writing in Greek to Greek-speaking readers, normally quotes the LXX rather than translating the Hebrew text.

[2] I have argued this position extensively in *Echoes of Scripture in the Letters of Paul* (New Haven: Yale University Press, 1989). See also D. A. Koch, *Die Schrift als Zeuge des Evangeliums: Untersuchungen zur Verwendung und zum Verständnis der Schrift bei Paulus* (BHT 69; Tübingen: Mohr-Siebeck, 1986); Christopher D. Stanley, *Paul and the Language of Scripture: Citation Technique in the Pauline Epistles and Contemporary Literature* (SNTSMS 69; Cambridge: Cambridge University Press, 1992); J. W. Aageson, *Written Also for Our Sake: Paul and the Art of Biblical Interpretation* (Louisville, KY: Westminster/John Knox, 1993); C. A. Evans and J. A. Sanders (eds.), *Paul and the Scriptures of Israel* (JSNTSup 83; Sheffield: JSOT Press, 1993); R. H. Bell, *Provoked to Jealousy: The Origin and Purpose of the Jealousy Motif in Romans 9–11* (WUNT, 2d Ser., 63; Tübingen: Mohr-Siebeck, 1994).

Rom 15:4. Paul is reluctant—for reasons that need no rehearsing here—to treat Scripture as a rule book. Indeed, he explicitly argues that various requirements of the Torah are not binding for his Gentile churches: circumcision (1 Cor 7:17–20; Gal 5:2–6), food laws (Rom 14:1–4, 14, 20), and probably the sabbath (Rom 14:5; Gal 4:9–11). The law, he says, was a παιδαγωγός [disciplinarian (NRSV); a slave given responsibility for conducting, or superintending a child] whose commission was valid and necessary until faith came, but now, since the resurrection of Jesus, the law is no longer necessary (Gal 3:23–25). Thus, when he is confronted with various problems of conduct in his churches (e.g., divorce, eating idol meat), he does not settle them in a rabbinic fashion by seeking to apply Torah casuistically. For example, in dealing with the issue of divorce in 1 Cor 7:10–16, he makes no reference to Deut 24:1–4, the Pentateuchal passage that was the focus of rabbinic discussions of the topic. The omission is perhaps not surprising, since Deuteronomy permits divorce, while Paul is seeking to restrict it.

Victor Furnish, after surveying a number of passages in which Paul does cite Scripture in his ethical arguments, summarizes the situation aptly:

> It is noteworthy that Paul never quotes the Old Testament *in extenso* for the purpose of developing a pattern of conduct. Except for a few instances in which a catena of passages from several different scriptural contexts is assembled, the citations are always brief. Moreover, and even of greater significance, they are never casuistically interpreted or elaborated. . . . There is no evidence which indicates that the apostle regarded [the Old Testament] as in any sense a source book for detailed moral instruction or even a manual of ethical norms.[3]

Instead, Paul seeks to commend his normative moral teachings on the basis of the gospel itself: right behavior is understood as "the fruit of the Spirit" (Gal 5:22–23), the natural outflow of the new life in Christ. Moral judgment becomes a matter not of obeying a written law but of discerning God's will in the new apocalyptic situation:

> I appeal to you therefore, brothers and sisters, by the mercies of God, to present your bodies as a living sacrifice, holy and acceptable to God, which is your spiritual worship. Do not be conformed to this world (or "age"; τῷ αἰῶνι τούτῳ), but be transformed by the renewing of your

---

[3] V. P. Furnish, *Theology and Ethics in Paul* (Nashville, TN: Abingdon, 1968) 33. More recently, P. J. Tomson (*Paul and the Jewish Law: Halakha in the Letters of the Apostle to the Gentiles* [CRINT III/1; Assen and Maastricht: Van Gorcum; Minneapolis, MN: Fortress, 1990]) has argued, to the contrary, that Paul's ethical teaching is deeply grounded in rabbinic traditions of halakhic scriptural interpretation.

minds, so that you may discern what is the will of God—what is good and acceptable and perfect. (Rom 12:1–2)

Thus, many scholars have argued, Scripture becomes *de facto* irrelevant—or at least a minor factor—for Pauline ethics.[4] Andreas Lindemann, for example, declares:

[Paulus] versteht aber das Alte Testament, seine Bibel, gerade nicht mehr als Tora in eigentlichen Sinne; sie ist ihm nicht mehr die Quelle der Weisungen Gottes für das Verhalten der Menschen, soweit sie Christen sind.[5]

Can this be correct? If so, how could Paul write Rom 15:4?[6] Or again, what are we to make of 1 Cor 10:11, which comments on the fate of Israel's wilderness generation?

These things happened to them typologically (τυπικῶς), and they were written down for our instruction (ἐγράφη δὲ πρὸς νουθεσίαν ἡμῶν), upon whom the ends of the ages have met. (Author's tr.)

Here Paul regards the written scriptural witness as a word for the instruction of his own community, a word intended by God precisely for the eschatological moment in which apostle and church now find themselves. The ethical import of this word for the situation Paul is addressing is very clear: the community is to flee from association with idols (10:14) and to beware of overconfident presumption upon the grace of God (10:12). In such a case, we see Paul appealing to Scripture very directly as a basis for ethical admonition to the church.

Clearly, a fresh look at the problem is needed. Lindemann and others are right that Paul does not use Scripture like the rabbis, yet there are numerous indications in Paul's letters that the Scripture somehow shapes his moral vision.[7] The conclusions drawn by Furnish in

---

[4] For an impressive roster of scholars who take this position, see the summary of B. S. Rosner, *Paul, Scripture and Ethics: A Study of 1 Corinthians 5–7* (AGJU 22; Leiden: Brill, 1994) 3–9.

[5] "Paul, however, no longer understands the Old Testament, his Bible, as Torah in the proper sense; it is for him no longer the source of God's directions for the behavior of human beings, insofar as they are Christians" (A. Lindemann, "Die biblischen Toragebote und die paulinische Ethik," in *Studien zum Text und zur Ethik des Neuen Testaments: Festschrift zum 80. Geburtstag von Heinrich Greeven* [ed. W. Schrage; BZNW 47; Berlin: de Gruyter, 1986], 242–65; here, 263–64).

[6] One solution to this problem is offered by L. E. Keck ("Romans 15:4—An Interpolation?" in *Faith and History: Essays in Honor of Paul W. Meyer*, [ed. J. T. Carroll et al.; Atlanta: Scholars Press, 1991], 125–36), who has argued that Paul did *not* write it. Keck proposes that the verse is a postpauline gloss.

[7] The work of Rosner (*Paul, Scripture and Ethics*) persuasively traces some of the ways in which Paul's teaching in 1 Corinthians 5–7 presupposes and alludes to biblical texts.

his discussion of the problem almost thirty years ago suggest a promising way forward:

> In fact, Paul's use of the Old Testament in his ethical teaching is not to be radically differentiated from his use of the Old Testament overall. In connection with ethical admonition and instruction, as elsewhere, an important presupposition is that the Old Testament is scriptural witness to the history of God's dealings with his people, his claim upon them, and his promises concerning their future. . . . While the Old Testament, then, is not a "source" for Paul's ethical instruction in a narrow sense, it is a source for it in a more basic way. . . . The Old Testament is not a source for his ethical teaching in that it provides him rules, aphorisms, maxims, and proverbs. Rather, it is a source for his ethical teaching in that it provides him with a perspective from which he interprets the whole event of God's act in Christ, and the concomitant and consequent claim God makes on the believer.[8]

Although Furnish does not develop this programmatic claim in detail, his basic insight merits fuller reflection: to understand the role of Scripture in Paul's ethics, we must widen our field of vision and consider the way in which Scripture renders a "world" for Paul, the way in which his symbolic universe is constituted by a particular reading of Israel's sacred texts.

I propose that we think about this problem by considering five ways in which Scripture informs Paul's ethics. Our treatment of these five aspects will move from the most global to the most particular roles played by the biblical texts in shaping Paul's moral world.

II. Some Functions of Scripture in Pauline Ethics

A. Scripture as Narrative Framework for Community Identity

Paul reads Scripture in light of a narrative hermeneutic as a grand story of election and promise, the story of δικαιοσύνη θεοῦ, God's covenant faithfulness reaching out to reclaim a fallen and broken humanity.[9] That is why his use of Scripture highlights the story of Abraham (the patriarch to whom God's universal promise was made), the climactic chapters of Deuteronomy (which promise covenant renewal and restoration of the people), and above all the prophetic passages known to us as Deutero-Isaiah (which promise the revelation of God's salvation to all flesh, the Jew first and then also all nations).

---

8 *Theology and Ethics in Paul*, 34. The present essay is dedicated to Victor Furnish with gratitude for his collegial support, as well as for his careful and generative work on Pauline ethics.

9 For fuller development and defense of these themes see Hays, *Echoes*, esp. 156–64.

The church is called to find its identity and mission within this epic story stretching from Adam to Abraham to Moses to Isaiah to Christ to the saints in Paul's own historical moment.

"What time is it?" "What is God doing in the world?" "What is our vocation as God's people?" These are the questions that Paul asks and answers on the basis of Scripture. A particularly powerful illustration of this way of reading Scripture is found in 2 Cor 5:17–6:2:

> So if anyone is in Christ, there is a new creation: everything old has passed away; see, everything has become new! All this is from God, who reconciled us to himself through Christ, and has given us the ministry of reconciliation; that is, in Christ God was reconciling the world to himself, not counting their trespasses against them, and entrusting the message of reconciliation to us. So we are ambassadors for Christ, since God is making his appeal through us; we entreat you on behalf of Christ, be reconciled to God. For our sake he made him to be sin who knew no sin, so that in him we might become the righteousness of God. As we work together with him, we urge you also not to accept the grace of God in vain. For he says,
>> At an acceptable time I have listened to you,
>> and on a day of salvation I have helped you.
> See, now is the acceptable time; see, now is the day of salvation!

What time is it? Now is the day of salvation announced by Isaiah (Isa 49:8), the time in which the Servant of the Lord will both raise up the tribes of Jacob and extend God's salvation to the ends of the earth (Isa 49:6). *What is God doing in the world?* God is reconciling the world to himself and actualizing the new creation that Isaiah prophesied (Isa 43:18–19; 65:17–25; 66:22–23). *What is our vocation as God's people?* Our vocation is to embody the message of reconciliation by *becoming* the righteousness of God (δικαιοσύνη θεοῦ). That is to say, the vocation of the community is to become a visible manifestation of God's reconciling covenant love in the world.[10] Such a description of the community's identity has wide-ranging implications for ethics, even though Paul does not spell them out fully at this point in 2 Corinthians. He does, however, in the apostolic self-description that follows immediately in 6:3–10, offer some hint of what it might mean to model the new creation in a world still hostile to God: hardships, suffering, and conformity to the example of Jesus.

Thus, Scripture provides an overarching proleptic vision of God's design to redeem the world and situates the community of believers within the unfolding story of this dramatic redemption. Every word of

---

[10] On δικαιοσύνη θεοῦ as covenant language, see R. B. Hays, "Justification," *ABD* 3.1129–33.

ethical guidance that Paul gives to his churches finds its ultimate warrant in this narrative framework. If ethical judgments are inseparable from foundational construals of communal identity, then any consideration of Pauline ethics must attend to the way in which Paul's understanding of the church's vocation is rooted in his reading of Scripture.

B. Scripture as Call to Righteousness and Love

Paul's vision of the church's identity carries with it the axiomatic conviction that the people of God are called to be a holy people whose conduct conforms to the will of God (cf. 1 Cor 1:2). Equally axiomatic for Paul is the conviction that the law—which is "holy and righteous and good" (Rom 7:12)—positively discloses God's will. Consequently, in several places Paul offers sweeping summary statements that construe the law in global fashion as a mandate for righteousness and/or love.

> Owe no one anything, except to love one another; for the one who loves another has fulfilled the law. The commandments, "You shall not commit adultery; You shall not murder; You shall not steal; You shall not covet" [Exod 20:13–17; Deut 5:17–21]; and any other commandment, are summed up in this word, "Love your neighbor as yourself" [Lev 19:18]. Love does no wrong to a neighbor; therefore, love is the fulfilling of the law. (Rom 13:8–10)

Here Paul cites Lev 19:18 as a summation of the content of the moral precepts of the Decalogue, thereby elaborating more fully what he meant in Gal 5:14 by saying, "For the whole law is summed up in a single commandment, 'You shall love your neighbor as yourself.'" It has often been observed that this appeal to Lev 19:18 as an encapsulation of Torah is formally similar to the teaching of R. Hillel: "What is hateful to you, do not do to your neighbor" (b. Šabb. 31a).[11] Our particular concern here, however, is not only to notice that Paul's strategy of summing up the law has parallels among his Jewish contemporaries but also to observe that he accomplishes this summation by citing another biblical text, interpreting Scripture by means of Scripture.[12] The hermeneutical reconfiguration of the law is achieved not through appeal to

---

[11] On Paul's use of Lev 19:18, see V. P. Furnish, *The Love Command in the New Testament* (Nashville, TN: Abingdon, 1972) 94, 97, 102–04, 107–11; W. Schrage, *Die konkreten Einzelgebote in der paulinischen Paränese* (Gütersloh: Mohn, 1961) 97–100, 249–71; A. Nissen, *Gott und der Nächste im antiken Judentum: Untersuchungen zum Doppelgebot der Liebe* (WUNT 15; Tübingen: Mohr-Siebeck, 1974).

[12] Whether Paul's singling out of Lev 19:18 was original with him or whether he was dependent on early Christian tradition, perhaps going back to Jesus himself (cf. Mark 12:28–34 parrs.), is a question that need not concern us here. See J. D. G. Dunn, *Romans 9–16* (WBC 38B; Dallas, TX: Word, 1988) 779.

the teaching of Jesus or to some other normative consideration but through a rereading of Scripture itself.

One remarkable feature of this global construal of the law is that it allows Paul to contend that Christians can "fulfill" the law without actually observing all the particular practices that it requires. This conviction—surely strange to Jews who shared Paul's own prior Pharisaic beliefs—underlies 1 Cor 7:19: "Circumcision is nothing, and uncircumcision is nothing; but what matters is keeping the command-ments of God." Since circumcision was one of the commandments of God, this affirmation can only have seemed bizarre and scandalous to Paul's Jewish contemporaries. Paul, however, had undergone a hermeneutical revolution in his reading of Scripture that allowed him to see Gentiles in Christ as fulfilling what the law requires. This is made explicit in Rom 2:26–29a:

> So, if those who are uncircumcised keep the requirements of the law (τὰ δικαιώματα τοῦ νόμου), will not their uncircumcision be regarded as circumcision? Then those who are physically uncircum-cised (= Gentiles) but keep the law will condemn you that have the written code and circumcision but break the law. For a person is not a Jew who is one in appearance, nor is circumcision a matter of appearance in the flesh. Rather, the (real) Jew is one who is one inwardly, and (real) circumcision is circumcision of the heart in the spirit, not in letter. (NRSV, with alterations by the author)

The interpretative move here is the same one that Paul makes in Phil 3:3 in his warning against Judaizers who "mutilate the flesh": "For it is we who are the circumcision, who worship in the Spirit of God and boast in Christ Jesus and have no confidence in the flesh." In both cases, rather than conceding that the honorific term περιτομή ("circumcision"—understood as a designation for God's elect) can be restricted to the Jewish people, Paul metaphorizes the term and claims it for the members of the new community that trusts in Jesus Christ. Even if they are physically uncircumcised, they nonetheless manifest the kind of obedience from the heart that the law commands. This is not merely an arbitrary hermeneutical sleight of hand: it is based, as the Romans 2 passage shows, on the biblical image of the "circumcision of the heart," which Paul finds prominently in Deuteronomy. Particularly important is Deut 30:6, which depicts the circumcision of the heart as God's gracious act of covenant renewal: "The Lord your God will circumcise your heart and the heart of your descendants, so that you will love the Lord your God with all your heart and with all your soul, in order that you may live" (cf. also Deut 10:16). If God has chosen now to circumcise the hearts of Gentile believers, as Paul maintains, that means that they must be full participants in the covenant community.

All of this is set forth strikingly in Rom 8:3–4:

> For God has done what the law, weakened by the flesh, could not do: by sending his own Son in the likeness of sinful flesh and as a sin-offering,[13] he condemned sin in the flesh, *so that the just requirement of the law* (τὸ δικαίωμα τοῦ νόμου: cf. Rom 2:26) *might be fulfilled in us*, who walk not according to the flesh but according to the Spirit. (Emphasis added.)

The general mandate to fulfill the law by walking in love is, on Paul's reading, to be found in Scripture itself. Thus, at a high level of generality, Scripture both commands and prefigures a certain "ethic," a way of life dedicated to God's service. Those in Christ—whether Jews or Gentiles—who walk in the Spirit now fulfill what the law requires, a life animated by the love of God.

C. Scripture as Implicit Source of Particular Norms

Of course, such a general mandate requires further behavioral specification. When Paul speaks of Gentiles fulfilling the law, he is making certain assumptions about the sort of moral conduct that is pleasing to God. He assumes, as Rom 13:8–10 indicates, that adultery, murder, theft, and covetousness are contrary to loving the neighbor and that "fulfilling the law" implicitly requires obedience to the commandments of the Decalogue. We see here, however, only the tip of the iceberg: Paul assumes without supporting argumentation a whole network of moral judgments and norms whose source lies ultimately in Israel's law.[14] These assumptions, rarely raised to the level of conscious reflection, appear offhandedly in Paul's occasional vice lists.

> Now the works of the flesh are obvious: fornication, impurity, licentiousness, idolatry, sorcery, enmities, strife, jealousy, anger, quarrels, dissensions, factions, envy, drunkenness, carousing, and things like these. I am warning you, as I warned you before: those who do such things will not inherit the kingdom of God. (Gal 5:19–21)

Paul makes no attempt to derive his condemnation of these behaviors explicitly from Scripture; he regards their negative character as self-

---

[13] The NRSV reads, "and to deal with sin"; on the above translation, see N. T. Wright, *The Climax of the Covenant: Christ and the Law in Pauline Theology* (Minneapolis, MN: Fortress, 1991) 220–25.

[14] See W. Schrage, *The Ethics of the New Testament* (Philadelphia: Fortress, 1988) 205: "There are instances where Paul as it were instinctively and without further justification presupposes certain conclusions deriving from Jewish thought based on the Torah."

evident (φανερά). Nor can every item in the vice list be traced to a particular Old Testament commandment. Nonetheless, some of the items are clear violations of biblical teaching: fornication, impurity, idolatry, sorcery. In such lists, even though Paul does not bother to draw clear distinctions between biblical norms and general common-sense moral standards, it is clear that Scripture has played a role in shaping his vision of the moral life.

Paul summons those who have become members of the Christian community to live a new kind of life, leaving behind immoral conduct that formerly characterized their existence:

> Do you not know that wrongdoers will not inherit the kindom of God? Do not be deceived! Fornicators, idolaters, adulterers, male prostitutes (μαλακοί), sodomites (ἀρσενοκοῖται), thieves, the greedy, drunkards, revilers, robbers—none of these will inherit the kingdom of God. And this is what some of you used to be. But you were washed, you were sanctified, you were justified in the name of the Lord Jesus Christ and in the Spirit of our God. (1 Cor 6:9–11)

The similarity of this list to that of Gal 5:19–21 is obvious, but the addition of μαλακοί and particularly of ἀρσενοκοῖται provides an interesting example of the "background" function of Scripture in Pauline ethics. Paul assumes a negative evaluation of same-sex intercourse that is rooted in distinctively Jewish attitudes which in turn depend upon the Old Testament law. Indeed, as Robin Scroggs has proposed, the term ἀρσενοκοῖται—not previously attested in Greek sources—is almost certainly a coinage derived from the language of Lev 18:22, 20:13 LXX.[15] Paul feels no need here, however, to cite chapter and verse or to make an ethical argument against homosexual acts. The Torah's condemnation of such behavior has become thoroughly diffused in Jewish culture and moral attitudes; Paul simply assumes that his readers will share this moral judgment, just as he expects that they will not need to be persuaded that stealing is wrong.

Similar assumptions underlie Paul's most extensively developed vice list in Rom 1:18–32, in which he depicts the plight of humanity in rebellion against their Creator.[16] The biblical subtexts here are manifold and complex: the condemnation of idolatry shows significant indebtedness to the Wisdom of Solomon (especially 12:23–14:31), but the idea that faithless humans have "exchanged" the glory of God for idolatrous images (Rom 1:18–23) draws upon Ps 106:20 ("They

---

[15] R. Scroggs, *The New Testament and Homosexuality* (Philadelphia: Fortress, 1983) 106–108.

[16] For fuller discussion, see R. B. Hays, "Relations Natural and Unnatural," *JRE* 14/1 (1986) 184–215.

exchanged the glory of God for the image of an ox that eats grass") and Jer 2:11:

> Has a nation changed its gods,
> even though they are no gods?
> But my people have changed their glory
> for something that does not profit.

This root sin of idolatrous rejection of the one true God leads humanity into a range of horrifying behavior, as God "gives them up" to follow their own devices and desires (Rom 1:24–32). Once again, Paul does not seek to adduce specific scriptural warrants for his condemnation of this catalogue of offenses; a negative judgment is assumed as part of the fabric of moral discourse. Yet there is no question that this fabric is woven with many threads drawn from Israel's Scripture.[17]

D. Scripture as Paradigmatic Narrative

Beyond specific norms and commandments, however, Scripture functions also in Paul's thought as a source of narratives that provide broader paradigms—examples of behavior, either positive or negative —for the life of the church. This is most evident in the passages where Paul explicitly reads the stories of Israel as prefiguring the experience of the church in his own day. I have contended in *Echoes of Scripture in the Letters of Paul* that this typological reading strategy—an ecclesio-centric hermeneutic for reading the Old Testament—is pervasive in Paul's letters.[18] The identity of the community is shaped by its identification with Israel.

Writing to a predominantly Gentile church at Corinth, Paul addresses them in a way that includes them within Israel's story and simultaneously reconfigures Israel's story in the light of the church's practices:

> I do not want you to be ignorant, brothers and sisters, that our fathers (οἱ πατέρες ἡμῶν) were all under the cloud, and all passed through the sea, and all were baptized into Moses in the cloud and in the sea, and all ate the same spiritual food, and all drank the same spiritual

---

[17] I do not mean to deny that Paul drew his moral judgments also from other sources, including Greco-Roman philosophical traditions. See, for example, Furnish, *Theology and Ethics*, 44–51; H. D. Betz, *Galatians* (Hermeneia; Philadelphia: Fortress, 1979), passim; J. Paul Sampley, *Walking Between the Times: Paul's Moral Reasoning* (Minneapolis, MN: Fortress, 1991) 94–98. The point is rather that Scripture is part of the mix, that the taken-for-granted account of righteousness and unrighteousness that Paul presupposes as normative is influenced in countless important ways by the moral world of Israel's Scripture.

[18] Hays, *Echoes*, 84–121.

drink. For they drank from the spiritual rock that followed them, and the rock was Christ. (1 Cor 10:1–4; NRSV, with alterations by the author)

The Gentile Corinthians are to recognize Israel's wilderness generation as "our fathers," and the story of their wanderings and misfortunes is now to be read as a prefiguration of the situation of the church. Even the supernatural spiritual events whereby God delivered Israel from captivity and preserved them in the desert could not serve as unconditional guarantees of God's favor; so, too, the Corinthians should not rely exclusively on baptism and the Lord's Supper as foolproof claims on God's grace.

The only biblical text actually quoted in 1 Cor 10:1–22 is a narrative description of the golden calf incident: "The people sat down to eat and drink, and they rose up to play" (Exod 32:6, quoted in 1 Cor 10:7). This single citation, however, evokes the larger story of Israel in the wilderness, and Paul follows it up with allusions to incidents described in Num 14:26–35; 25:1–9; 26:62; 21:5–9; and 16:41–50 (1 Cor 10:8–10). Each of these incidents is used by Paul in a hortatory fashion to warn the Corinthians against certain behavior: idolatry, sexual immorality, putting Christ to the test, and murmuring against God. In short, Paul uses the story of Israel here as a negative paradigm illustrating both rebellious behavior and its dire consequences.[19] The Corinthians should recognize themselves in the mirror of the biblical narrative and modify their behavior accordingly. If they fail to heed the warning, if they continue to flirt with idolatry by carelessly eating idol meat, they will be reenacting Israel's faithlessness. Paul subtly underscores the point by concluding the unit with a rhetorical question that echoes the Song of Moses (Deuteronomy 32): "Or are we provoking the Lord to jealousy (παραζηλοῦμεν)? Are we stronger than he?" (1 Cor 10:22). The full force of the question comes clear only when we recall the Deuteronomy text:

> They made him jealous with strange gods,
> with abhorrent things they provoked him.
> They sacrificed to demons, not God [cf. 1 Cor 10:20]. . . .
> The Lord saw it, and was jealous (ἐζήλωσε);
> he spurned his sons and daughters.

---

[19] Paul's deft way of retelling the wilderness story, however, will not allow for a supersessionist interpretation: Israel had Christ (v. 4) and the sacraments (vv. 1–3), and the church faces the same testing they did (vv. 12–13). Thus, the church is not in a superior position, despite their privileged eschatological vantage point (v. 11). Indeed, the rhetoric of Paul's typological reading seeks to lead the Corinthians to see themselves in the *same* situation as Israel in the desert. See Hays, *Echoes*, 91–104.

He said: I will hide my face from them. . . .
They made me jealous (παραζήλωσαν) with what is no god,
provoked me with their idols. (Deut 32:16–17a, 19–20a, 21a)[20]

Since the account of Israel's misadventures was written down "to instruct us, upon whom the ends of the ages have come" (1 Cor 10:11), the Corinthians should learn the lesson from the biblical story and shun "the table of demons" (10:21).

It is noteworthy that Paul argues the point here not by quoting commandments but by retelling the story and encouraging his readers to hear the resonances between the scriptural narrative and the contemporary problem. This passage in 1 Corinthians 10 is the most extensively developed illustration of this style of ethical argument in Paul's letters, but one could adduce numerous other examples. Paul reads Scripture as a vast network of typological prefigurations of himself and his communities. This allows him to use the scriptural stories as paradigms for his own mission (e.g., Rom 10:14–17; 11:1–6; Gal 1:15) and for the actions that he wants these communities to perform (e.g., Gal 4:21–5:1; 2 Cor 8:7–15).[21]

A special case of this strategy of reading scriptural narratives as ethical paradigms is Paul's use of the figure of Jesus—as prefigured in Scripture—as a pattern for imitation.[22] Paul sees in Scripture the story of Jesus Christ as the servant who suffers and relinquishes power for the sake of others. The clearest example is found in Rom 15:1–13, where Paul exhorts the strong to accept the weak for the sake of building up the community, in accordance with the example of Christ. The character of Christ's action is then explained by a quotation of Ps 69:9: "For Christ did not please himself; but, as it is written, 'The insults of those who insult you have fallen on me'" (Rom 15:3). Paul goes on to suggest in vv. 7–13 that Christ's welcoming of Jews and Gentiles alike is also prefigured in a string of scriptural passages: Ps 18:49, Deut 32:43, Ps 117:1, and Isa 11:10.[23] In light of this action of Christ, the Christians at Rome are exhorted to "Welcome one another . . . for the glory of God" (Rom 15:7).

One striking feature of this passage—the rhetorical summation of the letter to the Romans—is its portrayal of Christ as the speaker in the first-person quotations from the Psalms (Rom 15:3, 9). I have argued

---

[20] NRSV. Greek insertions demonstrate how the LXX rendered the pertinent words.

[21] See discussion of these passages in Hays, *Echoes*, 111–18, 88–91.

[22] On the importance of the *imitatio Christi* as a motif in Pauline ethics, see Furnish, *Theology and Ethics*, 217–23.

[23] Note once again that Deuteronomy 32 shows up in a climactic summary.

elsewhere[24] that the device of understanding the Messiah as the praying voice in the royal lament psalms was a widespread hermeneutical convention in early Christianity and that Paul's distinctive adaptation of that tradition here in Romans 15 is to interpret this motif in a *hortatory* (rather than apologetic) manner. In other words, Paul takes the suffering righteous figure of the Psalms as a pattern for the conduct of the church: "the community that learns to recognize the voice of the Messiah in the Psalms will learn finally to join in his suffering and in his song."[25] Once again, we see that Paul's fundamental reading of Scripture—in this case, the christological interpretation of the Psalter—yields a narrative that becomes paradigmatic for his ethical vision for the community.

E. Scripture as Specific Word Addressed to the Community

Finally, we may consider a number of passages in which Paul reads Scripture as a word of God spoken immediately to the situation of his community. What I have in mind here is not merely general moral advice that would apply always and everywhere, such as Rom 12:19–21, which quotes Deut 32:35 and Prov 25:21–22:

> Beloved, never avenge yourselves, but leave room for the wrath of God; for it is written, "'Vengeance is mine, I will repay,' says the Lord" [Deut 32:35]. No, "if your enemies are hungry, feed them; if they are thirsty, give them something to drink; for by doing this you will heap burning coals on their heads" [Prov 25:21–22]. Do not be overcome by evil, but overcome evil with good.

There is a sense in which this teaching of Scripture is addressed to the church, but the address is of a very general character. The appeal to Proverbs shows that Paul is drawing on a stock of generalizable moral wisdom in the service of paraenesis. To be sure, the force of such wisdom is enhanced for the early church by the teaching and example of Jesus, but there is no clear indication in the text of Romans that Paul regards this moral counsel as distinctively pertinent to the situation of the Roman Christians.

In other cases, however, Paul hears the word of Scripture as a word on target, a word spoken directly for the guidance of his churches, "on whom the ends of the ages have come." Probably the citation of Deut 25:4 in 1 Cor 9:9–12 fits this category:

---

[24] R. B. Hays, "Christ Prays the Psalms: Paul's Use of an Early Christian Exegetical Convention," in *The Future of Christology: Essays in Honor of Leander E. Keck* (ed. A. J. Malherbe and W. A. Meeks; Minneapolis, MN: Fortress, 1993) 122–36.

[25] Ibid., 136.

For it is written in the law of Moses, "You shall not muzzle an ox while it is treading out the grain." Is it for oxen that God is concerned? Or does he not speak entirely for our sake (δι' ἡμᾶς πάντως)? It was indeed written for our sake. . . . If we have sown spiritual good among you, is it too much if we reap your material benefits?

The law's commandment not to muzzle a threshing ox was written for the sake of the church, and its real referent is Paul and his apostolic colleagues. The hidden meaning of this law is that Paul as an apostle has the right to expect financial support from his churches.

Sometimes the word may be even more sharply targeted to the specific situation, as in Gal 4:30. What does Scripture say? Scripture (ἡ γραφή), virtually personified as a character, an intermediary spokesperson for God, addresses the Galatians directly, commanding them to "drive out the slavewoman and her son" (Gen 21:10), a command which, in light of Paul's allegorization of the Sarah-Hagar story, means that the Galatians are to expel the Jewish-Christian preachers of circumcision from their community.[26]

Not always, however, is the command of Scripture directed to a single action. In the opening chapters of 1 Corinthians, Paul repeatedly calls upon his readers to hear the word of Scripture as a *character-shaping* message that speaks precisely to the conflicts that are dividing the Corinthian church. Paul's first explicit quotation from Scripture in 1 Corinthians is adduced in support of his assertion that the word [NRSV reads: "message"] of the cross is, paradoxically, the power of God:

For the message of the cross is foolishness to those who are perishing,
but to us who are being saved it is the power of God. For it is written,
　"I will destroy the wisdom of the wise,
　and the discernment of the discerning I will thwart." (1 Cor 1:18–19)

This citation from Isa 29:14 is a pointed word of warning directed to those at Corinth who pride themselves on being σοφοί. Indeed, the metaleptically suppressed echo of the wider Isaiah context should rebound on the prideful Corinthians with particular force:

The Lord said:
Because these people draw near with their *mouths*
and honor me with their *lips*,
while their hearts are far from me,
and their worship of me is a human commandment learned by rote;
so I will again do amazing things with this people,
shocking and amazing.
The wisdom of their wise shall perish,

---

[26] For discussion of the passage, see Hays, *Echoes*, 111–18.

and the discernment of their discerning shall be hidden.
(Isa 29:13–14)

The Corinthians who glory in their speech gifts and their knowledge (cf. 1 Cor 1:6) are to hear themselves challenged directly by the word of Isaianic judgment that Paul adduces.

This is made even more explicit at the end of chapter 1 by Paul's next citation: Christ is said to have become "wisdom for us from God, and righteousness and sanctifiction and redemption, in order that, as it is written, 'Let the one who boasts boast in the Lord'" (1 Cor 1:30–31). God has chosen to reverse normal human standards of valuation, overturning wisdom and power and privilege, in order to remove all possible ground for human boasting (1 Cor 1:20–29). Thus, there can be no ground for boasting at all except for boasting in the Lord—that is, giving God praise for what he has done through the cross. The quotation that forbids boasting is usually thought to be derived loosely from Jer 9:22–23, a passage that occurs at the conclusion of a harsh judgment oracle against the unfaithful people of God.[27] An equally good case, however, can be made for hearing in 1 Cor 1:31 a citation of 1 Kgdms 2:10 (LXX), the conclusion of Hannah's song of praise to God for overturning human power and raising up the poor and needy.[28] (Cf. also 1 Kgdms 2:3: "Do not boast [μὴ καυχᾶσθε], and do not utter high things; Let not high-sounding words come out of your mouth, for the Lord is a God of knowledge, and God prepares his own designs.") In either case, regardless of the precise source, Paul's citation is to be heard by the Corinthians as a word spoken directly to them, calling them to humility and changed behavior.

The same themes are sounded again in 1 Cor 3:18–23, this time discouraging boasting in any particular apostles. The texts cited here are different (Job 5:12–13 and Ps 93:11 LXX), but the aim of these citations, as explained in 1 Cor 3:21, is to recall the concerns of the first chapter of the letter: "so that no one might *boast* (καυχάσθω) in human beings."

In light of these observations, we should conclude that the somewhat obscure comment of 1 Cor 4:6 refers back to these particular Scripture quotations:

> I have applied all this to Apollos and myself for your benefit, brothers and sisters, so that you may learn through us the meaning of the saying

---

[27] For a perceptive discussion of the rhetorical and theological implications of this intertextual link, see G. R. O'Day, "Jeremiah 9:22–23 and 1 Cor 1:26–31: A Study in Intertextuality," *JBL* 109 (1990) 259–67.

[28] The strength of the case for 1 Kgdms 2:10 as the source for Paul's citation was first brought to my attention in an unpublished paper by my student J. Ross Wagner.

"Nothing beyond what is written," so that none of you will be puffed up in favor of one against another.

Paul has spoken of his own relationship to Apollos in chapter 3 of the letter in order to illustrate what it would mean to be constrained by the scriptural mandate to boast only in the Lord, not in human gifts or personalities. The Corinthians should heed the Scriptural admonition against boasting as God's word directly to them and their situation.

A final example, also taken from 1 Corinthians, is Paul's deft use in 1 Cor 5:13 of the recurrent Deuteronomic refrain, "Drive out the wicked person from among you." Here in 1 Corinthians the directive stands—unmarked as a biblical quotation—at the conclusion of Paul's instructions to the Corinthian church to expel the man who is involved in a sexual relationship with his father's wife. Of course, in the context of Deuteronomy, this command is aimed at preserving the purity of Israel as a covenant community. Thus, by addressing the Gentile Corinthians as though they were members of Israel's covenant community, Paul makes a subtle theological point: the command of God to Israel applies to them not just by analogy but directly, because they really have been grafted into the people of God (cf. Rom 11:17–24). This command (ἐξαρεῖς τὸν πονηρὸν ἐξ ὑμῶν αὐτῶν, or its near equivalent) appears some nine times in Deuteronomy, prescribing the death penalty for conduct that would lead Israel into idolatry or impurity: Deut 13:5; 17:7,12; 19:19; 21:21; 22:21,22,24; 24:7.[29] The situation closest to the Corinthian case is the one treated in Deut 22:22: "If a man is caught lying with the wife of another man, both of them shall die, the man who lay with the woman as well as the woman. So you shall purge the evil from Israel." This section of the text (Deut 22:13–30) provides legislation dealing with various sexual offenses, culminating in v. 30 with a prohibition directly pertinent to the case of the Corinthian offender: "A man shall not marry his father's wife, thereby violating his father's rights." Although Deuteronomy does not explicitly prescribe a penalty for this case, it seems highly probable that Paul, thinking of this passage in relation to the problem at Corinth, simply appropriated the exclusion formula from the near context in Deut 22:22.[30]

---

[29] Paul changes the LXX's *future* active *indicative* second person *singular* form of the verb (ἐξαρεῖς) into an *aorist* active *imperative* second person *plural* (ἐξάρατε). This has the effect of rendering the LXX expression (which follows the LXX's tendency to use the future in place of the imperative) into more idiomatic Greek usage; at the same time, the change to second person *plural* more clearly emphasizes the church's communal responsibility to exercise discipline in this case.

[30] My treatment of this passage in *Echoes* (p. 97) refers only to Deut 17:7, which is the parallel noted in the margin of the Nestle-Aland text. Further study of the text has persuaded me that the echo of Deut 22:22 is of greater importance for understanding

45

In any case, the point is that Paul reads the Deuteronomy text as a word addressed directly to the Corinthians. They are called by Scripture to exercise community discipline by expelling the perpetrator of a form of sexual immorality (πορνεία) that is not found "even among the Gentiles" (1 Cor 5:1). They are to purify the community.

This example brings us full circle: the pertinence of this direct command to a Gentile church depends upon Paul's assumption of a grand framing narrative (see II.A, above). The covenant command of Deuteronomy can be heard as the word of God for the Gentile Corinthians only because God has acted to reconcile the world to himself and thereby bring them into "the Israel of God" (cf. Gal 6:16). Within that overarching story, Scripture provides the symbolic vocabulary for Pauline ethics. Paul's rereading of Scripture in light of God's reconciling work in Christ produces fresh imaginative configurations, calling on his Jewish contemporaries to read the text in surprising ways and calling his Gentile converts to read their lives anew within the story of Scripture. The generative power of this hermeneutical strategy is suggested by the remarkable metaphor that Paul articulates in 1 Cor 5:6–8: the church itself becomes the Passover bread, which must be purified by removal of the "old leaven of malice and evil," and Christ becomes the paschal lamb sacrificed to signify and celebrate the community's passage out of bondage into freedom. Because this sacrifice has already been made, the community's ethical action of purification through community discipline is now crucial so that the feast may be celebrated rightly. Such a "use" of the Old Testament in ethical reflection goes far beyond reading the text as a rule book and suggests that the community of the new creation must discover the will of God through boldly imaginative reading of the old story.

III. Conclusion

Our survey has shown that Scripture plays a major role in shaping Paul's moral vision. When we understand the meaning of "ethics" to include all the factors that shape a community's ethos and identity, we see that Scripture is crucial for Pauline ethics in a variety of ways. It provides the overarching narrative framework for the moral life, calls the community to aspire to love and righteousness, underwrites an implicit conception of the conduct that is pleasing to God, tells stories that model both negatively and positively the meaning of faithfulness, and speaks specific words of challenge and direction to the community.

Paul's use of the formula in 1 Cor 5:13.

Paul calls his churches to live within the world-story told by Scripture. They are to find their identity there as God's covenant people, bearing the message of reconciliation to the world and manifesting the righteousness of God through loving, self-sacrificial conduct that fulfills the law. Working out the specific behavior associated with this vision requires Spirit-led discernment and the transformation of the community's life. But Paul was convinced that the Spirit would lead his churches to become more discerning readers of Scripture, to hear themselves addressed directly by Scripture, and to shape their lives accordingly.

Paul's bold hermeneutical example may lead us in turn to reflect afresh on what it would mean for Scripture to shape our communities. If we followed Paul's lead, we would immerse ourselves in Scripture and ask how our lives fit into the ongoing story of God's reconciliation of the world through Jesus Christ. Ethics would not be a matter of casuistry, not a matter of reasoning through rules and priniciples, but of hearing the word of God and responding in imaginative freedom to embody God's righteousness. In order to do that with integrity, of course, we would have to believe that "whatever was written in former days was written for our instruction" and that we are those "upon whom the ends of the ages have come." The challenge of Pauline ethics to the church is to take these claims seriously and to put them into action.

The Crucial Event in the History of the Law (Gal 5:14)

J. Louis Martyn

I

Interpreters of Paul's letter to his Galatian churches are unanimously of the opinion that, in Gal 5:13–6:10, Paul addresses issues pertinent to the church's daily life. It is no surprise to see, then, that when these interpreters ask how that daily life is related to the law, they turn first of all to Gal 5:13–14, which in the NRSV reads as follows:

> For you were called to freedom, brothers and sisters; only do not use your freedom as an opportunity for self-indulgence, but through love become slaves to one another. For the whole law is summed up in a single commandment, "You shall love your neighbor as yourself."

Surprise sets in, however, with the discovery that in Gal 5:14 the NRSV committee offers "For the whole law *is summed up* in a single commandment" as the translation of ὁ γὰρ πᾶς νόμος ἐν ἑνὶ λόγῳ πεπλήρωται. The student of Greek knows that elsewhere in early Christian literature the verb πληρόω is almost always translated "to fulfill" (the RSV rendered Gal 5:14 "For the whole law *is fulfilled* in one word"). And the surprise deepens with the discovery that the NRSV was anticipated by the New English Bible—"can be summed up"—and by the Jerusalem Bible—"is summarised" (REB: "is summed up"). Why have the scholars responsible for these recent translations elected this new rendering?

Illumination arrives in Victor Furnish's perceptive and comprehensive work, *The Love Command in the New Testament*. For, after rendering the crucial verb of Gal 5:14 "has been epitomized," Furnish applauds the NEB and the JB (the NRSV had not yet appeared):

> The passive verb which I have translated "has been epitomized" (literally "has been fulfilled," cf. *RSV*) is equivalent to the verb "summed up" which Paul uses in Rom 13:9 (this is quite properly recognized in both *NEB* and *JB*). The law is "the law of faith" when its *essence* is recognized in the love commandment. . . . [For Paul] "God's commands" [1 Cor 7:19] are *summarized* in the one commandment of

Lev 19:18. When one is a new creature in Christ, he lives by a faith which becomes active in love, and that is *what really matters.*[1]

From several translations, then, and indeed from numerous studies parallel to that of Furnish, we know how Gal 5:14 reads if it is interpreted in the light of Rom 13:9.[2] That is to say, assuming Rom 13:9 to be a guide, one arrives at what is taken to be Paul's intention in Gal 5:14: When the law is *summarized,* its *essence*—that about it which really matters—emerges, and that essence is the love commandment of Lev 19:18. But how is Gal 5:14 to be read, if one interprets it—as the Galatians did—in the context of the letter in which it stands?

II

By the time he reaches Gal 5:13–14, Paul can take for granted three major elements that form the background for his words there.

A. *Galatians 5:3*

Speaking to the former Gentiles who make up his Galatian churches, and who are being tempted to accept circumcision, Paul says in 5:3 that the one who in this manner starts out on the route of the law must go all the way, observing the whole of the law (ὅλον τὸν νόμον ποιεῖν).[3] And in the next verse (5:4), he insists that to seek rectification in this observance of the whole law is to be separated from Christ. One sees, then, that, whereas in 5:14 Paul draws a positive link between "the whole of the law" and the life of the church, in 5:3 he says that observing "the whole of the law" can have nothing to do with the church's daily life.[4]

---

[1] Victor Paul Furnish, *The Love Command in the New Testament* (Nashville, TN: Abingdon, 1972) 97, emphasis added. Were the NRSV translators influenced in their rendering of Gal 5:14 not only by NEB and JB, but also by Furnish?

[2] In addition to Furnish, see, e.g., W. Schrage, *The Ethics of the New Testament* (Philadelphia: Fortress, 1988) 206–207; D. Lührmann, *Der Brief an die Galater* (Zürich: Theologischer Verlag, 1978) 87: "Zusammenfassung des Gesetzes." Reading Rom 13:9 into Gal 5:14 is a venerable practice, doubtless much older than its attestation (ἀνακεφαλαιοῦται) in the manuscript of 365 (twelfth or thirteenth century). The interpretation of Galatians in light of Romans remains very widespread in our own time, for the old assumption that Romans provides us with the quintessence of "Paul's theology" endures in the unconscious, even where it is consciously questioned.

[3] The *linguistic* difference between ὅλος ὁ νόμος (5:3) and ὁ πᾶς νόμος (5:14) is without significance, *pace* H. Hübner, *Das Gesetz bei Paulus* (Göttingen: Vandenhoeck & Ruprecht, 1978) 37–40. Regarding the expression "former Gentiles," see Gal 3:28.

[4] The tension between Gal 5:3 and 5:14 has frequently been "solved" by repeating the venerable tradition according to which Paul rejected the law as the way of rectification (5:3), while affirming it as the criterion for ethics (5:14). See, e.g., W. Schrage: "God

B. Galatians 4:21

This tension between the negative role of the law in 5:3 and its positive role in 5:14 leads us back to 4:21, where Paul speaks of a similar tension *internal* to the law.

> Tell me, you who wish to live under the power of the law! Do you really hear what the law says [when it speaks of children begotten by the power of the promise]?

Here the law as enslaving overlord stands in contrast with the law as promise. Indeed, an essential part of Paul's point in Gal 4:21–5:1 is that the law has two voices. The Galatians can come *under* the law, thereby being enslaved by the power of its subjugating and *cursing voice* (4:21a; cf. 3:10), or they can *hear* the *promising voice* with which the law speaks of the birth of circumcision-free churches among the Gentiles, thereby sensing their own true identity as children of God's promise (4:21b, 22, 27, 31).[5]

C. Galatians 3:6–4:7

From Gal 5:14, 5:3 and 4:21, then, we move further back into the letter, retracing certain aspects of Paul's exegetical argument in 3:6–4:7. For in constructing that argument, Paul again draws a sharp contrast between two voices. First, he portrays the contrast between the blessing/promising voice of God and the cursing/enslaving voice of the law. Second and equally important, Paul finds precisely the same two contrasting voices *in* the law. On the one hand, there is the law of Sinai, the law that forms one of the enslaving elements of the old cosmos by being paired with the not-law (4:3; 6:15; 3:28).[6] In Galatians 3 and 4,

---

'justifies without works of the law,' and the law has ceased to be a way of salvation . . . ; but this does not mean that Christians are dispensed from obeying the commandments (1 Cor 7:19). Therefore the Old Testament and its law are presupposed and enforced as the criterion of Christian conduct" (*The Ethics of the New Testament*, 205). Our honoree draws the same differentiation: "Paul rejects the law as a way of salvation, but he does not reject it as a norm for the conduct of one's life" (Furnish, *Love Command*, 95). And note more recently E. P. Sanders' distinction between "getting in"—one enters the church by faith rather than by the law—and "staying in"—one remains in the church by keeping the law (e.g., *Paul and Palestinian Judaism* [Philadelphia: Fortress, 1977] 513). Against this cherished tradition, one considers Paul's certainty that the church's daily life *is* the scene of God's rectification (so Gal 5:2–6:10). That is to say, God's act of making things right is for Paul "God's sovereignty over the world revealing itself eschatologically in Jesus . . . the rightful power with which God makes his cause to triumph in the world . . ." (E. Käsemann, *New Testament Questions of Today* [London: SCM, 1969] 180; cf. 188–195).

[5] Cf. J. Louis Martyn, "The Covenants of Hagar and Sarah," *Faith and History: Essays in Honor of Paul W. Meyer* (ed. J. T. Carroll et al.; Atlanta: Scholars Press, 1990) 160–192.

[6] On the paired expression "the law/the not-law," see J. Louis Martyn, "Events in Galatia," *Pauline Theology, Vol. I* (ed. J. M. Bassler; Minneapolis, MN: Fortress, 1991) 160–

this Sinaitic law *is* the enslaving and cursing voice of the law (3:10, 19–20; 4:4–5).

On the other hand, however, prior to the Sinaitic genesis of the law/ the not-law as one of the paired and enslaving cosmic elements, there was the promissory voice of the law.[7] This was the voice with which, speaking in God's behalf, the law (as ἡ γραφή) preached the gospel ahead of time to Abraham (and to Abraham's singular seed; 3:16–17) in the form, not of commandments, but rather of the covenantal promise: "In you all the Gentiles *will be blessed*" (Gal 3:8; Gen 12:3).[8]

Being nothing other than promissory, this original voice also pronounced the promise that is a statement of God's rectifying good news: "the one who is rectified by faith *will live*" (Gal 3:11; Hab 2:4).[9] We see, then, that Paul draws a clear distinction between that singular, true promise of the law's original voice and the false promise of the law in its plural and paired existence (Gal 3:12; Lev 18:5).[10] Thus, both from Gal

---

179; idem, "Christ, the Elements of the Cosmos, and the Law in Galatians," *The Social World of the First Christians: Essays in Honor of Wayne A. Meeks* (ed. L. M. White and O. L. Yarbrough; Minneapolis, MN: Fortress, 1995) 16–39.

[7] It may seem illogical to speak of a period prior to the existence of a cosmic element. For Paul, however, it is the cosmos of religion that has as one of its elements the law/the not-law. And Paul clearly considers the cosmos of religion to be younger than the cosmos created (in prospect) by God when he spoke his promise to Abraham (not to mention the cosmos God created in the time of Adam). For in Galatians, Paul's portrait of Abraham is that of a pre-religious and thus non-religious figure (see n. 13 below).

[8] Note especially Paul's use of the rhetorical stratagem of dissociation. In Gal 3:15–18, he links the word "covenant" to the Abrahamic promise, while divorcing that word from the Sinaitic law. See J. Louis Martyn, "Covenant, Christ, and Church in Galatians," *The Future of Christology: Essays in Honor of Leander E. Keck* (ed. A. J. Malherbe and W. A. Meeks; Minneapolis, MN: Fortress, 1993) 137–151. One could be tempted for the sake of clarity to summarize the argument of Gal 3:6–29 by means of a chronological narrative, beginning with creation (assumed); then God's promise to Abraham; then, 430 years later, the curse of the Sinaitic law; and finally the advent of Christ. One could then suggest that this narrative presents a redemptive-historical sequence: Both the promise and the law have their origin in God, even though they are not to be put on exactly the same level (so J. M. G. Barclay, *Obeying the Truth: A Study of Paul's Ethics in Galatians* [Edinburgh: T. & T. Clark, 1988] 99–100). In fact, however, Paul's distinction between the cursing voice *of the law* and the blessing voice *of God* makes this reading impossible (Gal 3:15–18; cf. 2:19). There is indeed a sequence: first God's covenantal promise to Abraham; then the advent of the cursing law; then Christ. What Paul finds in this sequence, however, is sure proof of the impotence of the later-arriving law to alter the earlier and potent promise (3:15, 21a). The sequence, then, is that of promissory potency and nomistic impotence, not that of a redemptive continuity.

[9] Caring nothing about what we would call the historical place of Habakkuk, Paul hears in Hab 2:4 (as in Isa 54:1; Gal 4:27) an element in the original utterance of the law (Gal 3:8). In the distinguishing of the two voices of the law, chronology plays a role (3:17), but one that is secondary to the role played by Christ. See n. 11 below.

[10] See J. Louis Martyn, "The Textual Contradiction Between Hab 2:4 and Lev 18:5,"

3:11–12 and from the two halves of 4:21, the reader of Galatians learns—before coming to 5:3 and 5:14—that, after hearing the promissory voice of the law testify successfully *against* the law's cursing voice, Paul cannot consider the law to be a monolith.[11]

Does the distinction between the law's two voices in Galatians 3 and 4 illuminate Paul's negative and positive pictures of the law in 5:3 and 5:14?

Two additional steps will prove helpful in our attempt to answer this question. First, we will ask whether the distinction between the law's two voices in Galatians 3 and 4 is related to the advent of Christ (III).

---

forthcoming in *From Tradition to Interpretation: Studies in Biblical Intertextuality in Honor of James A. Sanders* (ed. C. A. Evans and S. Talmon; Sheffield: Sheffield Academic Press, 1997).

[11] In the second and third centuries, the drawing of distinctions within the law became an important motif among Christian Jews, gnostics, and orthodox. See esp. the theory of false pericopies in the *Kerygmata Petrou* (in *New Testament Apocrypha: Revised Edition of the Collection initiated by Edgar Hennecke* [ed. Wilhelm Schneemelcher; 2 vols.; Louisville, KY: Westminster/John Knox, 1992] 2.533-35 [G. Strecker]); the *Letter of Ptolemy to Flora* (W. Foerster, *Gnosis* [ed. R. McL. Wilson; Oxford: Clarendon, 1972] 154–161); Irenaeus, *Adv. Haer.* IV, 24–29; and the *Didascalia Apostolorum* (R. H. Connolly, *Didascalia Apostolorum* [Oxford: Clarendon, 1929]). In the five books of Moses, Ptolemy found (a) the law of God (itself composed of three subparts), (b) the additions of Moses, and (c) the traditions of the elders. Perhaps influenced both by Galatians itself and by Ptolemy, the author of the *Didascalia* spoke repeatedly of a clean distinction between the eternally valid first law, which "consists of the Ten Words and the Judgments," and the *deuterosis*, the punitive Second Legislation with its cursing bonds of circumcision etc. Similarities and differences between these writings and those of Paul warrant more investigation than they have received.

Similarities: Three motifs in the *Letter of Ptolemy to Flora* and the *Didascalia* can be compared with motifs in Galatians: (1) The distinction(s) internal to the law have been *revealed by Christ* : "The words of the Saviour teach us that it [the law] is divided into three parts" (Ptolemy 4:1); "He teaches what is the Law and what is the Second Legislation" (*Didascalia* 6.15 [Connolly, 218]); cf. "If [one] accepts his [the true prophet's] doctrine, then will he learn which portions of the Scriptures answer to the truth and which are false," *Kerygmata Petrou* [*New Testament Apocrypha*, 2.534]). (2) Christ came in order to destroy the second law, with its injustice, thus *setting us loose from its curse* (Ptolemy 5:7; *Didascalia* 6.16–17 [Connolly, 224]). (3) In his act of making distinctions in the law and of liberating us from the second law, Christ fulfilled, *restored*, and *perfected* the law of God (Ptolemy 5:3, 9; *Didascalia* vi.16–17 [Connolly, 224]).

Two *differences* are also noteworthy: (1) Over against the second law, Ptolemy and the author of the *Didascalia* place not the singular Abrahamic promise, but rather the plural Decalogue, as its commandments were perfected by Christ. (2) For the catholic author of the *Didascalia*, God is expressly identified as the author both of the First Law and of the Second Legislation, whereas Ptolemy attributes the law of divorce, e.g., to Moses and the law of corban to the elders. In writing Galatians, does Paul come closer to preparing the way for Ptolemy? The apostle is, in any case, very far from linking God to the genesis of the Sinaitic law (Gal 2:19; 3:19–20; 4:24–25). For that reason, he "is not afraid to apply *to scripture* . . . the distinguishing of spirits demanded of the prophets in 1 Cor 12:10" (E. Käsemann, *Romans* [Grand Rapids, MI: Eerdmans, 1980] 286).

Second, returning to the matter of the translation of Gal 5:14, we will ask whether Paul's statement about the law in that verse is itself made in relation to Christ's advent (IV).

III

In Galatians, the law's relationship to Christ is a subject best approached by noting, first, that the law has done something to Christ, and, second, that Christ has done something to the law.

A. *What the Law Did to Christ*

In its old-age, paired existence with the not-law, the plural Sinaitic law formed the inimical orb into which Christ came. Thus, like every other human being, Christ himself was born into a cosmos enslaved under the power of that law (4:4; cf. Phil 2:7). Together, that is, with all others, Christ was subject to the curse of the law in its plural mode of existence (Gal 3:10; 4:3). But in his case there was also a head-on and climactic collision with that curse. As Christ hung on the cross, dying for the whole of humanity (1:4), the law pronounced a specific curse on him (3:13; Deut 21:23), doing that with the malignant power it possessed as one of the enslaving, paired elements of the old cosmos.

B. *What Christ Did to the Law*

Nothing in Galatians suggests that—unlike the other elements of the cosmos itself—the law has escaped the influence of Christ. Quite the reverse. Thus, when we turn the question around, asking what Christ did to the law, we see two motifs that are both distinct from and closely related to one another.

1. *Christ has defeated the cursing voice of the law.*

In the collision between Christ and the cursing voice of the Sinaitic law, Christ was distinctly the victor (3:13; 4:5; 5:1). In his crucifixion, Christ bore the law's curse for humanity, thus vanquishing the cursing voice of the law, confining it—properly speaking—to the era before his arrival (3:17).[12] Christ's victory over the law's cursing voice is, to a large extent, the good news that permeates the whole of the letter (cf. Col 2:14–15).

---

[12] To be precise, in Galatians the era of the law in its paired existence began 430 years after Abraham and ended with the arrival of Abraham's singular seed (3:17, 19). It is a paradox that to some extent the law's cursing voice survived its collision with Christ at the cross. Thus, even though greatly weaker than the promissory voice (3:17, 21), the cursing voice still poses a threat even to the baptized Galatians. For they can lose sight of what time it really is, thus becoming again slaves under the curse of the law (4:10; 5:3).

2. *Christ has enacted—and is enacting—the promise of the law's original voice, being the seed to whom, along with Abraham, the promise was spoken.*

a. The promise of the law's original voice in the time of Abraham. According to Galatians, the message that the law (as ἡ γραφή [the scripture]) preached ahead of time to Abraham did not consist of numerous commandments, or even of one commandment, such as covenantal circumcision.[13] In the time of Abraham, the law consisted solely of God's promise, and, for that reason, it preached nothing other than the singular gospel of Christ himself (3:8). For Christ is the singular seed of Abraham, and there is no gospel other than his (3:16; 1:6–7). From its Abrahamic inception, then, the original voice of the law was positively and closely related to Christ; and, from its inception, this voice was the singular, evangelical promise, not a plural series of commandments. By the same token, the true promise pronounced in Hab 2:4 was and is the promise of the gospel of the Christ who is now making things right by his faith and by the faith that his faith elicits (3:11).[14]

b. The promise of the law's original voice in the present. These affirmations themselves speak of the present connection between the promissory voice of the law and Christ. One is not surprised to see, then, that the circumcision-free mission, promised in the original, covenantal law

---

[13] In Galatians—ct. Rom 4:9–12—Paul totally and systematically ignores every aspect of God's dealing with Abraham, except the promise. He thus suppresses the Abrahamic covenant of circumcision (Gen 17:10–14), and he eclipses Jewish traditions in which God is said to have given the law itself to Abraham, thus enabling the patriarch to be observant prior to Sinai (*Jub.* 16:12–28; Sir 44:19–20). In this letter the figure of Abraham is emphatically pre-Sinaitic, pre-religious, and thus non-religious.

[14] In his own mind, does Paul locate Habakkuk chronologically between Abraham and Christ, even putting him after the genesis of the Sinaitic law? That is the sort of question to which Paul gives no attention. As we have noted above, a major concern in Gal 3:6–18 is the clean distinction between two voices, that of the cursing law and that of God's Abrahamic promise. In developing this distinction, Paul hears the voice of God in the scripture of Hab 2:4 (Gal 3:11), without naming or thinking of the individual through whom God spoke the rectifying gospel-word, and without thinking of that individual's date. In sharp contrast, Paul hears in Lev 18:5 (Gal 3:12) the false promise of the cursing and plural law ("The one who does the commandments will live by *them*"). He then returns in Gal 5:14 to the voice of God, hearing in another passage of Leviticus (19:18) an utterance of the singular law in its guiding function ("You shall love your neighbor as yourself"). Does Paul not know that the whole of Leviticus falls after Sinai, being in fact the major collection of the priestly laws? And if so, how can he hear in any part of Leviticus the voice of God, almost as though Lev 19:18 were included in God's utterance to Abraham? Those are questions to which we can respond only by noting that Paul's consistent point of departure for reading the law is the advent of Christ. It is *Christ* who has distinguished from one another the promising and cursing voices of the law. For that reason, Paul can find those voices in various parts of the scripture/law, paying no attention to what we might call the fine points of chronology. See nn. 9 and 11 above.

of Genesis 16–21 and Isa 54:1, is the mission in which the gospel of Christ is presently marching into the Gentile world, giving birth to churches among the Gentiles, and freeing them from the cursing voice of the law/the not-law (Gal 4:21–5:1). In that mission, the gospel of Christ has unleashed the promissory voice of the law (4:21b), affirming and enacting its distinction from the law's cursing voice (4:21a), and thus restoring it to the singularity it had in the time of Abraham.

IV

We can now return to Gal 5:14. In light of indications earlier in the letter that Christ has done something to the law—defeating its cursing voice and enacting its promissory voice—we may ask whether Paul words 5:14 as he does because he is still thinking of Christ's effect on the law. That question brings us back to Paul's use of the expression ὁ γὰρ πᾶς νόμος ἐν ἑνὶ λόγῳ πεπλήρωται (RSV: "For the whole law *is fulfilled* in one word"; NRSV: "For the whole law *is summed up* in one commandment"). Reading this expression in the context of the Galatian letter, how is one to translate the verb πεπλήρωται?

A. *The verb* πληρόω

In its literal use, the verb frequently refers to the filling of a container that was previously altogether or partially empty, the result being that the container is full (BAGD). Used as a trope, the verb has various shades of meaning, four of which could be suggested for Gal 5:14, where Paul employs the verb with reference to the law.

1. "is fulfilled." The New American Bible joins the RSV in the venerable tradition in which the verb πληρόω in Gal 5:14 is rendered "fulfill." Thus: the whole of the law "*is fulfilled*" in the one commandment of neighbor love, in the sense that the one who loves the neighbor is considered to have *completely observed* the *essence* of the law, thus fulfilling the law's *real* requirement. If there were reason to think that, in using the verb πληρόω, Paul was actually thinking of the verb קִיֵּם (pi. "to fulfill"), it could be pertinent to note that the rabbis sometimes used this verb to speak of the law's being *completely observed*.[15] But the

---

[15] E.g., *Yoma* 28b: "Abraham fulfilled the whole law." There are rabbinic traditions in which the whole law is said to be fulfilled in one commandment, but what is meant is either that that commandment is the "great principle" of the law or that that commandment is the point at which a non-Jew can enter into the law, its being presupposed in *both* cases that the rest of the law is also to be observed with undiminished rigor. These traditions have nothing to do, then, with what a post-Enlightenment thinker might identify as an "essence" that can serve as a stand-in for the rest of the law. If the expression "to fulfill the whole of the law" was current in Paul's time, it meant to keep the

broad context given by Paul's references to the law in Gal 2:16–5:4 precludes this interpretation, not least because, as H. D. Betz has emphatically noted, in wording 5:14, Paul uses the verb πληρόω rather than repeating from 5:3 the verb ποιέω ("observe"). About this verbal change, Betz remarks,

[In 5:14] the "whole law" is not to be "done" (ποιεῖν), as individual laws have to be done (cf. 3:10, 12; 5:3), but is rather "fulfilled" . . . According to him [Paul], the Jew is obliged to *do* the Torah (cf. 3:10, 12; 5:3; also 6:13), while the Christian *fulfills* the Torah through the act of love, to which he has been freed by Christ (5:1, 13).[16]

The comment of Betz is helpful. Fully to honor the verb πεπλήρω-ται, however, is to sense three grounds for avoiding the translation "is fulfilled." First, completely foreign to the text of Galatians 5 is Betz's reference to the Jew's obligation to observe the Torah, whereas the Christian fulfills it. Paul does not shift from the verb ποιέω to the verb πληρόω in order to speak of Jews and Christians! Second, in English parlance, the verb "fulfill" very often takes as its direct object the noun "requirements," the result being indistinguishable from "fully perform all required stipulations."[17] As noted above, it is precisely Paul's shift to the verb πληρόω that precludes in 5:14 the thought of law observance in that sense.[18] Third, to anticipate one of the major results to be

---

law completely, observing the commandments without exception. The expression would be precisely represented in a Jewish-Christian reference to keeping the whole of the law now found in James: "For whoever keeps the whole law (ὅλον τὸν νόμον τηρήσῃ) but fails in one point has become guilty of breaking all of it" (Jas 2:10). Cf. Gal 5:3.

[16] H. D. Betz, *Galatians* (Philadelphia: Fortress, 1979) 274–275. See also C. F. D. Moule, "Fulfillment Words in the New Testament: Use and Abuse," *NTS* 14 (1967) 293–320.

[17] It is not difficult to find instances in which, in the interpretation of Gal 5:14 and Rom 13:8–10, the verbs πεπλήρωται and ἀνακεφαλαιοῦται are equated—finally—with the English verb "to do," in the sense that by loving the neighbor, one *does* all of the requirements of the law.

[18] One of the most important motifs of Gal 5:14 is the singularity of its law, in contrast to the plural nature of the law of 5:3. Thus, one cannot link Gal 5:14 *in any way* to the fulfilling of discrete requirements and stipulations (*pl.*), not even via 1 Cor 7:19 and Rom 13:8–10. The latter two texts are to be read in the light of Gal 5:14 and 6:2, rather than vice versa. See Comment #48 in my forthcoming Anchor Bible on Galatians. See also the extraordinarily perceptive essay of A. Lindemann, "Die biblischen Toragebote und die paulinische Ethik," *Studien zum Text und zur Ethik des Neuen Testaments: Festschrift zum 80. Geburtstag von Heinrich Greeven* (ed. W. Schrage; BZNW 47; Berlin: de Gruyter, 1986) 242–265. Finding in Romans 14 a key to the interpretation of Rom 13:8–10, Lindemann remarks correctly, "Die Liebe bzw. 'das Lieben' dient also nicht etwa dazu, das Tun der Toragebote zu ermöglichen, sondern sie tritt an die Stelle dieser Gebote" (262; "Love—or the act of loving—does not somehow enable the doing of the law's commandments; rather it takes the place of the commandments"). Note also Lindemann's reference to an important comment of O. Hofius, "Paulus kennt keinen 'tertius usus legis', keinen 'neuen

reached below, by putting the verb in the *perfect passive*, Paul does not refer to something the Galatians are to do—as if, rather than observing the law, they are to fulfill it. The translation "is fulfilled" is therefore unacceptable.

2. "is summarized." As noted above, this translation is imported from Rom 13:9, rather than being an interpretation of Gal 5:14 in the setting provided by the remainder of the letter. We can now add that nothing in the letter suggests the rendering "is summarized."

3. "is brought to completion." The verb πληρόω can also be used in connection with a promise or a prophecy. A promise, for example, can be thought of as partially empty, until it is fulfilled by being *brought to completion* (Matt 1:22; John 13:18; cf. Rom 15:19; BAGD, "πληρόω" 3.; LSJ, III.3).[19]

4. "is made perfect." Finally, in a similar manner, πληρόω can have the connotation of bringing to perfection. Something can be thought imperfect, until it is *made perfect* by being "filled out," thus becoming what it was intended to be (so, for example, "your joy" in John 15:11; cf. Phil 2:2). Something could also be made perfect by being *restored* to its original identity, after having suffered some kind of deterioration or contamination.[20]

There are no purely lexicographical grounds for preferring one—or both—of the last two meanings. As we proceed, however, we will see that there are exegetical reasons for electing them.

B. The perfect tense of the verb πεπλήρωται

Interpreters are unanimous in taking the verb πεπλήρωται as an instance of the gnomic use of the perfect tense.[21] Gal 5:14 is taken, that is, to be a timeless aphorism. In the tradition of the RSV ("the whole law is fulfilled in one word"), Paul is understood to speak both in 5:13 and in 5:14 of the Galatians' action. First, he exhorts the Galatians to serve one another in love. Second, he provides an aphoristic explication of

---

ethischen Gebrauch der Mose-Tora für die christliche Gemeinde'" (262 n. 105; "Paul knows no 'third application of the law,' no 'new ethical use of the law of Moses for the Christian community'").

[19] See also *Mak.* 24b, where קום is used to refer to the bringing of a prophecy to completion.

[20] Note the passages in Thucydides and Aristotle from which LSJ arrives at a rendering of the passive of ἀναπληρόω: "to be restored to its former size or state." Note also ἀναπλήρωσις as "restoration," and cf. Gal 6:2, where Paul employs ἀναπληρόω essentially as a synonym for πληρόω. See, finally, the references in the *Letter of Ptolemy to Flora* (5:3 and 5:9) to the restorative perfecting of the law of God by Christ.

[21] Thus following, in effect, the texts in which the verb has been changed into the present tense (DFG et al.).

their act of loving service: you are to serve one another in love (v. 13), for it is always true—and thus true in your case as well—that when one loves the neighbor, one fulfills (the essence of) the law (v. 14).[22]

Could it be, however, that Paul selected the perfect tense in order to refer to the present state of affairs that is the result of a past action, the simple and most frequent sense of the Greek perfect?[23] On this reading, Paul intends in Gal 5:14 to speak of the present state of affairs with the law itself, as that state of affairs is the result of something that has happened to the law. In a word he speaks of a watershed event in the history of the law. To take the third and fourth meanings above, one would then find Paul saying, "The law is now completed, as the result of its having been brought to completion, thus being restored to its original identity."[24]

C. *The passive voice of the verb* πεπλήρωται

Had Paul put the verb in the active voice—"Someone has brought the law to completion"—how would he have identified the subject of that verb? He would scarcely have referred to an act performed by the Galatians, for his exhortation that they serve one another (5:13) is certainly not a plea that he bases on something they have already done to the law. In light of Paul's references to what Christ has done to the

---

[22] The translation "is summarized" is no less gnomic, for the summary is timeless. Interpreting the perfect tense as gnomic, a number of exegetes credit Paul, in effect, with being a child of the eighteenth-century Enlightenment, who refers both in Gal 5:14 and in Rom 13:8–10 to the law's *essential intention* (something done by no rabbi and by no early Christian; cf. n. 15 above). See, e.g., the references to W. Schrage and T. Holtz in A. Lindemann, "Die biblischen Toragebote und die paulinische Ethik," 243 n. 5.

[23] BDF, §340, §342. Citing Acts 5:28, "You have filled Jerusalem with your teaching," BDF remarks, "a perfect like πεπληρώκατε . . . may be resolved into ἐπληρώσατε καὶ νῦν πλήρης ἐστίν ('you filled it and it is now full')." See also R. Kühner and B. Gerth, *Ausführliche Grammatik der griechischen Sprache. Satzlehre I* (Leverkusen: Gottschalksche Verlag, 1955) 147.

[24] Note well that I have not said "thus being restored to its original intention." See n. 22 above. Since the translation I am suggesting is the most obvious way of taking into account the perfect tense in 5:14, its absence in the commentaries—even as a possibility—is astonishing. F. Mussner, *Der Galaterbrief* (Freiburg: Herder, 1974) may take a step in the direction of this reading: "Paulus denkt auch in der Ethik 'heilsgeschichtlich': Die ἀγάπη, die in Christi Opfertod sich beispielhaft geoffenbart hat, ist die eschatologische Erfüllung und Vollendung des Gesetzes" (370; "Also in ethics, Paul thinks in 'salvation-historical' terms: the love which manifested itself exemplarily in Christ's sacrificial death is the eschatological fulfillment and completion of the law"). In a footnote, however, he abandons even that modest step, taking Paul to be speaking of something the Galatians should do: "Das Perfekt πεπλήρωται ist wohl gnomisch in dem Sinn: das Gesetz ist immer dann erfüllt, wenn das Liebesgebot erfüllt wird" ["the perfect πεπλήρωται is surely gnomic in the sense that the law is always fulfilled when the love command is fulfilled"].

law (III above), an hypothesis virtually suggests itself: when Paul speaks in 5:14 of the effect of an event in the history of the law—it has now been brought to completion—he thinks of a state of affairs that is the result of a deed of Christ. Christ has brought the law to completion.

We recall that the freedom to which Paul refers at the outset of 5:13 is the freedom Christ has won for the Galatians (and all others); and this freedom is precisely liberation from the tyranny of the law's cursing voice: Christ has done something that has affected the law (5:1). Moreover, there is a clear link between 5:14, with its reference to the law's having been "brought to completion" (πεπλήρωται), and 6:2, with its reference to the future event in which the Galatians "will bring to completion" the law *of Christ* (ἀναπληρώσετε τὸν νόμον τοῦ Χριστοῦ).[25] Detailed exegesis of Gal 6:2—in light of Rom 8:2—would show that "The Law of Christ" is the law that has found its genesis in Christ's act vis-à-vis the law. In a word, it is the law in the hands of Christ.

That reading of Gal 6:2 takes us back to 5:14, with its positive announcement about the law. To honor that announcement in the context of the whole of Galatians is to find in it two crucial motifs. First, Paul presupposes Christ's deed in distinguishing from one another the two voices of the law (one could as well say distinguishing from one another the two laws, the original law of God and the later-arriving law of Sinai). Second, given that presupposed distinction, Paul refers in 5:14 to Christ's having brought the original law of God—the pre-Sinaitic law—to its completion. For in this announcement, Paul adds a crucial dimension to the portrait of that law he has painted in earlier passages. We have already seen that, restored by Christ to its pristine state, the original law proves to be the sure Abrahamic *promise* of God that is now *giving birth* to circumcision-free churches among the Gentiles (3:8; 4:21b–5:1). Now, in Gal 5:14, we see in addition that, thus restored, the original law is also the *one imperative* of God, a dependable *guide* for the daily life of those churches, precisely in the form of the love of neighbor.[26]

---

[25] In 6:2, Paul clearly speaks of something the Galatians themselves will do. In bearing one another's burdens, *they* will bring to completion "the law of Christ." How is their future deed related to the past deed of Christ? (a) Christ's having brought the law to completion (5:14) is the deed in which he took possession of the law, making it his own law, the law of Christ. (b) In bearing one another's burdens, the Galatians will themselves repeat Christ's deed, the major difference being that—as they follow in Christ's train—they will bring to completion the law that is now the law *of Christ*: "Bear one another's burdens, and in this way you yourselves will repeat Christ's deed, bringing to completion in your communities the law that Christ has already brought to completion in the sentence about loving the neighbor."

[26] It is significant that Paul calls this imperative a sentence, not a commandment. Even in Rom 13:8–10, Lev 19:18 proves to be the *one* imperative of God. See again A.

The nature of this imperative, however, is a matter of great import. *In the first instance*, that is, Paul does not speak in Gal 5:14 about the imperative that really matters, but rather about the imperative that really exists, having been caused to exist by God's act in Christ (cf. 3:28). What really exists for the church's guidance in everyday life is not the Sinaitic law, but rather the original law of God, as that original law has been brought to perfected completion by Christ.

Reading Gal 5:14 in its own letter, then, we are reminded in two regards of Paul's ubiquitous concern to differentiate anthropological possibility from christological power.[27] First, we sense that for Paul the difference between anthropological possibility and christological power is nowhere more evident than in the daily life of the church (cf. Gal 5:22–24). Second, we see that, in the church's life, that difference emerges precisely in relation to the question of the pertinence of the law. In Gal 5:14, that is to say, the guiding imperative of the law, Lev 19:18, is not the result of an insightful deed of *Paul*, his act of *reducing* the law to its essence (his achievement of the *reductio in unum*).[28] On the contrary, that guiding imperative is the result of the powerful deed of *Christ*, his act of *loosing* God's law from the law of Sinai, thereby

Lindemann, "Die biblischen Toragebote und die paulinische Ethik," 262–263.

[27] In this respect, one recalls a percipient comment of Furnish: For Paul Christians have been given "not just the *possibility* of a new life, but an actually and totally new existence" (*Theology and Ethics in Paul* [Nashville, TN: Abingdon, 1968] 225). On possibility and power, see notably E. Käsemann, *New Testament Questions of Today*, 173 n. 4 (the issue of the translation of δύναμις in Rom 1:16); J. Louis Martyn, "Paul and His Jewish-Christian Interpreters," *USQR* 42 (1988) 1–15 (12 n. 17).

[28] One can ask whether, in linking Lev 19:18 to "the whole of the law," Paul was influenced either by the sort of Jewish tradition we find in *Gen. Rab.* 24.7 (Akiba on Lev 19:18) or by Jewish-Christian tradition in which Jesus is credited with approving the link between Deut 6:4–5 and Lev 19:18 (cf. Furnish, *Love Command*, 94). The form of this latter tradition in Luke 10:25–28 suggests that the Jewish Christians who preserved it may have known the combination of Deut 6:4–5 and Lev 19:18 to be a Jewish formulation antedating Jesus. See J. A. Fitzmyer, *The Gospel According to Luke* (AB; Garden City: Doubleday, 1985) 879. In any case, both the Jewish tradition and the Jewish-Christian one are worlds removed from Paul's *announcement* in Gal 5:14 of an *event* in the history of the law. Moreover, for all of those traditioners the issue was that of the comparative importance *among* the many commandments. There was no thought of deleting or negating some of them (N.B. the strict Jewish-Christian tradition behind Matt 22:40: "On these two commandments hang *all* the law and the prophets"; cf. Matt 23:23). Cf. now the interpretation of the role of this Jewish-Christian tradition in Matthew's *mixed* church by T. L. Donaldson, "The Law That Hangs (Matthew 22:40): Rabbinic Formulation and Matthean Social World," *CBQ* 57 (1995) 689–709. In the setting of his mixed church, Matthew sees that significant aspects of the written Torah have been abrogated. In 22:40, then, Matthew uses "a rabbinic formulation in the service of an unrabbinic interpretation of the Torah" (696).

addressing it to the church.[29] The law taken in hand by Christ (Gal 6:2) is the law that Christ has restored to its original identity and power (Gal 5:14).

Paul can relate the law, therefore, both to the birth of the church (Gal 4:21–5:1), and to its daily life, because of Christ's powerful effect on the law. Stated as a guide for the church's daily life, then, Gal 5:14 refers climactically to *the christological event in the history of the law:*

> For you were called to freedom, brothers and sisters . . . through love, be genuine servants of one another. For the whole of the law has been brought to completion [by Christ] in one sentence: "You shall love your neighbor as yourself."

---

[29] My use of the verb "to loose" is intended to reflect the polemical cast of Gal 5:3 and 5:14, against the background of the same polemic in 3:10–18. The Teachers who invaded Paul's Galatian churches presupposed the integrity of the Abrahamic blessing/promise and the Sinaitic law. Paul sees that Christ has liberated the former from the latter. Note a partially similar reading in D. Lührmann's perceptive comment on Gal 6:2 (*Der Brief an die Galater*, 96–97): "The new teachers in Galatia may have used the expression 'the law of Christ' to indicate that the law of Sinai is still valid in the Christian church . . . [Paul, however, sees a] splitting of the law into the law of Sinai and the law of Christ, a view that is later completed in the opposition between 'the law of the Spirit of life' and 'the law of sin and death' in Rom 8:2. The 'law of Christ' is possible only through liberation from the law that was given on Sinai" (auth. tr.).

The present essay is tightly focused on Gal 5:14 and other texts in that letter, not least Gal 4:24–25; 5:3, where Paul draws a connection between the plural, *Sinaitic* law and enslavement. Were we to take account of 1 Cor 7:19 and Rom 13:8–10 (cf. Romans 7), we would see that, in settings different from the one that developed in Galatia, Paul could speak affirmatively of *some of the commandments in the Decalogue*, understanding them to be commandments *of God*. Noting, however, the reminiscence of Gal 5:14 and 6:2 in Rom 13:8–10—thus recalling Paul's certainty that Christ has distinguished the promising and guiding law from the cursing and enslaving law—we can arrive at a new paraphrastic translation of the *latter* text: "Owe no one anything at all, except to love one another. For the one who loves another has brought the law to completion (νόμον πεπλήρωκεν). What do we say, then, of the commandments, 'You shall not commit adultery; you shall not murder; you shall not steal; you shall not covet'? Like the whole of the law, these and all other commandments are brought to their completing sum-total (ἀνακεφαλαιοῦται) in this sentence: 'You shall love your neighbor as yourself.' Love does no wrong to a neighbor, such as the wrongs mentioned in the commandments. For that reason, taking the place of the commandments, love is the completion of the law (πλήρωμα νόμου)."

"The Law of Faith," "the Law of the Spirit" and "the Law of Christ"

James D. G. Dunn

In his classic study of Pauline theology and ethics, Victor Furnish has a section on "Paul and the 'Law of Christ,'" a discussion of Gal 6:2, in the course of which he refers briefly also to Rom 8:2 ("the law of the Spirit of life").[1] He concludes that both phrases refer not to any idea of the words of Jesus constituting a new Torah, but to "the law of love" and "the sum and substance of the law of Moses."[2] In a separate discussion of "the 'law of faith'" (Rom 3:27) he likewise shows willing to understand the reference as to the law: "by his faith in Christ . . . it (the law) ceased to be 'the law of works' and became 'the law of faith.'"[3] In his subsequent study of the love command he links all three phrases together: "Love is in fact 'the law of Christ' (Gal 6:2), a concept equivalent in Paul's thought to 'the law of faith' (Rom 3:27) and to 'the law of the Spirit of life in Christ Jesus' (Rom 8:2)."[4]

Other single-volume studies of New Testament ethics are also content to run the three phrases together and to see in them some reference to the Torah. Like Furnish, Eduard Lohse refers to them under the heading of "the Law of Christ" and writes of "the original significance of the Torah" and of the law's being able "once again (to) serve its original purpose of testifying to the 'holy, just, and good' will of God (Rom 7:12)."[5] Wolfgang Schrage's discussion is similarly brief and likewise takes it for granted that "the law of Christ" refers in some way to the Torah—"the law of the Old Testament must first become the 'law of Christ' and be interpreted with respect to its true intention (Gal 6:2); only then can it be the measure of Christian life"—though tantalizingly he also notes that "'law' in Paul does not always refer to the Torah," referring in a footnote to Räisänen's discussion of "the law of faith"

---

[1] *Theology and Ethics in Paul* (Nashville, TN: Abingdon, 1968) 59–65, esp. 62, 64.

[2] Furnish, *Theology*, 235.

[3] Furnish, *Theology*, 191–94.

[4] *The Love Command in the New Testament* (Nashville, TN: Abingdon, 1972; London: SCM, 1973) 100.

[5] *Theological Ethics of the New Testament* (Minneapolis, MN: Fortress, 1991), quotations from 161–62.

(Rom 3:27) and "the law of the Spirit" (Rom 8:2).[6] Equally brief, but more circumspect is Rudolf Schnackenburg. He follows the regular route of identifying "the law of Christ" with the love commandment as the "fulfilling of the law" (Rom 13:10). But then he adds: "Es ist eine übertragene und paradoxe Ausdrucksweise, die doch auf die letzt-gültige sittliche Norm christlichen Handelns weist. Es ist jenes vom Geist ausgehende 'Gesetz', das sich in einem mit Christus verbundenen Leben verwirklicht (Röm 8,2), 'Gesetz' nicht im Sinn des zwanghaften, zu Sünde und Tod treibenden Mosegesetzes, sondern im Sinn des befreienden, zum Tun des Willens Gottes hindrängenden, durch den Geist ermöglichten Lebensvollzuges."[7]

In contrast, where the focus has been on the issue of Paul and the law these same references have been seen as particularly problematic: could Paul indeed regard the law of Moses, the Torah, in such a positive light, as such a positive factor, even when qualified as in the above studies? Given the fundamental law/gospel antithesis of Reformation theology, the tendency to deny the law/Torah any role in Christian discipleship would seem to be almost inescapable. In consequence there has been a strong trend in recent studies on Paul and the law to deny that these references to "the law" can be understood in terms of the law of Moses, the Torah. Either a different law must be in view, or the term νόμος should not be translated as "law."

So, for example, Hans Hübner argues that the "whole" law (ὁ πᾶς νόμος) of Gal 5:14 cannot be the same as the "whole" law (ὅλος ὁ νόμος) of Gal 5:3, but must refer to such a radical and unheard of reduction of the Torah (to the love command) that it can hardly be called "the law of Moses," perhaps as a play on the word νόμος.[8] Stephen Westerholm, arguing more consistently that for Paul the law of

---

6 Schrage, *The Ethics of the New Testament* (Minneapolis, MN: Fortress; Edinburgh: T. & T. Clark, 1988) 206–7. Cf. Peter Stuhlmacher's distinction between "the Torah from Sinai" and the "Zion torah," the latter corresponding eschatologically to the former; so in the "torah of Christ the spiritual intention of the Torah from Sinai reaches its goal" ("The Law as a Topic of Biblical Theology," in his *Reconciliation, Law, and Righteousness: Essays in Biblical Theology* [Philadelphia: Fortress, 1986] 110–33; here, 125).

7 ["It is a figurative and paradoxical mode of expression, which points to the ultimate-ly valid ethical norm of Christian action. It is that 'law' which proceeds from the Spirit and operates in a life bound up with Christ (Rom 8:2)—'law,' not in the sense of the coercive law of Moses, which brings about sin and death, but in the sense of the conduct of life which is liberating, leading to the doing of God's will, and made possible by the Spirit."] *Die sittliche Botschaft des Neuen Testaments.* Band 2: *Die urchristlichen Verkündiger* (Freiberg: Herder, 1988) 43–44; but there is no reference to Rom 3:27.

8 *Biblische Theologie des Neuen Testaments.* Band 2: *Die Theologie des Paulus* (Göttingen: Vandenhoeck & Ruprecht, 1993) 103–5, referring back to his earlier *Law in Paul's Thought* (ed. J. Riches; Edinburgh: T. & T. Clark, 1984) 36–40.

Moses has been replaced by the Spirit, not another law, deduces that the phrase "law of Christ" "is used loosely, by analogy with the Mosaic code, for the way of life fitting for a Christian."[9] Still bolder exegetically is Frank Thielman: "the law of faith," "the law of the Spirit" is a different law from the law of Moses; it refers to Christ's atoning work; it is "the new covenant established by the sacrifice of Christ."[10]

Of the second approach, the most significant and influential example is the work of Heikki Räisänen. He has argued that νόμος in the two Romans passages (3:27 and 8:2) should be regarded as a word-play and in the key phrases should be translated as "order of faith," "order of the Spirit."[11] Such a range of use and metaphorical use he has demonstrated from his search of Greek literature.[12] So too with Gal 6:2, νόμος "is being used in a loose sense, almost metaphorically, much as it is used in Rom 3:27 or 8:2. To fulfil the *nomos* of Christ is simply to live the way a life in Christ is to be lived. . . . [T]he 'law' of Christ is not literally a law."[13]

The conflict and tension between the two sets of studies, the one on New Testament ethics, the other on Paul and the law, is an interesting feature in itself, which deserves more study. Could it be, for example, that the discussion of New Testament ethics has disregarded emphases in Paul's theology which the narrower focus on Paul and the law brings out more clearly? Alternatively, could it be that the discussion of Paul and the law has treated the subject in a too narrowly theological way and has ignored the ethical question: How then should the believer live? At all events the all too brief treatment of these passages in studies of New Testament ethics and the dismissal of them as a witness to Paul's evaluation of the Mosaic law in studies of Paul and the law suggest that they deserve closer attention.

The Law of Faith

The phrase, "the law of faith," appears in Rom 3:27–31 and in a slightly different form in Rom 9:30–32.

> Rom 3:27–31: Where then is boasting? It has been excluded. By what kind of law? Of works? No, on the contrary, by *the law of faith.* For we reckon

---

[9] *Israel's Law and the Church's Faith* (Grand Rapids, MI: Eerdmans, 1988) 214 n. 38.

[10] *Paul and the Law: A Contextual Approach* (Downers Grove, IL: IVP, 1994) 201–2.

[11] "Das "Gesetz" des Glaubens und des Geistes," *NTS* 26 (1979–80) 101–17; ET: "The 'Law' of Faith and the Spirit," in his *Jesus, Paul and Torah: Collected Essays* (JSNTSup 43; Sheffield Academic Press, 1992) 48–68; *Paul and the Law* (WUNT 29; Tübingen: Mohr-Siebeck, 1983) 50–52.

[12] "Paul's Word-Play on νόμος: A Linguistic Study," in his *Jesus, Paul and Torah,* 69–94.

[13] *Paul and the Law,* 80–81.

that a man is justified by faith, apart from works of the law. Or is he God of Jews only? Is he not also God of Gentiles? Yes, of Gentiles too, since, after all, "God is one," who will justify circumcision from faith and uncircumcision through faith. Do we then make the law invalid through faith? Not at all. On the contrary, we establish the law.

Many commentators find it difficult to believe that Paul would link the law with faith in a phrase like "the law of faith" (νόμος πίστεως). After all, the more familiar link between law and faith in Paul is that of contrast: the promise came not through the law but through faith (Rom 4:13); "the law is not from faith" (Gal 3:12); and so on. In consequence the commentators usually infer that Paul is playing on the word νόμος and using it here in its alternative sense of "order"[14] or "principle."[15] So, for example, the NIV translates: "Where, then, is boasting? It is excluded. On what principle? On that of observing the law? No, but on that of faith."

But this will hardly do. To take νόμος in the sense of "order" or "principle" actually destroys the point Paul is making in the paragraph. By "the νόμος of works" Paul must mean the Torah understood in terms of the works it required of Israel. Only so can we make sense of Paul's argument, that such emphasis on the law of works leads to the inference that God is God of the Jews only (Rom 3:29). As I have observed elsewhere, to focus the law in the works it required meant in practice to reinforce Israel's distinctiveness and favored status before God over against the other nations.[16] Paul, however, turns this argument on its head. He starts from the fundamental Jewish confession, that "God is one" (the *Shemaꜥ*, Deut 6:4), and infers from that that God must be God of Gentile as well as of Jew. Which means in turn that God treats the two in the same way: he justifies the circumcision from faith and the uncircumcision through faith (3:30). To round off the line of thought (οὖν) Paul asks finally, does this affirmation that Gentile and Jew are on equal footing before God in terms of faith therefore invalidate the law? Not at all, he replies, on the contrary faith establishes the law (3:31).[17]

---

[14] See especially Räisänen cited above (nn. 11–12); also W. Schmithals, *Der Römerbrief* (Gütersloh: Mohn, 1988) 129; T. R. Schreiner, *The Law and its Fulfillment: A Pauline Theology of Law* (Grand Rapids, MI: Baker, 1993) 34–36.

[15] E.g., L. Morris, *The Epistle to the Romans* (Grand Rapids, MI: Eerdmans, 1988) 144; J. A. Fitzmyer, *Romans* (AB 33; New York: Doubleday, 1993) 363.

[16] See, e.g., my "Yet Once More—'The Works of the Law': A Response," *JSNT* 46 (1992) 99–117; and for more detailed exegesis see my *Romans* (WBC 38; Dallas, TX: Word, 1988) 193–94.

[17] Rom 3:31 is clearly the conclusion to 3:27–31 and should not be separated from its preceding context to be taken as the introduction to chap. 4, a suggestion rightly

Paul's very line of argument shows how well aware he was that his argument must seem contradictory. He knew that his emphasis elsewhere, including the present context, set the Torah and faith in contrast. But he nevertheless makes the bold affirmation that the (Jewish) law is established by faith. Despite the antithesis between the Torah and faith elsewhere, Paul evidently also wanted to affirm a positive connection between them. The point for us is that this conclusion, that faith establishes the law, wraps up the line of argument begun in 3:27. It is in effect the answer to his opening question, by what kind of law is boasting, Israel's boasting in its privileged position (2:17, 23), excluded? Paul's answer is, by the law of faith, i.e., the law established by faith. The final sentence simply expands our key phrase: Paul can speak of "the *law* of *faith*" because he believed that *faith* establishes the *law*. In such a direct and integrated line of argument the νόμος of 3:27 cannot be other than the νόμος of 3:31.[18]

We see just the same line of thought later on in Romans 9:30–32:

> What then shall we say? That Gentiles who do not pursue righteousness have attained righteousness, the righteousness which is from faith, whereas Israel pursuing the law of righteousness has not reached the law. Why so? Because they did so not from faith but as if it was from works.

What is so astonishing here for many commentators is that Paul can speak of Israel "pursuing the law of righteousness" and failing to reach that law. Quite clearly it is the law, the Torah, which is in view. And Paul refers to it in a wholly positive way: Israel pursued the law, and it was a good and proper goal to pursue—"the law of righteousness." They failed to reach that law, but no criticism of the law is contained in that conclusion.

The text seems so surprising that even conservative translations like the RSV and NRSV have turned the Greek round into what they think Paul really said, or ought to have said: so NRSV—Israel strove "for the righteousness that is based on the law," making "righteousness" the object of Israel's striving rather than "the law."[19] But Paul's meaning is

---

rejected, e.g., by Schmithals (*Römerbrief*, 131) and Fitzmyer (*Romans*, 366).

[18] It is surprising that so few commentators recognize that the meaning of νόμος in 3:27 must be the same as that in 3:31. Among recent studies see particularly P. von der Osten-Sacken, *Die Heiligkeit der Tora: Studien zum Gesetz bei Paulus* (München: Kaiser, 1989) 23–33; P. Stuhlmacher, *Paul's Letter to the Romans* (Louisville, KY: Westminster/John Knox, 1994) 66–67. Contrast D. Moo, *Romans 1–8* (Chicago: Moody, 1991) who argues that Paul makes a "clear principial distinction" between faith and the Mosaic law (252), a claim applicable only to the law (τῶν or ἐξ ἔργων), as the comparison of 3:27 with 9:31–32 indicates.

[19] For other attempts to weaken or avoid the obvious sense, see my *Romans*, 581;

clear: "the law" can be described as a legitimate goal; the entirely positive term "righteousness" can be complemented or expanded as "the law of righteousness." And his point is also clear: Israel's mistake was not that they pursued the law, but that they did so as though that goal was to be achieved in terms of works; whereas it could only be achieved "from faith." Israel had not reached the law. Why? Because they pursued the law of righteousness not from faith but as if it was from works. Here, clearly, is simply an alternative way of putting our key phrase: the law pursued in terms of faith is another way of saying "the law of faith."[20]

When we recognize that "the law of faith" has a positive meaning for Paul it helps make sense of what otherwise is another somewhat puzzling phrase elsewhere in Romans. In Rom 1:5 Paul describes his apostolic commission as intended to bring the nations to "the obedience of faith." The same phrase is used in the final doxology in the letter, in what is generally regarded as a later addition, but nevertheless a good summary of Paul's own thought, which speaks of the mystery of God long concealed but now made manifest through the gospel and "made known for the obedience of faith for all the nations" (Rom 16:26). Again there is an instinctive reaction among some commentators: to talk of "faith" and "obedience" in the same breath is in danger of undermining the character of faith and of confusing it with some kind of merit-seeking work.[21] But Paul evidently had no such qualms; he expresses this as the objective of his missionary work right at the beginning of the letter, without qualification and without any hint that this might be a controversial formulation. Faith can be described as a form of obedience. Such an attitude, of course, is wholly of a piece with the summary phrase, "the law of faith."

What then does Paul mean by "the law of faith"? How is it that he can put these two terms together in such a positive way? The clue is almost certainly given by Romans 4—the passage which follows from his use of

---

Schmithals, *Römerbrief*, 363; and Fitzmyer, *Romans*, 578.

[20] We can perhaps illustrate Paul's argument and distinctions in these two passages visually:

Romans 3 - law
{ works → boasting → God only of Jews
{ faith → God of Jews and Gentiles → establish law

Romans 9
{ Israel → works → law of righteousness
{ Gentiles → faith → law of righteousness

[21] Fitzmyer prefers to translate "a commitment of faith" (*Romans*, 237–38). On the meaning of the phrase see now D. B. Garlington, "Faith's Obedience: The Meaning of ὑπακοὴ πίστεως," *Faith, Obedience and Perseverance* (WUNT 79; Tübingen: Mohr-Siebeck, 1994) 10–31.

the phrase itself and which explains what he meant in saying "faith establishes the law."

Romans 4 is the greatest and clearest statement of Paul's understanding of faith. As is obvious and well known, the chapter is a midrash or exposition of Gen 15:6: "Abraham believed God and it was reckoned to him for righteousness." Important for us is the fact that we know how this text was understood in the Judaism of Paul's day. A typical exposition took the various passages about the promise made to Abraham, from Genesis 12 through to Genesis 22, and interpreted them in the light of each other. In particular, Abraham's believing, his faith, was interpreted in the light of his later act of obedience in being willing to offer up his son Isaac at God's command. Thus we find it expounded by Mattathias in 1 Macc 2:52 as part of his recall of the heroes of the covenant and heroes of zeal: "Was not Abraham found faithful when tested, and it was reckoned to him as righteousness?" In other words, Abraham's faith was understood as his faithfulness. Abraham was being presented as a model of the faithful Jew, who remains loyal to the covenant, who defends Israel's distinctive status (1 Maccabees 2). Abraham's faithfulness, we might say, was his obedience understood in terms of works; this Abraham represents Israel pursuing the law of righteousness as if it was from works.[22]

Paul's exposition is different. For him faith means total and unconditional reliance on God. "Abraham believed God" means that Abraham believed God's promise that he would have a child, despite the fact that he and his wife were long past child-bearing (Abraham was about 100 years old and his wife not much younger). Neither of them could do anything about the barrenness of Sarah's womb. Humanly speaking the promise was impossible of fulfillment; they had nothing to hope for. Yet Abraham believed; "against hope, in hope 'he believed'. He did not doubt the promise of God, but was strengthened in faith, giving glory to God, being fully convinced that what God had promised he was able also to do" (Rom 4:18–21). In other words, faith for Paul meant complete trust in God, total reliance on God's enabling. *That* is the root of obedience for Paul; unless obedience springs from that, it is misdirected. The "obedience of faith" is that obedience which lives out the sort of trust and reliance on God which Abraham demonstrated.

The law of faith, then, is the law in its function of calling for and facilitating the same sort of trust in God as that out of which Abraham lived. This is not a reference only to sections or parts of the law but

---

[22] Hence the importance of understanding Jas 2:18–24 as an intra-Christian debate, James responding to and complementing Paul. Otherwise James appears more as a restatement of 1 Macc 2:52, the attitude to which Paul was objecting in Romans 4!

describes the function of the law as a whole. Thus we can recognize the criterion by which Paul judged the relevance of the law as a whole and in any of its particulars. Whatever commandment directed or channelled that reliance on God or helped bring that reliance to expression in daily living was the law still expressive of God's will. Conversely, whatever law required more than faith, whatever commandment could not be lived out as an expression of such trust in God alone, whatever ruling hindered or prevented such faith, that was the law now left behind by the coming of Christ. With the gospel now making it possible for *all* to express such faith in God through believing in Christ, the law which was understood to demand more than that faith was in fact the enemy of that faith and should be regarded as redundant.[23]

The Law of the Spirit

We should not make a parody of the Jewish or Old Testament attitude to the law. It is all too easy to take some of Paul's more negative-sounding statements on the law and to extrapolate from them "the Jewish view of the law"—as though all Paul's predecessors treated the law in a superficial way, or observed the letter but disregarded the spirit. In fact, however, there is a widespread recognition in Israel's scriptures that the law can be treated in a superficial way, and there are frequent warnings against that danger. We need think only of the repeated warnings of the great eighth century prophets that mere observance of festival and fast was a totally inadequate way of keeping the law (Isa 1:12–14; Hos 6:6; Mic 6:8). Paul's own warning that "not the hearers of the law are righteous before God, but the doers of the law shall be counted righteous" (Rom 2:13) is in fact thoroughly characteristic of Old Testament and Jewish concerns.[24] Paul, in other words, was by no means the first Jew to make distinctions between attitudes to the law or between different levels of keeping the law.

One of the most striking ways in which this Old Testament and Jewish concern was expressed was in the recognition that the law must penetrate to the heart. The obedience to the law for which Yahweh looked was obedience from the heart. Thus for example the repeated call to "circumcise the foreskin of your heart,"[25] and the promise that "the Lord your God will circumcise your heart and the heart of your

---

[23] So also Rom 14:23, "everything which is not from faith is sin"; note that faith has a defining role in regard to sin just as the law had earlier—hence "the law of faith." See further my *Romans*, 828–29.

[24] Cf., e.g., Deut 4:1, 5–6, 13–14; 30:11–14; 1 Macc 2:67; 13:48; Philo, *Cong.* 70; *Praem.* 79; Jos. *Ant.* 20.44; *m. ʾAbot* 1:7; 5:14.

[25] Deut 10:16; Jer 4:4; 9:25–26; Ezek 44:9; 1QpHab 11:13; 1QS 5:5; 1QH 2:18; 18:20; Philo, *Spec. Leg.* 1.305.

descendants, so that you will love the Lord your God with all your heart . . ." (Deut 30:6). The most famous expressions of this hope are, of course, the prophecies of the new covenant in Jer 31:31–34 and of a new heart in Ezek 36:26–27.

This hope for Paul was fulfilled in the gift of the Spirit. The fulfillment of this hope in his converts is clearly what he has in mind in his distinction between the "letter" (γράμμα) and the "Spirit."

> Rom 2:28–29: the true Jew is not the one visibly marked as such, nor circumcision that which is performed in the flesh, but one who is so in a hidden way, and circumcision is of the heart, in Spirit not in letter.
> Rom 7:6: we have been released from the law, having died to that by which we were confined, so that we might serve in newness of Spirit and not in oldness of letter.
> 2 Cor 3:3, 6: you show that you are a letter of Christ . . . written not with ink but with the Spirit of the living God, not on tablets of stone but on tablets of human heart . . . (so that we are) ministers of a new covenant, not of letter but of Spirit.
> Phil 3:3: it is we who are the circumcision, who worship in the Spirit of God and boast in Christ Jesus and have no confidence in the flesh.

Coming clearly to expression in these passages is the conviction that in the gift of the Spirit these earliest Christians had experienced the hoped-for circumcision of the heart of Deuteronomy, had experienced the hoped-for new covenant of Jeremiah,[26] had experienced the hoped-for new heart and new spirit of Ezekiel.

What must be noted, however, is that this hope did not refer to another law or another Torah. Its fulfillment was not perceived by any prophet as dispensing individuals from keeping the law. On the contrary, it was understood as the only way to ensure a more effective keeping of the law. Only a circumcision of the heart would enable an adequate obedience of the law (Deut 30:8–10). Contrary to popular perception, the promise of the new covenant in Jeremiah is not of a new or different law; the promise is plain: "I will put my law within them, and I will write it on their hearts" (Jer 31:33). Likewise the new heart and spirit promised in Ezekiel has in view a more effective keeping of the law: "I will put my spirit within you, and make you follow my statutes and be careful to observe my ordinances" (Ezek 36:27). It is this hope, precisely this hope, which Paul claims was fulfilled in the gift of the Spirit to those who put their faith in Messiah Jesus. The coming

---

[26] For the view that 2 Cor 3:3, 6 in particular alludes to Jer 31:31–34 and other bibliography, see, e.g., V. P. Furnish, *II Corinthians* (AB 32A; New York: Doubleday, 1984) 181, 183–84, 196–97; Thielman, *Paul and the Law*, 110–11 and n. 32.

of Christ and of faith in Christ has brought emancipation from the law in its temporary, constrictive function (Gal 3:19–4:7), of course.[27] But nothing that Paul says indicates that Christ has brought emancipation from the law as God's rule of right and wrong, as God's guidelines for conduct.

The issue is nicely posed in Paul's choice and exposition of Deut 30:12–14 in Rom 10:6–8. For Deut 30:11–14 is all about how *easy* it is to obey the *law*.

> Surely this commandment that I am commanding you today is not too hard for you, nor is it far away. It is not in heaven, that you should say, "Who will go up to heaven for us, and get it for us that we may hear it and observe it?" Neither is it beyond the sea, that you should say, "Who will cross to the other side of the sea for us, and get it for us so that we may hear it and observe it?" No, the word is very near to you; it is in your mouth and in your heart so that you may observe it.

In Romans 10, however, Paul takes this passage and expounds it in reference to the word of *faith*. The point is that this exposition should not be seen as totally wrenching the passage away from its original sense.[28] Paul is not setting the word of faith and the law as such in antithesis; certainly he contrasts the word of faith and the law understood ὡς ἐξ ἔργων [as if on the basis of works] (9:32; 10:5); but not the word of faith and the law understood ἐξ πίστεως [on the basis of faith] (9:32). The word of faith *is* that law. The faith that springs from the heart is what talk of the law written in the heart had in mind.

It is from the same sequence of Pauline thought that the phrase "the law of the Spirit" emerges. It appears as part of Paul's defence of the law in Rom 7:7–8:4. There, as the line of argument clearly indicates, Paul defends the law by portraying it as the dupe of sin, as abused by the power of sin (7:7–13). The human "I" is split—split between the "I" that wants to observe the law of God, and the "I" as flesh, weakened in any good resolve to obey the law by its all-too-human appetites and desires. It is important to note, however, that the law is also split—split between the law as still God's law in which the "I" delights with the mind, and

---

[27] For Paul's more carefully circumscribed understanding of the negative role of the law, see my "Was Paul Against the Law? The Law in Galatians and Romans: A Test-Case of Text in Context," in *Text and Contexts. Biblical Texts in Their Textual and Situational Contexts. Essays in Honor of Lars Hartman* (ed. T. Fornberg and D. Hellholm; Oslo: Scandinavian University Press, 1995) 455–75.

[28] That Paul was probably familiar with and drawing upon a well-established line of Jewish interpretation of Deut 30:12–14 (Bar 3:39–40; Philo, *Post* 84–5; Targum Neofiti on Deut 30:11–14) is well known (see, e.g., my *Romans*, 603–5).

the law used by the power of sin to enslave the "I" as flesh (7:22–23, 25).[29]

This is where our controversial second phrase enters the exposition: "the law of the Spirit of life in Christ Jesus has set you free from the law of sin and death" (Rom 8:2). Here again, as with the previous phrase, "the law of faith," many commentators find it impossible to think that Paul should refer to the law, the Torah, in such a positive way. How could Paul, after saying so many negative things about the law, actually describe it as "the law of the Spirit of life" and attribute to it the decisive role in liberating the Christian from the law?[30] The solution once again would be to read here a play on the word νόμος, understood again as "rule" or "principle."

Once again, however, such a reading simply undermines the flow of Paul's argument.

> The law of the Spirit of life in Christ Jesus has set you free from the law of sin and death. For what the law was unable to do in that it was weak through the flesh, God sent his own Son in the very likeness of sinful flesh ... and condemned sin in the flesh, in order that the requirement of the law might be fulfilled in us who walk not in accordance with the flesh but in accordance with the Spirit. (Rom 8:2–4)

To be noted is the way in which reference to the law is woven throughout these three verses (Rom 8:2–4).[31] In fact, this passage is nothing other than the climax of Paul's defence of the law which began in Rom 7:7. Who can doubt that "the law of sin and death" (8:2) is the law abused and misused by sin to bring about death (as described in 7:7–13)? The law weakened through the flesh is the good law of God, but defeated by the combination of sin's power and the weakness of the similarly divided "I." But what then of the law freed, like the "I," from the power of sin and death? This in fact is the most obvious way to take the phrase "the law of the Spirit of life," that is, as a reference to the law in its capacity as the law of God, but no longer caught in the nexus of human weakness and sin's power. The law is "spiritual" (πνευματικός— 7:14) because it can be the vehicle of the Spirit (πνεῦμα). As 3:31 answers to 3:27, so 8:2 answers to 7:14. "The law of the Spirit," in other

---

[29] The possibility (I would say probability) that some at least of the multiple references to νόμος in Rom 7:7–8:4 are to be explained in terms of a split in the law equivalent to the split in the "I" has not been given sufficient attention in discussions on this text; see my *Romans*, 377 and below, n. 32.

[30] So especially Räisänen, "Law," 66 and *Law*, 51–52, followed particularly by Moo, *Romans 1–8*, 505–6; for the debate and bibliography see Räisänen, "Law"; Dunn, *Romans*, 416–18; and Moo, *Romans 1–8*, 504–7.

[31] In what follows cf. particularly Osten-Sacken, *Die Heiligkeit der Torah*, 19–23.

words, is one of the ways in which Paul refers to what we might call the positive side of the divided law.[32] Perhaps most striking of all, the purpose for which God sent his Son is explicitly stated as to bring about the fulfillment of the law's requirements. For Paul, the objective of God's saving action in Christ was to make possible the keeping of the law. What makes the difference and what defeats the power of sin and the weakness of the flesh is the Spirit. "The requirement of the law (is) fulfilled in us who walk not in accordance with the flesh but in accordance with the Spirit." It would appear, then, that "the law of the Spirit" is simply a summary way of speaking of the requirement of the law fulfilled by those who walk in accordance with the Spirit.[33]

It is precisely as the law of the Spirit, the law understood as guidelines for Spirit-directed conduct, the law thus freed from the misconceptions which gave the power of sin its leverage and from the weakness of the flesh which so disempowered it, that the law can be experienced as a liberating power. It is the law thus rightly perceived and experienced which sets free from the law of sin and death.

And what does this mean in practice for Paul? Paul presumably had in mind a conduct informed and enabled out of a direct and immediate apprehension of the divine will. This is the contrast he draws in Romans itself. On the one hand stands the claim to know God's will, as part of the Jewish boasting of which he disapproves: "you are called a 'Jew' and rely on the law and boast in God, and know his will and approve things that matter (γινώσκεις τὸ θέλημα καὶ δοκιμάζεις τὰ διαφέροντα) being instructed from the law" (Rom 2:18). On the other stands the knowing of God's will which comes from the renewed mind: "Do not be conformed to this age, but be transformed by the renewal of your mind, so that you may ascertain what is the will of God (εἰς τὸ δοκιμάζειν ὑμᾶς τί τὸ θέλημα τοῦ θεοῦ)" (Rom 12:2). Here the contrast is between an obedience instructed by the law, and an obedience instructed by the renewed mind. But it is obviously equivalent to the contrast

---

[32] To take νόμος as other than "the law" would mean that a *third* νόμος is now in view in 8:2 (G. D. Fee, *God's Empowering Presence: The Holy Spirit in the Letters of Paul* [Peabody, MA: Hendrickson, 1994] 552), which does not exactly make Paul's meaning more lucid.

[33] The double line of thought in Paul's defence of the law in Rom 7:7–8:4 can be illustrated in two ways:

```
(1)   law         law         (2)          flesh
       ↓           ↓                     ↗        ↘
     flesh        mind        law                  fulfillment
       ↓           ↓                     ↘        ↗
      sin         Spirit                  Spirit
       ↓           ↓
     death        life
```

between the law of sin preventing the will of God and the law of the Spirit enabling its fulfillment.

The same point is made, again in different terms, without reference to the Spirit as such, in Paul's prayer in Phil 1:9–10: "This is my prayer, that your love may overflow more and more with knowledge and full insight so that you may determine what is best." What Paul had in mind is what Oscar Cullmann expressed as "the capacity of forming the correct Christian ethical judgment at each given moment,"[34] the sense or instinct for what is right and appropriate in any given situation. For Paul this knowledge of God's will was not something which could be read off from a law code or rule book. It required much more spiritual sensitivity, what Col 1:9–10 speaks of as "spiritual wisdom and understanding." And yet in so saying, Paul had the same objective in mind as the law—the doing of God's will. So once again we can say that Paul wanted what God, in giving the law, wanted: that God's will might be done. The law of God and the Spirit of God had the same objective, however much it had been thwarted and corrupted.

Clearly there is also a link between "the law of the Spirit" and the subject of the previous section, "the law of faith." In both cases Paul uses the term "law" because he wanted to underline the vital importance of doing, obeying God's will. And in both cases the qualifier, "of faith," "of the Spirit," indicates in a summary way how that obedience is made possible. In Paul's solution to the problem of human weakness and sin's power, faith and Spirit are the two sides of the same coin. The human trust is met by the power of the Spirit. The obedience that God looks for and makes possible is, in a phrase, human receptiveness (faith) to divine enabling (Spirit).

To formulate the point from a slightly different angle, both phrases, "the law of faith" and "the law of the Spirit," can be defined by their contrasting phrases. As the law of faith is different from the law understood in terms of works, so the law of the Spirit is different from the law understood as letter (γράμμα). Both "works" and "letter" emphasize the visible, public character of what is being required and done, where the tendency or danger is always for that visible element to become the dominant feature of the obedience so expressed and for the obedience to become divorced from obedience from the heart.[35] As one who believed that he had himself succumbed to that danger, Paul emphasized the law of faith and the law of the Spirit as a way of

---

[34] *Christ and Time* (3d ed; London: SCM, 1962) 228.

[35] It should surely be obvious that γράμμα and νόμος are *not* synonymous in Paul's thought and that γράμμα involves some failure in understanding of the law's purpose and function.

reaffirming the obedience which is required by God; at the same time, he insists that the only obedience which actually does God's will and fulfills the law of God is an obedience which is the outworking of faith and enabled by the Spirit.

The Law of Christ

One other Pauline "law" phrase has caused puzzlement and confusion for many, viz. "the law of Christ." Like the other phrases this one occurs only once or twice in Paul. In Gal 6:2 he calls on the Galatians: "Bear one another's burdens and thus you shall fulfill the law of Christ (τὸν νόμον τοῦ Χριστοῦ)." And in 1 Cor 9:21 he describes his personal policy: "to those under the law I became as one under the law, not as being myself under the law but in order that I might win those under the law; while to those outside the law I became as one outside the law, not as being outside the law of God but as being within the law of Christ (ἔννομος Χριστοῦ), in order that I might win those outside the law." Here again, as with the phrases discussed above, there is a widespread feeling that Paul cannot be referring to the Torah when he spoke of "the law of Christ." Once again he must be playing with the term νόμος, in order to contrast the νόμος of Christ with the Torah itself. Because the antithesis with the law elsewhere in Paul seems so absolute ("I died to the law," Gal 2:19; "under the law" equivalent to "under slavery," Gal 3:19–4:10; etc.), it would seem strange for Paul to use the phrase "the law of Christ" in reference to the Jewish law. Whatever else "the law of Christ" means, it cannot refer to the Torah. Such would be a typical train of thought for many Pauline commentators.[36]

Once again, however, the positive strand of Paul's teaching on the law has been missed or too heavily discounted. So far as Gal 6:2 is concerned, there is a striking parallel in thought at this point between Romans and Galatians. In Rom 13:8–10 Paul sums up his ethical teaching to that point with the words:

> Owe nothing to anyone except to love one another; for he who loves the other has fulfilled the law. For the commandment, "You shall not

---

[36] See, e.g., H. Lietzmann, *An die Galater* (4th ed.; HNT; Tübingen: Mohr-Siebeck, 1971) 41 and D. Lührmann, *Der Brief an die Galater* (Zürcher Bibelkommentare; Zürich: Theologischer Verlag, 1988) 97. Hence H. D. Betz, *Galatians* (Hermeneia; Philadelphia: Fortress, 1979) 300–1, somewhat incoherently: "Paul took over the notion from the opponents . . . and used [it] here polemically"; and J. L. Martyn, "A Law-observant Mission to Gentiles: the Background of Galatians," *SJT* 38 (1984) 307–24 (here 315): an expression coined by the other missionaries. Prior to Hübner (*Biblische Theologie*; see above, n. 8), E. Bammel, "Νόμος Χριστοῦ," *Studia Evangelica* III (ed. F. L. Cross; TU 88; Berlin: Akademie, 1964) 12–28 suggests that the phrase "the law of Christ" was coined "in an almost playful manner."

commit adultery," "You shall not kill," "You shall not steal," "You shall not covet," and any other commandment, is summed up in this word, in the command, "You shall love your neighbor as yourself." Love does no wrong to the neighbor; therefore the fulfillment of the law is love.

Then, a chapter and a half later, Paul again sums up, this time his extensive treatment of the problem of food laws, in a similar call for concern for the neighbor:

We the strong ought to support the weaknesses of those without strength, and not to please ourselves. Let each of us please his neighbor with a view to what is good, for upbuilding. For the Christ too did not please himself . . . . (Rom 15:1–3)

Since this is the only other occasion on which Paul speaks of concern for the "neighbor" (except in the Galatians passage we will turn to in a moment), it is not too hard to see a train of thought running between the two Romans passages. Jesus' refusal to please himself was depicted by Paul as an example of pleasing the neighbor, which is another way of saying "Love your neighbor as yourself," which in turn is a fulfillment of the law.

What is striking is that Paul seems to follow the same train of thought in Galatians. In Gal 5:14 he says something very similar to Rom 13:8–10: "Through love serve one another. For the whole law is fulfilled (πεπλήρωται) in one word, in the well-known, 'You shall love your neighbor as yourself'" (Gal 5:13–14). And then, just half a chapter later, he calls for his audience to "Bear one another's burdens and thus you will fulfill (ἀναπληρώσετε) the law of Christ" (Gal 6:2). We can make precisely the same deduction as before. To fulfill the law of Christ is to bear one another's burdens, which is a particular example of loving the neighbor, which fulfills the law. The point should be obvious: in the parallel trains of thought "the law of Christ" (Galatians) is equivalent to Jesus' refusal to please himself (Romans).[37] Which presumably means that in Paul's mind "the law of Christ" includes some reference to Jesus' own example.

A second consideration has to be added. That is the likelihood that this repeated emphasis on love of neighbor as fulfilling the whole law is a conscious echo of Jesus' teaching on the two great commandments: "'You shall love the Lord your God with all your heart . . .' (and) 'You shall love your neighbor as yourself'. There is no other commandment greater than these" (Mark 12:30–31). Or in Matthew's version, "On these two commandments depend the whole law . . ." (Matt 22:40). The

---

[37] Romans: fulfill law—love neighbor—please neighbor—follow Jesus' example;
Galatians: fulfill law—love neighbor— bear other's burden—fulfill law of Christ.

idea that the law could be encapsulated in one or a few commandments is not unique to Christianity.[38] But the evidence of the Romans and Galatians passages indicates that this emphasis on love of neighbor as summing up or fulfilling the whole law had become an established feature in Pauline paraenesis (if not Christian paraenesis more generally). And given that the same emphasis is clearly established within the Jesus tradition it would be somewhat perverse to look to another source for the subsequent Christian emphasis at this point.

The deduction is then obvious: that by "the law of Christ" Paul will have been thinking particularly of the love command. To bear the other's burden is obviously to love the burdened neighbor. And since bearing the other's burden fulfills the law of Christ it is a wholly natural deduction that "the law of Christ" is a way of speaking of the command to love the neighbor. Understandably, therefore, there is a broad consensus on this point.[39] Adding this point to the one already made, however, the fuller deduction can also be made: that by the law of Christ Paul had in mind both Jesus' teaching on the love command and Jesus' own example in living out the love command.

We may therefore gather together our findings thus far on our third phrase, "the law of Christ," under three heads. (1) First, the clear implication of Rom 13:8–10 and Gal 5:13–14 is that Paul had *not* discarded the law or abandoned the law or broken with the law. In both passages he talks about the "fulfilling" of the law as something obviously desirable on the part of Christians. Indeed he indicates clearly that he is talking about the whole law. Not just the moral commands within the ten commandments are in view, but "any other command" too (Rom 13:9). His concern was not just with the particular command to love the neighbor, understood as abstracted or separated from other commands, but the "whole law" was in mind as worthy and necessary of fulfillment (Gal 5:14). To fulfill the law of Christ is to fulfill the law. In other words, our consistent thesis in this paper is given still further support: Paul still saw a positive role for the law in Christian conduct.

(2) Second, at the core of the whole law is the love command. If the whole law is to be fulfilled, the way in which it is to be fulfilled is by love of neighbor, with, presumably, love of God as the unstated presupposition. Particularly noticeable in Galatians is the fact that within a few verses Paul can speak both of "doing the whole law" as something entirely *un*desirable for Gentile Christians, and yet also of "fulfilling the whole law" as something entirely desirable for Christians (Gal 5:3, 14). Gal 5:3—"Everyone who is being circumcised . . . is obligated to do the

---

[38] See those cited in my *Romans*, 778–79.

[39] See not least Furnish in the opening paragraph above.

whole law. You have been estranged from Christ . . . ." Gal 5:14—"The whole law is fulfilled . . . in the well-known, 'You shall love your neighbor as yourself.'"[40] If these two statements are contradictory, Paul assuredly cannot have been unaware of that contradiction. It must rather be the case that he had in mind the same twofold way of looking at and living in relation to the law to which we have now grown accustomed. The one was a misunderstanding of the role of the law in relation to Israel, all that Paul summed up under the terms "works" and "letter." But the other was a wholly acceptable and necessary appreciation of the law's continuing importance—the whole law, but as summed up and expressible in and through the command to love the neighbor. Where requirements of the law were being interpreted in a way which ran counter to the basic principle of the love command, Paul thought that the requirements could and should be dispensed with. On the other hand, it was still possible in his view for the *whole* law, and *all* its commandments to be fulfilled in a way which did not run counter to the love command.

We may add that this presumably was the theological logic which lay behind Paul's own principles of mission and conduct as articulated in the other "law of Christ" text, 1 Cor 9:21. To live "under the law" (ὑπὸ νόμον) was not an impossible thing for even Paul to do. And when he speaks of living "outside the law" (ἄνομος) he quickly qualifies himself: even outside the law he remains still within the law of Christ (ἔννομος Χριστοῦ). Here is an understanding of life in relation to the law which is not *de facto* antithetical to loving the neighbor. On the contrary, it was the principle of loving the neighbor which made it possible for Paul to live as one under the law. One could love the neighbor, the Jewish neighbor, *by* living under the law. As one could fulfill the law by loving one's neighbor, so one could love the neighbor by keeping the law.

(3) Third, it follows from our analysis that Jesus himself provided Paul with a model for such conduct in relation to the law. Jesus' teaching, itself summed up in the love command, and Jesus' example, understood as an expression of life lived in accord with the love command, together provided clear illustration of what living in accord with the love command actually meant in practice.

---

40 Hübner's distinction between ὁ πᾶς νόμος of Gal 5:14 and ὅλος ὁ νόμος of Gal 5:3 (see above, n. 8) cannot be sustained; see my *Galatians* (BNTC; London: A. & C. Black, 1993) 290. Compare and contrast also the various wrestlings with the otherwise problematic character of Paul's conception of Christians "fulfilling the law"—Hübner, *Law*, 83–87; J. M. G. Barclay, *Obeying the Truth: A Study of Paul's Ethics in Galatians* (Edinburgh: T. & T. Clark, 1988) 135–42; Westerholm, *Israel's Law*, 201–5; Schreiner, "The Fulfillment of the Law by Christians," *Law*, 145–78.

This third conclusion runs counter to a large consensus that Paul knew and cared little for the teaching of Jesus and for the way Jesus lived prior to his passion. The subject is one I have addressed elsewhere and may simply summarize the chief considerations.[41] In the first place, it is not simply a question of the eight or nine echoes of Jesus' teaching in the paraenesis of Romans, 1 Corinthians and 1 Thessalonians, which are widely recognized.[42] For this finding still leaves a problem, which has been decisive for most.[43] If Paul did know and does allude to Jesus tradition, why did he not identify it as such? What could have given his paraenesis more authoritative weight than a citation of Jesus' own teaching?

This question, however, reveals a failure to understand how tradition works in a community. A community, almost by definition, has its shared language and metaphors and technical terms and memories. These form the common currency of conversational exchange within the community. They enable the discourse within the community to be abbreviated to a kind of shorthand, where allusions to what is common knowledge can function as allusions and do not need to be spelled out every time. The closer the community, the more allusive the conversations can be. Indeed, it is precisely the character of such discourse as allusive which enables it to function as a kind of glue bonding the community together. It is one's knowledge of the tradition which enables one to recognize the allusions and which thus attests one's membership in the community. Those who do not recognize the allusions thereby demonstrate that they are still outside the community. One enters the community, in effect, by "learning the language," that is by learning the community's tradition in order to make and recognize the allusions to it, and thus to function within the community's discourse.

The point should be obvious. It stands to reason that early Christian communities, which had believed in Christ and taken the name of Christ, should have been instructed in the life and teaching of this Christ in at least some measure. Paul's allusions to his own role in passing on founding traditions (e.g., 1 Cor 11:2; 1 Thess 4:1–2) confirm what we would have had to assume anyway. In consequence Paul could

---

[41] "Jesus Tradition in Paul," in *Studying the Historical Jesus: Evaluations of the State of Current Research* (ed. B. Chilton & C. A. Evans; Leiden: Brill, 1994) 155–78.

[42] The most commonly cited are Rom 12:14, 17; 13:7; 14:13, 14; 1 Cor 13:2; and 1 Thess 5:2, 13, 15. Furnish, *Theology*, 57 does not include 1 Cor 13:2.

[43] See particularly N. Walter, "Paul and the Early Christian Jesus-Tradition," in *Paul and Jesus: Collected Essays* (ed. A. J. M. Wedderburn; JSNTSup 37; Sheffield: JSOT Press, 1989) 51–80, for whom the decisive consideration is that Paul seems to show no consciousness that he was referring to sayings of Jesus.

assume a fair degree of knowledge about Jesus' life and teaching. And because it was common knowledge he did not need to cite Jesus' authority when making such allusions. Indeed, had he cited Jesus' authority every time he referred to something Jesus said or did he would have undermined the force of the allusion as allusion. The allusion which has to be explained has lost its bonding effect; it no longer functions to separate those who recognize the allusion, and thus attest their competence in the Christian "language," from those who fail to recognize it, and thus attest that they are "unbelievers" or "uninstructed" (cf. 1 Cor 14:23–24). In contrast, it is noticeable that in regard to the only two pieces of paraenesis which Paul does explicitly attribute to Jesus, he does so in order to make it clear either that his own instruction goes beyond what Jesus taught (the teaching on divorce in 1 Cor 7:10–16), or that his own practice disregards what Jesus commanded (the evangelist should be provided with financial support by the church, in 1 Cor 9). By way of contrast, then, the fact that all Paul's other references are allusions indicates his acceptance of their authority. In other words, the allusiveness does not weaken the authority of the reference to the Jesus tradition; on the contrary it recognizes and affirms its authority for the community of Jesus.

On the basis of this conclusion we can gain a fairly clear idea of what living in accordance with "the law of Christ" meant for Paul and his addressees. "The law of Christ" alludes to the Jesus tradition which each church received from its founding apostle and which helped constitute it as the church of Jesus Christ. The Christian wanting to live in accord with that law could refer to the Jesus tradition known widely in the church, or in particular to the teachers of the community, whose primary function within the community was to act as depository for and instructor in that tradition. This tradition would provide a model of what it meant to live in accord with the law as summed up in the love command. In this phrase, "the law of Christ," then, we have further confirmation that the law continued to have paraenetic force for the first Christians. But it was the law as taught and lived out by Jesus, as known to the church through its founding traditions.

Conclusions

We may sum up our conclusions briefly under two points. First, it surely follows that for Paul the law, the Jewish law, the Torah, continued to have a positive function to play for the first Christians. The widespread impression that Paul's attitude to the law was essentially or wholly negative has been gleaned by reading the negative comments, which he certainly does make, as though they were the whole story or the primary story. Despite the thousands of pages devoted to the subject, too little attempt has been made to integrate the undeniably positive affirmations Paul also makes concerning the continuing role of the law in the life of the believer.

The solution I have offered here is that the negative thrust of Paul's teaching on the law is clearly focused and circumscribed. It is directed primarily against the way in which the power of sin in concert with the weakness of the flesh has been able to subvert the role of the law as a measure to deal with sin. Even so, that subversion is for a limited time, since the law will still be the measure of judgment when the power of sin and death are themselves brought under the final judgment. But in the meantime, the law, weakened by the flesh and subverted by sin, stands on the negative side of the salvation equation.

This ineffectiveness of the law was particularly focused in its relation to Israel. The temporary role of the law, during Israel's minority as heir of the promise, had been allowed to degenerate into the law understood in terms of works, the law as γράμμα. Paul's own conversion experience had brought home to him that the promise confined to Israel was the promise denied its eschatological fulfillment. And the law insofar as it reinforced that limitation and restriction was itself counter to the promise and purpose of God. It was the law thus understood, that the coming of faith, the coming of Christ had brought to an end.

At the same time, the law, freed from the power of sin and liberated from its role as marking off Israel from the other nations, could and did still have a positive role to play in the life of believer and church. Not in the form of separate commands pulled away from the law as a whole, and not as the moral law distinct from the law's ritual commands, but as the whole law—the whole law lived out of and expressive of faith, the whole law as from the heart in the enabling of the Spirit, the whole law as summed up in the love command and documented in real life by the traditions of Jesus' own teaching and mission.

Second, when we put all three phrases together we gain a surprisingly clear picture of how Paul actually envisaged the law as functioning in this continuingly positive way for Christians.

The law could only be fulfilled out of faith, that is, out of a deep-rooted consciousness of creaturely dependence on the Creator, constantly expressed and nourished in and through worship of the Creator. Where any particular command of the law in a given situation ran counter to that faith it could and perhaps should be dispensed with. For most Gentiles that meant in practice an abandonment of laws of circumcision, clean and unclean foods, sacrifice, etc. But such abandonment might not be necessary in every case; the norm of faith remained; the law of faith remained; and where faith was expressed in and through obedience to a command, that command was still the law of faith.

The law could be fulfilled only in the enabling of the Spirit. Since true obedience could only come from the heart, only by the Spirit could it be effectively offered. This is simply the other side of the coin from the assertion of faith as dependence. It is the Spirit which meets that faith and sustains it and enables it to be expressed in the law, without the law's degenerating into "letter" or "works" or being caught once again in the nexus of the power of self-seeking and the weakness of fleshly appetite.

And finally, the Jesus tradition provides a constant stimulus for living, and a check on what it means to live, in accord with the law of Christ. The Gospels provide many examples of one who lived by the law in terms of recognizing and operating in accord with fundamental principles to be applied in the light of the circumstances (love being the primary principle) rather than by rules to be obeyed whatever the circumstances. No wonder, then, that such living can only be sustained in the context of the community which reveres and steeps itself in that Gospel and in the first Christians' memories of what Jesus taught and how he lived.

A final thought. For most of us brought up in the tradition of Protestant theology it is an astounding thing that Paul himself actually linked the much abused term "law" with three terms which are so much at the centre of his gospel—"faith," "Spirit" and "Christ," or love. But that is what he did! It is in the clarification of this surprising linkage, in the resolution of this surprising paradox, that we find the key to Pauline ethics, and perhaps also to Christian ethics as a whole.

A Partner in the Gospel:
Paul's Understanding of His Ministry

Morna D. Hooker

My original intention was to use as the title for this essay a phrase from 1 Cor 9:22 which is familiar to us all in the translation immortalized by the King James' Version—"All things to all men." The phrase occurs in a passage in which St. Paul is discussing his ministry, and it is highly relevant to my theme, but clearly the sexist language of that version would not do. And it is in fact the translation which is at fault, not Paul, for in Greek his phrase is terse and impartial: τοῖς πᾶσιν γέγονα πάντα. The word "man" simply does not occur! So I toyed with the possibility of using the non-sexist, but flabby translation in the NRSV—"All things to all people"—but then I realized that there were other problems with the traditional rendering, in addition to the feminists' very proper objection to its masculine language. First, the phrase is meant to sum up the list of different categories of people whom Paul has been listing in the previous verses: Paul has put himself out, in different ways, for each individual group in turn, and this is simply not conveyed by the traditional translation, which suggests rather that Paul has become everything at once to everyone on earth. The REB attempts to catch the original meaning, but needs twice as many words as did Paul: "To them all I have become everything in turn." But none of these translations avoids the danger that the verse might be understood to be suggesting something almost dishonest in Paul's dealings with men and women, as though he were a kind of prototype of the Vicar of Bray, willing to adapt his principles according to circumstance: and whatever Paul is meaning in this passage, he is surely not suggesting, as Henry Chadwick once neatly put it, that he is "a mere weathercock."[1]

So what *is* the argument that Paul is attempting to sum up in this phrase? We need to begin at v. 19. The context is Paul's discussion of his rights and privileges as an apostle—rights and privileges which he has gladly foregone for the sake of winning men and women for the Gospel. This chapter has sometimes been seen as a digression from the

---

[1] H. C. Chadwick, "All Things to All Men," *NTS* 1 (1955) 261.

main argument in 1 Corinthians 8 and 10, which concerns the question of whether or not it is permissible to eat meat that has been offered to idols. But, of course, the argument is highly relevant to that topic, for in chapter 8 Paul has urged the Corinthians, too, to give up freedom for the sake of their fellow-Christians. In support of his insistence that concern for one another is far more important than their freedom to do what they believe to be permissible as Christians, he points to the way in which he has denied himself the rewards due to an apostle. The behavior he urges on them may prevent the downfall of a fellow-Christian; the behavior he himself has adopted has helped to *win* men and women for the Gospel.

In 9:19ff. he explains what this has meant. He has, he says, though free, enslaved himself in order to win others; to Jews, he became as a Jew, in order to win Jews; though he himself was not under the law, he became as one who was under the law for the sake of those who were under the law, in order to win those who were under the law, while to those outside the law he became as though he were outside the law, even though he was not himself outside the law, in order to win those who were outside the law; finally, to those who were weak he became weak, in order that he might win the weak. Five times over, then, Paul spells out the same theme: he became what others were, in order to win them for the Gospel. Five times over, he uses the verb κερδαίνω [gain/win], introduced each time by the word ἵνα [in order that]. The first of his five points—that though he was in fact free, he made himself a slave to all—picks up the theme of the previous chapter, and may well have made his readers uncomfortable: some, at least, of the Corinthians have been glorying in their freedom; Paul gladly gives his freedom up for the sake of the Gospel. The last point also—his willingness to share the weakness of the weak—echoes the theme of that section; it is the "weak" in Corinth—that is to say, those who are hesitant about how to act in particular circumstances—who are afraid to eat idol meat, and who could be made to fall if those of their fellow-Christians who are more confident and whose consciences are therefore more robust are not prepared to limit their freedom—to "share," as it were, in the weakness of others. The second, third and fourth statements are the most problematic, and therefore the most interesting. To Jews, says Paul, he became "as a Jew," in order to win Jews. This time he cannot, of course, say that he became a Jew, because he was by birth a Jew; rather, he became "as a Jew." Perhaps because he realizes that his readers may be puzzled, he immediately explains what he means in another way: to become "as a Jew" means that he put himself under the law, even though he was not under the law. Similarly, for Gentiles—for those outside the law—he became as one outside the law; but once again, he immediately qualifies his statement: though he put himself outside the law, he was not outside the law of God, for he was under the law of Christ. But whatever qualifications Paul needs to add, the point he is making is clear: as far as possible he has deliberately identified himself with those whom he has sought to win for the Gospel.

So when Paul says, in v. 22, that he has become all things to them all, he is summing up his missionary endeavors. He has done it all in order—once again he uses the word ἵνα—to save some of them. The form of the statement is parallel to the previous five, except that the verb σώζω [save] replaces κερδαίνω [gain]. Then, in v. 23, he repeats this statement and defines it: "I do it all," he says, "for the sake of the Gospel, in order that I may be a participant in it"—ἵνα συγκοινωνὸς αὐτοῦ γένωμαι. What does Paul mean by describing himself as a συγκοινωνός in the Gospel? The literal meaning of the word is "participant" or "partner."[2] Almost all the commentators believe that it means one who participates in the *benefits* of the Gospel, and the majority of the translators agree.[3] They understand Paul to be saying: "I do it all for the sake of the Gospel, so that I may share in its blessings." But is this the most likely interpretation? Has Paul undertaken all his missionary endeavors merely so that he himself may share in the benefits of the Gospel? Is it not strange that the climax of the argument should prove to be a statement that what seemed like selfless activity undertaken to win men and women for the Gospel should have as its ultimate aim his own personal salvation?

No doubt there were some evangelists, then as now, who preached a message which concentrated on the personal benefits which come to those who accept the Gospel, but Paul himself has scathing things to say about this perversion of the Gospel—not least in 1 Corinthians! If we understand συγκοινωνός in this way, as one who participates in the benefits of the Gospel, then we must certainly stress the force of the συν-. Paul does not say simply that his aim is to be a κοινωνὸς τοῦ εὐαγγελίου [participant in the gospel] but a συγκοινωνὸς τοῦ εὐαγγελίου [fellow participant in the gospel], which suggests that his purpose is that others should join him in these benefits.[4] In this case, we should understand Paul to be saying, not "I do all this for the sake of the Gospel, so that I may share its benefits," but "I do all this for the

---

[2] For the adjective, LSJ gives the meaning "partaking jointly of"; for the noun, "partner."

[3] But see R. St John Parry, *The First Epistle of Paul the Apostle to the Corinthians* (CGTC; Cambridge: Cambridge University Press, 1916) 143; NEB: "All this I do for the sake of the Gospel, to bear my part in proclaiming it."

[4] Cf. the other occurrences of συγκοινωνός in the New Testament: Rom 11:17; Phil 1:7; Rev 1:9.

sake of the Gospel, so that *others* may share in its benefits *with me.*" This emphasis is not normally brought out in either the translations or the commentaries however: rather, Paul is assumed to be referring primarily to his own salvation.[5]

The word συγκοινωνός can be understood in a passive sense, therefore, provided that the phrase is emphasized in this way. But are the commentators right in understanding the word to mean a passive participant? I have suggested already that Paul's accounts of his mission in vv. 22b and 23 belong together. Is it not far more logical to suggest that coming as it does at the climax of the argument of vv. 19–23, this twin statement of Paul's intentions means that in becoming "all things to all people," he is sharing in the Gospel, not simply passively but actively also? The fact that the structure of vv. 22 and 23 is parallel to the structure of the previous five statements suggests that the meaning, also, is parallel: Paul has become all things to all people *in order to* save some; he has done it all for the sake of the Gospel, *in order to* be a sharer in the Gospel—and logic suggests that this means sharing in its work of salvation. Why is it, then, that neither the commentators nor the translators agree with me on this point? Why is it that they understand Paul to be introducing a new idea here, describing himself as receiving a share in the *benefits* of the Gospel?

First, it has to be acknowledged that the overall theme of 1 Corinthians 9 is that of reward. In pointing to himself as an example of one who has deliberately limited his freedom and refused to demand his "rights" for the sake of the Gospel, Paul stresses the rewards that are his due as an apostle. Might we not expect him to continue this theme in v. 23? But the whole point of Paul's argument is that he has *refused* to accept any reward—save that of preaching the Gospel without charge (vv. 12, 15–18). The last thing we expect to be told, therefore, is that the reward he is aiming for is his own salvation. Rather, we would expect him to insist once again that his only "reward" is to preach the word, and to win men and women for the Gospel.

Secondly, immediately after this verse, in vv. 24–27, Paul goes on to speak of the reward that comes to those who compete in the games, and says that he disciplines his own body lest, after preaching to others, he is himself rejected. Here we certainly have the idea of Paul himself hoping to share in the benefits of the Gospel. Does v. 23b, then, look forward to this idea? We suggest not: firstly, because the idea that Paul's *aim* in preaching was to secure his own salvation is far removed from the *hope*

---

[5] Thus C. K. Barrett, A *Commentary on the First Epistle to the Corinthians* (HNTC; New York: Harper & Row; London: Black, 1968) 216 translates: "that I too may have my share in it."

he expresses in v. 27; secondly, because vv. 24–27 introduce a new argument, backed up by a new metaphor, as to why the Corinthians should discipline themselves. The reference to Paul having preached to others is incidental to the main argument, though understandable in view of the theme of the chapter.

Thirdly, there is the question of the precise meaning of the phrase ἵνα συγκοινωνὸς αὐτοῦ γένομαι. The word συγκοινωνός, as we have seen, means "partner," a term which implies both giving and receiving: a partner in a firm is obliged to contribute something in terms of finance and labor, but can expect to share in the firm's profits.[6] The word here could thus refer either to participation in the *benefits* of the Gospel, or to sharing in the *work* of the Gospel, which seems highly appropriate in the present context. This second interpretation is generally ruled out as impossible.[7] Nevertheless, the active sense is a possible one for συγκοινωνός, and it makes good sense to understand it here as "one who participates in the work of the gospel."[8] The word αὐτοῦ [in/of it] refers to εὐαγγέλιον, a term which normally refers to the *content* of the Gospel; but although it is frequently used with a verb to denote the preaching of the Gospel, it is sometimes used without a verb to refer to the *proclamation* of the Gospel.[9] In the present passage, Paul is very much concerned with his own proclamation of the Gospel. He says that he is anxious that no obstacle should obstruct [the spread of] the Gospel of Christ (v. 12); he reminds the Corinthians of the Lord's instruction that those who preach the Gospel should live by the Gospel [i.e., be paid for preaching it] (v. 14); and he says that his aim is that in preaching the Gospel he should do so without charge, in order not to make full use of his authority in the Gospel [i.e., as a preacher of it] (v. 18). The meaning that we are suggesting for v. 23 understands εὐαγγέλιον in the same sense. The phrase could thus signify that Paul sees himself as a partner with others in the work of preaching the Gospel—in which case he is presumably referring to the group alluded

---

[6] The word κοινωνός is used in that sense in Luke 5:10.

[7] C. K. Barrett, *First Corinthians*, 216, who comments simply that this is not what Paul means. Cf. W. G. Kümmel, who states that "Die Übersetzung 'Mitarbeiter am Evangelium' ist unmöglich; συγκοινωνός heisst niemals 'aktiver Teilnehmer,' [the translation, 'co-worker in the gospel' is impossible; συγκοινωνός never means 'active participant']" (H. Lietzmann, *An die Korinther I–II* [5th ed., rev. W. G. Kümmel; HNT 9; Tübingen: Mohr, 1969] 180). For the active sense, however, we need only turn to Rev 1:9, where John describes himself as the συγκοινωνός of his readers in tribulation and sovereignty and endurance.

[8] Cf. the reference to Titus as κοινωνὸς ἐμός in 2 Cor 8:23; also to the κοινωνία of the Philippians εἰς τὸ εὐαγγέλιον in Phil 1:5.

[9] Cf. Rom 1:1, 9; 2 Cor 2:12; 10:14; Gal 2:7; Phil 2:22; 4:15. I am grateful to Mr. G. M. Styler for pointing out the relevance of this in relation to 1 Cor 9:23.

to in v. 1 of this chapter of those people who also claim to be apostles and to have seen the Lord. As so often, Paul is on the defensive about his apostleship throughout this section, and it would not be surprising if he here claims that his labors for the salvation of the Gentiles are the proof that he is a "partner in the Gospel" in the sense that he, too, shares in the work of proclaiming it.

Yet Paul's understanding of what apostleship involves clearly differs from that of some of these other apostles: is he here perhaps going beyond the mere claim that, like them, he shares in the proclamation of the Gospel? If he has refused to claim his "rights," this is because he is determined to put no obstacle in the way of the Gospel (v. 12): in other words, his behavior is governed by the Gospel itself. There is, in fact, yet a third possible way of understanding the phrase συγκοινωνὸς τοῦ εὐαγγελίου which underlines this point, and this is to take it as meaning that Paul is a partner of the Gospel in the sense that he and the Gospel are 'partners' in a common enterprise."[10] In other words, he is a συγκοινωνός with the Gospel itself (which is in effect personified), working with a common purpose.[11] Paul does more than proclaim the Gospel: his involvement with it is such that he is in a sense identified with it. This idea comes out clearly in many of his letters: he has been crucified with Christ,[12] and carries round in his body the death that Jesus died.[13] If this is what he means here, then he is saying that his task as a partner in this enterprise is to share in the work of the Gospel by bringing men and women to salvation. This would in effect sum up all that he has been saying in the previous verses; if this is correct, then Paul is claiming that by his manner of life in identifying with others he in fact proclaims the Gospel, and thus wins men and women for Christ.

---

[10] The idea is not entirely without parallel in Paul, though elsewhere he speaks of his co-operation with God. Cf. 1 Cor 3:9, where θεοῦ γάρ ἐσμεν συνεργοί may mean "we are fellow-workers with God," and 1 Thess 3:2, where Timothy is described as τὸν ἀδελφὸν ἡμῶν καὶ συνεργὸν τοῦ θεοῦ, a phrase which is normally interpreted as meaning "our brother and God's fellow-worker." C. K. Barrett, *First Corinthians*, 216, argues that in 1 Cor 9:23 this sense would require a dative, but if the word is treated as a noun rather than a participle, a genitive is the only case possible. In two of the three other occurrences of συγκοινωνός in the New Testament the genitive is used of the person with whom one is a partner or fellow-participant. See Phil 1:7 and Rev 1:9. Cf. 2 Cor 8:23. In 1 Corinthians 10 the phrase κοινωνοὶ τοῦ θυσιαστηρίου used in v. 18 with the sense "partners *in* the altar," followed in v. 20 by the phrase κοινωνοὺς τῶν δαιμονίων with the sense "partners *with* demons."

[11] So Einar Molland, *Das Paulinische Euangelion: Das Wort und die Sache* (Oslo: Jacob Dybwad, 1934) 53f.

[12] Gal 2:20.

[13] 2 Cor 4:10.

If the idea that Paul may be a "partner *with* the gospel" is a startling one, this is perhaps because it is at odds with the Lutheran insistence that Paul saw himself simply as the passive recipient of God's grace, doing nothing: how can Paul *share* in the work of salvation? In fact, however, Paul has already described himself, in v. 22b, as saving others. It is not this that makes this particular interpretation difficult, but rather the need to personify the Gospel, which has no parallel in Paul. Yet he comes close to doing so elsewhere: he describes it in Rom 1:16 as "the power of God which brings salvation,"[14] and like the word of God in the Old Testament, the Gospel brings life and death.[15] Paul can speak of "preaching the Gospel" or of "preaching Christ crucified,"[16] and the latter, like the former, is "the power of God."[17] He tells the Corinthians that he begat them διὰ τοῦ εὐαγγελίου [through the gospel],[18] and describes himself as a διάκονος [servant] of the Gospel[19] and as being engaged in the priestly service of the Gospel.[20] It is possible, then, that in describing himself as a συγκοινωνὸς τοῦ εὐαγγελίου, Paul is claiming to be a partner *with* the Gospel, sharing in the work of the Gospel itself.

Whichever of these interpretations of the phrase may be the correct one, it seems highly likely that when Paul applies the word συγκοινωνός to himself, he does so because he sees his role not simply as that of a passive participant in the Gospel, but as an active partner. The Gospel of course brings benefits, which Paul expects to receive, but it must also be shared with others, and the receiving and the sharing cannot be separated; the term συγκοινωνός having an active as well as a passive meaning, describes both aspects admirably. Far from being a selfish statement that the ultimate motive he has for working as an evangelist is in order to have his share in the benefits of the Gospel, he is surely saying here that the only way to receive those benefits is to share in *ministry*—to be a *partner* in the Gospel in every sense of the term.

There is, I suggest, interesting support for this interpretation in the remarkable parallel between the statements concerning Paul's ministry which we have just been analyzing and those summaries of the Gospel which Paul uses from time to time which are sometimes described as

[14] Cf. 1 Cor 15:1f.
[15] 1 Cor 1:23f.; 2 Cor 2:15f.
[16] 1 Cor 1:17, 23; Gal 1:6–9 and 3:1f.
[17] 1 Cor 1:24.
[18] 1 Cor 4:15.
[19] Col 1:23; cf. Eph 3:7.
[20] Rom 15:16.

expressing a notion of interchange. Now the term "interchange" is not an ideal one, though I confess to having used it myself, for want of a better word, more than most: "interchange" suggests a total reversal of roles, a substitution of the kind that takes place in A *Tale of Two Cities,* when Sydney Carton takes Charles Darnay's place on the scaffold. In fact, what Paul describes is the self-identification of Christ with men and women which, in turn, results in their sharing in what he is. In becoming what men and women are, Christ does not cease to be what he eternally is. Irenaeus expressed this idea tersely and admirably when he said that Christ became what we are, in order that we might become what he is.[21] The passages in Paul where this idea is most clearly spelled out are as follows:

> 2 Cor 5:21: God made Christ sin for our sake, though he knew no sin, in order that we might become the righteousness of God in him.
>
> 2 Cor 8:9: Christ became poor for our sake, though he was rich, in order that we might become rich through his poverty.
>
> Gal 3:13: Christ redeemed us from the curse of the law, having become a curse for us, in order that the blessing of Abraham might come upon the Gentiles, in order that we might receive the Spirit.
>
> Gal 4:4–5: God sent his Son, born of a woman, born under the law, in order that he might redeem those who were under the law, in order that we might receive adoption as sons.

Similar ideas are expressed elsewhere:

> Rom 8:3–4: God sent his own Son in the likeness of sinful flesh and . . . condemned sin in the flesh, in order that the righteous command of the law might be fulfilled in us.
>
> Phil 2:6–8: Christ, being in the form of God, emptied himself, taking the form of a slave; and humbling himself, he became obedient to a slave's death on a cross. (The result is spelled out at the end of chapter 3, where Christians are transformed into the likeness of Christ's glorious body.)

The common structure of these passages is as follows:

First, Christ became something (or God made him to be something); in other words, Christ accepted a state of existence which was not normal to him. He became poor, became sin, was born as a man, under the law, came under a curse; he came in the likeness of sinful flesh, took the form of a slave. The fact that he was accepting a condition that was foreign to him is reflected in the way in which Paul often hedges his statements around with apologetic explanations. He became poor—

---

[21] *Adv. Haer.* V. praef.

though of course he was rich; he became sin—though of course he knew no sin; he came *in the likeness of* sinful flesh; he took the *form* of a slave: we should not misunderstand μορφή in this last statement as though it referred to something unreal; the phrase may perhaps be best interpreted as indicating status: in other words, Christ accepted the status of a slave. Only in Galatians, where Paul tends to be blunt in everything he says, does he fail to put things delicately: Christ was born of a woman (nothing docetic about that!), he was born under the law, and he became a curse—and what endless problems that last, stark statement has caused for commentators who wanted to escape from its blunt reality! In all these statements, whether the idea is expressed bluntly or more carefully, Christ is identified with the condition of men and women.

Secondly, the purpose of this identification, introduced in every case (except in Philippians) by the word ἵνα [so that], is that men and women might share in what Christ is: might share, not in what he became in being identified with us, but in what he essentially was and is. Through the redemptive kenosis of Christ they share what he was willing to abandon; he was rich, and they too become rich; he knew no sin, and they become the righteousness of God in him; the Son of God abandoned the privileges of sonship when he came under the curse of the law, but those who are redeemed from the curse of the law receive a blessing instead of a curse, and have become the children of God. When he came in the likeness of sinful flesh, Christ destroyed sin in the flesh, and so allowed the righteous command of God to be fulfilled in men and women, just as it was in himself. And because the one who was in the form of God took the form of men and women, their bodies of humiliation will be conformed to his body of glory.

We begin to understand now how this "interchange" works: it is not that Christ changes place with men and women. Though he identifies with them, he remains what he is—without sin, Son of God, in the form of God. And when they become what he is it is because they are now identified with him—or, to use the crucial Pauline expression, because they are "in Christ."

Let us return to those seven parallel statements about Paul's ministry in 1 Corinthians 9. Straight away, we see that there is an obvious parallel between them and our "interchange" formulae. Christ became what we are, he was made what we are, he was sent into our condition, *in order that* we might become what he is. Paul, in turn, became what the men and women to whom he was proclaiming the Gospel were, in order that he might gain them for the Gospel. And just as some of the statements about what Christ became needed modification—he became sin, *though he knew no sin,* and he came *in the likeness of* sinful flesh, where the word "likeness" prevents us thinking of him as sinful—so, too, in the case of Paul. He came under the law, *even though he was not under the law;* he became as one without law, *even though he was not without God's law.* Only the last part of the statements is different: in those about Christ, Paul spells out the interchange: we become rich, we become children of God, and so on. But in the statements in 1 Corinthians about his own ministry, his aim—in six of the seven—is said to be that he may gain—or save—the men and women to whom he preaches. And in the seventh, it is that he may be a partner in the Gospel.

Commentators are often puzzled by the paradoxical nature of these statements: how can Paul be under the law, even though he was not under the law, and be as one without law, even though he was not without God's law? Perhaps the realization that he sees himself, in Christ, as sharing in some sense in the paradox of the incarnation may provide us with the clue. What I am suggesting is that the summary of events which lies at the heart of Paul's kerygma is seen by him as the pattern for his own ministry. The apostle, sent by his Lord, acts as his representative. He proclaims the Gospel, not simply in word, but in action. He is conformed to the pattern of Christ's own kenosis. Far from being a simple recipient of the benefits of the Gospel, he is a partner in it. We should not be surprised to find Paul seeing his ministry in this light, for after all, there is a sense in which he sees the whole of Christian existence in these terms. In earlier studies, I have sought to show how, paradoxically, the Christian shares the kenosis of Christ in order to share the benefits which that kenosis brought about.[22] Christ shared our condition in order that we might share his, yet we need, in turn, to share his humiliation and suffering. He shared our death, in order that we might share his life, yet in order to share his life, we need to share his death. The Christian is summoned to die with Christ, to suffer with Christ, to become like him in his obedience and self-emptying. Christian atonement is never a simple matter of substitution, and neither is Christian living. It is hardly surprising, then, if Christian ministry is seen as a sharing in the pattern provided by Christ.

But if Christ is a pattern, then there is a sense in which Christians are called to imitate him. Now it is my conviction that the notion of imitation is much more significant in Pauline thought than has often been allowed. Commentators have sometimes tended to shy away from it, partly perhaps because, like Luther, they have felt that the idea of imitating Christ suggests human endeavor, and so conflicts with the belief that the Christian depends for salvation on the grace of God

---

[22] See M. D. Hooker, *From Adam to Christ* (Cambridge: Cambridge University Press, 1990) 1–69, 88–100.

alone and can do nothing on his or her own; and partly perhaps because they have thought that in 2 Cor 5:16 Paul denies any earthly knowledge of the earthly Jesus. [23] But the theme of imitation is found relatively frequently in Paul. [24] More often than not, of course, Paul points to *himself* as the pattern for others to follow. When he urges his converts to imitate him, as he does in 1 Cor 4:16 and Phil 4:9, [25] we may well conclude that he is being immodest, but at least it does not offend Protestant theological principles. But why does he set himself up as a pattern for other believers to imitate? The answer is set out most clearly in 1 Cor 11:1, where Paul urges the Corinthians to become imitators of him, *even as he is an imitator of Christ*. This is a particularly interesting passage, and we shall come back to it in a moment. Meanwhile, we note that in Phil 3:17, Paul urges the Philippians to become fellow-imitators, but this time his meaning is ambiguous, for the word he uses is συμμιμηταί, and if, as is most natural, the μου which follows is a subjective genitive, then he must mean that they are to become fellow-imitators *with* him; he is suggesting, that is, that they should imitate Christ together. [26] Once again, however, I find that I am out of step with the commentators and the translators in taking the passage this way, since they almost all understand Paul to mean here that it is the Philippians who are to join together in imitating *him:* in other words, they are to be fellow-imitators with one another. And I have to admit that Paul *does* appeal to himself as an example in the last four words of the verse, where he says "even as you have us as a model." But

---

[23] The article contributed by W. Michaelis to *TWNT* has been extremely influential, especially in Germany. Cf. *TDNT* 4:672f.: "When Paul calls himself a μιμητὴς Χριστοῦ, or when he tells the Thessalonians they must show themselves to be μιμηταὶ τοῦ κυρίου, the point is that both he and they are followers of their heavenly Lord. There is thus no thought of an imitation, whether outward or inward, of the earthly life of Jesus in either individual features or total impress. The call for an *imitatio Christi* finds no support in the statements of Paul. . . . Paul does not speak of true imitation of Christ or God. His reference is simply to obedient following as an expression of fellowship of life and will." Cf. H. D. Betz, *Nachfolge und Nachahmung Jesu Christi im Neuen Testament* (BHT 37; Tübingen: Mohr-Siebeck, 1967) 137–89; E. Lohse, *RGG* 4 (3d ed.; 1960) col. 1287f.

[24] See the discussions in E. J. Tinsley, *The Imitation of God in Christ* (London: SCM, 1960) 134–65; E. Larsson, *Christus als Vorbild* (Uppsala: Almsquist & Wiksells, 1962) 232–70; V. P. Furnish, *Theology and Ethics in Paul* (Nashville, TN, and New York: Abingdon, 1968) 218–24; D. M. Stanley, "'Become imitators of me': The Pauline Conception of Apostolic Tradition," *Biblica* 40 (1959) 859–77, and "Imitation in Paul's Letters: Its Significance for His Relationship to Jesus and to His Own Christian Foundations," in *From Jesus to Paul: Studies in Honour of Francis Wright Beare* (ed. Peter Richardson and John C. Hurd; Waterloo, ON: Wilfrid Laurier University Press, 1984) 127–41; L. W. Hurtado, "Jesus as Lordly Example in Philippians 2:5–11," in *From Jesus to Paul*, 113–26.

[25] Cf. also 2 Thess 3:7, 9.

[26] See the references in my *From Adam to Christ*, 177.

perhaps Paul was not merely repeating himself here: he was a model for the Philippians; but the context makes clear that *his* model was Christ; is it not logical, then, that he should appeal to them to be fellow-imitators of Christ with him?

Even if I am wrong about this passage, however, we find when we turn to 1 Thess 1:6–7 that Paul says quite clearly that the Thessalonians have become imitators both of himself *and of the Lord,* and that in so doing they have, in turn, become the pattern for other believers to imitate. The context makes clear that this "imitation" involved suffering, which suggests that in this respect, at least, it is not something which is undertaken deliberately. A somewhat similar statement is made in 1 Thess 2:14, where Paul comments that the Thessalonians "became imitators of the churches of God in Judaea which are in Christ Jesus"— not, to be sure, deliberately—but because they suffered the same things from their countrymen as did the Jews from theirs, who also killed the Lord Jesus and the prophets. Here again, Paul reminds the Thessalonians that they are sharing the same fate as the Lord himself. And that, of course, is a theme which Paul elaborates in terms of his own ministry in 2 Corinthians, where he speaks of carrying about in his body the dying of the Lord Jesus. But though in 1 Thessalonians he uses the language of "imitation," the idea that Christians suffer in the same way that their Lord suffered is similar to that which Paul elsewhere expresses in terms of "being conformed" to Christ's sufferings.

These passages in 1 Thesssalonians describe an imitation of Christ which has been forced on believers by circumstance. Elsewhere, it is something to be deliberately pursued. Meanwhile, we note that there are several other passages where Paul recalls the saving activity of Christ, and urges his readers to take it as a pattern to be copied. In Rom 15:1–3, he argues that "we who are strong ought to bear with the failings of the weak, and not to please ourselves; let each of us please our neighbor, in order to build up the community . . . even as Christ did not please himself." The advice is repeated in v. 7: "Accept one another, as Christ accepted us." Again, in 2 Corinthians 8, where Paul is appealing to the Corinthians to contribute to his collection for the saints in Jerusalem, he reminds them of the grace of the Lord Jesus: "though he was rich, yet he became poor for your sake, in order that you, through his poverty, might become rich." This is a passage we have looked at already; but notice how it continues. They, in their turn, must show the same kind of generosity—in other words, they are to follow Christ's example. In chapter 10, at the very point where Paul suddenly becomes very cross with the Corinthians, he appeals to them "by the gentleness and magnanimity of Christ"—and goes on to argue that it is this same gentleness and magnanimity which have governed his own behavior in dealing with them: he has followed the example of Christ.

The best-known example, however, is to be found in the introduction to the so-called "hymn" in Philippians 2, where Paul's readers are urged to "have the mind of Christ Jesus." Now in fact, ever since Käsemann's influential study of this passage, the relevance of this exhortation to our theme is often denied. Käsemann argued that Paul's appeal was not to the example of the earthly Jesus, but to the events of the saving kerygma,[27] and many commentators have followed him.[28] Käsemann is certainly right to insist that the Pauline ethic does not consist *simply* in an exhortation to be like Jesus; rather it depends on the saving events of the Gospel, and on the fact that the believer now lives in Christ. But the antithesis he draws between these two ideas is unnecessarily sharp: it is not a case of either/or but of both/and. This passage is one of the most difficult in the Pauline epistles, but certainly we may say that Paul sees *some* connection between Christ's self-emptying and self-humiliation and the behavior which he thinks proper in the Christian community: the behavior of those who are in Christ must conform to his.[29] And it is not just the self-emptying of the heavenly Christ which is to be our pattern, but the obedience of the earthly Jesus, which led him to death on a cross.

It is perhaps worth mentioning that appeals to emulate the love of Christ are found in Eph 5:2, 25, and that the first of these is linked with an appeal to imitate God himself (5:1). And before we dismiss these passages as simply post-Pauline, we should note the same idea in Rom 14:1–3, which introduces the argument about the necessity for the strong in the congregation to care for the weak: if the strong are to accept the weak, that is because God himself has already received them.

It is surely no accident that when we examine the context of all these passages, we find that this is concerned with the behavior which is expected among Christians, and in particular with the way in which they deal with one another. It is in their lifestyle that Christians are to be imitators of Christ; moreover, in imitating him they benefit one another. Just as Christ's actions brought benefit to Christians, so the actions of his followers bring help to their fellow-Christians.

---

[27] E. Käsemann, "Kritische Analyse von Phil 2:5–11," *ZTK* 47 (1950) 313–60; ET: *JTC* 5 (1968) 45–88.

[28] Among these are F. W. Beare, *A Commentary on the Epistle to the Philippians* (BNTC; London: Black, 1959) 73–78; R. P. Martin, *Carmen Christi: Philippians ii.5–11 in Recent Interpretation and in the Setting of Early Christian Worship* (Cambridge: Cambridge University Press, 1967) and *Philippians* (NCB; London: Oliphants, 1976).

[29] See M. D. Hooker, *From Adam to Christ*, 88–100.

We should not be surprised, then, to find that Paul applies this idea of *imitatio Christi* to his own ministry—or to discover that it is the pattern of kenosis which he sees as the model to which he should be conformed. But does he in fact link those statements in 1 Corinthians 9 (about becoming what others are in order to win them for the Gospel) with the example of Christ? He does.

If we turn to the end of chapter 10 we find the idea repeated, in v. 33, in language which echoes 1 Cor 9:22; this time, Paul says that he tries to please everyone in every matter (πάντα πᾶσι), seeking their advantage rather than his own, and that he does it in order to *save* them. The interesting thing about this passage is that it is followed immediately, in 1 Cor 11:1, by the appeal we noted earlier—an appeal to the Corinthians to imitate him, *as he imitates Christ.* The language, moreover, about "pleasing others," echoes what he says about Christ in a similar context in Romans 15. Here is clear evidence that Paul modeled his own ministry on that of Christ; in becoming "all things to all people," he was consciously conforming to the example of Christ. And indeed the link is made once again in Romans 15, for there Paul uses this appeal to Christ's example to back up a statement that those who are strong ought to bear with the failings of the weak, and not to please themselves (Rom 15:1); in the context, the meaning of this is clear. Those who are strong in faith (and Paul associates himself with them) must be prepared to identify with the weakness of those whose faith is weak. The strong must be as though weak, for the sake of the weak. Why? The reason is spelled out in the preceding chapter: "don't let what you eat destroy the fellow-Christian for whom Christ died . . . it is not right to eat meat or drink wine or to do anything that makes a fellow-Christian stumble" (Rom 14:15, 21). Notice that the motive expressed positively in 1 Corinthians 9—the desire to save others—is here expressed in negative terms. Notice, too, that this ministry of self-identification with others is not something which stops at Paul, but is extended to the members of his congregation: they, too, are to become as others are, in order that others may be saved. And when we turn back to 1 Corinthians, we find that in chapter 8, Paul urges the Corinthians, in effect, to share the weakness of the weak. Why should they do so? Because if they do not, their behavior may destroy their fellow-Christians, for whom Christ died: once again, it is something Paul himself is prepared to do: "if food causes my brother's downfall, I will abstain from meat for evermore, lest I cause him to stumble" (8:13).

Now both 1 Corinthians 8–10 and Romans 14–15 are about the problems of what may be eaten and drunk. But this is not the only context in which Paul uses this idea that he, like Christ, identifies himself with those whom he hopes to save for the Gospel. The fact that in 1 Corinthians 9 he spoke of coming "under the law" or being "outside the law" for the sake of others might perhaps reflect the fact that questions about clean and unclean food were at stake, but it could suggest that wider issues are involved. So let us turn to Galatians, where Paul grapples with the problem of the law. In 4:12, we find him appealing to the Galatians to become as he is, because he has become *as they are:* here is a fascinating echo of the interchange formulae. Its meaning is that Paul has become "without the law" for the sake of his Gentile converts, and it follows very quickly after the statement that Christ himself came *under the law* in order to set free those under the law. At first sight, Paul seems to be doing something diametrically opposite: Christ came under the law for the sake of others; moreover, he came under the curse of the law. But Paul puts himself *outside* the law! That means, of course, that he too comes under its curse. What is important, however, is that in preaching the Gospel, *Paul shares the condition of those to whom he ministers,* and so is conformed to the pattern of his Lord.

There are other passages, too, in which Paul appears to be claiming that his ministry is modeled on that of Christ. Let us look again at Philippians, where Paul spells out in chapter 2 the self-emptying of Christ, and then describes in the following chapter how he himself has abandoned everything he prized for the sake of Christ. Here he spells out the benefits of the Gospel which he enjoys—the surpassing worth of knowing Jesus Christ his Lord, and the hope of resurrection. But it is not his own salvation alone that is his concern, for in the service of that Gospel, he has learned (as did Christ), how to be abased and how to abound (4:12): we are perhaps not surprised to find that Paul's somewhat extravagant language here echoes the verb used of Christ's self-humiliation in 2:8.[30] The Gospel is not merely something to which he has responded and whose benefits he enjoys; it has stamped its pattern on his whole life: he shares in the self-emptying of Christ.

Or take 2 Cor 6:10, where he describes himself as poor, yet making many rich. Here is a clear "echo" of what he will go on to say about Christ himself in 8:9. This verse is part of the many in 2 Corinthians where Paul speaks of his ministry in terms of sharing in the sufferings of Christ for the sake of others. He carries around in the body the dying of the Lord Jesus, and he is always being given up to death for Jesus' sake; but what is the end result? "Death is at work in us, but life in you" (2 Cor 4:10–11). The theme is spelled out in the opening chapter of the epistle: Paul shares abundantly, he says, in the sufferings of Christ, and through Christ shares abundantly in comfort too; but, he goes on, "if we

---

[30] ἐταπείνωσεν – ταπεινοῦσθαι.

are afflicted, it is for your comfort and salvation, and if we are comforted, it is for your comfort." Like Christ himself, Paul knows both suffering and comfort; and his experience is used by God for the comfort and salvation of others. As Victor Furnish admirably expressed it: "Paul's suffering and serving as an apostle are to be regarded as a sort of "parable" of Christ's own saving death and resurrection."[31]

But the most remarkable passage of all is Col 1:24, where Paul (if it is Paul) speaks of his sufferings on behalf of the Colossians (ὑπὲρ ὑμῶν), and says that these sufferings fill up what is lacking of the afflictions of Christ in his flesh. We can be sure that Paul does not mean that the sufferings of Christ himself were in any sense inadequate. Yet he understands himself to be called to share the sufferings of Christ—and it is for the sake of his body, the Church. *Because they are Christ's sufferings,* they can bring benefit to others. [32]

Now one of the reasons why expositors have often been so wary of the notion of imitation is clearly the suspicion that it could be thought to undermine the uniqueness of God's saving action in Christ. If grace stands over against human endeavor, how can we "imitate" the work of Christ? If salvation is through Christ alone, how can the sufferings of others be in any sense redemptive? The answer, of course, is that if imitation is attempted at an external level, like the imitation of the latest fashion in hair styles or pop music, one cannot: this is indeed a version of the belief that one can save oneself by works. But the imitation Paul is describing depends on the fact that the believer is in Christ. He is thinking, that is, not of counterfeit copies, pirated without permission, but of authentic replicas which bear the stamp of the original. Perhaps, rather than talking about imitation, we should speak of Christians being conformed to the pattern of Christ—language with which Paul is certainly equally at home. To suppose that what we term "imitation" is impossible is to ignore Paul's fundamental belief in the believer's participation in Christ. For the imitation of Christ depends on union with him, and takes place within that union: it is thus a

---

[31] Furnish, *Theology and Ethics in Paul,* 222f.

[32] Cf. W. F. Flemington, "On the interpretation of Colossians 1:24," in *Suffering and Martyrdom in the New Testament: Studies presented to G. M. Styler by the Cambridge New Testament Seminar* (ed. William Horbury and Brian McNeil; Cambridge: Cambridge University Press, 1981) 84–90. See p. 89: ". . . the Cross is representative and capable of being reflected and mirrored in the life of Christians. The love of God in Christ that there embraced sacrificial suffering is the pattern for the Christian. By incorporation 'in Christ' he must continually seek more and more completely to reproduce it in his own life, and St. Paul believes that this can bring benefit to the Body of Christ." Cf. also those passages where Paul describes himself or others as suffering ὑπὲρ Χριστοῦ [for the sake of Christ]: 2 Cor 12:10; Phil 1:29.

question of believers being conformed to his image, not of copying an external pattern: what Paul desires for his converts above all else is that "Christ be formed in them" (Gal 4:19). But if Christ is truly formed in the Christian community, does this not mean that its members will share in *his* redeeming work?

Whatever we may wish to say about Christ's death as a unique saving act is not diminished by the recognition that what he does *for* us has to be worked out *in us*. Christ's uniqueness as the one on whom salvation depends is in no sense affected, for whatever men and women are enabled to do derives from him. It is an old heresy—and one with which Paul was all too familiar—to imagine that the doctrine of salvation by grace meant that one was now free to live as one liked; to suppose that because Christ had reconciled men and women to God through his death, the Christian life meant living like kings; that particular version of the heresy can unfortunately still be heard on certain American television stations. In contrast, Paul insists that Christians were set free (from sin and the flesh) to live "in Christ," which certainly involves being like him; he insists, too, that being a follower of Christ means sharing in his sufferings; and dares to suggest that, precisely because they are Christ's sufferings, they can bring life and comfort to others. But whatever men and women are enabled to do as channels of salvation derives from him. The "interchange" works only for those who are in Christ, as we can see in a remarkable passage where Paul expresses a wish to be identified with others, but cannot be. The passage in question is Rom 9:3, where Paul declares that he could wish to be *anathema*, cut off from Christ, for the sake of his fellow-Jews. Commentators recognize an echo of Moses' prayer in Exod 32:32. But notice also an echo of the interchange formulae: Paul is willing to become anathema for the Jews—ὑπὲρ [τουτῶν], "for their sake"—just as Christ became a curse for our sake. But this particular longing necessarily remains unfulfilled, for at this point he cannot imitate his Lord. By becoming a curse, Christ was able to bring blessing to others; by being made sin, he was able to become the source of righteousness. But *it is only those who are in Christ* who are able to share in what he is and who are able to be channels through whom this life can be passed on to others. However much Paul may identify with his fellow-Jews, therefore, he cannot help them *by being cut off from Christ,* for were he to be cut off, he could not be the means of bringing them blessing. The paradox is that it is his union with Christ which causes him to long to save his countrymen, even were it to be at the cost of losing his own salvation.

Perhaps the key to Paul's understanding of what it means to be a minister, a partner in the Gospel, is to be found in Gal 1:16, where Paul refers briefly to what we tend to describe as his conversion, but which he clearly thinks of as his call to be an apostle. He refers here to what he terms "the time when it pleased God to reveal his son in me, in order that I might proclaim him among the Gentiles." Once again, I find myself at odds with many of the commentators and translators, who tend to ignore the fact that Paul speaks of God revealing his son *in* him: this is surely deliberate. The revelation of Christ which is given to Paul is stamped on him, so that he himself, by his life as well as by his words, becomes the means by whom Christ is revealed to the Gentiles.

Paul's summons to his converts to imitate him was not the result of immodesty; rather it sprang from his conviction that the whole Christian community should reflect the love and compassion of Christ: there was no distinction here between apostle and community, except that the role of the apostle was to be a subsidiary model. The Gospel was to be proclaimed both by Paul and by the community, not simply through the preaching of the word, but in every believer's life.

Paul's teaching on ministry has often been misunderstood—not least, perhaps, because in the final chapters of 2 Corinthians he is led to lay down the law and exert his own authority because of the problems facing him in Corinth. People tend to remember those passages, and ignore the teaching we have been examining here. But there is another reason why little attention has been paid to what I believe to be his real understanding of ministry. The inhibition about recognizing Christ as an example has led many to ignore Paul's emphasis on Christ as a pattern to which they should be conformed. Is it not paradoxical that in shying away from this idea, Christians have looked for other models for ministry—and those models have tended to be about status and authority, instead of about kenosis? Paul, I think, would claim that when that happens, men and women have misunderstood, not simply Christian ministry, but the Gospel itself.

Mother's Milk and Ministry in 1 Corinthians 3

Beverly Roberts Gaventa

C. H. Dodd once observed that Paul "lacks the gift for sustained illustration of ideas through concrete images (though he is capable of a brief illuminating metaphor). It is probably a defect of imagination."[1] The analogy Paul uses in the opening lines of 1 Corinthians 3 would seem to support Dodd's claim. The NRSV translates as follows: "And so, brothers and sisters, I could not speak to you as to spiritual people but rather as people of the flesh, as infants in Christ. I fed you with milk, not solid food, for you were not ready for solid food. Even now you are still not ready. . . ."

If this analogy does not compete with Rom 7:1–6 for sheer logical difficulties, it nevertheless raises a number of questions. How can "people of the flesh" be simultaneously "infants in Christ," since those who are in Christ are supposed to have put away living according to the flesh? Does Paul understand there to be varying kinds or degrees of Christian instruction, corresponding to milk and solid food? Is the proclamation of "Jesus Christ, and him crucified" (2:2) to be equated with infant's milk? If so, then what constitutes the "solid food" of those who are more mature in faith?

These are the questions that arise most often in scholarly discussion of this passage, but I want to press the importance of yet another question concerning the passage: What is the significance of Paul's referring to himself as the nursing mother of the Corinthians? In this essay I shall argue that we cannot understand the drama presupposed in 1 Cor 3:1–2 until we take into consideration both of the characters— not only the child who may or may not be ready to begin eating solid food but also the mother who has thus far nursed the child with milk. That is, Paul's presentation of himself as a nursing mother suggests that 1 Cor 3:1–2 illumines Paul's understanding of the nature of the apostolic task.[2] When Paul employs the image of a nursing mother in self-

---

[1] C. H. Dodd, *The Epistle of Paul to the Romans* (London: Hodder and Stoughton, 1932) 121.

[2] To a limited degree, my proposals are anticipated in the work of J. Francis ("'As

reference here, he accomplishes several things. First, the use of maternal imagery reinforces the imagery of family that appears throughout 1 Corinthians, language that serves to upbuild the Corinthian community. Second, the use of this image undermines the culturally-approved masculine role and, hence, renders Paul susceptible to attack as weak and ineffective. Third, this metaphor of the nursing mother introduces the later series of metaphors in which apostles are compared with farmers and builders, and prepares the way for further remarks about the nature of the apostolic task.

As noted above, most scholarly discussion of this passage has focused on questions about the diet of the Christian community at Corinth. Many interpreters, taking their cues from the reference in 2:6 to speaking wisdom among the "mature," identify milk with Paul's initial instruction in the gospel and solid food with his more extensive instruction in wisdom.[3] Other interpreters have rightly pointed to the difficulties inherent in this two-tiered system of Christian diet. For Paul there is only one Christian gospel, that of the crucified, and this gospel itself contains all the wisdom needed (1:18, 24; 2:1). As Morna Hooker nicely puts it, "the fundamental contrast in Paul's mind is . . . between the true food of the Gospel with which he has fed them (whether milk or meat) and the synthetic substitutes which the Corinthians have preferred."[4] At most, the solid food Paul refers to may be a more profound understanding of the gospel rather than some mystery tradition.[5] In addition, some interpreters appeal to 14:20 as evidence that the Corinthians have not made sufficient progress in their faith.

Babes in Christ'–Some Proposals Regarding 1 Corinthians 3.1–3," *JSNT* 7 [1980] 41–60), who notes the claims to authority implicit in Paul's use of what Francis refers to as the "nurse image." I contend that Paul is not merely reinforcing his own claims to authority but laying the groundwork for a radically different understanding of authority.

[3] See, for example, the following discussions: H. A. W. Meyer, *Critical and Exegetical Handbook to the Epistles to the Corinthians*, Vol. 1: *First Epistle* (2 vols.; Edinburgh: T. & T. Clark, 1877) 83–84; Archibald Robertson and Alfred Plummer, *A Critical and Exegetical Commentary on the First Epistle of St. Paul to the Corinthians* (2d ed.; ICC; Edinburgh: T. & T. Clark, 1914) 52–53; Hans Lietzmann, *An die Korinther I-II* (HNT; Tübingen: Mohr-Siebeck, 1923) 15; Johannes Behm, "βρῶμα," *TDNT* 1:642–45; Heinrich Schlier, "γάλα," *TDNT* 1:645–47; Ulrich Wilckens, *Weisheit und Torheit: Eine exegetisch-religionsgeschichtliche Untersuchung zu 1. Kor. 1 und 2* (BHT 26; Tübingen: Mohr, 1959) 52–53.

[4] Morna Hooker, "Hard Sayings: 1 Corinthians 3:1," *Theology* 69 (1966) 19–22; here, 21. Hooker suggests that it is the Corinthians who have introduced the "milk and meat" imagery into the conversation, accusing Paul of giving them only baby food. Paul employs their language but turns it against them. J. Francis characterizes the problem as "not a failure of progression but a failure of basic comprehension" ("As Babes in Christ," 57).

[5] C. K. Barrett, for example, contends that the teaching among the mature "rests on" proclamation of the cross, "but it is a development of this, of such a kind that in it the essential message of the simple preaching of the cross might be missed, or perverted, by

These views of 3:1–2 share a focus on the Corinthians and their wisdom or maturity (or the lack thereof). The majority of scholars agree that Paul is saying something like, "*You* are not mature enough for the special wisdom [or the more mature forms of the kerygma] that we dispense among a few. It is time now for *you* to grow up and grasp the gospel as mature adults."

What I find intriguing is that none of these interpretations of the passage attends to the fact that Paul casts his remarks in the first person. At most, the occasional commentator suggests that the κἀγώ ("and I") in v. 1 implicitly contrasts Paul with other Christian teachers. But Paul speaks here in first person of himself as the mother of the Corinthians: "I could not speak to you. . . . I fed you with milk, not solid food . . . ." Indeed, the "milk and solid food" analogy would work better as a reprimand if Paul had omitted the reference to himself at the beginning of v. 2 and substituted something like, "you are still drinking milk when you should at least be ready for cereal." In other words, using the first person actually confuses things, or at least it does *if Paul's primary concern is the maturity of the Corinthians or their readiness for advanced instruction*. The oddness and intrusiveness of Paul's "I fed you with milk" suggests that we need to attend a little more closely to the use of first person in this passage.

Milk and Solid Food Elsewhere

Support for my claim that we need to pay attention to the use of first person in this passage comes from a surprising source. The food imagery in this text is not unique to Paul, of course. Virtually every interpreter of this passage, regardless of the position taken on "milk, not solid food," makes reference to other Hellenistic texts that employ the contrast between milk and solid food. To the best of my knowledge, however, no one has recognized the most significant difference

---

the inexperienced." He concludes that the two teachings differ in form but not in content, just "as meat and milk are both food" (*A Commentary on the First Epistle to the Corinthians* [HNTC; New York: Harper and Row, 1967] 81). See also: Calvin, *First Epistle of Paul the Apostle to the Corinthians* (tr. John W. Fraser; Edinburgh: Oliver and Boyd, 1960) 66; C. F. Georg Heinrici, *Der erste Brief an die Korinther* (MeyerK; Göttingen: Vandenhoeck & Ruprecht, 1896) 116; Rudolf Schnackenburg, "Christian Adulthood According to the Apostle Paul," *CBQ* 25 (1963) 356–57; Karl Maly, *Mündige Gemeinde: Untersuchungen zur pastoralen Führung des Apostels Paulus im 1. Korintherbrief* (SBM; Stuttgart: Katholisches Bibelwerk, 1967) 58; Wilhelm Thüsing, "'Milch' und 'feste Speise' (1 Kor 3,1f. und Hebr 5,11–6,3): Elementarkatechese und theologische Vertiefung in neutestamentlicher Sicht," *TTZ* 76 (1967) 235–38; Rolf Baumann, *Mitte und Norm des Christlichen: Eine Auslegung von 1 Korinther 1,1–3,4* (NTAbh; Münster: Aschendorff, 1968) 267; Gordon Fee, *The First Epistle to the Corinthians* (NICNT; Grand Rapids, MI: Eerdmans, 1987) 124–26; Wolfgang Schrage, *Der erste Brief an die Korinther* (2 vols.; Zurich: Benziger, 1991–95) 1.280–82.

between the texts adduced and 1 Cor 3:1–2: unlike the parallels, Paul speaks of himself as the one supplying the milk.

It will be instructive to review some of the passages cited most often so that the differences from 1 Corinthians 3 will be apparent. In Heb 5:12–14 the author complains:

> For though by this time you ought to be teachers, you need someone to teach you again the basic elements of the oracles of God. You need milk, not solid food; for everyone who lives on milk, being still an infant, is unskilled in the word of righteousness. But solid food is for the mature, for those whose faculties have been trained by practice to distinguish good from evil.

And the author of 1 Peter admonishes: "Like newborn infants, long for the pure, spiritual milk, so that by it you may grow into salvation" (1 Pet 2:2 NRSV).

These two early Christian instances of the milk and solid food metaphor are customarily read alongside several texts from Philo and Epictetus:

> Philo, *Quod omnis probus liber sit* 160: But souls which have as yet got nothing of either kind, neither that which enslaves, nor that which establishes freedom, souls still naked like those of mere infants, must be tended and nursed by instilling first, in place of milk [γάλα], the soft food of instruction given in the school subjects, later, the harder, stronger meat [τροφή], which philosophy produces. (LCL 363:100–101)

> Philo, *De congressu quaerendae eruditionis gratia* 19: Observe too that our body is not nourished in the earlier stages with solid [τροφή] and costly foods. The simple and milky [γαλακτώδης] foods of infancy come first. Just so you may consider that the school subjects and the lore which belongs to each of them stand ready to nourish the child-hood of the soul, while the virtues are grown-up food, suited for those who are really men. (LCL 261:466–67)

> Philo, *De agricultura* 9: But who else could the man that is in each of us be save the mind, whose place it is to reap the benefits derived from all that has been sown or planted? But seeing that for babes milk [γάλα] is food, but for grown men wheaten bread, there must also be soul-nourishment, such as is milk-like suited to the time of childhood, in the shape of the preliminary stages of school-learning, and such as is adapted to grown men in the shape of instructions leading the way through wisdom and temperance and all virtue. (LCL 247:112–13)

Philo, *De migratione Abrahami* 29: In this country there awaiteth thee the nature which is its own pupil, its own teacher, that needs not be fed on milk [γαλακτώδης] as children are fed, that has been stayed by a Divine oracle from going down to Egypt and from meeting with the ensnaring pleasures of the flesh. (LCL 261:148–49)

Philo, *De Somniis* 2.10: The noble company is led by Isaac who learns from no teacher but himself, for Moses represents him as weaned, absolutely disdaining to make any use of soft and milky food [γαλακτώδης] suited to infants and little children, and using only strong nourishment fit for grown men, seeing that from a babe he was naturally stalwart, and was ever attaining fresh vigour and renewing his youth. (LCL 275:446–47)

Epictetus, *Discourses* 2.16.39: Are you not willing, at this late date, like children, to be weaned and to partake of more solid food [τροφή], and not to cry for [mothers] and nurses—old wives' lamentations? (LCL 131:332–33)

Epictetus, *Discourses* 3.24.9: Shall we not wean [ἀπογαλακτίζειν] ourselves at last, and call to mind what we have heard from the philosophers? (LCL 218:186–87)

1 Cor 3:1–2 shares with these passages the image of milk and solid food. As should be clear from my earlier summary of the discussion, commentators debate the adequacy of these ostensible parallels, particularly on the question whether Paul thinks there are two tiers of Christian instruction.[6] What the discussion of these parallels completely neglects is the fact that Paul is himself the nurturer, a feature that appears in none of the examples adduced. Paul does not speak with Philo's detachment about what food the soul requires or about the "shape of instruction." Neither does Paul cajole the Corinthians to cease their crying "for mothers and nurses." Instead, he images himself as the mother who nurtures, the one who knows what food is appropriate for her children. In other words, even though the image of milk and meat was current, Paul does something distinctive with it: he presents himself as the mother of the Corinthians.

Attending to the use of first person in 3:1–2 alters the way in which we read this passage. It is no longer about the single issue of what the

---

[6] In addition to the literature cited above, see the discussions of the New Testament usage of this imagery in Walter Grundmann, "Die ΝΗΠΙΟΙ in der Urchristlichen Paränese," *NTS* 5 (1959) 188–205; Thüsing, "'Milch' und 'feste Speise,'" 233–46, 261–80; and Ronald Williamson, *Philo and the Epistle to the Hebrews* (ALGHJ; Leiden: Brill, 1970) 277–308.

Corinthians eat; it also concerns the one who feeds them. And the language is unequivocal: Paul is the nursing mother of the church.

That point would seem to be obvious from the phrase γάλα ὑμᾶς ἐπότισα ("I gave you milk to drink"). Prior to the advent of infant formula and baby bottles, it is the mother or the wetnurse who feeds milk to an infant. Commentators overlook or at least underinterpret this point, preferring to focus instead on the paternal imagery at the end of chapter 4. Some will even connect this use of maternal imagery with the later passage, as if the nursing mother were somehow a father.[7] Paul does not use the two kinds of images interchangeably, however. In 3:1–2, as elsewhere, he uses maternal imagery to refer to the on-going process of nurturing Christian faith. Paternal imagery, as in 4:15–16, he employs for the initial act of missionary preaching.[8]

Paul as Male Nurse?

Before exploring the implications of this use of maternal imagery, one possible objection requires attention. In a recent article on parents and children in the letters of Paul, O. Larry Yarbrough contends that the figure of a male nurse (*nutritor*), rather than a nursing mother or wetnurse, stands in the background of 1 Cor 3:1–2. The male nurse might have fed his charges with a mixture of goat's milk and honey (presumably in the absence of an available wetnurse).[9] Inscriptional evidence suggests that male nurses were often fondly remembered by their charges, so that Paul's imagery in this passage suggests the intimate connection between himself and the Corinthians.[10]

Yarbrough's identification of 1 Cor 3:2 with male nurses depends on Keith R. Bradley's study of male involvement in child care at Rome.[11]

---

[7] Our honoree, I am pleased to note, carefully distinguishes the two in his annotations to 1 Corinthians in *The HarperCollins Study Bible* (ed. Wayne A. Meeks; San Francisco: HarperCollins, 1993) 2144–45.

[8] On this distinction, see the discussion in Gaventa, "Our Mother St. Paul: Toward the Recovery of a Neglected Theme," *Princeton Seminary Bulletin* 17 (1996) 29–44.

[9] In situations where neither mother nor wetnurse was available, preparations of honey mixed with goat's milk or even water were substituted. Apparently, the dangers of these substitutes were recognized, and they were used only in emergencies (see Ralph Jackson, *Doctors and Diseases in the Roman Empire* [London: British Museum Publications, 1988] 102).

[10] O. Larry Yarbrough, "Parents and Children in the Letters of Paul," *The Social World of the First Christians: Essays in Honor of Wayne A. Meeks* (ed. L. Michael White and O. Larry Yarbrough; Minneapolis: Augsburg Fortress, 1995) 126–41, discussion of the *nutritor* is on pp. 132–33.

[11] Keith R. Bradley, "Child Care at Rome: The Role of Men," in *Discovering the Roman Family: Studies in Roman Social History* (New York: Oxford University Press, 1991) 37–75 (orig. publ. in *Historical Reflections/Réflexions Historiques* 12 [1985] 485–523).

Bradley examines both literary and inscriptional evidence for the figures of the *paedagogus*, the *educator*, and the *nutritor* or male nurse. In the single case of C. Mussius Chrysonicus is someone identified as *nutritor lactaneus* (or male nurse who fed milk to his charges).[12] Bradley himself observes that *nutritores* were sometimes foster fathers. More often they appear to have been figures who *assisted* wetnurses with very young children, perhaps because the *nutritor* and *nutrix* (wetnurse) were married to one another.[13] Bradley also speculates that the *nutritor*'s role involved watching over children who were no longer confined to the women's quarter with the *nutrix*.[14] Bradley himself makes no claim that the *nutritor* offered babies a substitute breast milk.[15] In other words, the Roman male nurse as Bradley reconstructs him seems quite removed from the direct acts of feeding an infant that are involved in the metaphor of 1 Cor 3:2.

It appears that Yarbrough has either misunderstood Bradley or exaggerated the importance of one small sample in Bradley's study. In addition, Yarbrough does not take into account those other instances in which Paul speaks of himself in unambiguously maternal terms (e.g., Gal 4:19, 1 Thess 2:7).

Paul as Nursing Mother

The preceding remarks might be dismissed as a severe case of overkill, an elaborate attempt to persuade readers of 1 Cor 3:1–2 to take seriously two small words: κἀγώ [and I] and ποτίζειν [cause to drink]. What warrants such extended attention to such minute details?

In the first place, this essay developed from a larger project of retrieving Paul's use of maternal imagery and exploring the importance of that imagery in Paul's thought. Not only 1 Cor 3:1–2, but Gal 4:19, 1 Thess 2:7, Rom 8:22 and 1 Cor 15:8 are among those passages that have routinely been overlooked or unaccountably lumped together with passages in which Paul uses paternal imagery. As students of Paul continue to explore Paul's remarks about women, the roles of women in the Pauline churches, and the implications of Paul's letters for women, this cluster of passages merits consideration in its own right.[16]

---

[12] Ibid., 40–41.

[13] Ibid., 49–51.

[14] Ibid., 61.

[15] In an earlier article, Bradley does comment that a *nutritor lactaneus* "may have fed infants from a bottle, though the evidence that bottle-feeding was practised at all is very slender" ("Wet-Nursing at Rome: A Study in Social Relations," *The Family in Ancient Rome: New Perspectives* [ed. Beryl Rawson; Ithaca: Cornell University Press, 1986] 214).

[16] On the maternal imagery in these texts see Gaventa, "The Maternity of Paul: An Exegetical Study of Galatians 4:19," in *The Conversation Continues: Studies in Paul and John*

Beyond that initial task of retrieval, the image of the nursing mother in 1 Cor 3:1–2 contributes in specific ways to the case Paul develops in this letter. To begin with, there is in this letter an extensive network of what might be termed "family imagery," language that serves to reinforce Paul's urgent appeal for unity in Corinth. The letter opens by invoking "God our Father" (1:3) and "his Son, Jesus Christ" (1:9). It discusses relationships between husbands and wives (7:1–16, 11:2–16),[17] it refers to meals eaten at home (11:22), and it refers to believers in households (1:16, 16:15, and probably 1:11).[18] One extraordinary passage recalls "our ancestors" (lit. "all our fathers," 10:1) who wandered in the wilderness, boldly claiming for an assorted group of Corinthian Gentiles the ancestors of Israel.

Most prominent in this network of family language in 1 Corinthians is Paul's use of ἀδελφός, "brother and sister" in the NRSV.[19] This is a regular feature of Paul's letters, of course, but the term occurs thirty-nine times in this letter, as compared with nineteen times in Romans and twelve times in 2 Corinthians. From the opening of the letter (1:1, 10, 11) through to the very end (16:11, 12, 15, 20), Paul speaks to and about his siblings in the faith.[20]

Paul's references to himself as the nursing mother and begetting father of the Corinthians are also part of this network of family language.[21] It seems unlikely that this extensive network is merely accidental. Instead, it serves to reinforce Paul's concerns about factions in the Corinthian church.[22] If believers in Corinth accept Paul's designation of themselves as "brothers and sisters," if they understand

---

in Honor of J. Louis Martyn (ed. Robert T. Fortna and Beverly R. Gaventa; Nashville, TN: Abingdon, 1990) 189–201; "Apostles as Babes and Nurses in 1 Thessalonians 2:7," *Faith and History: Essays in Honor of Paul W. Meyer* (ed. John T. Carroll et al.; SP Homage Series; Atlanta: Scholars Press, 1990) 193–207; and "Our Mother St. Paul."

[17] I omit 14:33b–36 because, along with many commentators, I regard this as a non-Pauline interpolation. On that question, see Fee, *1 Corinthians,* 699–708, and the literature cited there.

[18] For a suggestive treatment of the household language in 1 Corinthians, see Stephen C. Barton, "Community Formation in Corinth," *NTS* 32 (1986) 225–46.

[19] ἀδελφή (sister) itself occurs in 7:15 and 9:5.

[20] On this feature of Paul's letters, see Klaus Schäfer, *Gemeinde als "Bruderschaft": Ein Beitrag zum Kirchenverständnis des Paulus* (Frankfurt: Peter Lang, 1989).

[21] Yarbrough's article, "Parents and Children in Paul," helpfully surveys this aspect of Paul's family language in 1 Corinthians and elsewhere and speculates on its moral implications. In my judgment, however, he considerably understates the significance of the maternal language in Paul.

[22] On the factionalized nature of the Corinthian congregation, see the excellent work of Margaret Mitchell, *Paul and the Rhetoric of Reconciliation: An Exegetical Investigation of the Language and Composition of 1 Corinthians* (Louisville, KY: Westminster/John Knox, 1991).

themselves to have Paul as their begetting father and their nurturing mother, if they affirm their connection with Israel's ancestors and, most important, if they agree that God is the father of them all, it should prove far more difficult for them to maintain their divisiveness.

Even within this impressive array of family language, however, Paul's self-designation as the nursing mother of the Corinthians is particularly striking. To state what is manifestly obvious: Paul may have been a biological father, but he surely did not nurse an infant (his own or anyone else's). The very incongruity of the imagery presses the question of how the Corinthians might have heard it. What would they make of a male speaking of himself in what are unmistakably female tones?

Answers to this question will need to be couched in exceedingly cautious terms. If we have difficulty identifying Paul's "intentions," how much more complicated is it to construct the responses of the Corinthians, from whom we have not even a single scrap of evidence? Some tantalizing clues appear, nevertheless, in the burgeoning literature on gender-construction in the Greco-Roman world. Thomas Laquer has identified a "one-sex" model of sexuality that dominated the ancient world, a model in which women are understood to be "inverted" males. On this view, "the standard of the human body and its representations is the male body."[23]

For the purposes of this study of 1 Corinthians 3, what is important about this one-sex model is the way in which it dominates not only understandings of physiology but every aspect of appearance and behavior.[24] For example, the *Physiognomics* attributed to Aristotle identifies an amazing array of physical characteristics associated with persons of varying dispositions (including men who are shameless, orderly, insensitive, morbid, and so forth). In this elaborate scheme, a "real man" (σκληρὸς ἀνῆρ) possesses such identifiable traits as stiff hair, erect carriage, a strong neck, and a fleshy broad chest. One who is less manly (μαλακός) may be identified by his soft hair, sedentary habits, weak eyes, and small legs (*Physiognomics* 807a-b [LCL 307:98–99]). Seneca claims that men who dress like women and attempt to look young and boyish behave contrary to nature (*Epistle* 122.7 [LCL 77:414–17]). Quintilian complains that when a speaker's style and content are inconsistent with one another, "it is as if men deformed themselves by wearing necklaces, pearls, and long flowing robes, which are feminine

---

[23] Thomas Laquer, *Making Sex: Body and Gender from the Greeks to Freud* (Cambridge: Harvard University Press, 1990) 62. According to Laquer, this one-sex model dominated understandings of sexual differences until the end of the seventeenth century.

[24] For a fascinating reading of 1 Corinthians in light of this discussion of the body, see now Dale B. Martin, *The Corinthian Body* (New Haven: Yale University Press, 1995).

adornments . . ." (*Institutes* 11.1.3 [cf. LCL 127:154–55]).[25] Dio Chrysostom purports to be able to identify males of bad character and disposition from such features as "voice, glance, posture . . . style of haircut, mode of walking, elevation of the eye, inclination of the neck, the trick of conversing with upturned palms" (*Discourse* 33.52 [LCL 358:322–23]).

Later physiognomists such as the second-century Polemo prided themselves on their ability to identify those males who were not "real men," no matter how much such persons labored to conceal their identity. In her study of Polemo and Favorinus, Maud W. Gleason concludes that the polarized gender distinctions they used "purported to characterize the gulf between men and women, but actually served to divide the male sex into legitimate and illegitimate members . . . ."[26]

John J. Winkler has characterized these concerns as reflecting the belief that "male life is warfare, that masculinity is a duty and a hard-won achievement, and that the temptation to desert one's side is very great."[27] In this view, the female is not only an inverted male but a threat to masculine identity. A male who transgresses the boundaries in dress, behavior, deportment, even in physical features may be accused of "going AWOL from [his] assigned place in the gender hierarchy."[28]

Given this environment, I find it reasonable to imagine that "I fed you with milk" (that is, "I was your mother or wetnurse") would cause the sensitive among the Corinthians to suspect that Paul himself was not a "real male." By actively taking upon himself a role that could only be played by a woman, he effectively concedes the culturally predisposed battle for his masculinity.[29] This environment may help to explain why Philo and Epictetus do not speak in first person when they invoke the milk and meat image, lest their own masculinity likewise be called into question.

---

[25] See the discussion of Quintilian in Maud W. Gleason, *Making Men: Sophists and Self-Presentation in Ancient Rome* (Princeton: Princeton University Press, 1995) 113–21.

[26] Maud W. Gleason, "The Semiotics of Gender: Physiognomy and Self-Fashioning in the Second Century C.E.," in *Before Sexuality: The Construction of Erotic Experience in the Ancient Greek World*, (ed. David M. Halperin et al.; Princeton: Princeton University Press, 1990) 412. See also Gleason, *Making Men: Sophists and Self-Presentation in Ancient Rome.*

[27] John J. Winkler, *The Constraints of Desire: The Anthropology of Sex and Gender in Ancient Greece* (New York: Routledge, 1990) 50.

[28] Ibid., 21.

[29] This is not to claim, of course, that Paul was consistently indifferent to gender distinctions. His argument in 1 Cor 11:2–16 that it contravenes nature for women to have heads uncovered and for men to wear their hair long is prime evidence that he was very much influenced by such social constructs.

Why would Paul risk such a perception while dealing with the Corinthians? We can best assess the function of the maternal imagery here by looking ahead to Paul's comments about the apostolic role later in this chapter and in chapter 4. Paul introduces the topic in v. 5 with the question, "What then is Apollos? What is Paul? Servants [διάκονοι] through whom you came to believe, as the Lord assigned to each." He promptly elaborates on this notion of servanthood through the analogies of planting and building (vv. 5–16), but the discussion as a whole needs to be read over against the question of v. 4: "For when one says, 'I belong to Paul' [ἐγὼ μέν εἰμι Παύλου], and another, 'I belong to Apollos' [ἐγὼ ᾿Απολλῶ], are you not merely human?" The Corinthians belong, not to Paul or Apollos, but to Christ, as becomes clear in 3:23: "you belong to Christ" (ὑμεῖς δὲ Χριστοῦ). Over against any perception that Paul and Apollos are, even figuratively, owners of the Corinthians, Paul responds, "But we are *mere* servants."[30]

That Paul and Apollos are mere servants may seem to be contradicted by the imagery that follows. When Paul identifies himself as the planter or the architect and the Corinthians as the field or building, he places himself in a role that appears active and authoritative over against the Corinthians who are mere recipients. Elizabeth A. Castelli finds in the passage

> a clear hierarchical separation between the apostles on the one hand and the community on the other. . . . While Apollos and Paul are the fellow workers of God, the community is characterized as the passive object of that apostolic work. Also, while there is no equality being expressed here, neither is there any expression of reciprocity: the community is the recipient of the apostles' work.[31]

Another reading is possible, however, and ever preferable. Paul does not say that the Corinthians are his field or Apollos's building; they are God's field, God's building (v. 9). Indeed, vv. 16–17 raise the volume of the metaphor, making the Corinthians into God's own holy temple. Anyone who destroys that temple will be destroyed. Paul is not the authoritative ruler, then, but the servant commissioned by the proprietor, a servant who stands under the threat of destructive judgment should that possession be violated. The issue at stake in this passage is not who is active and who is passive, but to whom the Corinthians belong and to whom Paul and Apollos are accountable. Dale Martin gets it right:

---

[30] Fee nicely underscores this point (*1 Corinthians*, 129–30).

[31] Elizabeth Castelli, *Imitating Paul: A Discourse of Power* (Louisville, KY: Westminster/John Knox, 1991) 105.

In 3:5–17 he relativizes the position of apostles: they are only workmen, planters or waterers, whereas the Corinthians are God's field, the object of his care. . . . Paul portrays the Corinthian church as God's temple and himself and other teachers as mere architects or builders.[32]

The ironic remarks of 4:8–13 confirm this reading of the apostolic task as found in 3:5–17. Apostles are not identified with those people and things normally perceived as wealthy, strong, and honorable. In fact, the apostles are the polar opposite: "last of all, as though sentenced to death . . . a spectacle to the world, to angels and to mortals" (4:9). It seems appropriate that Paul introduces this view of apostolic ministry in the language of the nursing mother. The metaphor expresses the bond of affection and care that characterizes the relationship and simultaneously places Paul at the margins of what is perceived to be "genuine" manhood.

Conventional interpretations of 3:1–2 read backwards; that is to say, they take their cues primarily from the discussion of wisdom in chapter 2 and see in 3:1–2 the sharp expression of Paul's concern for the Corinthians' maturity. I have argued that the passage *also* must be read forward, as it contributes to Paul's immediate argument about what constitutes authentic apostolic ministry.[33] By speaking in first person, Paul anticipates his comments about his own work as διάκονος (servant). By speaking in first person as a nursing mother, Paul compromises his own standing as a "real man," anticipating the loss of standing that later emerges as he depicts his ministry as that of a planter of someone else's field, a servant of someone else's building, the "dregs of all things" (4:13). If we are to read 3:1–2 backward, then we need to read back as far as 1:18, for the images of apostolic ministry Paul employs in chapter 3 have their origin in his proclamation of the crucified Jesus, who is no more a "real man" by the world's standards than is a nursing Paul.[34]

---

[32] Dale B. Martin, *The Corinthian Body*, 64.

[33] In a sense, this interpretation contributes to the case of those who see 1 Cor 3:1–4 as a transition from chap. 2 to chap. 3 (over against those who identify 3:1–4 as the conclusion to the argument in chap. 2 and others who identify it as the introduction to chap. 3). Most of those who read 3:1–4 as transitional, however, see it as marking a shift from the discussion of wisdom to a renewed discussion of factions at Corinth. Both of those issues are present, of course, but so is the nature of apostolic ministry; on this point, see Brendan Byrne, "Ministry and Maturity in 1 Corinthians 3," *AusBR* 35 (1987) 83–87. For 3:1–4 as transitional, see Conzelmann, *1 Corinthians* (Hemeneia; Philadelphia: Fortress, 1975) 71; Fee, *1 Corinthians*, 121–22; David W. Kuck, *Judgment and Community Conflict: Paul's Use of Apocalyptic Judgment Language in 1 Corinthians 3:5–4:5* (NovTSup 66; Leiden: Brill, 1992) 155.

[34] In a private communication, C. Clifton Black writes: "Paul's maternal language registers as a stunning, altogether appropriate image for the stewardship of God's mysteries

The Afterlife of a Metaphor

Shelves of modern commentaries on Paul contain scarcely a hint that the milk of Paul's ministry is mother's milk, but earlier generations of interpreters did take seriously the maternal language of 1 Corinthians 3. A striking example appears in a sermon by the twelfth century Cistercian, Guerric of Igny. Commenting on the tradition that milk rather than blood flowed from Paul's body at his execution,[35] Guerric explains:

> Truly there was no element of blood but the whole was of milk in him. . . . [H]e abounded with such a wealth of loving kindness that he yearned not only to impart the milk of his spirit in its totality to his children but also to give them his body.[36]

Although we may have long overlooked the importance of the maternal language in 1 Corinthians 3, Guerric does not. He rightly sees its relationship to the work of ministry and the role of an apostle.[37]

(4:1), which, like Christ, must appear by worldly standards of judgment scandalous and utterly foolish."

[35] See the account in "The Acts of Paul," which is conveniently available in *New Testament Apocrypha: Revised Edition of the Collection initiated by Edgar Hennecke* (ed. Wilhelm Schneemelcher; 2 vols.; Louisville, KY: Westminster/John Knox, 1991–92) 2.237–70.

[36] Guerric of Igny, "Sermon 45: The Second Sermon for Saints Peter and Paul," *Liturgical Sermons* (2 vols.; Spencer, MA: Cistercian Publications, 1970–71) 2.154.

[37] It is a pleasure to contribute this essay in honor of Victor Paul Furnish, from whose own work I have learned much about Paul and his letters. I am grateful for the assistance of C. Clifton Black and Patrick J. Willson, who graciously read and commented on an earlier version of this essay.

Reasoning From the Horizons of Paul's Thought World: A Comparison of Galatians and Philippians

J. Paul Sampley

We have become increasingly conscious of the situational, occasional character of Paul's letters and of the importance of factoring that exigence into our interpretation of any letter and its contents. Now we should become more aware of Paul's own assessment of his recipients and, more specifically, of his evaluation of where his audience[1] in any letter stands with regard to the two horizons of Paul's thought world, from Christ's death and resurrection on the one side to the parousia on the other. Many of Paul's most fundamental convictions cluster around those two horizons, and Paul reckons from these clusters in primary ways. As we have seen elsewhere,[2] Paul views the life of faith as a "walk," as a movement, as a growth from being babies in faith to being mature in faith. Believers' "improvement" (προκοπή; Phil 1:25)—indeed, their becoming strong in faith like their father Abraham grew strong in his (Rom 4:20)—is the expected path along which all believers are moved by God's grace and power toward the completion of God's purposes.

Each of Paul's letters allows an assessment of where he thinks his auditors are in this pilgrimage. In some letters he tends to view them as nearer the one horizon or the other and, in his engagement with the recipients, draws upon the clusters of convictions that stand on either horizon. In order to demonstrate that Paul reveals his assessment of his readers' standing vis-à-vis the two horizons and that each horizon provides its own special convictions from which Paul reasons, I have chosen to look closely at Galatians and Philippians. And, as a way of honoring Victor Furnish[3] and our shared interest in Paul's moral reasoning, I will

---

[1] Or significant portions of that audience, as might be most obvious in 1 Corinthians, for example.

[2] J. Paul Sampley, *Walking Between the Times: Paul's Moral Reasoning* (Minneapolis, MN: Fortress, 1991) 46–49, 75–76.

[3] It was my special privilege to be a student in Victor Furnish's very first class on Paul the year he joined the faculty at Perkins School of Theology.

selectively highlight in Galatians and Philippians some of the ways in which Paul gains moral leverage from each of the two horizons.

To accomplish these goals, I first sketch the two horizons between which Paul thinks that believers comport their lives. Then I show that Paul thinks of the Galatians as standing close to the turning event of their sharing Christ's death and resurrection and that he considers the Philippians to be more directly oriented toward the culminating event of Christ's parousia. Finally, I highlight some ways in which Paul builds moral suasion by reasoning from the two distinct horizons reflected in these letters.

I. The Two Horizons of Paul's Thought World: From Peace to Parousia

The Turning Event	*The Culminating Event*
Christ's death and resurrection;	Christ's coming;
Sharing Christ's death	Sharing a resurrection like his

These two events, the one ending enmity and enabling peace with God and the other bringing to fulfillment God's redemptive purposes, frame the way Paul thinks about life. The one event lies in the past for all believers; the other remains future for all of them. These are the decisive events and, by God's grace and power, the former points directly and inexorably toward the latter. Because these two events structure Paul's thinking, they also give foundation to Paul's most important convictions and richly ground his imagery.

Clusters of Convictions and Images Around the Two Horizons	
Already/Now	*Not Yet/Goal*
(A Result of the Turning Event)	*(Anticipated with the Culminating Event)*
Died with Christ	Share a resurrection like his
(Baptism)	
(Receive Holy Spirit)	
(Down Payment)	
Babies/God's children	Adult/mature
(Adoption)	(Receive inheritance)
Reconciliation/justification	Salvation/eternal life
Call	Judgment
	Day of Christ
	(Stand)
	(Be presented)
	(Be without blemish)
	(Be glorified with Christ)
	(Share the glory of God)

The left column acknowledges a point of radical change when one's former way of living in alienation from God was overcome by God's grace. The recipients of all of Paul's letters would have shared the conviction that their new life in Christ accorded with the word-picture on the left: Having died with Christ to the power of sin, they have received God's call, they have been baptized, have received the Holy Spirit, have become God's children; they are justified, reconciled with God.

Paul assumes that believers make progress, by the working of the Holy Spirit and by the mutual care among believers, toward maturity, toward salvation which will fully and finally occur at the day of Christ, at the judgment when, by God's grace they will be glorified with Christ and receive eternal life. Paul's letters address people who have already been granted entry to the standing depicted on the left and urge them to comport their daily lives with a view to the impending glory portrayed on the right. Images of progress, growth, and movement prevail as Paul delineates the life appropriate to such a grand design.

Between the turning event and the culminating event Paul describes believers as moving, changing, struggling, growing. One of Paul's favorite images for the life of faith is "walking" which in itself suggests movement from one point to another. *How* one walks becomes Paul's focus: "in love," "in newness of life," "according to the Spirit." The athletic images—running, seeking the prize or crown—convey the same idea as do the battle images of conflict (Phil 1:30), affliction (1 Thess 3:3), and warfare (2 Cor 10:4). A host of other motifs in Paul reflect his conviction that the life of faith involves process or movement and is lived toward a goal: "bearing fruit for God," improvement, upbuilding, completion (Phil 1:6; cf. 3:3), growth, maturing.

Paul expects no one to have reached what is depicted on the right column above—even he of the visions and of the heavenly transit has not done so (Phil 3:12). Appropriately he writes in future tenses when he details the right-column convictions, or he reminds readers that they have "not yet" arrived at the completion of God's plan (cf. 1 Cor 4:8–12). Practically the reality depicted in the right column is proleptically experienced now; it cannot be fully realized, however, until the (imminent) consummation of God's redemptive purposes.

Short of the parousia, however, Paul thinks that people can grow in faith and that some people are simply more mature, more advanced, in their faith than others, though no believer has so small a measure of faith as to remove one's responsibility for stewarding and nourishing that faith. Abraham grew strong in faith (Rom 4:20); all have different measures of faith (Rom 12:3). The same conviction is expressed through the notion of maturity: some are more adult in faith while others resemble babies in faith. He counts himself among the mature (τέλειος; Phil 3:15); he does speak "wisdom to the mature" (1 Cor 2:6). [4] But even with himself there is room for growth, for completion: he has not yet achieved the resurrection; so he is not yet completely τέλειος in that sense, but he eagerly presses on toward it (Phil 3:11–12). Surely some similar notion is present when he thinks of some people as spiritually advanced, calling them "those who are spiritual" (cf. 1 Cor 2:13, 15; 14:37; Gal 6:1). In fact, he chides the Corinthians because they are *not* "spiritual people" (as he would hope them to be and as some of them perhaps think they are), but instead they are babies (3:1). Passages such as 1 Cor 4:8–10 not only suggest that Paul's estimate of the Corinthians may be at dissonance with their self-estimation, but more importantly for our purposes also show that he and they have come to accept such categories of gradation with regard to progress in the life of the Spirit. Paul and the Corinthians know that the life of faith is one of growth and progress; they simply disagree where at least some of the Corinthians are along the continuum of growth from babies to adults.

II. Paul's Assessment of the Standing
of the Galatians and of the Philippians

Paul thinks of the audiences of Galatians and Philippians as being oriented to the opposite horizons described above. The Galatians and their issues cause Paul to see them at the horizon of the start of faith; they are in the position of babies in the faith. The Philippians, however, and their issues lend themselves to consideration in light of the other horizon, the finishing up of adulthood, of maturity in faith. Accordingly, the remainder of this paper will first seek to establish the claim that Galatians ought to be read primarily in light of the left horizon and Philippians is best interpreted principally against the vista of the last horizon, and then the study will assess some resources for moral reasoning with each audience that Paul finds in each cluster of convictions.

A. Galatians: A Letter Written to People
Considered Near the Turning Event

1. *Paul's depictions of the Galatians' location.* Paul pictures them as living in proximity to their call (1:6; 5:8), near the inception of their faith. They are people who formerly "did not know God" and they were

---

[4] Translations are mine unless otherwise indicated.

"enslaved to beings which by nature were not gods" (4:7). In Paul's view, they have not moved far from the formative event when "faith came" to them, when "Christ came" to them, undoubtedly in Paul's illness-induced preaching to them (3:23–25; 4:13–14). In fact, such a spatial image is appropriate to his asking them "How can you turn back (ἐπιστρέφετε; a change of course) to the feeble and impotent elemental spirits to whom you once again want to be enslaved?" (4:9). He revisits the image of reversion to slavery in 5:1: "Stand your ground, then, and do not again be loaded down with a yoke of slavery." Paul considers that the Galatians stand near the border between faith and unfaith and are tempted to cross back over, like undisciplined military recruits who desert, turn away, apostasize (1:6), rather than stand their ground.

2. *Paul's portrayal of the Galatians' status.* Slaves they were; now they are children of God. "No longer slave, but son" (4:7). In a recurring motif the Galatians are called "sons" (υἱοί) whose status is derived from the ones of whom they are said to be sons (Abraham, 3:7; God, 3:26; the free woman, 4:30). But in most respects that is what one would expect to find in Pauline letters. What is noteworthy in Galatians, however, is the pointed way that Paul drives the issue by calling them νήπιοι (babies, 4:1, 3) and τέκνα (children, 4:19). To be a "son" of someone does not in itself suggest the age of the person so designated; it points to affiliation, to identification. But a νήπιος is an infant, a young child, and by its usage in Galatians Paul refines his more general idea of sonship to highlight the Galatians' immaturity. A word of caution: we know from 1 Cor 3:1 that Paul can call believers "babies" even when by all accounts they should have been more grown up, so his portrayal of the Galatians as "sons," "children," and "babies" does not necessarily indicate that they were recent converts, just that they had not advanced in maturity. Thus the Galatians are pictured by Paul as having the status of youthful, immature believers; so no matter how long they have been faithful they have remained, in effect, near the point at which they entered, near where "faith came" to them.[5]

3. *Paul's emphasis on baptism and the Holy Spirit.* As is true elsewhere in the Pauline corpus (Rom 8:14–17) so in Galatians the believers' new status as God's children is made expressible by the working of the Spirit (4:6). Likewise, when Paul wants to focus the issue—"This alone I want to ask of you" (3:2)—that he sees at the heart of the Galatian problem, he casts it as a question of the mode of the Spirit's reception. Receiving

---

[5] Paul's depiction of the Galatians as babies thus gives no clue regarding how long the Galatian churches have been in existence at the time of the letter's writing.

the Spirit is the hallmark of the believers' inclusion in Christ, into the community of faith. Paul's rhetoric shows that he and they know they have received the Spirit and that the Spirit is the telltale sign of belonging; the point at issue between Paul and them is how they came by the Spirit.

Reception of the Spirit is the dominant point-of-entry talk for Paul: "Having made a beginning with the Spirit . . ." (3:3).[6] Hinged to it is the assertion that the Galatians have become "sons of God, through faith" (Gal 3:26 RSV); the predominantly Gentile Galatian believers know that their adoption (υἱοθεσία; 4:5) as God's children was confirmed by the Spirit's enabling presence within them (4:6–7). In recounting the Galatians' biography, Paul pinpoints faith's coming (3:23), Christ's coming (3:24), faith's having come (3:25) to them as the time of their deliverance, when they became "children of God through faith" (Gal 3:26 NRSV). Reflections of their baptismal liturgy reinforce the image. They were "baptized into Christ"; their vestment is taken to be their "putting on" Christ; and the traditional formula of unity (3:28) is recited.[7]

4. *Paul's emphasis on the crucifixion.*[8] Christ's death, the cross and crucifixion are mentioned throughout Galatians. When Paul wants to bring the "bewitched," "foolish" Galatians back to the heart of the issue he reminds them that it was before their eyes that "Jesus Christ was publicly exhibited as crucified" (3:1 NRSV). In such powerful preaching, focused on the crucified Lord, the gospel and their faith came to them (3:23–25). Paul's boast is confined to "the cross of our Lord Jesus Christ" because that cross demarcates between "the new creation" (6:15) and works of the flesh (5:19–21), between the believer and the world. The cross is a powerful perspective keeper: through the cross "the world is crucified to me and I to the world" (6:14). The cross takes away the world's allure and obviates the world's power over believers. Paul exemplifies solidarity with Christ: "I have been crucified with Christ" (2:19). And the exemplification extends beyond that: as a result of that shared death, Paul—and by implication the Galatians as well—now lives differently in the flesh. As Romans puts it, he walks in "newness of life" (6:4). More on exemplification later.

---

[6] Gordon D. Fee, *God's Empowering Presence. The Holy Spirit in the Letters of Paul* (Peabody, MA: Hendrickson, 1994). Cf. idem, *The First Epistle to the Corinthians* (NICNT; Grand Rapids, MI: Eerdmans, 1987) 603: "For Paul the reception of the Spirit is the *sine qua non* of Christian life."

[7] Cf. 1 Cor 12:13, where the connection of baptism and reception of the Holy Spirit is explicit. See Fee, *First Epistle*, 604–606.

[8] B. R. Gaventa, "The Singularity of the Gospel," *Pauline Theology, Vol. I* (ed. J. M. Bassler; Minneapolis, MN: Fortress, 1991) 156–157.

By contrast, there is only one, fleeting reference to Christ's resurrection in all of Galatians: Paul's apostleship is credited to "God the Father who raised him [Christ] from the dead" (1:2).[9] Apart from that, the focus is entirely on the crucifixion, not on the resurrection. Some interpreters account for the paucity of resurrection claims in Galatians with the far-fetched idea that Paul had not yet got the idea of the resurrection securely in his theological lexicon at the time of the writing of Galatians.[10] Much closer to hand is the realization that, while Paul always claims that Christ has died and has been raised, when he talks about believers' relationship to that death and resurrection, he regularly affirms that believers have died with Christ but *have not yet shared a resurrection like Christ's.* As noted at the outset of this study, Paul lodges the origin of the life of faith clearly in the turning point event of Christ's death and resurrection; believers, by their baptism, enact their dying with Christ. The sharing of Christ's resurrection, however, is located by Paul in the future, at the parousia, at the consummation of God's purposes. So why is the resurrection not featured more prominently in Galatians? Because Paul consistently depicts the Galatians as being situated precisely at the beginning of the life of faith, in their sharing of Christ's death. They are babies; Christ is barely formed in them; they may cross back over the divide and be re-enslaved to the elemental spirits; they may turn their backs on their new sonship and its promised inheritance; they may reject the promptings of the Spirit and engross themselves in works of the flesh; and Mother Paul may have to give birth to them again (4:19). Throughout Galatians Paul sees his audience as teetering on the edge between standing as relative newborns in the gospel or falling back into the slaveries that still lie so close at hand. The Galatians' problem is one of staying in the faith, not one of developing and growing toward maturity; if this letter is successful in preventing their falling from faith, then Paul will have an opportunity to move his attention toward the future. For now, however, the focus is entirely on the present and whether they will stand firm or desert. Galatians is cast in the categories of the start of the gospel, not in those

---

[9] Cf. also 2:20 and J. C. Beker, *Paul the Apostle: The Triumph of God in Life and Thought* (Philadelphia: Fortress, 1980) 58.

[10] This view was voiced in the discussion of the Pauline Theology Group at the Society of Biblical Literature meeting in 1988 at Chicago. Practically I find more convincing Robin Scroggs's observation about Paul's silence on a given topic in one of his letters: "That dimension of his thought does not appear in the letter because it was not relevant to the matters at hand" ("Salvation History: The Theological Structure of Paul's Thought (1 Thessalonians, Philippians, and Galatians)," in *Pauline Theology, Vol. 1: Thessalonians, Philippians, Galatians, Philemon* [ed. Jouette M. Bassler; Minneapolis: Fortress Press, 1991] 212-26; here, 220).

of its refinement, advancement or growth. Accordingly, death, crucifixion, the cross—and not resurrection—predominate.

B. Philippians: A Letter Written to People Considered More Focused On the Culminating Event

Though we cannot be sure when Paul established the church at Philippi, we can see from the letter that he enjoyed a long, positive relationship with the believers there. The letter is replete with friendship terms;[11] more words per page are formulated with the συν-[together] prefix than in any other Pauline letter, identifying Paul ever so closely with the Philippians so that their story is also his story and vice versa. They are Paul's "joy and crown,"[12] his "beloved" (2:12; 4:1). The first note in Paul's thanksgiving is for their "partnership in the gospel from the first day till now" (1:5). Toward the end of the letter, when he acknowledges their recent gift of support to him, he recounts their unique relationship with him: "And you yourselves, Philippians, know that in the beginning of the gospel, when I left Macedonia, no other church partnered by keeping accounts except you alone" (4:15) and as an index of that arrangement he cites their twice-sent aid to him in Thessalonica (cf. 2 Cor 11:9). The Philippians and Paul got along swimmingly from the day he first preached the gospel to them. More than any other church represented in the corpus, the Philippians grew and matured in faith such that they were truly like him from early on in their relationship.

1. *The Philippians' location.* Recurrent in Philippians are formulations that refer to past, solid performance as a means of encouraging its continuation into the future. Paul views them as "joint-partners with me of grace" and expects them to continue to be so (1:7). The love which has characterized them is to "abound more and more" (1:9 RSV). They have "always obeyed" and should continue to do so (2:12). They have been concerned about Paul in the past and their recent gift shows their continued commitment to him (4:10).

Paul assumes that the Philippians are lasered onto God's culminating purposes. The thanksgiving is framed with references to the day of Christ, the time of judgment. First there is Paul's conviction that God will complete, on that day, the good work begun in the Philippians (1:6; cf. 2:13). Second, Paul reports his prayer that they be "pure and

---

[11] See S. K. Stowers' helpful elaboration of Philippians as a "hortatory letter of friendship" in "Friends and Enemies in the Politics of Heaven," *Pauline Theology, Vol. I*, 107–114.

[12] Crown itself is a metaphor of victory at the end of the race; cf. BAGD 767.

blameless," as proper sacrifices of thanksgiving (cf. Rom 12:1), at the day of Christ (1:10; 2:15). They and he[13] will stand before the judgment. No doubt the same orientation is presumed in Paul's cryptic reference to the fellow workers "whose names are in the book of life" (4:3).

Whereas Galatians viewed its auditors as (too) near the point of entry into the faith and thereby exceedingly vulnerable to falling away, Philippians, though it supposes a long, tried-and-true record of faithful living, reckons not from the past ("forgetting what lies behind"; 3:13) but from the near and impending future. Verbs of "pressing on," "pursuit," "prevailing," "completing" (ἐπιτελεῖν; 1:6)[14] and "filling out" (πληρεῖν; 1:11; 2:2; 4:19) characterize Paul's location of the Philippians as moving, or rather being providentially moved, toward God's consummation.

2. *The Philippians' status*. The Philippians are not neophytes. The only reference to their being "children" (τέκνα θεοῦ; 2:15; perhaps an echo of Deut 32:5 LXX) has to do with what Paul elsewhere calls being "babies with respect to evil" (1 Cor 14:20), living an unblemished life in a sinful world. Paul, in an open call to self-imitation, invites any and all of them to think of themselves as "adults," "mature" in the faith: "As many as are mature . . ." (3:15). The Philippians are tried and true believers. They have attained much and they should hold onto it as the end draws near (3:16).

As in Paul's contemporary world where the games and battle are intrinsically interrelated, so the Philippians are soldiers and athletes for Christ. Employing a battle metaphor,[15] Paul expects them to "stand" (1:27; 4:1; cf. Ephesians 6), "not being frightened in anything by the adversaries" (1:28) and knowing that the "enemies of the cross of Christ" face annihilation (3:18–19). Paul's fellow agonists are "in the midst of an unscrupulous and depraved generation" (2:15); there believers are to "discharge" their "obligations as citizens" (1:27),[16] but theirs is an alien citizenship whose commonwealth is heaven (3:20)— and appropriately its call is an "upward call" (ἄνω κλήσεως; 3:14)— and its Lord is at hand (3:5). The Philippian believers, citizens of

---

[13] Later in the letter he sees his own fate at the day of Christ tied directly to whether they are indeed "blameless and innocent . . . without blemish" (Phil 2:15–16 NRSV).

[14] The contrast with Galatians is clear here: both Galatians and Philippians speak of starting or beginning, but Galatians assumes that the danger lies in a *wrong* completion, namely back into slavery, while Philippians assumes a proper completion at the day of Christ.

[15] E. M. Krentz, "Military Language and Metaphors in Philippians," in *Origins and Method: Towards a New Understanding of Judaism and Christianity* (ed. B. H. McLean; JSNTSup 86; Sheffield: Sheffield Academic Press, 1993) 105–127.

[16] BAGD 686.

heaven, discharge that citizenship, like warriors and athletes, among a crooked generation. Euodia and Syntyche, the two women who are having some problem (4:2–3), are described as persons who have contended or struggled alongside Paul in disseminating the gospel (συνήθλησαν; 4:3) and in that respect they are depicted as persons who, at least before they encountered their present antagonism, fit Paul's call for proper citizenship (1:27) in the gospel: such persons "stand firm" and they strive "side by side for the faith of the gospel" (συναθλοῦντες; 1:27 RSV). Though Philippians lacks any explicit identification of the crooked generation with darkness, Paul's description of his audience as φωστῆρες ἐν κόσμῳ, "light-giving or heavenly bodies in the world," reinforces the believers' identity as cosmically important in God's purposes. Their not being frightened by enemies is proof or a sign (ἔνδειξις; 1:28) of their impending salvation which they are to "work out" or work to attain because God is at work in them (2:12–13). Though for Paul salvation is not a present possession of believers, but promised to them, references to salvation in Philippians serve to position the hearers and to guide them toward proper comportment.

Paul is persuaded that the God who is working in the Philippians (2:13; cf. 1 Thess 2:13) "inaugurated a good work among you" and "will bring it to completion right up to the day of Christ Jesus" (1:6). Sharing Christ's death is presupposed (3:10), but the focus is on attaining the resurrection from the dead, that *telos* toward which the Philippian believers are, like Paul, properly and maturely striving (3:12–15).[17]

III. Some Examples of Paul's Moral Leverage From Each Horizon

It remains for us to sample some ways in which Paul gains moral suasion with his auditors by focusing on the distinctive horizons. Galatians, with its vision targeted on the incipience of faith, reasons from what the Galatian believers know of their rebirth into Christ and appeals to them not to be led astray from what they have already received. Philippians, written to a relatively mature and stable community of believers, capitalizes on their track record, focuses on the *telos* toward which they have been moving, and appeals to them not to let worldly opposition and internal bickering distract them from the avid pursuit of that goal. Galatians is written to believers near the starting line; Philippians is penned for believers well along the course.

---

[17] "Nowhere [in Philippians] is there any description of the period before Christ." D. J. Lull, "Salvation History," in *Pauline Theology, Vol. 1*, 259.

A. Galatians: Moral Reasoning from the Turning Event

1. *Holy Spirit.* Paul's basic question ("This alone I want to ask you"; 3:2), how did they receive the Spirit, supposes that they and Paul know that they did receive it. Its presence in their lives is a given; Paul's leverage from it is our interest.

a. The Spirit establishes them as God's children ("born according to the Spirit," 4:29), and enables them to cry from the heart "Abba! Father!" (4:6). The moral leverage: they are no longer slaves (4:7) and therefore should not revert to their former slavery to the puerile elemental spirits that used to govern their lives (4:8–9; 5:1).

b. They received the Spirit by faith (3:2; 5:5), not by works; from this Paul can reason that the Galatians do not need to resort to circumcision.

c. The Spirit generates a *telos* ("Having begun with the Spirit, are you now ending up with the flesh?" 3:3), but, ironically, the Galatians are in danger of straying from the proper goal and ending up where they started, namely in sin. Moral leverage: Believers, endowed with the Spirit, live by the Spirit, align themselves with the Spirit (5:25), walk by the Spirit (5:16), and bear the fruit of the Spirit (5:22–23). The Spirit governs their lives and their comportment together so that "love, joy, peace, forbearance, kindness, goodness, faithfulness, considerateness and self-control" all are manifested in their lives (5:22–23). Those "who are spiritual" ought to employ that very "spirit of considerateness" in restoring one who has stumbled (6:1). So walking by the Spirit has direct application to the way believers relate and come to the aid of one another.

d. The agricultural metaphor behind the notion of "fruit of the Spirit" powers cautionary words toward the end of the letter: "God is not to be treated with contempt: for whatever one sows, that shall he reap" (6:8). Paul sees only two possible sowings, to the flesh or to the Spirit. A crop will come either way: sow to the flesh and one reaps ruin or destruction (φθορά; 6:8); sow to the Spirit and "from the Spirit one shall reap eternal life" (6:8). Thus we can observe that, by a carefully traced argument across the last three chapters of Galatians, Paul seizes on the Spirit's reception as the symbol of the Galatian believers' own turning point and by references to the Spirit not only encourages the Galatians to eschew a return to slavery but also to point them toward true freedom (5:1, 13) and the proper fruition of the Spirit in their lives now and for all eternity.[18]

---

[18] Cf. the same point as expressed by J. D. G. Dunn, "The Theology of Galatians," *Pauline Theology, Vol. I,* 131: "The expression of life within the covenant should be

2. *Paul's biography and theirs.* It is not uncommon in Paul's letters for him to recount his life, or more precisely, a carefully selected portion of his life with a view to its exemplary value for exhortation. And so it is in Galatians.[19] His life, like theirs, hinged on a radical change, what some might term a call or conversion; his new life and its work, like theirs, was challenged by others who raised the very same question of circumcision;[20] his life, like theirs, had to be lived steadfastly despite pressure from individuals who should have known better (even Cephas and Barnabas, Gal 2:11–21) but who got cloudy vision concerning the truth of the gospel and about the relationship of faith and works (2:16);[21] as surely as persons have tried to lead the Galatians back to bondage, so it was for Paul (2:4); as Paul has been crucified with Christ and therefore Christ lives in him (2:20), so it should be with the Galatians (4:19). But he prevailed; he did not turn back; he did not "nullify the grace of God" (2:21). Paul expects no less of them.[22] Paul explicitly notes the overlap in their stories and his: "Become as I am because I have become as you" (4:12).

3. *Rival endings of the Galatians' story.* Paul has to deal with the dissonance he is experiencing regarding the Galatians. When he first preached to them they responded with zeal to the gospel and to him. Paul's travail over them resulted in a good birth (4:19). They got off to a good start: "You were running well" (5:7). But now they are being lured away to another gospel which Paul considers no gospel (1:6–9). What should have been the turning point from which their new lives developed and grew out toward the culminating point has instead become an ironical turning point where they are in danger of falling away from grace (5:4), of throwing away what has so richly and freely been given to them. Note his expressions of this: "Having started with the Spirit, are you now ending with the flesh?" (3:3 NRSV). "But now . . . having been known by God, how can you turn back to the feeble and impotent elemental spirits to whom you once again want to be

---

consistent with its beginning."

[19] Cf. G. Lyons, *Pauline Autobiography: Toward a New Understanding* (SBLDS 73; Atlanta: Scholars Press, 1985) 171: In Galatians "Paul presents his 'autobiography' as a paradigm of the gospel of Christian freedom which he seeks to persuade his readers to reaffirm in the face of the threat presented by the troublemakers." On Paul's carefully selected retelling of aspects of his life, see pp. 226–227.

[20] By his claim to have excellence in his standing among his Jewish peers and in his zeal for the traditions (1:14), he subverts a possible charge that his avoidance of circumcizing Gentiles comes from his ignorance.

[21] Even Abraham's story is told in such a way as to bear on theirs: the centrality of faith, not works; and their being his children by faith through the free woman (3:6–9; 4:21–31).

[22] His story and theirs are explicitly coordinated in passages such as 4:3–5.

enslaved?" (4:9). Little wonder that he fears he has worked among them in vain (4:11). In order to steer them back in the right direction, toward what he thinks is the proper end to which they ought to be oriented, Paul develops two complementary arguments.

a. He describes the wrong way, which he is careful to indicate was already their own until faith came to them, and which he projects will be theirs again unless they come to their senses. His reminders of their former life without Christ are designed to highlight *via negativa* what they now enjoy in Christ. In Christ, their social status has been radically changed: they were slaves, now they are children. They were in bondage to puny elemental spirits (4:3, 9) who were not gods (4:8). For emphasis, he challenges the assumption that living "from works of the law" or that being under the law is a blessing; instead, perhaps shockingly for his audience, he labels living that way as a curse (κατάρα; 3:10; cf. 3:13).

b. He describes the right end or goal. Granted, he merely hints at it; he points at it without developing it. His inklings of the right goal function to heighten the sense of what they put in jeopardy by their contemplated move toward circumcision and the law, or as Paul would put it, back to where they were before faith came to them. One fundamental allusion to the proper target is grounded in the Spirit's making believers God's children: because they are adopted into God's family as children, believers have every right to expect their full share of the inheritance. Paul puts it most economically: "you are no longer a slave but a son, and if a son, also an heir through God" (4:7; 3:29). When people become God's children they are in line for the inheritance. Paul reasons from the assurance of inheritance to suggest the grandeur of what the Galatians risk in flirting with turning their backs on the gospel (4:1–7). A second allusion, suggesting much the same as inheritance but in contrast focusing on the responsibility of the readers, not God, is the harvest metaphor. "Whatever one sows, that shall he reap" (6:7). The way Paul develops the argument, there is no question that each one will sow; at issue is whether one will sow to the flesh or to the Spirit. Likewise, Paul never questions whether there will be a crop. There will be a harvest: either destruction/ruin (φθορά) or eternal life (6:8). And the crop depends directly upon that to which one sows. Sowing, labor, and harvest all hang together. Paul's moral leverage from that supposition is direct and simple: "In doing the good let us not lose heart, for in its own time we shall reap if we do not give out. So then, as we have occasion/opportunity, let us do the good to all people" (6:9–10).

B. Philippians: Moral Reasoning From the Culminating Event

1. Paul's biography and theirs. Once again Paul tells his own story—again a selectively edited version of it—as an exemplification of the stance he hopes the Philippians will adopt. Paul offers himself as a model for the Philippians. Here his story is told in three scenes. In the first autobiographical scene (1:12–26), Paul is in prison (1:7, 12–14) and sees it as a context for him to live true to his calling, so he is preaching the gospel to good effect (1:12–14). Like the Philippians, he has people who would cause him affliction (1:15–17; 1:28–30). But, undaunted, he rejoices and contemplates *where this will lead* (ἀπο-βαίνω; 2:19), namely to his σωτηρία (deliverance or salvation; the ambivalence probably intentional). In the same prison scene of his biography Paul next depicts himself as weighing alternate futures for himself: whether to go directly to be with the Lord full-time, his preference, or to "remain in the flesh" for them (1:21–26). Eschewing what might seem best to him and opting for what serves the needs of others he puts himself fully in accord with Jesus Christ (2:5–11); so do Timothy (2:20–22) and one of their own, Epaphroditus (2:29–30).[23]

In scene two (3:4–14) Paul parades his worldly criteria of honor. Though it might appear that he has reason to look back with pride—he says as much (3:4)—on his scrupulous and zealous religious accomplishments and heritage, he dismisses them and, in an open appeal for emulation (3:17: "Brothers and sisters, become fellow-imitators of me"), pictures himself as turning his back on what lies behind and straining forward (ἐπεκτείνομαι; 3:13) to what lies ahead. Forceful language intensifies that claim: "Toward the goal [σκοπός] I pursue [διώκω, hasten, run] the prize [of victory]."

The third and final autobiographical scene (4:10–20) is introduced by the Pauline corpus's most comprehensive injunction to emulation, paratactically aligned for emphasis, reaching back and embracing all the encouragement to emulation found earlier in the letter: "What you have learned and received and heard and seen in me, these things do!" This last scene encourages abiding the vagaries of life, as Paul does, with joy grounded in the confidence that the divine power enables him, and presumably all believers, to cope with everything (4:11–13).

The Philippians' biography coordinates with Paul's regarding opposition. We are not told the specifics of the external opposition because the Philippians already know about it. Paul makes a direct association of their struggle (ἀγών) with his own (1:30) and thereby invites them to

---

[23] For imitation (and the integrity of the letter as well), see R. A. Culpepper, "Co-Workers In Suffering. Philippians 2:19–30," *RevExp* 77 (1980) 349–358.

model the way he has not been distracted or distressed by his opponents (1:15–18). The particular moral leverage he exerts from this shared fight builds from the just-reported first scene of his autobiography: he hopes they will "stand firm in one spirit, in one mind contending together for the faith of the gospel" (1:27).

Their story should coordinate with his in another way: they should seek what is good for others and should subordinate self-interest to the greater good of the community. Scene one of Paul's biography already epitomized that mode of living and choosing. Despite Paul's preference to be delivered from the struggles (ἀγῶνα) of being in this world, the need of others, namely of these very Philippians, overrides his own preference. Then, like hammer blows spaced out across much of the letter, other exemplifications of this overarching concern for the needs of others appear: Christ (2:5–11), Timothy (2:19–24), Epaphroditus (2:25–30). The exemplifying portrait of Christ (see esp. 2:1–5) elaborates the unity that Paul expects to be paramount in internal church relations (2:1–5).

Both of these biographical connections with Paul provide a context for Paul's entreaty to Euodia and Syntyche to "be of the same mind in the Lord" (4:2 NRSV; a direct reprise of the "same mind" exhortations in 2:1–5). His description of them as "contending alongside me in the gospel" (4:3) is a direct echo of Paul's hope for the "one spirit . . . one mind" that he feels is necessary "for the faith of the gospel" (1:27). Paul's description of these two fellow workers is designed to reinforce the need for them to be of one spirit and one mind—because that unity is appropriate to the gospel and to the life it fosters. His explicit treatment of the problem of the two women draws on the resources and strengths of the rest of the community as additional leverage.

2. *Forgetting what lies behind and pressing on.* The second scene of Paul's autobiography exemplifies this posture toward the past and provides Paul with the moral leverage to address Euodia and Syntyche. His past, as theirs, could be construed as praiseworthy and laudatory: he was of sound pedigree; he was scrupulously religious and zealous for the traditions; he even defended the traditions against subversion. What did he have? "A righteousness of my own" (3:9 RSV), not "the from-God righteousness" (3:9). Euodia and Syntyche, who are entreated just after scene two of Paul's biography, have the same need to let go of the past where their dispute is grounded. Like Paul, they should strain forward (ἐπεκτείνομαι; 3:13) to what lies ahead. They ought to let bygones be bygones, but more importantly they need to stretch out toward what lies ahead, and the way to do that is to fall back into line, "contending alongside" Paul and Clement and "the rest of my fellow workers whose

names are in the book of life" and live with the appropriate unity of spirit and mind that the gospel enables and requires. The call to do so also fits the larger sweep of the vision of Philippians where Paul points all the Philippians toward the future where salvation will be achieved and granted (2:12–13).

3. *True, eschatological citizenship and appropriate comportment in an alien setting.* Every Roman citizen, and countless persons who coveted such citizenship, knew that citizenship was identity, power, right and obligation. The Philippian congregation, lodged in that proud, grand capital city, were attuned to those socio-political dynamics, or at least Paul supposes them to be. Accordingly, he reminds them that, as ones with an "upward call" (3:14), their citizenship is in heaven. That heavenly citizenship, itself an implied critique of earthly citizenship, involves "discharging the obligations of citizens" (πολιτεύεσθε; 1:27) in an alien world, contending with opposition (συναθλοῦντες; 1:27–30; cf. 4:3), standing firm in one spirit (1:27) in the Lord (4:1). These athletic/ battle metaphors function: a) to encourage continued identification with the struggle, and b) to point the believers, without mentioning victory explicitly, to the time when the victory will be complete. Instead of victory images, Paul transposes to the last judgment, a prominent motif of the culminating event, as a way of calling the believers to take stock of their present lives, to deal with the internal strife around Euodia and Syntyche, and to bring their behavior in line with the gospel under whose banner they march and have citizenship. Paul's opening affirmation in the thanksgiving expresses his confidence that "the one who began this good work in you will bring it to completion right up to the day of Christ" (1:6). The same thanksgiving closes with Paul's prayer that the Philippians may be able to "discern what really matters, that you may be pure in motive and blameless for the day of Christ" (1:10). The next reference to the day of Christ (2:16) reaffirms the blemishlessness and innocence that they as God's people should manifest right up to the day of Christ. That motif prepares for what Paul says immediately after he has explicitly encouraged the community and Euodia and Syntyche to reclaim the harmony appropriate to the gospel: "The Lord is near!" (4:5), meaning "Get your house in order!"[24]

One other item needs attention. References to the past function rather differently in these two Pauline letters. In Galatians, the past is remembered and portrayed vividly; it functions doubly, as a reminder of that slavery from which they have been delivered, and as an index of

---

[24] Pheme Perkins' reflections on 4:5 (in "Philippians," *Pauline Theology, Vol. I,* 103–104) are worthy of note.

what they actually enjoy in their new life in Christ. "No longer" confirms and enhances the "now" and warns against a return to the past's imprisonment. In Philippians, the past is treated ambivalently. On the one side, the letter abounds in positive recitations of past accomplishments and high standards of moral life. The Philippians are the ones who "have always obeyed" (2:12), who have been "in partnership in the gospel from the first day until now" (1:5), who can bring Paul's joy to completion (2:2), who have sent Epaphroditus (2:25) and missions of support for Paul (4:16). On the other side, Paul pictures himself, with the second scene of his biography to support it, as one who "forgetting what lies behind" (3:13) hastens on or runs (διώκω; 3:12, 14, bracketing the "forgetting") to seize (καταλαμβάνω; 3:12, 13) perfection or the prize (3:14). So what is and is not involved in "forgetting what lies behind"? Because positive references to the past pervade Philippians, forgetting the past cannot mean some sort of evangelical amnesia in which the past is totally discounted; Paul is not advocating faith without history.[25] Instead, "forgetting what lies behind" should be seen for what it is, namely, practical pastoral advice aimed to encourage Paul's two women co-workers, Euodia and Syntyche, and the congregation around them to let bygones be bygones. Forgetting what lies behind allows a re-collecting around the shared pursuit of the goal toward which life in Christ ought to be lived, namely to be blameless, without blemish, to be of one mind, one spirit on the day of the Lord. Behind the notion and driving it is probably Paul's conviction that love does not keep score but instead "throws a cloak of silence over what is displeasing in another person" (1 Cor 13:7).[26] Euodia and Syntyche, encouraged by Paul and the community to practice love, should forget what lies behind and press on toward the "prize of the upward calling" appropriate to citizens of heaven.

So, in conclusion, Galatians and Philippians depict congregations that are at the extreme horizons of Paul's picture of God's action from the death and resurrection of Jesus Christ until his return.[27] Paul views the Galatians, because of their temptation to turn back from his gospel, as babies, as persons who started running well, as persons who are hovering altogether too close to the point where faith began, and

---

[25] But note J. L. Martyn's thoughtful reflections on the problems of faith and history in Galatians, along with what he calls a "side glance at Philippians," in "Events in Galatia," *Pauline Theology, Vol. I*, 173–174.

[26] BAGD 766.

[27] The differences between Paul's stance in Galatians and in Philippians is a sign not of change or development in his thought but of his differing assessments of the respective audiences' locations along the path between the two horizons of Paul's thought world.

therefore as persons who are in danger of falling back into their former slavery to sin. On the other extreme, he views the Philippians, whom he knows to be tried and true, as mature believers, as persons who are, in general, properly oriented toward living the gospel, as persons who have proved themselves to be ready for the parousia and the judgment it brings. True, the Philippians have an external and an internal challenge to deal with, but their resources are viewed as great.

Accordingly, with the Galatians Paul focuses on their liberating, shared death with Christ, their receipt of the Spirit, and their status as babies; for the same reasons he writes them not about resurrection, salvation, the parousia, or the judgment day. And with the Philippians Paul holds up considerations of the culminating event by which they are to take a present measure of themselves and reorient themselves so that they stand side by side in one spirit and one mind, blameless and blemishless and so that they are ready for the consummation of God's purposes; culmination, completion, finishing are the dominant motifs; for these reasons there is no depicting of the Philippians as babies, limited attention to Christ's death, and (almost) no reference to their lives before faith came to them.

The Continuing Quest for Coherence in St. Paul: An Experiment in Thought

Paul J. Achtemeier

The past decade and a half have seen a number of proposals regarding Pauline theology and the Jewish background from which the apostle himself came, proposals that have given impetus to new ways of understanding that theology. Two of the foremost among them are 1) the argument that Pauline theology is constructed within the perspective of an adapted form of Jewish apocalyptic, set forth in considerable detail by J. C. Beker, the way for which was in many ways prepared by the magisterial commentary on Romans by Ernst Käsemann; and 2) the convincing demonstration by E. P. Sanders that the Judaism of the first century understood itself principally as a religion of covenantal grace rather than human accomplishment. A problem yet to be resolved, however, despite a century or so of discussion, is whether or not one can use the term "coherent" when one speaks of Pauline theology.[1] That is, is there an underlying conceptual unity which gives birth to the many and disparate discussions found in Paul's letters? In this context it is well to remind ourselves that what we know of the way Paul carried on his theological thinking is derived not from treatises on theology or even chapters from such a theology, but rather from letters of primarily pastoral intent, letters whose goal was, in most cases, the resolution of certain problems which had arisen within the Christian communities to which those letters were addressed. The one possible exception is Romans, which by its nature—seeking to enlist the Roman Christians in support of Paul's proposed mission to Spain—seems likely to give us a clearer insight into the broad scope of his theological thinking. Yet even Romans bears the clear stamp of Paul's situation as it was being composed, so that in the end it is not qualitatively different from the other letters.

Given, therefore, the situational nature of the letters, with their varying theological approaches and conclusions, and the almost accidental

---

[1] This problem has occupied members of the SBL Group on Pauline Theology from time to time, a group in which Prof. Furnish has played a significant and creative role. This article is in partial acknowledgment of what I have gained from his careful and creative scholarship over the years.

way in which some were preserved and others lost,[2] the key question for anyone interested in Paul's theology is the question of the coherent center of that theology. What, amid the myriad situationally-conditioned ("contingent") expressions contained in his letters, constitutes the coherent center which will make sense of the variety of theological assertions? Put another way, can we, who have only the situationally-conditioned statements present in Paul's letters, deduce the coherent central core of Paul's theology which, itself coherent, lends to the multitude of situation-conditioned statements their coherence?[3]

I

A classic attempt to arrive at such a coherent center of Pauline theology is to locate it in the doctrine of justification by faith. That is to say, at the core of all of Paul's theological thinking lies the notion that one gets right with God through faith in Jesus Christ. Finding in this doctrine the structural element in the arguments put forth in Paul's letter to Galatia, and locating it as the theme of Paul's letter to the Romans (1:17), one can argue that here we have the center of Paul's theology. That doctrine is further to be understood in terms of its opposite, namely that one is to be justified before God by works of the law. This understanding of the center of Paul's thought found powerful support from Martin Luther's personal struggle to satisfy himself that he had confessed, and done penance for, all the sins he had committed (Vulgate: *paenitentiam agite* for Greek μετανοεῖτε). That attempt to satisfy for all his sins only led Luther further into despair until he was transformed by the realization that such justification came by God's grace through trust in Christ. Equating Luther's struggle with that confronting Paul in his attempt to fulfill the law, this view argues that despair on Paul's part in his attempt to fulfill the law similarly led him finally to realize that one got right with God only through faith in the divine son Jesus Christ. This view found justification in the struggle with the law portrayed in Romans 7, with its despairing cry "Wretched person that I am, who will deliver me from this body of death?" (7:24). Here then is both the personal center of Paul's religion and the doctrinal center of Paul's thought.

---

[2] For example, we no longer have the earlier letter to the Christians in Corinth which Paul mentioned in 1 Cor 5:9.

[3] For the sake of maintaining a sharper focus, I shall limit my discussion to those letters generally acknowledged to have come directly from Paul, i.e., Romans, 1 & 2 Corinthians, Galatians, Philippians, and 1 Thessalonians.

There are a number of problems with that solution to the coherent center of Paul's theology, however. There is first the assumption in this scenario that Judaism, and especially the term "works of the law," meant the Jew had to accomplish more good works than bad to get right with God. Yet that is not the case, as Sanders has shown. Rather, Judaism understood itself primarily in terms of Deut 7:7; God had chosen Israel out of love, not for any of its accomplishments, and Judaism therefore knew itself a people graced by God. To be born a Jew meant to be born into that grace; the law, nothing more nor less than a sign of that grace, informed Israel of God's will for it, and the Jews, grateful for God's gracious election of their people, happily followed it. The Jews therefore did not despair in the law, they gloried in it as a visible sign that God had chosen them.

That is, quite apparently, also the view Paul the Pharisee had held of the law. In his autobiographical description in Philippians 3, he tells his readers that as far as righteousness under the law was concerned, he knew himself to be blameless (3:6). Far from despairing in his inability to fulfill the law, therefore, Paul had gloried in the fact that he had in fact fulfilled it perfectly. Nor can one appeal to Rom 7:13–25 as an indication of such despair. There is remarkable agreement among most recent commentators (e.g., Käsemann, Dunn, Fitzmyer) on Romans that whatever else Romans 7 may be, it is not a description of Paul's conscious despair at his inability to fulfill the law; its contradiction to the admittedly autobiographical statement in Philippians 3 will not permit it. Let me simply assert for the moment that what Romans 7 does describe is not subjective feelings, but the objective situation of the person who seeks to do God's will by relying on the law. More on that later.

Finally, if justification by faith as opposed to justification by works of the law is in fact the center of Paul's theology, then one would expect some consistency in the way Paul describes the origin and function of the law. Yet such is precisely not the case. For example, Paul gives no single reason, but several, for the purpose of the law: 1) it was intended to be the Jews' (or maybe everyone's) custodian until Christ came, to keep people headed in the right direction (Gal 3:23–24), so that after Christ came, it was no longer needed; 2) it was given to furnish people with a knowledge of what sin is, to help them identify it for what it is (Rom 3:20); that means that where there is no law, sin may exist, but it cannot be kept track of (Rom 5:13; cf. 4:15, 7:7; perhaps in this sense 5:20); 3) the law was introduced actually to foster the increase of sin, not just to aid in its identification (Rom 7:5, 8, 11); thus it is the law that gives to sin the power that it has (1 Cor 15:56). Paul can also in different contexts speak of faith as upholding the law (Rom 3:31) and of the law as not resting on faith (Gal 3:12), and he can, as some have argued, use it in some instances to mean the Jewish law, in others to mean law of a different sort, i.e., law of Christ, in still others to mean not law at all but simply "principle" (e.g., Rom 3:27, 7:21). Whether or not this last interpretation is valid, and I do not think it is, it is nevertheless clear that for a concept that constitutes the center of his theology, Paul is remarkably loose in his various discussions of the law. On the basis of such evidence, one can draw one of two conclusions. The one is that if Paul is that inconsistent on a central point of his theology, i.e., the law, one can hardly use the word "coherent" to describe his theology. One must therefore give up the notion of a coherent center of Paul's theology, and admit that one cannot describe Paul as a coherent theologian.[4] The alternative conclusion is that justification by faith does not constitute the doctrinal center of Paul's theology, a point supported by the virtual absence of discussion of it in the majority of Paul's letters, and the unlikelihood that it constitutes the theme of Romans, appearing as it does in 1:17 in a grammatically subordinate position.[5] That is hardly the place one would expect a theme to be announced. Again, let me simply assert, once more with the support of many recent commentators, that the theme of Romans is in fact the conviction that in Christ, God has extended divine election beyond the bounds of the Jewish people, to include within God's people all who trust in Christ.

II

Rather than locate the center of Paul's thought in some doctrinal statement, perhaps it would be more appropriate to locate it in the content of a tradition concerning the fate of Jesus that Paul shares with the early church, and that underlies, and gives coherence to, the various theological discussions in which he engages. Central to such a tradition would be the death of Jesus, or more precisely, the death of Jesus on the cross, as Paul himself shows in his letters. Not only is the death of Jesus mentioned more widely in his letters than, say, justification by faith; Paul himself identifies it as central to his understanding of Jesus Christ. He tells the Corinthian Christians that when he undertook his mission among them, he decided that the central element of his preaching would be the crucified Christ (1 Cor 2:2: "I decided to know nothing among you but Christ, and this one as

---

[4] That is the conclusion, e.g., of the Finnish scholar Heikki Räisänen.

[5] The theme of justification by faith hardly appears in 1 & 2 Corinthians, Philippians, 1 Thessalonians, or Philemon, and it is the third element in a compound enthymeme that runs from Rom 1:16 at least through 1:18, and perhaps further.

crucified"). In identifying the reason for his wonderment that the Galatians have abandoned the gospel Paul preached among them, he notes, apparently as the central element of that gospel, that Christ was publicly portrayed before them as the crucified one (Gal 3:1). The reason for such centrality was Paul's conviction that it was the cross that protected against any misunderstanding that the power of Paul's message came from his own lofty rhetoric or wise arguments (1 Cor 1:25–2:5; cf. 2 Cor 4:7). Paul can identify his apostolic conduct as a life lived by faithfulness to the Son of God "who gave himself for me," (Gal 2:20), and can argue that the death of Christ had universal significance: he died for all people (Rom 8:32; 2 Cor 5:14). Paul can use the cross in a variety of circumstances, ranging from the centrality of what he preached to the reason why people ought to give generously to the point of self-impoverishment to the offering for the Christians in Jerusalem.[6] Negatively, Paul identified the cross as that point hardest for his contemporaries to accept; it represented foolishness to Greeks and a stumbling-block to Jews (1 Cor 1:18, 23; cf. Gal 5:11). The fact that he would not alter that point in his preaching attests to its importance for his theological understanding.

Yet once again, there is a problem in identifying Christ's death on the cross as the central core of Paul's theology, and that problem rests in the fact that while there is a rich variety in the meanings Paul finds in Christ's death on the cross, there is no consistency in the meanings he finds there. Paul can argue, for example, that Christ is our paschal lamb, whose sacrifice, on the analogy of Israel in Egypt (Exod 12:7, 12–13), allows us to escape the death visited upon others (1 Cor 5:7). He can also argue that Christ is the sacrifice that is necessary for the initiation of a (new) covenant, as a sacrifice was necessary for the initiation of the Mosaic covenant at Mt. Sinai (Exod 24:5–8; cf. Gen 15:9–10, 17–18). He does that specifically in such a passage as 1 Cor 11:24–25, where the bread is Christ's broken body, and the cup the new covenant in his blood (cf. 2 Cor 3:6, where Paul identifies himself as the minister of a new covenant). He can argue that point in a more general way by saying Christ's death allowed us to become "righteous," itself a term drawn from covenantal language in the Old Testament, as in Rom 5:9: we are made righteous through Christ's blood; or, comparing the two covenants, old and new, he can say that if righteousness came through the law, then Christ died to no purpose (Gal 2:21), clearly implying that a new covenant, inaugurated by his death, was necessary.

---

[6] ". . . though he was rich, yet for your sake he became poor, so that by his poverty you might become rich" (2 Cor 8:9).

Again, Paul can identify Christ's death as a sin offering, an analogy to a sacrifice for those already within the covenant (Leviticus 4–7), not the sacrifice which enables people to enter into it (Rom 4:28 "Christ was put to death for our trespasses"; cf. Rom 6:10; 1 Cor 15:3). On a different tack, Paul can affirm that Christ's death delivered us from the law, but he is not consistent in whether it: 1) delivered us from the law as such, i.e., we need no longer follow it (as seems to be the case in Rom 7:4, where Christians have died to the law through Christ's death); or 2) delivered us from the curse that hangs over anyone who does not fulfill the law (as in Gal 3:13, where Christ himself, by hanging from a tree, i.e., the cross, became himself a curse for us, thus killing it with his death); or 3) enabled us in fact to fulfill the law (as in Rom 8:3 where God, sending his Son in the likeness of sinful flesh, thus condemned sin in the flesh so that the just requirement of the law could be fulfilled in us). 4) A final example: Paul is clear that Christ, by dying on the cross, acted in obedience to a divine command (Phil 2:8), and by that act of obedience Christ annulled the effects of the disobedience of Adam which had brought death for all human beings (Rom 5:19). Thus yet another reason for Christ's death is cited, one unrelated to covenant or sin offering.

Now to be sure, all of those points may be valid, and some may simply be different expressions of the same concept, but that is not true of all of those explications. If the death was the way into the covenant, then it could hardly also be the sacrifice for sin for those within the covenant. Again, if it was a representative death, then it could hardly be understood as the sacrifice that made possible a new covenant. That is the way one might use an analogy, i.e., to make a variety of points, but it is not the way one would expect the central theological core to be handled. If it were central, one would expect Paul to be consistent in the way he explained the significance of that death within the framework of his theology. Once again, we can conclude either that Paul was simply an inconsistent thinker, unable to provide any kind of coherent explication of his theology, or that the crucifixion of Jesus did not constitute the central conceptual core of his theology.

There are other concepts one could investigate as possible constituents of the doctrinal or conceptual core of Pauline theology, e.g., righteousness, Christology, ecclesiology, but the result would be the same. We would find no consistency in the way Paul employs these various theologoumena in his letters. There is another way we may approach the question of the coherence of Paul's theology, however, and it is that route that I would like to explore in what follows.

III

The fluidity of the various theological concepts Paul uses suggests that we are not likely to find the coherent center of his theology in terms of any of those concepts, whether singly or in combination. For that reason, I should like to alter the terms of our search. Instead of looking for a doctrinal center whose content provides coherence to Paul's varied theological discussions, we ought rather, I think, to look for what I should like to call the "generative center" of Paul's theology. That is, we should look for that central conviction out of which Paul's theology grows, and which will then help explain the way he theologizes about such things as, say, Jewish law and Christ's death.

While it is conceivable that Paul could have held this central conviction which was the generative core of his theology without ever making it thematic or even mentioning it, such a case would be unlikely on the face of it, and were it the case, that generative core would prove evanescent to the point of invisibility. Is there, then, any conviction Paul expresses without which in his view the Christian faith would not be possible, which lay at the heart of his own self-understanding as a Christian and as an apostle, and which could therefore serve as the generative center for his other theological positions? I think there is, and I take it to be the conviction that Jesus rose from the dead, and that God was the one who brought it about. The *generative center of Paul's theology, as it is his own self-understanding as apostle*, I want to argue, *is his conviction that God raised Jesus from the dead*.

That Christ's resurrection is important for Paul's theology is evident from a reading of Paul's letters. It is Christ's resurrection that guarantees a more glorious future for those who belong to him; that promises that death will not have the last word. Because of that resurrection, Christians also will be raised to a life in the presence of God. So 1 Thess 4:14: As Jesus died and rose again, so will Christians who have died; 2 Cor 4:14: we know that the one who raised the Lord Jesus will raise us also with him; 1 Cor 7:14: God raised the Lord and will also raise us up; so also 1 Thess 5:10; 1 Cor 15:20. Part of that future is the transformation of our bodies of flesh into bodies of Spirit, which again are patterned after the risen body of Christ; that is the point of Phil 3:20–21—we await the Lord Jesus Christ, who will change our lowly body to be like his glorious body—as it is the point of the discussion in 1 Cor 15:35–57. The point is that as God is Spirit, and flesh and blood cannot survive in the divine presence (so 1 Cor 15:50), it will be necessary for human beings to share in the spiritual existence of God's kingdom if they are to have part in it. Hence the necessity for the redeemed to have spiritual bodies if they are to have any kind of life in the presence of

God, and those spiritual bodies in their turn depend for their (future) existence on the glorious body of the risen Christ.[7]

That coming glory, with its defeat of death and its life in the presence of God, makes itself felt already in the present, however. For the Christians who have died with Christ through baptism into his death, the only life they can now live must be empowered by that risen Christ. So Paul can say that because of his being crucified with Christ, it is no longer he who lives but Christ who lives in him (Gal 2:20). Indeed, one important aspect of the power of the risen Christ is to enable Christians, despite life in an as-yet unredeemed world, to act in ways acceptable to God: to "bear fruit for God" is the language Paul uses (Rom 7:4). But because that power comes from the spiritual reality that is the primal characteristic of the future age, everything in the Christians' life worked by the power of the Spirit is ultimately for Paul to be traced to the ability of the risen Christ already to affect reality in this unredeemed age.

From all of this it is clear that the resurrection of Christ is important for Paul, but then so is Christ's crucifixion and the idea of being justified by faith. What sets the resurrection apart as being of central importance is the fact that this is the one event about Christ, as it is the one element of the Christian confession that Paul singles out as of absolute foundational importance. It is the one event the absence of which would render the Christian faith of no importance whatsoever. Paul says that not once but twice to the Corinthian Christians: if Christ is not raised, our preaching is vain, your faith is vain (1 Cor 15:14), and again, if Christ is not raised, your faith is futile, you are still in your sins (15:17). It was in fact, says Paul, the resurrection which constituted Jesus as Son of God in power (Rom 1:4), which made him Lord of all (Rom 14:7), and which gave him the very divine name itself that allowed him, like God, to be worshipped (Phil 2:9–11). Because of his resurrection and presence with God, he can now intercede for the faithful (Rom 8:34) and in the future deliver them from the divine wrath which will accompany the final judgment (1 Thess 1:9–10).

Yet the key here is not simply that Jesus rose from the dead. That in itself had no particular meaning for the Hellenistic world. Any magician worth his salt had at least one story told about his revivifying a corpse. The point is therefore not primarily that Jesus *rose* from the dead; rather, the point is that he *was raised* from the dead, and that he was raised from the dead *by God*. That is the key for Paul: that it was *God* who raised Jesus from the dead, as he says in Rom 10:9. That is why the

---

[7] That Paul could not conceive of any form of human existence without a body is here presumed, as it is everywhere in his thought.

resurrection is also the goal of Paul's apostolic ministry, simply because it is the central fact of the Christian faith, without which the whole enterprise would be rendered nugatory.

While there is a paucity of first-hand reporting concerning Paul's conversion from an opponent to a proponent of the Christian faith, what little there is points in the direction that it was the realization that God was the one who had raised Jesus from the dead, that constituted the core of that experience. Paul has remarkably little to say about that key event in his life, but when he does mention it, it is linked to the resurrection: at his conversion, when as he says, God "was pleased to reveal his son to me" (Gal 1:15–16), his goal became to know Christ and the power of his resurrection (Phil 3:10). The accounts in Acts of Paul's conversion (9:4–5; 22:7–8; 26:14–15) point in the same direction with their reports of a confrontation between Paul and the risen, glorious Jesus of Nazareth. The heart of Paul's theology—that God raised Jesus from the dead—very likely therefore derives from the event that changed Paul from an opponent to an apostle of Jesus Christ.

Yet however important the resurrection may be for Paul, there could have been no resurrection if there had not been a preceding death on the cross. And there could have been no death on the cross had people not found reason to stand in lethal opposition to him. Now, it is precisely that train of thought that offers us a way of reconstructing the path of Paul's theological reflections resulting from his conviction that it was God who had raised Jesus from the dead. If that conviction is the generative center of his theology, it ought to give us a clue as to how he reached his other theological convictions, and presented them as he does in his letters. It ought thus to allow us to catch sight of some aspects of the theological coherence that finds its contingent expression in Paul's letters. In what follows, I will limit the sketch to accounting for Paul's presentation of Jesus' death, and his thought about the law.

IV

If God raised Jesus from the dead, several implications clearly follow. One implication would be that since Jesus was involved in a resurrection, that event would have to be understood within a theological framework within which resurrection from the dead has more than passing significance. Such a framework was ready to hand in the apocalyptic outlook which had been formed out of the heritage of prophetic traditions concerning divine justice and God's sovereignty over history, and the question of the sages concerning the fact that all too often those who follow God's will suffer and those who do not, prosper. The solution was to posit a series of ages, over which God remained sovereign but did not directly intervene in the cause of divine justice, culminating in a final judgment in which all injustices rampant in prior ages were set right. Such a judgment was, in turn, the prelude to a new order of reality in which God would be immediately present, and hence no further injustice could exist. But for all injustices to be set right, there had to be a resurrection of the dead, so that everyone, not only those who remained alive at the time of the last judgment, would share in it. That judgment, finally, occurred at the conclusion of the old age and the inception of the new. Clearly, in such a framework, resurrection played a key role, and it was thus that framework that Paul adopted, and adapted. Since Christ had been raised from the dead, and since such a resurrection was the necessary prelude to the general judgment, and the transformation of the age, that must mean that the new age had already begun. Yet the transformation of reality that accompanied the new age had not yet occurred. That meant that while the new age had begun, the old had not yet come to an end. Paul's solution was to collapse old and new eras into each other for a period prior to the final transformation, which Paul then assumed would occur with the return of Jesus. In the present era, therefore, forces of both the old age (flesh, sin, death, injustice) and of the new age (spirit, salvation, life) were present. It was within that adapted framework that Paul worked out both his theological and ethical understanding. The fact that acceptance and adaptation of such a framework for Christian theology was not limited to Paul is manifest in that strange Matthean tradition (Matt 27:52–53) about many others rising from the dead at the time of Jesus' passion. In its (to us) bizarre way, it points to the fact that with Jesus in fact the new age, with its general resurrection, has already gotten underway.

A second implication drawn from the fact that God raised Jesus from the dead is that there must have been something true about Jesus that was not true about any number of other Jewish martyrs who had died over the centuries. Here, the apocalyptic framework may have provided the clue. In some apocalyptic traditions, a divine figure would appear at the time of the final judgment and the transformation of the age. If with Jesus' resurrection, the new age was already under way, then apparently Jesus was that figure, that one anointed by God to inaugurate it. Because he alone of all those who had functioned as agents of God through the ages had been raised by God from the dead, there was something unique about Jesus. That uniqueness came to be understood in terms of Jesus' sharing in God's own divine nature. Whether his divinity was granted or confirmed by the resurrection, the risen Jesus was himself divine, and could be worshipped as God since he bore the divine name (Phil 2:9–11).

A third, and perhaps most obvious, implication of the fact that God raised Jesus from the dead is that God did not want Jesus to remain dead. That means that God did not agree with the judgment of those responsible for Jesus' death, namely that Jesus had blasphemed God and falsely declared himself a unique representative of the divine will. That in its turn meant that: 1) the death was not deserved as a result of Jesus' transgressions, and 2) the basis on which his opponents reached their decision led to conclusions that were at odds with God's will. Let us, by way of conclusion, look at each of those points in turn.

1) Jesus' death was not deserved as a result of his own transgressions. Paul affirms that all of humanity shares in the primal sin of Adam (1 Cor 15:49), which was disobedience to the will of God (Rom 5:19), that as a result all people have to die (Rom 5:12), and that, further, death is the price required by sin (Rom 6:7). Yet Jesus as Son of God was free from sin during his life (2 Cor 5:21) because he was obedient to God (Phil 2:8); hence his death was not required as payment for his sin. If his death was not required by his sin, and hence he derived no benefit from it, then that death must have been for the sin of others, and hence others may benefit from it. It is the working out of that conclusion that is represented in the variety of ways Paul describes Christ's death. In every instance, at the core of Paul's thought about Jesus' death is the notion that it was for the benefit of others, whether as a reenactment of the deliverance from death at the time of the Exodus, or to begin a new covenant, or to deliver human beings from the power of sin, or from the law. Depending on what kind of analogy was most appropriate for the situation Paul was addressing, he described the death of Jesus as an event which was for the benefit of others. At the heart of such "inconsistent" analogies in Paul's understanding of the benefit of Jesus' death, lies the fact that Jesus' death is not the generative center of Paul's theology. That center is Christ's resurrection by God's power. Rather, Paul's thought about Jesus' death lies at one remove from that center, as a first level derivative, as it were, and thus can be interpreted as needed, and as the situation requires, even if those interpretations do not necessarily represent a single, monolithic viewpoint on the benefits provided by Christ's innocent death. There is thus not so much inconsistency as variety in the way Paul understands that death, an understanding situated, as I have suggested, at one remove from the generative center.

2) If God did not want Jesus to remain dead, and if as Son of God his death was not deserved because of some disobedience to God, then those who put him to death as one who opposed God's will were wrong. Now, the basis for their condemnation of Jesus as one who opposed God was their view of the law, which in their eyes represented the

complete will of God, and which, also in their eyes, Jesus contravened. It was because of their view of the law, therefore, that the Jewish leaders condemned, and caused the execution of, Jesus.[8] That has as a corollary that it was precisely their view of the law that led them astray when it came to understanding Jesus as one who acted in accordance with the will of God. It appeared to Paul, therefore, that either one understood the law as the complete expression of God's will, or one understood Jesus as that expression. On that point there could be no compromise.

Yet the law had been given by God; it was, as Paul admitted, the thing which set Israel apart as the people with whom God had first communicated his will (Rom 3:2). Yet if the law was intended to communicate God's will, and Jesus was the final expression of God's will, then how could it be that the law led those who called upon it as their fundamental national heritage and the holy expression of the will of God, to oppose Jesus? The answer Paul arrives at is the conclusion that the law had been overpowered by sin, and that as a result, in that state, and as interpreted by sinful human beings, it now led in the opposite direction it had been intended to lead, namely away from, not toward, God's will. It is that insight, incidentally, that lies at the root of Paul's understanding of sin as a power or force, rather than as a moral shortcoming or disobedience to specific commands. That the law led away from, rather than toward, God's will was in its turn demonstrated by the Jewish religious leaders, who accused Jesus repeatedly of not obeying the law. But it was also confirmed by Paul's own life. Prior to his confrontation with the risen Jesus, Paul himself, in the name of the law, had persecuted the followers of Jesus. It is, I think, no accident that when Paul speaks of his life prior to becoming an apostle, he announces in succession that his zeal led him to persecute the church and that as to any righteousness to be had under the law he was blameless (Phil 3:6). That is, it appears, the zeal which led him to oppose Christ was accompanied by a feeling that in doing so he was fulfilling God's will as expressed in the law. His position is further illustrated, I would want to argue, in Rom 7:13–25, which is an objective description of the dilemma confronting the person who relied on the law: wanting to follow God's will, which is good, by adhering to the law, one is led to oppose Christ, and because Christ is the final expression of

---

[8] Paul shared this condemnation of Jesus when, as he confesses, he was a persecutor of the church (Phil 3:6a). That his view of the law was a motivating factor for such persecution (cf. Acts 8:3, where the persecution Paul took part in was caused by Stephen's view of the law [6:14b]) is made evident when Paul contrasts the righteousness he gave up, which caused him to persecute the church, namely a righteousness based on law (Phil 3:9) with the righteousness he found in Christ, a righteousness, be it noted, intimately linked with Christ's resurrection (Phil 3:10–11).

God's will, following the law led one, in the name of doing the good, i.e., following God's will, to do just the opposite, i.e., oppose God's will. The good that the person wanted (viz., to follow God's will), the person did not do, and the very thing the person hated (viz., opposing God) is what devotion to the law as the means of being in a right relationship with God—the covenant—brought about. No wonder Paul can say of such a person that with respect to the law, whenever one wants to do good, i.e., to follow God's will, evil lies close at hand, i.e., opposing Christ (Rom 7:21).

It is necessary here to be clear on what Paul meant by the word νόμος, "law." He did not understand it as the principle of legislation, as the establishment of rules, as though the very establishment of such rules led people astray. His apostolic admonitions indicate that not to be the case. Rather Paul, good rabbi that he was, understood by "law" the Hebrew word "Torah," which at its root means "teaching." As such, Torah could be limited to the designation of the first books of the Hebrew Scriptures, the "books of the law," but it could be understood more broadly as the divine teaching about what God wanted. As such it included the whole of the Hebrew Scriptures, prophets and writings as well as Pentateuch. That is clear from the way Paul uses the term "law" to designate not only the first five books, but also to designate quotations from Psalms (Rom 3:10–13) and from the prophet Isaiah (Rom 3:15).

Torah therefore has as its purpose the communication of God's will. That means when Paul uses the word "law," he means the divine expression of the divine will, and hence he can use it to refer to God's will expressed in Christ (1 Cor 9:21; Gal 6:2) as well as in the Hebrew Scriptures. As the expression of God's will, therefore, the law is holy (Rom 7:12). That also means that when Paul uses the term "works of the law" to describe a way of doing what God wants, he is referring to obeying the commands of the Torah, not to human accomplishments which are intended to earn the favor of God. For that reason, "works of the law" can be accomplished only by Jews, since obeying the Torah was open only to Jews. And it was open only to Jews since to them alone the law had been given (Rom 9:4). Relying on "works of the law" for being right with God is thus open only to Jews, not to Gentiles, a point made clear in Rom 3:28–29, where Paul argues that if one could be right with God by doing such works of the law, God would be the God of the Jews alone. The revolution of Christ, which caused Paul to regard as trash all his former religious orientation, was that being right with God was now a matter of trusting Christ, and hence open to all people, not just to Jews, whose birthright was the law. That also means, I suspect, that for Paul the word "law" means only Torah, understood as the various expressions of God's will, nuanced in a variety of ways, and never something like "principle" or "rule." In the broadest sense, it means the communication of God's will; in contexts where the Jewish religion is at issue, it means Hebrew Scriptures. To show that would require a much longer paper than this one, and I shan't attempt it here, but I do think the case can be made, as it already has been, for example, by James Dunn and Hendrikus Boers, among others.

Thus, Paul can use the term "law" in a variety of ways, again depending on what in his judgment is most appropriate for the circumstances. He has the freedom to do this because law lies at two removes, as it were, from the generative center of Paul's theological thinking, namely the resurrection. "Law" is, in a sense, a second level derivative for Paul, deriving from the circumstances of Jesus' death, itself a derivative, and so Paul is freer to construe "law" in a variety of ways, some apparently at odds with others, since the law does not belong to the heart of the generative center of Paul's theology.

V

To summarize, I have sought in this experiment in thought I have been conducting to show that one can understand Paul's theological thought as coherent if one starts from the generative center of that theology, namely the resurrection of Jesus by God's power, and if one then proceeds to see how the implications of that generative center account for other theological positions Paul has taken. I am tempted to illustrate the relation between Paul's coherent generative center and the various contingent expressions in his letters in terms of the hub and spokes of a wheel. The coherence is not to be found in the individual spokes which proceed from their common center in the hub, so that all spokes must be equal in all respects, but rather the coherence is to be found in the hub from which the spokes radiate. It is their common center that gives them coherence as individual spokes. The spokes are, as it were, the contingent expressions of a unity that finds its expression in the hub as the generative center. Yet such an analogy lacks the dynamism I think was present in Paul's theologizing. Perhaps it is better simply to state that in my view, Paul's letters represent the theologizing prompted by one who, convinced that God has raised Jesus from the dead, sought to think through, and express, the implications of that event in a variety of circumstances. In that way, I have tried to argue, the coherence of Paul's theology lies at its generative center, from which Paul's thought on a variety of theological problems emanates. It may be, therefore, that Paul was not the muddle-headed dummy he is sometimes made out to be.

Changes of Thought in Pauline Theology? Some Reflections on Paul's Ethical Teaching in the Context of His Theology

Eduard Lohse

In most traditional interpretations of Pauline theology the thoughts developed by the apostle are seen as constituting a relatively homogeneous unity. In his ethical instructions Paul made use of traditional material drawn from his Jewish background as well as from Hellenistic presuppositions. But he integrated that material into his preaching of the gospel in order to explain what it meant to conduct one's life in a Christian manner. Confronted with different situations in his churches, the apostle shaped his arguments in the context of his theology. His teaching was not characterized by the elaboration of a theoretical system of thought but was unfolded as he answered concrete questions and thus explained the central meaning of the good news and its implications for the behavior of those who believe in Christ.

Recent scholarly research, however, has seriously questioned this understanding. Was Paul's theology so clearly shaped from the beginning—springing from Paul's basic theology like the fully-armed goddess Athena from Zeus's head? Or can we still find within the Corpus Paulinum some general lines pointing to a process in which Paul was evaluating the expression of his theological thoughts step by step? Some scholars are inclined to make a clear distinction between the earliest letter from Paul's hand, which was sent to the Thessalonians, and the last epistle, which he wrote to the Christians in Rome. Between these fixed points we find the main corpus of documents which, one after the other, show how the apostle was attempting to come to terms with the different topics he faced.

Looking at the letters in this way, one may raise the question whether in 1 Thessalonians eschatology so dominates the discussion that even the ethical instruction is entirely shaped by Paul's understanding of the coming parousia—whereas later, when Paul became increasingly aware that the last judgment probably would not take place as soon as he had once expected, his ethics took a corresponding turn of direction. Such a question is by no means new, for some exegetes pointed to problems of development in Paul's thought years ago.[1] But while it is admittedly probable—as V. P. Furnish has remarked—"that a writer's thought has undergone some modifications or even perhaps decisive shifts over a period of time in the course of altered conditions or even as a result of new insights,"[2] readers are rightly warned not to overemphasize any particular observations. If this warning is not heeded, ancient authors can be seen simply as pragmatic persons who changed their minds whenever it proved useful in handling difficult affairs. So one must be careful when considering whether there were changes or developments of thought in Paul's theology.

These considerations notwithstanding, some scholars argue that we can detect changes within the apostle's theological thinking.[3] So S. Schulz, in his voluminous work on New Testament ethics, distinguishes sharply between an early phase of Pauline ethical instruction which is found in 1 Thessalonians and a later stage represented in Romans, with a middle phase in between.[4] Not only Paul's eschatology but also his understanding of the role of the law is taken as evidence for speaking of changes in the apostle's ethical thought. So it is supposed that in 1 Thessalonians the law of Moses as way of salvation and the ethical relevance of the commandments are closely connected with each other. God's will is to be found in general morals applied to the Christian life. And it is the spirit which gives one the power to fulfill the demands of God. At the same time, it is argued that no hints of Paul's theology of justification can be detected in 1 Thessalonians. Rather, this understanding of the Christian kerygma was developed by Paul only in later letters when, as a consequence, his paraenetical comments were shaped to fit the new theoretical framework. At an even later stage, the final and definitive description of Pauline ethics was expounded in Romans.[5]

But is this really a convincing perspective for interpreting Paul's thought? Are we, as critical interpreters, actually in the position of being able to observe how Paul was learning, at successive periods of his apostolic ministry, to express his preaching and teaching? Or should

[1] See, e.g., C. H. Dodd, "The Mind of Paul: Change and Development," *BJRL* 18 (1934) 69–110, repr. in Dodd, *New Testament Studies* (3d ed.; Manchester: University of Manchester Press, 1967) 83–110; C. Buck and G. Taylor, *Saint Paul, A Study of the Development of His Thought* (New York: Charles Scribner's Son, 1969).

[2] V. P. Furnish, "Development in Paul's Thought," *JAAR* 38 (1970) 289–303; here, 289–90.

[3] Cf. U. Schnelle, *Wandlungen im paulinischen Denken* (Stuttgart: Katholisches Bibelwerk, 1989).

[4] S. Schulz, *Neutestamentliche Ethik* (Zürcher Grundrisse zur Bibel; Zurich: Theologischer Verlag, 1987).

[5] Ibid., 301–33.

one hesitate before differentiating among three or even more phases of Paul's theological thinking?

I

When one examines the Corpus Paulinum as a whole, certain changes of thought stand out to such a degree that they constitute some of the important reasons for distinguishing between Pauline and deuteropauline epistles. Thus in the Pastorals we find not only that Paul's work is brought into a different situation—a situation which does not fit into the chronology of the authentic Pauline writings and the Acts of the Apostles—but also that some shifts in theological argument have occurred. Time was passing, and the church had to develop appropriate patterns of living in its changing world. A constitution of the church had to be developed, different ministries had to be described, and certain requirements had to be met by those responsible for the Christian congregations. So there are good arguments for interpreting the Pastorals as documents composed within a Pauline school in which the apostle's theology was transmitted and rethought in order to define the position of the church in post-apostolic times. One has to suppose, therefore, that in the Pauline school an intensive discussion was going on about the adequate expression of early Christian theology.

Not only the Pastorals but also Colossians and Ephesians are to be characterized as deuteropauline documents and ascribed to members of a Pauline school—not to the apostle himself, and not to a secretary whom Paul might have authorized to speak in his name. In these two epistles as in the Pastorals, early Christian theologians were handling some important problems of their time. Eschatology was no longer emphasized. A doctrine of the church was formulated in which Christianity was seen as the worldwide body of Christ, embracing its members wherever they were. Former Jews and Gentiles were united in Christ. These documents' ecclesiology drew upon Pauline ideas but developed those ideas in the context of a late-first century vision of the role of the church. It was a difficult task, indeed, to reject the influence of a so-called syncretistic philosophy, as Colossians had to do, and to explain the reality of the new life of those who had been baptized in Christ. The ethical instruction has to be seen in close relation to the Pauline paradigm of indicative and imperative as the base of Christian behavior: Those who live in Christ are to "put to death whatever in [them] is earthly: fornication, impurity, passion, evil desire and greed" (Col 3:5), for "[they] have died and [their] life is hidden with Christ in God" (3:3). They "have been raised with Christ" (3:1); thus they are to

148

"seek the things that are above" and "as God's chosen ones, holy and beloved, clothe [them]selves with compassion, kindness, humility, meekness and patience" (Col 3:1, 12).

And finally 2 Thessalonians also has to be judged as a deuteropauline text. Whereas 1 Thessalonians expresses a vivid eschatological hope, 2 Thessalonians presents a critical commentary to correct false ideas which might come from an enthusiastic interpretation of such eschatological expectation. The author of 2 Thessalonians must have known the earlier letter because he made use of the style in which 1 Thessalonians was written. Speaking in the same language as Paul in 1 Thessalonians, the author of 2 Thessalonians offers his comments so that misunderstandings might be excluded as far as possible.

Modern scholarship has attained a far-reaching critical consensus that 2 Thessalonians, Colossians, Ephesians and the Pastorals come, not from the apostle himself but from the Pauline school tradition. Formerly, when scholars tried to understand these epistles as authentic documents written by Paul himself, they were forced to think of changes of thought in the apostle's theology and to see these texts as coming from Paul after he had grown old. On this view, Paul had to re-formulate some central theological topics, and give new expression to what he had said earlier in other ways.[6] But attempts at describing the theology of the whole Corpus Paulinum made it more and more evident that such changes of thought took place, not within Paul's lifetime but later, as theologians who had learned from him tried to restate his message in ways they thought he might have done to address the late-first century Christian situation. Hence we may now affirm that there are only seven authentic Pauline letters: 1 Thessalonians, Galatians, 1 and 2 Corinthians, Philippians, Philemon and Romans.

Before some theological topics are considered under this perspective a statement about the chronology should be made. 1 Thessalonians is probably the earliest document we have from Paul's hand, written about AD 50, and Romans must be seen as the last letter he composed, about AD 56 or 57. So when we ask whether the Pauline letters represent a concise theology, we must not forget that these letters were composed within a fairly short period of time.

---

[6] See, e.g., A. Schlatter, *Neutestamentliche Theologie II: Die Lehre der Apostel* (Calw & Stuttgart: Verlag der Vereinsbuchhandlung, 1910) 381–407, dealing with stages in the development of doctrine from 1 Thessalonians up to the Pastorals.

II

Paul had been a trained Jewish scribe before he became Christian. So a fundamental change of thought must have occurred when he was converted and called to be an apostle of Christ. Paul himself described this total renewal of his whole life and thinking when he mentioned how he had behaved as a pious Jew and member of the Pharisaic movement: "If anyone else has reason to be confident in the flesh, I have more: circumcised on the eighth day, a member of the people of Israel, of the tribe of Benjamin, a Hebrew born of Hebrews; as to the law, a Pharisee; as to zeal, a persecutor of the church; as to righteousness under law, blameless" (Phil 3:4–6). The critical point of view was implicit in this enumeration. For what Paul as a Jewish scribe had thought and done resulted in his decision to persecute the church. This persecution—and hence the viewpoint that occasioned it—had proven to be absolutely wrong.

That is why Paul expressed so sharply the contrast with his new understanding, an understanding which now originated from his confrontation with the crucified and risen Christ: "Yet whatever gains I had, these I have come to regard as loss because of Christ. More than that, I regard everything as loss because of the surpassing value of knowing Christ" (3:7–8). Reflecting the starkness of his incredible change of thought, Paul concludes: "For his sake I have suffered the loss of all things, and I regard them as rubbish, in order that I may gain Christ and be found in him" (v. 9).

These sentences may be characterized as the center of Paul's theological thinking from which all subjects discussed in his letters have to be explained.[7] Not only his new understanding of the early Christian kerygma, but also the wellspring of Paul's ethical teaching is to be found here. V. P. Furnish expresses it well: "Can a convincing explanation of Paul's conversion be achieved without reference to a changed stance towards the law—the decisive point of reference for the devout Jew, and for Paul himself in his pre-Christian days, as he more than once says?"[8] So Philippians 3 opens "a new and determinative Pauline insight," indeed the key to his whole theology.[9]

This fundamental change of thought happened right at the beginning of Paul's preaching and teaching as an apostle of Christ, a

---

[7] Cf. J. Jeremias, *Der Schlüssel zur Theologie des Apostels Paulus* (Calwer Hefte 115; Stuttgart: Calwer Verlag, 1971), and Ch. Dietzfelbinger, *Die Berufung des Paulus als Ursprung seiner Theologie* (2d ed.; Neukirchen: Neukirchener Verlag, 1989).

[8] V. P. Furnish, "Development in Paul's Thought," 301; cf. idem, *Theology and Ethics in Paul* (Nashville, TN: Abingdon, 1968) passim.

[9] Furnish, "Development in Paul's Thought," 303.

fact which must be kept in mind as one examines the theological topics relevant to the question of whether changes of thought are evident within the sequence of Paul's letters. In what follows, we shall examine, in connection with Paul's ethical teaching, his understanding of eschatology, his interpretation of the law, and his doctrine of justification by faith.

III

Paul did not construct a fixed system of thought which could, in textbook fashion, have served to provide predetermined answers to all questions which might arise. Confronted with different situations and changing problems, Paul was forced to rethink again and again how the Christian kerygma should be understood and applied to actual problems. It is this vivid dialogue which is reflected in the Pauline epistles.

a) Eschatological expectation. When he wrote 1 Thessalonians, Paul evidently believed that the parousia was imminent and, indeed, would occur within in his own lifetime. It was, in fact, a common conviction of Christians during that early period that this world would come to an end very soon and that the end would bring final judgment and their own ultimate salvation. In the church of Thessalonica, however, Christians were concerned whether those who had recently died would partake of the final salvation. In the face of their lively hope, the continuing reality of death provoked the question, what about those who die before the last day dawns?

Paul picked up this question and gave an answer which was rooted in the very center of the Christian confession. He pointed to the early Christian creed which affirmed "that Jesus died and rose again" (1 Thess 4:14), and moving from this common Christian conviction, he concluded, "God will bring with [Christ] those who have died" (v. 14). The argument which followed was based upon a Jesus-logion taken from the oral tradition. From this saying Paul concluded that in the last day the dead in Christ would rise and then "we"—the Christians, including Paul—"who are alive, who are left until the coming of the Lord, shall be caught up in the clouds together with them to meet the Lord." That is to say, all were expected to partake of the final salvation; the dead would be raised, the living would meet the Lord in the air, and all would be with the Lord forever (vv. 15–17).

It was doubtless Paul's opinion that he himself was among those who would be alive when the final day came. Nevertheless he offers no apocalyptic speculations about end-time conditions. The christological

151

confession is held fast and interpreted so as to allay uncertainty about the future.

In Philippians we find a different situation. Paul was in prison and faced the possibility that he might be condemned and sentenced to death. He did not shrink before this danger but was full of hope that he would soon be with the Lord. He left to God's will any decision about his future. The only important point was that "Christ . . . be exalted now as always in my body, whether by life or by death" (Phil 1:20). "For to me," Paul continued, "living is Christ, and dying is gain. If I am to live in the flesh, that means fruitful labor for me; and I do not know what I prefer. I am hard pressed between the two: my desire is to depart and be with Christ, for that is far better; but to remain in the flesh is more necessary for you" (1:21–24).

So Paul—some years after the composition of 1 Thessalonians—no longer expected that the parousia would come during his own lifetime but reckoned with his death before that event. This means, of course, that a change of thought had occurred, and it is a change which can be observed in other Pauline passages as well (cf. 1 Cor 15:51–57; 2 Cor 5:1–5). Nevertheless the firm conviction remained unchanged: "the Lord is near" (Phil 4:5). This hope, consistently maintained, provided the real reason for rejoicing even in suffering and hard times. The nearness of the κύριος [Lord] was not fundamentally an apocalyptic concept. Paul may have used some apocalyptic terms in the context of his eschatological teaching—the trumpet, angels, the raising of the dead etc.—but these terms were not intended to describe an apocalyptic drama; rather, they illustrated the worldwide relevance of the eschatological event. Paul was not speculating about the limit or the periods of time as was normally done in Jewish apocalyptic writings. Confessing Christ as the κύριος did not include calculations about an eschatological timetable. The only important concern was that of obeying the exalted Lord and trusting in him.

This understanding of eschatology was preserved by Paul in all his letters right to the end. So in Romans 13 we read: "You know what time it is, how it is now the moment for you to wake from sleep. For salvation is nearer to us now than when we first became believers" (13:11). In this passage Paul also expressed his belief that the last day was not far away. Looking forward to the coming event, Christians expected that "the appointed time has grown short" (1 Cor 7:29). What conclusions were to be drawn from this understanding? Paul gave a short and clear answer: Christians ought to live in obedience to the commandments of the Lord, keeping in mind that the time God gave should be used to proclaim the good news throughout the world.

Summing up Paul's statement about the eschatological hope, we find a consistent line of unabated expectation. A clear change is only evident with respect to the length of time remaining, i.e., with respect to whether Paul thought he would still be alive at the parousia or whether he had begun to reckon with the possibility that he might die before that event. His vivid hope was, however, by no means dependent on speculations about space and time; instead, it was entirely bound to Christology. Thus Paul's understanding of eschatology has to be seen as a consequence of interpreting the common Christian creed. There is no evidence for stages of thought which would have developed over the years during which Paul was writing.

b) What about Paul's *interpretation of the law* and its relevance for Christian faith and life? Whereas in earlier expositions of Paul's theology scholars tried to describe his view as more or less uniform, H. Räisänen has argued that Paul offered no clear and definitive insight about the law's relevance.[10] Paul did not work from a consistent theological position but reacted as a pragmatic missionary and preacher, formulating his statements according to the different situations and problems with which he was confronted. H. Hübner has shown the inadequacy of describing Paul's interpretation of the law by reference to Romans alone and the necessity of paying due attention to the special and critical arguments of Galatians. In Hübner's view, it is more correct to proceed from the other direction and read Galatians first. [11]

In the churches of Galatia some teachers had tried to persuade the newly converted Christians to acknowledge the full relevance of Israel's Torah. One of their main claims was that Paul had withheld this material from his preaching because he wanted to please people (Gal 1:10). But the complete gospel had to include the law, and that meant that circumcision had to be practiced (5:2; 6:12), the Jewish calendar had to be observed (4:10) and rules concerning food and ritual purity had to be followed (2:11–21). Only those who did the works demanded by the Torah could be righteous before God.

Paul formulated his response very sharply. Whoever accepted this teaching would be obliged to keep the whole law (5:2). But in so doing they would fall back into that slavery in which they had once lived as pagans (4:9–10). Living under the dominion of the law was, in the end, no better than being subjected to the tyranny of the elemental spirits, as the Galatians had been in the past. This statement clearly constitutes a

---

[10] H. Räisänen, *Paul and the Law* (2d ed.; Tübingen: Mohr-Siebeck, 1987).

[11] H. Hübner, *Das Gesetz bei Paulus - ein Beitrag zum Werden der paulinischen Theologie* (3d ed.; Göttingen: Vandenhoeck & Ruprecht, 1982); ET: *Law in Paul's Thought* (ed. John Riches; Edinburgh: T. & T. Clark, 1984).

very polemical description of life under the law. The strict antithesis is quite evident.[12]

In Romans Paul was not engaged in a controversy as in Galatians but was presenting more general reflections. There are, of course, critical statements: "through the law comes knowledge of sin" (3:20); "the law brings wrath" (4:15); "law came in, with the result that the trespass multiplied" (5:20); etc. But in Romans we find not only negative remarks about the law, but also some positive statements: "the law is holy, and the commandment is holy and just and good" (7:12). Paul thought that if the awful alliance between sin and law were broken then the original goal of the law could be seen anew. And there is the summarizing declaration: "We uphold the law" (3:31), which is to say that in Paul's Christian preaching the original intention of the law was made evident, and thus the law itself became effective in the sense in which God, at the beginning, had given it.

It is Hübner's thesis that a change or a development of thought took place between Galatians and Romans. On his view, Paul was engaged in an ongoing evaluation of arguments which led, in the end, to the more sophisticated view represented in Romans. Surely Paul was not bound to a fixed system of dogmatic principles in his doctrine of the law; nonetheless there are weighty doubts about whether a real change of thought occurred. It seems by far more plausible to interpret the different statements as dependent on the respective situations of the addressees to which the apostle had to react.[13]

Paul did not change his thinking from one stage of his missionary work to the other. He was, on the contrary, an outstanding theologian arguing from a clear theoretical perspective. So also in Galatians, we find not only negative but also positive statements about the law: "the whole law is summed up in a single commandment, 'You shall love your neighbor as yourself'" (5:14). That is to say, God's commandments remained as valid as they had always been, so that Christians must fulfill the "law of Christ" (6:2). Whenever Paul was talking about the relevance of the law, either in Galatians or in Romans, it was absolutely clear that justification could never be gained by doing the works of the law, but could only be received as God's gift of mercy, accepted by faith.

---

[12] Paul's understanding of the law is treated in several contributions to the recent debate; see U. Wilckens, "Zur Entwicklung des paulinischen Gesetzesverständnisses," *NTS* 28 (1982) 154–90; G. Klein, "Werkruhm und Christusruhm im Galaterbrief und die Frage nach einer Entwicklung des Paulus. Ein hermeneutischer und exegetischer Zwischenruf," in *Studien zum Text und zur Ethik des Neuen Testaments. Festschrift H. Greeven* (Berlin/New York: de Gruyter, 1986) 196–211; P. Zeller, "Zur neueren Diskussion über das Gesetz bei Paulus," *TP* 62 (1987) 481–99.

[13] Cf. K. Niederwimmer's critical review of Hübner's book, *TLZ* 105 (1980) 896–98.

Justification included, however, the strong obligation to live in obedience to God's will. And it is just in this connection that the positive statements about the persistent authority of the law are linked with the arguments for Christian ethics.

c) The special terminology related to Paul's understanding of *justification by faith* is not found in all of his letters, but mainly in Galatians, Philippians and Romans. How is this fact to be evaluated? Some scholars have revived critical viewpoints which were noted in our earlier discussions. So they suppose that Paul did not teach a doctrine of justification from the beginning of his missionary work but was forced by the confrontation in the Galatian churches to develop his understanding of this theme. [14] It is true enough that 1 Thessalonians does not expound a theology of justification, but the problem is how to interpret this fact. Is it that Paul, in his earliest letter, had a deeper understanding of the Christian creed, confessing that the crucified and resurrected Christ is Lord, and that his doctrine of justification developed later in the polemical situation into which he was thrust in writing to the churches in Galatia?

There are, it seems to me, some important objections to be made to this thesis. For Paul was not restricted to employing a special terminology in all cases. In the Corinthian correspondence, his theology of the cross and of redemption became the vehicle for explaining the central relevance of the gospel. In comparison with Galatians, Philippians, and Romans, we find in Corinthians a different terminology, but that does not necessarily point to a different theological understanding. On the contrary, in 1 Thessalonians as well Jesus is described as the savior "who rescues us from the wrath that is coming" (1:10).

This conviction proceeded from the common Christian confession. For Paul argued—as was mentioned earlier—that "since we believe that Jesus died and rose again, even so, through Jesus, God will bring with him those who have died." (1 Thess 4:14) This verse reveals how, right from the beginning of his missionary work, the apostle was interpreting the early Christian kerygma. For he not only referred to Christ's death and resurrection, but at the same time he pointed to its meaning for those who believed and trusted that this message was true. H. Conzelmann was therefore right when he stated that Paul always

---

[14] See esp. G. Strecker, "Befreiung und Rechtfertigung. Zur Stellung der Rechtfertigungslehre in der Theologie des Paulus," in *Rechtfertigung. Festschrift für E. Käsemann* (Tübingen: Mohr-Siebeck; Göttingen: Vandenhoeck & Ruprecht, 1976) 479–508, repr. in *Eschatologie und Geschichte. Aufsätze* (Göttingen: Vandenhoeck & Ruprecht, Göttingen, 1979) 229–59. Strecker mentions especially W. Wrede and A. Schweitzer, who had discussed this problem earlier.

explained the Christian confession in a way that related Christology and anthropology to one another. Nowhere did he make christological statements *per se* but he always emphasized that the content of the gospel is directed to us.[15] When the faithful answer is given, the real meaning of the message is accepted and understood.

This fundamental structure of theological interpretation is found in all of Paul's letters without any change of thought. Paul uses varying terms to express this central relevance of the good news, but the interrelation between Christology and anthropology was described most convincingly in Paul's theology of justification. When he had to refute the false doctrine of those teachers who had come to Galatia, Paul drew upon the example of Abraham and the faith by which he trusted in God's promise: "and it was reckoned to him as righteousness" (Gal 3:6). The long explanation which Paul gives about this Old Testament story must have been developed earlier in intensive discussions about this most important biblical passage. In those discussions Paul could make use of some early Christian formulations in which the meaning of righteousness and justification had been expressed already. For Christ "was handed over to death for our trespasses and was raised for our justification" (Rom 4:25; cf. further Rom 3:25–26; 1 Cor 6:11). We should not, therefore, suppose that it is only when he was confronted with judaizing positions that Paul had to develop his understanding of justification. Rather, it had been the consistently central structure of his thinking which was fundamental for his preaching and teaching.

These arguments lead one to agree with F. Hahn when he says that one finds no development in the understanding of justification in the authentic Pauline epistles.[16] The apostle may use different words and terms to express the central meaning of the gospel, but the structure of his thinking did not change. On the contrary, Paul's understanding of the gospel and his doctrine of justification are identical, in regard both to its intention and to its content.

IV

Reading one Pauline letter after the other, one will observe a scarlet thread running from beginning to end. On the one hand, each letter is a document all its own. But on the other, the inner continuity will not

---

[15] H. Conzelmann, "Die Rechtfertigungslehre des Paulus. Theologie oder Anthropologie?" in *Theologie als Schriftauslegung* (Munich: Chr. Kaiser, 1974) 191–214; here, 196.

[16] See F. Hahn, "Gibt es eine Entwicklung in den Aussagen über die Rechtfertigung bei Paulus?" in *The Truth of the Gospel (Galatians 1:1–4:11)* (ed. J. Lambrecht; Mon. Series of "Benedictina," 12; Rome: St. Paul's Abbey, 1993) 187–232 = *EvT* 53 (1993) 342–66.

be fully understood when one tries to examine the special theology of each letter separately without looking at the connections with the others. [17] For in the end scholars engaged in this enterprise will not only present different opinions about the interpretation of each individual letter, but will find it even more problematic to delineate the outlines of Pauline theology as a whole. On the contrary, it is necessary to describe the main lines of the apostle's theological thinking.

A very stimulating thesis was put forward by J. C. Beker in his profound book, *Paul, the Apostle. The Triumph of God in Life and Thought.*[18] Since then he has further explained his interpretation in some essays which should be read in connection with his book.[19] Beker is describing a "via media" between two extremes: a sociological analysis on the one side and a dogmatic imposition of a specific center on Paul's thought on the other side. The fundamental structure of thought is characterized as "the truth of the gospel, i.e. the apocalyptic interpretation of the Christ event in its significance for the eschatological triumph of God."[20] This consistent understanding is applied to the different challenges Paul encountered in his churches. So the coherent answers Paul gave to the various problems are to be seen in their relation to the consistency of his guiding theological interpretation.

Beker's "via media" quite helpfully avoids extremes which will not do justice to Paul's theology. But one has to ask whether Beker gives too much weight to the role of apocalypticism in his description of the final triumph of God. It seems to me more convincing to say that it was not an apocalyptic worldview but the christological message of the gospel which formed the leading idea out of which the whole of Paul's theological thinking developed. The central relevance of the gospel was underlined in all his epistles, even in the short letter to Philemon. Although Paul declared emphatically that he was called "neither by human commission nor from human authorities, but through Jesus Christ and God the Father, who raised him from the dead" (Gal 1:1), he did his work in solidarity with the other apostles and evangelists. And although he was convinced that he neither received the gospel from a human source nor was taught it, but "received it through a revelation of

---

[17] This is done in *Pauline Theology, Volume I: Thessalonians, Philippians, Galatians, Philemon* (ed. J. M. Bassler; Minneapolis, MN: Fortress, 1991); and *Pauline Theology, Volume II: 1 and 2 Corinthians* (ed. David M. Hay; Minneapolis, MN: Fortress, 1993).

[18] J. C. Beker, *Paul, the Apostle. The Triumph of God in Life and Thought* (2d ed.; Edinburgh: T. & T. Clark, 1984).

[19] Cf. J. C. Beker, "Paul's Theology: Consistent or Inconsistent?" *NTS* 34 (1988) 364–67; idem, "Recasting Pauline Theology. The Coherence-Contingency Scheme as Interpretive Model," in *Pauline Theology, Vol. 1,* 15–24.

[20] "Paul's Theology: Consistent or Inconsistent?" 375.

Jesus Christ" (Gal 1:12), he did not hesitate to characterize the content of this message by quoting formulas which had been shaped already by earliest Christianity (1 Cor 15:3–5; Rom 1:3–4 and others). For by doing so he was able to demonstrate that there is one and only one gospel (Gal 1:6–9). This good news was proclaimed by all messengers wherever they preached (1 Cor 15:11).

The gospel was not proclaimed by quoting a fixed formula as a sacred text, but the good news had to be addressed to the audience and interpreted in order to underline its concrete meaning. So whenever Paul picked up preshaped texts, he added his comments in order to express the actual meaning of the Christian message. This was Paul's understanding of his missionary work, as can be seen from a comparison of two texts in which he spoke of his appointment as an apostle of Christ. First in Galatians, he wrote of "when God, who had set me apart before I was born and called me through his grace, was pleased to reveal his Son to me, so that I might proclaim him among the Gentiles . . ." (1:15–16). That means that Paul was entrusted to confess and to preach Christ as Son of God. Then in Philippians, Paul referred to the same event using the terminology of justification: "not having a righteousness of my own that comes from the law, but one which comes through faith in Christ, the righteousness from God based on faith" (3:9). When these two passages are compared with one another it is clear that preaching the gospel means interpreting its relevance by pointing to justification by faith. Certainly both texts were written a good while after Paul's conversion. There are, however, no reasons to distrust Paul's statements when he described his call in this way. For as a Pharisee he had been familiar with the problems of law and justification. But in his encounter with the crucified and risen Lord, it was revealed to him that law and justification would be understood rightly only when they were interpreted entirely in the light of Christology. It was exactly this new understanding by which Paul was guided in his apostolic preaching without any change of thought.

It may have taken some time before Paul evaluated all the consequences of his new insight. But there was a long span of years, about which very little news is preserved, before Paul composed his first extant letter. By the time he began writing, he was by no means a beginner, but a theologian who had for many years thought about his understanding and interpretation of the gospel.[21] If some development of

---

[21] One should, therefore, not make too sharp a distinction between the message of 1 Thessalonians and that of the following epistles, as some scholars are inclined to do. Cf. Th. Söding, "Der erste Thessalonicherbrief und die frühe paulinische Evangeliumsverkündigung. Zur Frage einer Entwicklung der paulinischen Theologie," *BZ* 35 (1991) 180–203.

thought occurred, it must have taken place before 1 Thessalonians was composed, but not during the six or seven years in which Paul's authentic letters were written. It is an important testimony to the high rank of Paul's thinking that he was neither bound to a fixed system of doctrine nor dependent on changing influences from outside. On the contrary, he was able to respond to different situations and to formulate the actual relevance of the gospel again and again by taking into consideration the problems which had to be answered in each congregation and church.

A very important part of his preaching and teaching was Paul's ethical instruction which is as consistent as his whole theology. There are no convincing arguments to show that 1 Thessalonians embodies a less developed understanding of ethical obligation than the following letters. For the law of Moses, to which some scholars point in this connection (see above, p. 147), is in fact nowhere mentioned in the whole letter. In this epistle as in all other Pauline ethical comments the same structure and understanding of paraenesis is found. That means that ethical teaching was unfolded under the eschatological perspective of Paul's theology, which is closely related to Christology.

We read that Paul had spoken in Thessalonica of how Christians "ought to live and to please God" (1 Thess 4:1). "For," the apostle says, "you know what instructions we gave you through the Lord Jesus" (v. 2). To this general instruction was added a series of individual exhortations which, in turn, were strengthened by the reminder "to aspire to live quietly, to mind your own affairs, and to work with your hands, as we directed you, so that you may behave properly towards outsiders" (vv. 11–12). These statements include references to tradition, to specific commandments, and to that which is generally accepted as right conduct. The confession of Jesus as Lord was to be validated to "outsiders" by the credible conduct of Christians. If a positive evaluation of Christians by "outsiders" was expected, this meant that the rules that governed moral conduct in general were also to be observed by Christians. "To live in accordance with the instructions given through the Lord Jesus" (cf. 4:2) was, in brief, the content of Christian ethics. It referred to conduct of the individual as well as to the common life in the community, without separating either from the other. The commanding authority of the Lord applied to all realms of the life of the believers.[22]

In our last preserved Pauline document as in the first one, the ethical instruction was presented from an eschatological perspective: "the night

---

[22] Cf. E. Lohse, *Theologische Ethik des Neuen Testaments* (Stuttgart: Kohlhammer, 1988) 9–10; ET: *Theological Ethics of the New Testament* (Minneapolis, MN: Fortress, 1991) 2–3.

is far gone, the day is near. Let us then lay aside the works of darkness and put on the armor of light" (Rom 13:12). Christians are people who belong to the day; that is, they live their lives in the light of the dawning day of the Lord. They must therefore "keep awake" and "be sober" (1 Thess 5:5–6). What can be done stealthily in the darkness does not even come into consideration for Christians: reveling and drunkenness, debauchery and licentiousness, quarreling and jealousy. The appropriate response to the time is "to put on the Lord Jesus Christ" (Rom 13:13–14). Such words in fact leave no doubt: by pointing to the ultimate day of the Lord and the kind of life it demands in the present age, one can derive clear directions for leading one's life.[23]

So it is evident that there is a consistent understanding of Christian ethics in all the authentic Pauline epistles. Christians are charged with the responsibility of living their life "in a manner worthy of the gospel of Christ" (Phil 1:27). By pointing to the central relevance of the gospel, Paul integrated his ethical teaching into the context of his whole theology. The eschatological basis of ethical instruction affirms that the future salvation has already come near (Rom 13:11). All the same, the confidence of this expectation is not dependent on calculating how far advanced the hands of the world clock may be. Whether the Lord would come during the lifetime of the apostle or only after his death was a matter of no importance. The sole decisive thing was the conviction that Christians belong to the Lord, who has delivered his own from darkness and placed them in the clear light of day. They cannot therefore continue in the works of darkness, but must put on the armor of light (Rom 13:12).[24]

Paul may have changed his way of speaking to the various churches and the terminology by which he explained the common Christian kerygma,[25] but he did not change his fundamental theological thought.[26] That means that Paul's theology "is best described not as lineal and developing but as complex and dialectical."[27]

---

[23] Cf. Lohse, *Theologische Ethik*, 33 (ET, 42–43).

[24] Cf. Lohse, *Theologische Ethik*, 73 (ET, 112).

[25] Cf. W. G. Kümmel, "Das Problem einer Entwicklung in der Theologie des Paulus," *NTS* 18 (1971/72) 457–58.

[26] W. Schrage, *Ethik des Neuen Testaments* (2d ed.; Göttingen: Vandenhoeck & Ruprecht, 1989) 169; ET of 1982 ed.: *The Ethics of the New Testament* (Philadelphia: Fortress, 1988).

[27] Furnish, "Development in Paul's Thought," 303. Cf. further G. Lüdemann, *Paulus der Heidenapostel* I (Göttingen: Vandenhoeck & Ruprecht, 1980) 21 n. 11 and 228 n. 52.

Deuteropauline Ethics:
Some Observations

C. K. Barrett

If we begin by excluding the historical Paul, known to us by means of the certainly genuine letters, there appear to be two lines of ethical tradition running through the later parts of the New Testament. The sharp contrast between them makes it possible to take a clearer view of each, and it will therefore be rewarding to begin with a brief consideration of that line which does not constitute the major theme of this paper. This line is to be found in the gospels or, more specifically, in the Synoptic Gospels; John may be excluded from the present discussion since, so far as that Gospel may be said to rest upon early tradition, it has absorbed and reinterpreted the tradition in accordance with the specifically Johannine outlook and material. In the Synoptic Gospels there is a vein of radical ethical material, attributed to Jesus, which is neither philosophically systematic nor adapted to the variety of practical situations. Precepts are given which have the effect not of giving the hearer directions that will enable him or her to choose between ethical alternatives but of placing the hearer in the presence of a God who always requires nothing less than total obedience. To quote one who has given classical—and it may be, in some respects, exaggerated— expression to this understanding of the teaching of Jesus, Jesus'

> ethic . . . is strictly opposed to every humanistic and value ethic; it is an ethic of obedience. He sees the meaning of human action not in the development toward an ideal of man which is founded on the human spirit . . . the concept of an ideal or end is foreign to him . . . he sees only the individual man standing before the will of God . . . This really means that *Jesus teaches no ethics at all* in the sense of an intelligible theory valid for all men concerning what should be done and left undone.[1]

The requirement of obedience is from time to time illustrated in practical terms: the command to love one's enemies (which surely must on occasion mean correcting or restraining them) may be fulfilled by going an extra mile with one who commandeers one's services. But

---

[1] R. Bultmann, *Jesus and the Word* (London: Nicholson & Watson 1935) 84.

there are also commands which, taken literally and applied universally, would lead to the breakdown of society. Sell all that you have and give to the poor (thereby creating another penniless person); if anyone comes to me and does not hate his own father and mother and wife and children and brothers and sisters . . . he cannot be my disciple. Such commands are not serious ethics but a very powerful—and paradoxical—statement of the all-embracing claim made by Jesus in the name of God. This radical claim is made with an authority, for the most part undefined, which is the basis of all Christological development, and both the ethical content and the doctrinal foundation of the claim are accessible to inference rather than to explicit interpretation. The Christological element and the ethical element stand in close relation to each other; what we are dealing with here is Christological ethics.

This is of course not a complete account of the ethics of the gospels. As a counterpart to Bultmann's interpretation we may put E. Käsemann's essay "Sätze Heiligen Rechtes im Neuen Testament,"[2] though Käsemann does little to pursue his theme within the Synoptic Gospels. There are places where a primitive tradition, absolute in form, is accommodated to practical circumstances and thereby turned into observable law. A familiar and clear example is provided by Mark 10:2–12, on marriage and divorce. The teaching is provided by Mark with a setting (v. 2) which, describing the Pharisees as tempting Jesus, presents the material as controversial. So in itself it is, for Jesus contradicts the teaching of Moses (Deut 24:1) and represents marriage as indissoluble. This is done by means of a reference to creation. God created man and woman to be joined together as one flesh, and the conclusion follows: ὃ οὖν ὁ θεὸς συνέζευξεν, ἄνθρωπος μὴ χωριζέτω [therefore what God has joined together, let no one separate]. This is the core of the tradition; Mark explains it, using an inquiry by the disciples (v. 10) as his means of introducing the piece of sacred law: If you divorce your wife and marry another you are committing adultery. Therefore, don't do it. This was a hard command, hard not only by reason of the desires of flesh and blood but also because it contradicted Moses. Matthew accordingly modifies the teaching by assimilating it to the terms of current Jewish discussion.[3] Moses permitted divorce; yet it disrupts families and clearly ought to be avoided if possible. We must therefore ask, in what circumstances is divorce permissible? Matthew (19:9) answers, divorce is wrong because it leads to adultery and must be avoided except where the marriage has already been broken by sexual unfaithfulness (μὴ ἐπὶ πορνείᾳ). Mark has a different addition

---

[2] *NTS* 1 (1955) 248–60.

[3] Cf. the well-known disagreement between Hillel and Shammai (*Giṭṭin* 9.10).

(probably unknown to Matthew and Luke). What applies to men applies also to women: If she who has divorced her husband marries another, she commits adultery. In Jewish law, women were not able to divorce their husbands; Mark 10:12 is a practical inference providing legislation for the Hellenistic world in which they had this right. As for men, remarriage meant adultery and was therefore forbidden. It was, however, easier to be specific over religious than over ethical requirements; easier for example to declare that no food entering the stomach could defile the eater than to be specific about those things that come out from within and do defile. Some indeed are clear enough—fornication, theft, murder, adultery, deceit, lasciviousness—but others are not. In this context, however, the words of Mark 7:19, καθαρίζων πάντα τὰ βρώματα [he declared all foods clean], point back to the personal authority of Jesus. What Moses declares unclean he declares clean. The ethics, the ethically expressed theological assertion, is based on the assertion of the authority of Christ, in whom God in his kingdom draws near in judgment and mercy.

The historical Paul was prepared to handle specific ethical problems when they were presented to him, whether by those who sought instruction in what they should do or by those who were able to report problems that had arisen in the churches. Thus, 1 Corinthians 7 contains treatment of the problems of marriage and divorce analogous (though not identical) with that in Mark 10. But it is more characteristic of Paul that he too deals (though in a way different from that of the synoptic tradition) with the Christological roots of ethics. The essence of the matter is that one died for all in order that those who are alive should live no longer for themselves but for him who on their behalf died and was raised (2 Cor 5:15). Paul's lists of vices (works of the flesh, Gal 5:19–21) and of virtues (fruit of the Spirit, Gal 5:22f.) are similar to those of Mark 7. We are given no examples of the ways in which love, joy, peace, and the rest are to be manifested. As soon as we step into the deuteropauline letters a change is apparent. Colossians and Ephesians both contain sets of household rules: for husbands, wives, children, parents, slaves, and masters. Neither of these epistles is unaware of the spiritual depth and ethical spontaneity of life lived in Christ, but in these passages (Col 3:28–4:1; Eph 5:22–6:9) Christians are provided with a code; and there is other ethical material of the same kind.

The tendency to codify Christian behavior appears much more strongly in the Pastorals. According to M. Dibelius[4] the Pastorals are characterized by "Bürgerlichkeit," a word that defies translation: it describes the character and attitude of the good, honest, decent,

---

[4] *Die Pastoralbriefe* (HNT 13; Tübingen: Mohr-Siebeck, 1955) 7.

ordinary citizen. Household rules reappear, though the family is now the church rather than the natural family: thus 1 Tim 5:1 (how to treat an older man, younger men, older women, younger women) and Titus 2:2–6 (rules for old men; rules for older women, who must instruct younger ones; rules for younger men). Most important in this respect are the social and moral qualifications required in church officers— bishops (or elders) and deacons. These, as has long been recognized, present many parallels with the qualifications that were looked for in candidates for civil office (see, e.g., Dibelius, *Pastoralbriefe*, 42–48). There is certainly nothing to complain of here. It was—and is— desirable that Christian ministers should be as upright and as intelligent as members of the civil service. The lists of qualifications are both more explicit and less inspiring than "We do not proclaim ourselves; we proclaim Jesus Christ as Lord, and ourselves as your slaves for Jesus' sake" (2 Cor 4:5). The minister must be "free from reproach, faithful to his one wife,[5] sober, sensible, dignified, hospitable, good at teaching, not given to wine or violence, but gentle, peaceable, no lover of money, presiding well over his own household, having children who are kept in order and fully respectful, . . . not a new convert . . . he must have a good reputation with those outside the church" (auth. tr.). These are the requirements of an ἐπίσκοπος [bishop] in 1 Tim 3:2–7; διάκονοι [deacons] must show similar virtues (3:8–12). They are admirable qualities, whether in Christian ministers or in city councillors. Paul would (perhaps unwisely—people sometimes let him down) have taken them for granted. In addition to these passages the Pastorals are full of good, sensible advice, calculated to produce Christians who will win the respect of all honorable and intelligent men. There is no space here to give it in detail.

In Acts there is little explicit ethical teaching. It is true that hearers of the apostolic message are urged to repent (Acts 2:38 *et al.*), but apart from the implication that those responsible should repent of killing Jesus we are not told of what sins they should repent. Nor are we told with what virtues they should replace their vices. It is clear enough that some people are regarded as "good" and others are not. Barnabas does well in selling his property for the benefit of others (4:36–37); Ananias and Sapphira are not good when they try to deceive the Holy Spirit (5:1–11). It is clearly implied that to flog and imprison Paul and Silas was a bad thing[6] and that to wash their wounds and feed them was good (16:19–34). This is scarcely advanced casuistry, though as ethics it may

---

[5] There are other interpretations of this obscure phrase.

[6] But why? because they were innocent? because they had not had a judicial hearing? because they were Roman citizens?

perhaps be regarded as being on the same level as the simple but adequate theology of Acts. Christians who look to God for forgiveness should perform works worthy of repentance (26:20). And it is assumed that we all know well enough what that means.

These observations are superficial, but they may lead to a further step in the discussion. In our glance at the Synoptic Gospels, it was possible to use Bultmann's perhaps exaggerated understanding of the tradition. Here we may make a similar critical use of E. Haenchen's comment on Acts 23:1 (ἐγὼ πάσῃ συνειδήσει ἀγαθῇ πεπολίτευμαι τῷ θεῷ ἄχρι ταύτης τῆς ἡμέρας [up to this day I have lived my life with a clear conscience before God]). He writes, "Diese Theologie des 'guten Gewissens' wird in der nachapostolischen Literatur beliebt," and in a footnote refers to 1 Tim 1:5, 19; 3:9; 2 Tim 1:3; 1 Pet 3:16, 21; Heb 9:14; 13:18.[7] Earlier in his note he has referred to the close parallel in Acts 24:16 (ἀσκῶ ἀπρόσκοπον συνείδησιν ἔχειν [I do my best always to have a clear conscience]). It is not clear what Haenchen means by "this theology of the 'good conscience,'" or indeed whether *theology* is an appropriate word. In the two passages quoted, Paul is simply asserting that he has at all times behaved as a good Jew, though his understanding of what being a good Jew meant had suffered a violent change when he discovered that God had raised Jesus from death. This is an important factor in Paul's view (or what Luke believed Paul's view to have been) of the relation between Christianity and Judaism, but neither Luke nor Paul asserts that Paul's relationship with God depends on his having maintained a good conscience (though Acts contains no such vigorous disclaimer as 1 Cor 4:4). The word συνείδησις [conscience] occurs nowhere else in Acts; it does occur six times in the Pastorals (1 Tim 1:5, 19; 3:9; 4:2; 2 Tim 1:3; Titus 1:15), but it also occurs fourteen times in Romans and 1 and 2 Corinthians, so that as a word it cannot be regarded as postpauline. It is true that the conscience plays a somewhat different role in the Pastorals from that which it plays in the genuine letters; this provides at least a partial justification (as Acts does not) for Haenchen's view of its popularity and distinctiveness. Love, faith, and a good conscience commend us to God; beware lest your conscience become seared or defiled. Too much should not be made of this. The 'good conscience' may have the effect of devaluing love and faith, but the reverse process also is in operation. "Das gute Gewissen ist somit mehr als das schlichte reine Herz der alttestament-

---

[7] ["This theology of the 'good conscience' is popular in the post-apostolic literature."] E. Haenchen, *Die Apostelgeschichte* (KEK III; Göttingen: Vandenhoeck & Ruprecht, 1977) 609; E.T. of 14th German ed. (1965): *The Acts of the Apostles: A Commentary* (Philadelphia: Westminster, 1971) 637.

lichen Frommen . . . . So sind an diesem Punkte die Pastoralbriefe nicht nur das Produkt christlicher Bürgerlichkeit, sondern ebenso das bewusste Echo des paulinischen Rechtfertigungsbotschaft, aus der heraus sie gewachsen sind."[8] What we may take out of the two verses in Acts and use as the starting-point for future inquiry is not so much the use of συνείδησις as of the verbs that accompany it, πολιτεύεσθαι [to live, conduct one's life] and ἀσκεῖν [to practice, engage in something]. These in turn suggest a number of others: ἀγών (+ ἀγωνίζεσθαι); ἀθλεῖν; γυμνάζειν (+ γυμνασία); ἐγκράτεια (+ ἐγκρατεύεσθαι, ἐγκρατής); προκοπή (+ προκόπτειν).[9]

Most of these words have their primary reference to the games, to the life and effort of the athlete; in the New Testament they are of course used metaphorically, or in similes. Paul himself had done this; for example, at 1 Cor 9:25–27, and probably at Phil 1:27, 30. The deuteropauline use however is different. In 1 Corinthians and Philippians the thought concentrates upon the fierce and disciplined contest itself. You must run hard and fight hard; behind the exhortation lies Paul's awareness of a contest into which he has to enter with himself; ὑπωπιάζω μου τὸ σῶμα [I punish my body]. In Philippians (cf. Colossians), the ἀγών [struggle] is rather with external circumstances. Paul's own circumstances are made clear in the epistle itself. He is in prison (1:13, 17) and facing the possibility of death (1:21–23); and he has reason to think that his readers are in a comparable situation; they are sharing the same ἀγών (1:30) and in it he urges them to join unitedly in the contest (συναθλοῦντες).[10] This basic sense is of course inseparable from the language used, but the general image of athletics is wide, and, on the whole, the later writers choose to emphasize another aspect of it.

In the two Acts passages referred to above the verbs are πολιτεύεσθαι and ἀσκεῖν. The former may not be significant. Though it referred originally to the conduct of the citizen in relation to his πόλις [city], it came to mean no more than *to conduct oneself*. Here it need not mean more than this. It does, however, seem to have been used with special reference to behavior in relation to the Jewish πολιτεία

---

[8] C. Maurer, "σύνοιδα, συνείδησις," *TWNT* 7.917—putting the matter perhaps a little too strongly. [*TDNT* 7:918 – "(The good conscience) is also more than the pure and simple heart of the OT righteous. . . . At this point, then, the Pastorals are not the product of Christian respectability; they are a deliberate echo of the Pauline message of justification out of which they grew."]

[9] [contest, struggle (+ to struggle); to compete; to exercise (+ training); self control (+ to control oneself, self-controlled) progress (+ to progress)]. More could be added; those mentioned here suffice for a brief sketch.

[10] Cf. also Col 1:29; 2:1; 4:12, where Pauline authorship cannot be reckoned certain.

[community, body politic], and this seems to be the sense that Luke is putting into Paul's mouth. From the beginning up to the present day he has conducted himself conscientiously in strict accordance with the Jewish way of life, which he follows as understood by Pharisees (23:6). This has nothing to do with a "theology of the good conscience," or with the point that will emerge as we proceed.

Ἀσκεῖν, which occurs nowhere else in the New Testament, is different. It may mean *to work curiously, to form by art, to dress out, to trick out,* but its most characteristic meaning is *to practice, exercise, train,* "properly of athletic exercise."[11] From this the metaphorical use developed, and it was used of training, exercise, in truth, righteousness, virtue. "Diese Bedeutung von ἀσκεῖν ist schon dem klassischen und hellenistischen Griechisch geläufig."[12] "I see that as those who do not train their bodies (τοὺς μὴ τὰ σώματα ἀσκοῦντας) are not able to do the things proper to the body, so those who do not train the soul (τοὺς μὴ τὴν ψυχὴν ἀσκοῦντας) are not able to do the things of the soul."[13] This use of ἀσκεῖν (and of ἄσκησις) continued into the post-classical age; thus, for example in the Cynic Epistles, *Epistle* 19, to Patrocles (68.26), . . . ἐπὶ τῷ τὴν ἀρετὴν ἀσκῆσαι ἀνδρεῖον [. . . courageous in the practice of virtue]. Acts 24:16 goes further than 23:1. Paul does not simply assert that his conscience is clear; he trains his conscience in order to keep it clear, a particularized version of Xenophon's training of the soul.

The imagery of other words is even more explicit. Thus, in 1 Tim 4:7, 8 there occurs the pair γυμνάζειν [to exercise], γυμνασία [training]. Their original sense requires no illustration. There is a neat parallel to "Paul's" use with the reflexive pronoun in Epictetus, *Discourses,* 2.18.27, where Epictetus is emphasizing the importance of attention to what is true over against mere appearance. "This is the athlete concerned for truths (ὁ ταῖς ἀληθείαις ἀσκητής; see ἀσκεῖν above), he who exercises himself (ὁ . . . γυμνάζων ἑαυτόν) against such appearances." Over against σωματικὴ γυμνασία [bodily exercise], which has its uses, 1 Timothy sets piety, εὐσέβεια, the practice of which involves serious training. 1 Tim 4:8 is to be connected with v. 10, to which v. 9 provides the emphatic pointer, you know this is true, and you must accept it. To this end we labor and strive (κοπιῶμεν καὶ ἀγωνιζόμεθα—the latter

---

[11] Liddell and Scott, 257. See also F. Pfister, "Ἄσκησις," in *Festgabe für Adolf Deissmann* (Tübingen: Mohr-Siebeck, 1927) 76–81; H. Dressler, *The Usage of ἀσκέω and Its Cognates in Greek Documents to 100 A.D.* (Washington, DC: Catholic University of America Press, 1947).

[12] H. Windisch, "ἀσκέω," in *TWNT* 1.492 (TDNT 1:494 – "This sense of ἀσκεῖν is already current in classical and hellenistic Greek").

[13] Xenophon, *Memorabilia* 1.2.19; see the whole paragraph, 1.2.19–28.

167

another word derived from athletics); the attainment of piety is not easy, and the training for it includes hope and faith.

The Pastorals use another related word, ἀθλεῖν (2 Tim 2:5). The literal meaning of the verb is *to take part in the games, to contend for a prize*. No athlete can win unless he contends νομίμως [lawfully]. Again there is a parallel in Epictetus, *Disc.*, 3.10.8; God speaks: δός μοι ἀπόδειξιν, εἰ νομίμως ἤθλησας [Give me proof, whether you have striven lawfully]. The words that follow bring out the meaning of νομίμως: εἰ ἔφαγες ὅσα δεῖ, εἰ ἐγυμνάσθης, εἰ τοῦ ἀλείπτου ἤκουσας ["whether you have eaten what is prescribed, taken exercise, heeded your trainer"; LCL 218:75]. That is, to contend *lawfully* is to observe the rules of training. It is implied that there are rules of training for the Christian athlete, and whoever does not observe them will not receive the promised crown. This is interesting and important in itself, in that it indicates an attitude to and understanding of Christian life. It is important too in that it points out the correct interpretation of 1 Tim 1:8: the law is good ἐάν τις αὐτῷ νομίμως χρῆται [if one uses it legitimately]. That is (one may suggest), the law is good if one uses it as a means of training in the good life, the life of piety. The law is no threat to a good person who thus uses it for instruction in the way of obedience; it is a threat only to those who disregard it, who are ἄνομοι, and express their lawlessness in the various ways listed in vv. 9, 10, which (as we say) "break training." It is in agreement with this that a vital constituent in training for the Christian life is ἐγκράτεια ("self control"; Acts 24:25), and that the *episcopus* must be ἐγκρατής (Titus 1:8). Self-control, self-discipline, is an essential quality of the Christian athlete, whose aim must be to fight the καλὸν ἀγῶνα ("good fight"; 1 Tim 6:12; 2 Tim 4:8; cf. 1 Tim 1:18). The use of ἀγών and ἀγωνίζεσθαι [fight and to fight] points, in the Pauline fashion, rather to the contest itself than to the training undergone in preparation for it.

This sketch of some of the background material is enough to show that the deuteropauline works, especially Acts and the Pastorals, are related to earlier and contemporary moral philosophers in their concept of training for the good life. They have of course a somewhat different (not entirely different) concept of what the good life is, but they agree that it is not achieved automatically or without effort. As the athlete exercises self-control and obeys the rules laid down by his trainer (ἀλείστης), so as a Christian, one must obey the laws that God has given and be prepared to deny oneself and stand firm in faith in order to make sure of receiving the crown that God has promised to all who have set their hearts on Christ's appearing (2 Tim 4:8). To this must be added a further observation.

168

This language and this framework of thought had already been taken up in Judaism. To complete the quotation from Windisch given above, "Diese Bedeutung von ἀσκεῖν ist schon dem klassischen und hellenistischen Griechish geläufig, ebenso dem jüdischen Hellenismus."[14] Windisch rightly adds, "Begriff und Sache hat dann Philo in die theologische Ethik eingeführt."[15] The evidence is plentiful, notably in Philo's description of Jacob as ὁ ἀσκητής [the athlete]. Among the patriarchs Abraham represents μάθησις [learning], Isaac φύσις [nature], Jacob ἄσκησις [exercise, training]. He is the one who learns by practice, who trains himself in virtue; ἀσκητής, the man in training, is suggested by ἀθλητής, the man who practices athletics, and Jacob is shown to be such a man by the story of Gen 32.24–32, Jacob's wrestling match with the mysterious figure at the brook Jabbok. The outcome of the process of ἄσκησις is Jacob's change of name; he becomes Israel, which Philo interprets as ὁρῶν θεόν, the one who sees God. The end of moral and spiritual training is the vision of God. Thus for example *Mig.* 200, 201: παλαίοντος γὰρ καὶ κονιομένου καὶ πτερνίζοντος Ἰακώβ ἐστιν ὄνομα, οὐ νενικηκότος· ὅταν δὲ τὸν θεὸν ὁρᾶν ἱκανὸς εἶναι δόξας Ἰσραὴλ μετονομασθῇ . . . [For "Jacob" is a name belonging to one wrestling, and preparing for the arena, and tripping up his adversary, not of one who has won the victory. But when, now deemed capable of seeing God, he shall have received the new name of "Israel" . . . (LCL 261:249)]. This spiritual advance is προκοπή, progress. At *Ebr.* 82 Jacob is introduced as ὁ ἀσκητής [The Man of Practice]; his is a name for learning and progress (μαθήσεως καὶ προκοπῆς); but Israel is a name for perfection (τελειότητος); ὅρασιν γὰρ θεοῦ μηνύει τοὔνομα ["for the name expresses the vision of God" (LCL 247:359)].

Other words that have been considered can be found in Philo. *Spec. Leg.* 2.183 will cover at once two words. The priests' privileges may be γέρας ἀγώνων, οὓς ὑπὲρ εὐσεβείας ἀθλοῦσιν [a reward for the contests they take part in for the sake of piety]. Philo comes near to a more literal understanding of training when he says that the law is concerned περὶ τοῦ γυμνάσαι καὶ συγκροτῆσαι ψυχὴν πρὸς ἀνδρείαν (*Virt.* 18 ["to train and exercise the soul to manly courage," LCL 320:421]). In *Vit. Mos.* 1.48 he combines the theoretical and the practical (θεωρητικὸν καὶ πρακτικόν) in a sentence full of relevant words: τοὺς ἀρετῆς ἄθλους Μωυσῆς διῆθλει τὸν ἀλείπτην ἔχων ἐν ἑαυτῷ λογισμὸν ἀστεῖον, ὑφ᾿ οὗ γυμναζόμενος πρὸς τοὺς ἀρίστους βίους [Moses was carrying out the exercises of virtue with an admirable

[14] See n. 12 (. . . and also in Jewish Hellenism).

[15] Ibid., 493 (*TDNT* 1:494 – "Philo introduced both the term and the reality into theological ethics").

trainer, the reason within him, under whose discipline he labored to fit himself for life in its highest forms (LCL 289:301)].[16] Moral training, ἄσκησις, requires self-discipline. Those who obtain true wealth, the wealth that is the result of controlled desire, are ὀλιγοδεΐαν καὶ ἐγκράτειαν ἀσκήσαντες (*Praem. Poen.* 100 ["(the ones who) practice frugality and self-restraint," LCL 341:373]).

So far I have quoted only Philo; given the extent of his works within the field of Hellenistic Judaism this was inevitable. Other examples of the use of the words that have been considered here are not easy to find, no doubt in part because athletics was a suspiciously Greek and un-Jewish pastime. There are however a number of examples in the Epistle of Aristeas of the use of ἀσκεῖν. Thus at § 168, the law commands us to do evil to no one, ἀλλ᾽ ἵνα δι᾽ ὅλου τοῦ ζῆν καὶ ἐν ταῖς πράξεσιν ἀσκῶμεν δικαιοσύνην πρὸς πάντας ἀνθρώπους [but to the intent that through the whole of our lives we may also practice justice toward all people in our actions]. Cf. § 225: ἠσκηκὼς πρὸς πάντας ἀνθρώπους εὔνοιαν καὶ κατεργασάμενος φιλίας [practicing good will toward all people and forming friendships]; § 255: . . . τὴν εὐσέβειαν ἀσκοῦντι [practice piety]; § 285: . . . πᾶσαν ἠσκηκὼς καταστολήν [well versed (practiced) in all restraint].[17] Josephus uses γυμνάζειν in the literal sense of bodily training, but gives to ἀσκεῖν a moral sense, for example at *Antiquities* 3.309, where τοῖς ἀρετὴν ἠσκηκόσιν [those trained in virtue] are soldiers trained not only in military skills but in courage and determination; 4.294 is similar, though the construction is different. It is worthwhile to note also the words of Trypho, in Justin, *Dialogue* 8.3. It would be better, he says, for Justin to adhere to Plato or to some other philosophical discipline, ἀσκοῦντα καρτερίαν καὶ ἐγκράτειαν καὶ σωφροσύνην, ἢ λόγοις ἐξαπατηθῆναι ψευδέσι . . . [practicing patience, self-control, and moderation, rather than to be deceived by false words] . . . .

The upshot of this study is that the deuteropauline works in the New Testament (and these could have been extended to include 1 and 2 Peter and Hebrews) differ from the genuine Pauline letters in their concern for disciplined training in the ethical and spiritual life, in which progress, προκοπή, is made in ἀρετή [virtue] and εὐσέβεια [piety]. This is not to say that Paul would have actively disapproved of such ἄσκησις [training]. Faith includes obedience, and he was aware of the fact that obedience is not easy. He was probably aware also of the

---

[16] It is interesting that neither the New Testament nor any of the other works covered in Bauer-Aland's *Wörterbuch* makes any use of the ἀλείπτης, the trainer, or coach.

[17] The translations of Aristeas are adapted from *The Old Testament Pseudepigrapha* (ed. James H. Charlesworth; Garden City, NY: Doubleday, 1985) 2:24–31.

fact that the professional athlete (in moral matters) is in danger of generating a good opinion of his achievements which may be more perilous than the occasional cropper of the enthusiastic but unthinking amateur. The course, however, was set for the following generation, and the Apostolic Fathers take up the language of disciplined progress. A few examples must suffice.

1 Clement, *2 Clement*, and *Barnabas* all use ἀγωνίζεσθαι [to strive] in an exhortation. *1 Clem.* 35.4 shows that what is in mind is a continuing effort: ἀγωνισώμεθα εὑρεθῆναι ἐν τῷ ἀριθμῷ τῶν ὑπομενόντων αὐτόν [Let us strive to be found among the number of those who wait for him]. This is the way to share in the promised gifts. *2 Clem.* 7.1–5 sketches the whole process: ἀγωνισώμεθα ... ὁ ἀγών ... οὐ πάντες στεφανοῦνται εἰ μὴ οἱ ... καλῶς ἀγωνισάμενοι [Let us contend ... the contest ... not all are crowned save those who ... have contended well (LCL 24:139)]. In *Barnabas* 4.11 the struggle is to keep the commandments: φυλάσσειν ἀγωνιζώμεθα τὰς ἐντολὰς αὐτοῦ [let us strive to keep his commandments]. Ἀσκεῖν [to practice] is used with a number of objects: δικαιοσύνην (righteousness; Herm. *Mand.* 8.10); πᾶσαν ὑπομονήν (all endurance; Pol. *Phil.* 9.1); ἀκακίαν (guilelessness; Papias, fragment 8). Surprisingly, the *Epistle to Diognetus* uses ἀσκεῖν in a bad sense: Christians do not practice a distinctive manner of life (βίον παράσημον, 5.2); γνῶσις [knowledge] is an appropriate way to pursue (12.5). In *Mart. Pol.* 18.3 ἄσκησις is especially training for martyrdom. The "birthday" of the martyr is observed εἴς τε τὴν τῶν προηθληκότων μνήμην καὶ τῶν μελλόντων ἄσκησίν τε καὶ ἑτοιμασίαν ["both in memory of those who have already contested, and for the practice and training of those whose fate it shall be"; LCL 25:337]. Ἀθλητής [the one who contends] and ἀθλεῖν [to contend] are used in *1 Clem.* 5.1f. of the martyrs Peter and Paul. This application of the language of athletics reaches its climax when it is applied to Christ himself: ὁ εἰς πολλοὺς ἀγῶνας ὑπὲρ ἡμῶν ἀγωνιζόμενος καὶ νικᾶν ποιῶν ἡμᾶς ἐν πᾶσι· ὁ ἀληθὴς ἀθλητὴς ἡμῶν καὶ ἀήττητος (*Acts of Thomas* 39). [18]

These observations about the contrast between the ethical teaching of the historical Paul, with his "sin shall no more have dominion over you" and his "become what you are," and deutero-Paul, whose converts are expected to enter into training for the ethical and spiritual life cannot of themselves prove, but fit well into, an historical situation

---

[18] "who in many battles dost fight for us, and make us conquer in them all, our true and invincible champion"; *New Testament Apocrypha: Revised Edition of the Collection initiated by Edgar Hennecke* (ed. Wilhelm Schneemelcher; 2 vols.; Louisville, KY: Westminster-John Knox, 1992) 2.356.

which on other grounds seems probable. The author of Acts seems to have regarded Paul as a successor to, a replacement of, the Hellenist Jew Stephen; the Areopagus speech which he puts into Paul's mouth is best explained (as also is Stephen's speech in Acts 7) as a Hellenistic Jewish sermon, turned into a Christian Jewish sermon by the addition of a somewhat obscure reference to Jesus. If this is true, it suggests that in the generation after Paul's death there was a tendency to understand him as a member of the Hellenistic Jewish Christian group. This he was not; he was not a Hellenist but a Hebrew, as he himself asserts. The mistake was probably an honest one, certainly an understandable one. The Hellenistic Jews already before they became Christians exercised a mission to the Gentiles; as Christians they became more ardent missionaries. Paul was notoriously the apostle of the Gentiles. It was an almost inevitable, though in part it was a mistaken, conclusion that he had himself been one of the Hellenistic Jewish Christians. If so, he will have shared their approach to the Gentiles; hence, the Areopagus speech. If so, he will not have left his churches to themselves to sort themselves out and settle their problems under the guidance of the Spirit; he must have set out a clear-cut organization based on the ministry of presbyter-bishops and deacons. If so, he will not have left his young churches to the guidance of the Spirit under such basic commands as: "Love your neighbors"; he will have instituted training programs in ethics and spirituality. The historical Paul was not a Hellenistic Jew,[19] and had not absorbed Stoicism on the way to Christian faith.

It is not strictly relevant to this paper, but I cannot forbear to add that this observation helps me with a problem. M. D. Goulder's *Tale of Two Missions*,[20] though popular in style, is a very serious restatement of something like the position of F. C. Baur. It is to be taken seriously, and welcomed. Most of it I believe to be true, but I have found difficult the assertion that in the conflict between "Paulines" and "Petrines" it was Paul who won. This puzzles me; it seems to me that Paul lost. If, however, we may take the "Paul who won" to be not the historical Paul but the unhistorical, or, more accurately, the not-quite-historical Paul, the difficulty disappears, or at least is diminished. But this is a matter that I have discussed and hope to discuss further in other places.

---

[19] He was of course a Hellenistic Jew in the sense that he was a Jew born in the Hellenistic city of Tarsus (according to Acts 22:3); I refer here to his attitude.

[20] M. D. Goulder, *A Tale of Two Missions* (London: SCM, 1994).

"He remains faithful" (2 Tim 2:13a)

Jouette M. Bassler

One of the relatively few places in the Pastoral Epistles where the author of these pseudonymous letters seems to remain faithful not only to Paul's theology but almost to his very words is in the hymn quoted in 2 Tim 2:11–13.[1] Indeed, scholars have focused on this happy circumstance to such an extent that they have tended to neglect a cardinal rule of exegesis of the epistles: "trace the flow of the writer's argument in order to understand any single sentence or paragraph."[2] Especially with regard to the surprising conclusion of the fourth line of the hymn, "if we are faithless, *he remains faithful*" (v. 13a), commentators have sought its meaning in Paul's letters and not, by and large, in the argument of 2 Timothy itself.

Although my colleague, Victor Furnish, has not focused his research on the Pastoral Epistles, he has always insisted that the study of the theology of a letter should begin with a careful analysis of the argument of that letter[3] and has zealously advocated fidelity to the exegetical

---

[1] A. T. Hanson says that "the theology implied in the hymn is thoroughly Pauline" (*The Pastoral Epistles* [NCB; Grand Rapids, MI: Eerdmans, 1982] 132). Hejne Simonsen agrees: "Den stärksten Einfluss paulinischer Tradition finden wir im 2 Tim. . . . In diesem Zusammenhang hat das Traditionsstück 2,11f. eine zentrale Bedeutung" (["We find the strongest influence of Pauline tradition in 2 Timothy. . . . In this context the traditional element in 2:11f. has a central significance"] "Christologische Traditionselemente in den Pastoralbriefen," *Die Paulinische Literatur und Theologie* [ed. S. Pedersen; Teologiske Studier 7; Göttingen: Vandenhoeck & Ruprecht, 1980] 62); see also Norbert Brox, *Die Pastoralbriefe* (RNT 7.2; Regensburg: Pustet, 1969) 244.

[2] Gordon D. Fee, *New Testament Exegesis: A Handbook for Students and Pastors* (rev. ed.; Louisville, KY: Westminster/John Knox, 1993) 28.

[3] "If Paul's theology is to be understood as his reflection about the gospel—hence, as a process—then it can only be found as one follows and engages the dynamics of his argument" (Victor P. Furnish, "Theology in 1 Corinthians," *Pauline Theology, Volume II: 1 & 2 Corinthians* [ed. D. M. Hay; Minneapolis, MN: Fortress, 1993] 62). He is speaking, of course, of the theology in the undisputed letters; but the procedure is the same for the pseudonymous letters, provided one acknowledges at least a minimal theological competence of the author. Though the theological competence of the author of the Pastorals has, in fact, been seriously questioned on occasion (see, e.g., Hanson, *Pastoral Epistles*, 38), that assessment has changed somewhat in recent years. See, e.g., Frances Young, *The Theology of the Pastoral Letters* (New Testament Theology; Cambridge: Cambridge University Press, 1994); Lewis R. Donelson, *Pseudepigraphy and Ethical Argument*

process.[4] Thus I offer to him, on the occasion of his sixty-fifth birthday, this study of the meaning and import of the Pauline-sounding words concerning divine faithfulness within the deuteropauline context of 2 Timothy.[5]

I

The meaning of v. 13a is not the only disputed issue in this portion of 2 Timothy. Most commentators—but not all[6]—agree that vv. 11b–13a were part of an early Christian hymn, and that the original setting for this hymn was the rite of baptism. There is some debate, however, over how much a message of martyrdom pervades the passage and whether it

in the Pastoral Epistles (HUT 22; Tübingen: Mohr-Siebeck, 1986); Philip H. Towner, *The Goal of our Instruction: The Structure of Theology and Ethics in the Pastoral Epistles* (JSNTSup 34; Sheffield: JSOT Press, 1989).

4 "There is, of course, a place for understanding Paul, however much or little he can be understood. It is in his letters, read critically and in context. Every scholarly hypothesis and reconstruction, every churchly claim about him, has finally to be tested with reference to his own writings. Apart from encountering Paul in these—and this means, if one may be pardoned for using an old-fashioned term, *exegetically*—there is no way to put him in his place" (Victor Paul Furnish, "On Putting Paul in his Place," *JBL* 113 (1994) 12; emphasis his). The explicit reference, again, is to the homologoumena, but the applicability of the comment to the deuteropauline letters is obvious.

5 Though there are several studies that affirm the Pauline authorship of 2 Timothy, but not 1 Timothy or Titus (see, e.g., J. Murphy-O'Connor, "2 Timothy Contrasted with 1 Timothy and Titus," *RB* 98 [1991] 401–18; Michael Prior, *Paul the Letter-Writer and the Second Letter to Timothy* [JSNTSup 23; Sheffield: Sheffield Academic Press, 1989]), and a number of recent commentaries continue to insist on the authenticity of all three (see, e.g., Gordon D. Fee, *1 and 2 Timothy, Titus* [New International Biblical Commentary; Peabody, MA: Hendrickson, 1988]; George W. Knight III, *Commentary on the Pastoral Epistles* [NIGTC; Grand Rapids, MI: Eerdmans, 1992]; Luke T. Johnson, *1 Timothy, 2 Timothy, Titus* [Knox Preaching Guides; Atlanta: John Knox, 1987]; Philip H. Towner, *1–2 Timothy and Titus* [IVP New Testament Commentary Series; Downers Grove, IL: InterVarsity, 1994]), the arguments in favor of the pseudonymity of all three seem to me to be compelling (see, e.g., Brox, *Pastoralbriefe*, 22–66; Jürgen Roloff, *Der erste Brief an Timotheus* [EKK 15; Neukirchen-Vluyn: Neukirchener Verlag, 1988] 23–39).

6 Jürgen Roloff argues that while the structure of the passage might suggest a hymnic origin, its content identifies it as a piece of catechetical material ("ein katechetisches Traditionsstück") instead ("Der Weg Jesu als Lebensnorm [2 Tim 2,8–13]: Ein Beitrag zur Christologie der Pastoralbriefe," *Anfänge der Christologie: Festschrift für Ferdinand Hahn zum 65. Geburtstag* [ed. C. Breytenbach and H. Paulsen; Göttingen: Vandenhoeck & Ruprecht, 1991] 155–67, esp. p. 164). J. L. Houlden, on the other hand, thinks the verses fit so well into the argument that "it is a moot point whether these lines come from the writer himself or from his stock of revered formulas" (*The Pastoral Epistles: I and II Timothy, Titus* [TPI New Testament Commentaries; Philadelphia: Trinity Press International, 1989] 119). These remain, however, minority opinions.

was a part of the original hymn.[7] There is even some debate over whether the hymn is the faithful saying referred to in v. 11a,[8] and whether the comment, "for he cannot deny himself" (v. 13b), was a part of the original hymn.[9] In this paper, however, I will only be concerned with the meaning and import of the fourth line of the quoted piece, which contains a surprising paradox: "If we are faithless, he remains faithful." Read in isolation, of course, the line is not at all surprising. Indeed, it reproduces quite faithfully Paul's point in Rom 3:3 ("What if some were unfaithful? Will their faithlessness nullify the faithfulness of God? By no means!"). The surprise is generated by its association with the other three lines of the hymn.

The hymn is very carefully composed. Each line has the same structure: a brief conditional clause (εἰ + indicative verb) is followed by a result clause. The content of the first two lines is nearly identical: conditional statements about faithful suffering are followed by promises of future reward:

If we have died with him, we will also live with him;
If we endure, we will also reign with him.

The third line, however, establishes a new pattern. The conditional statement refers to denial instead of faithful endurance, and the result clause promises rejection instead of reward:

If we deny him, he will also deny us.

This new pattern seems to continue in the fourth line when it opens with another conditional statement about human faithlessness, and this leads to the expectation of an overall *aabb* pattern to the hymn and thus closure with another statement of divine rejection. Instead there is a

---

[7] Knight, e.g., sees the baptismal message of spiritual union with Christ dominating the passage (*Pastoral Epistles*, 405); Victor Hasler finds only the message of martyrdom there (*Die Briefe an Timotheus und Titus [Pastoralbriefe]* [Zürcher Bibelkommentare; Zurich: Theologischer Verlag, 1978] 65); and Arland J. Hultgren argues that both messages were present in the hymn—and the passage—from the beginning (*I-II Timothy, Titus* [Augsburg Commentary on the New Testament; Minneapolis, MN: Augsburg, 1984] 122–24).

[8] Because the word γάρ ("for") is found in its first line, the hymn seems logically to serve as a warrant for describing *another* saying (either v. 8 or v. 10b) as "sure" ("The [previous] saying is sure, *for* . . ."). Most, however, identify the hymn with the saying mentioned in v. 11a, taking γάρ in a weakened sense ("namely") or as part of the quoted text (see George W. Knight III, *The Faithful Sayings in the Pastoral Epistles* [Kampen: Kok, 1968] 112–15).

[9] Knight, e.g., insists that "it must have been part of the original saying" (*Pastoral Epistles*, 407), while Hanson concludes that "it is probably the author's own comment" (*Pastoral Epistles*, 133).

reference—surprising now in this context—to what appears to be a positive conclusion:

If we are faithless, he remains faithful.

What is implied by this final line?

The basic issue is whether the expected parallelism between lines three and four of the hymn determines the meaning of the final line or whether the statement in line four reverses or qualifies in some significant way the harsh response articulated in line three. The general consensus, at least among contemporary scholars, is that line four does *not* simply reiterate or reinforce the message of line three. That is, scholars generally reject an interpretation of "he remains faithful" in terms of faithfulness to the requirements of divine justice that demand appropriate punishment.[10] Most commentators assume that v. 13a represents "the triumph of grace,"[11] a word of promise that offsets in some way the message of rejection in v. 12b. In spite of human faithlessness, God (or Christ) remains faithful.[12] But what is the reference point and what are the consequences of this faithfulness?

Since we do not know and cannot determine the entire contents of the quoted hymn or even its original wording,[13] speculations about the meaning of v. 13a within the original hymn are fruitless. We can only ask what meaning it has within this letter. What significance, if any, does the author of the Pastoral Epistles find in the affirmation, "If we are faithless, he remains faithful"? To determine this we must investigate the surrounding argument.

There have, of course, been numerous attempts to clarify the connection between the hymn and its context. Houlden viewed the entire hymn as an integral part of the surrounding argument,[14] but most

---

[10] Such an interpretation has been proposed, e.g., by J. H. Bernard, *The Pastoral Epistles* (Cambridge Greek Testament for Schools and Colleges; Cambridge: Cambridge University Press, 1899) and W. Lock, *A Critical and Exegetical Commentary on the Pastoral Epistles* (ICC; New York: Scribner, 1924). See also Towner, *1–2 Timothy and Titus*, 178–79.

[11] Hultgren, *I-II Timothy*, 124.

[12] Attempts to resolve the apparent contradiction between lines three and four of the hymn by finding a significant difference between denial (i.e., unbelief) and faithlessness (i.e., the momentary lack of trust of a believer) can best be described as solutions of desperation (see, e.g., Knight, *Pastoral Epistles*, 405–7; Fee, *1 and 2 Timothy*, 250–52). In the Pastorals, ἀπιστία and ἄπιστος unambiguously refer to those outside the faith (1 Tim 1:13; 5:8; Titus 1:15).

[13] Fred Gealy suggests that in v. 13 the original language of the hymn may have been modified, presumably by the author of the letter ("II Timothy: Exegesis," *IB* 11.486). See also Gottfried Schille, *Frühchristliche Hymnen* (Berlin: Evangelische Verlagsanstalt, 1962) 17–18.

[14] Houlden, *Pastoral Epistles*, 119; see note 6 above.

others have found more modest connections. Spicq, for example, links the reference to "dying together" (v. 11b) to the good soldier motif in 2:3,[15] but the most commonly noted connection is that between the hymn's promise to those who endure (v. 12a) and the statement in v. 10 about Paul's own endurance.[16] When it comes to assessing the significance of v. 13a, however, commentators rarely explore the surrounding argument. Instead they appeal to pious generalities or to the Pauline corpus.

The most common assumption is that the passage refers to God's faithfulness to the covenant or to the promises, and this interpretation is usually confirmed by citing Rom 3:3.[17] Alternatively, commentators simply appeal to the general message of love and forgiveness that characterizes the New Testament in general or the Pastoral Epistles in particular as the "explanation" of the verse.[18] What is consistently lacking, however, is a careful analysis of 2 Timothy 2 to see whether the wider argument sheds any light on what the author of this letter might have understood to be the theological and ethical import of the phrase. Since the promises articulated in lines one and two of the hymn fragment have clear connections with the argument in the rest of the letter,[19] it is reasonable to expect that the comment on divine faithfulness finds expression and application there as well.

---

[15] C. Spicq, *Les épîtres pastorales* (Ebib; 2 vols.; Paris: Lecoffre, 1969) 2.749.

[16] See, e.g., Knight, *Pastoral Epistles*, 402; J. Jeremias, *Die Briefe an Timotheus und Titus* (NTD 9; Göttingen: Vandenhoeck & Ruprecht, 1981) 55; Towner, *1–2 Timothy and Titus*, 179; Roloff, "Der Weg Jesu," 164; Hultgren, *I-II Timothy*, 124.

[17] So, e.g., M. Dibelius and H. Conzelmann, *The Pastoral Epistles* (Hermeneia; Philadelphia: Fortress, 1972) 109; Jeremias, *Briefe*, 55; and Spicq (assuming that his otherwise inexplicable citation of Rom 3:13 is a typographical error; see *Epîtres pastorales*, 2.750); see also Hultgren, *I-II Timothy*, 124; Gottfried Holtz, *Die Pastoralbriefe* (THKNT 13; Berlin: Evangelische Verlagsanstalt, 1965) 169; and Helmut Merkel, *Die Pastoralbriefe* (NTD 9/1; Göttingen: Vandenhoeck & Ruprecht, 1991) 65. Hasler offers the odd suggestion that Christ "bleibt seinem unter Pilatus abgelegten Heilszeugnis treu [remains faithful to his sacred testimony before Pilate]," an apparent reference to 1 Tim 6:13 (*Briefe*, 66). Knight, on the other hand, relates God's faithfulness to a host of issues and cites a variety of texts, both Pauline and non-Pauline, in support of this view: "Paul does not mention God's faithfulness as a basis for the certainty that the faithless will be punished, but as the basis for the assurance of the gospel promises (2 Cor 1:18–20), for safety in temptation (1 Cor 10:13), for protection from the evil one (2 Thess 3:3), and for the sanctification and preservation of God's people (1 Thess 5:24; cf. also Heb 10:23; 11:11; 1 Pet 4:19; 1 John 1:9; Rev 1:5; 3:14; 19:11)" (*Pastoral Epistles*, 407).

[18] So, e.g., Gealy, "II Timothy," 487; Hanson, *Pastoral Epistles*, 132.

[19] In addition to 2:10, see especially 3:10–11; 4:8, 18

II

The hymnic fragment mentions neither God nor Christ explicitly, but the reference to dying together (v. 11a) and the close connection between the message of the fragment and "the salvation that is in Christ Jesus" (v. 10b) point to Christ as the one who "remains faithful." The echo of Rom 3:3, however, encourages an identification of the faithful one as God, and commentaries reflect this confusion.[20] In fact, there is in the Pastoral Letters a great deal of overlap between the roles of God and Christ: both are called "Savior" (see, e.g., Titus 1:3–4) and "Lord" (see, e.g., 1 Tim 6:15; 2 Tim 1:2; 2:19); Christ is (apparently) called "God and Savior" (Titus 2:13);[21] and the advent of Jesus is described as the appearance of the grace of God (Titus 2:11). In light of this, one can expect a reference to Christ's faithfulness, especially one that echoes a reference to God's, to be worked out in the argument either in terms of God's actions or Christ's.

Some have rejected out of hand, however, any connection between v. 13a and the surrounding argument. Gealy, for example, asserts that this line is "without much point in the context";[22] Merkel claims that the final lines of the hymn do not suit the paraenetic tenor of the passage;[23] and Dibelius and Conzelmann insist that "the idea of v. 13 does not belong in the context of 2 Tim 2."[24] Roloff makes the same point somewhat more expansively:

> Der Vf. der Past hat diese Schlusszeile sicherlich inhaltlich bejaht, obwohl er sie nur infolge des Zitationszwanges übernommen haben dürfte. Sein Motiv für die Übernahme des Traditionsstücks lag zweifellos darin, dass ihm dessen beide erste Zeilen die Möglichkeit gaben, die christologische Aussage von V. 8 seiner Intention gemäss zu ergänzen und in den Kontext einzubringen.[25]

---

[20] Knight, in his commentary, says that "obviously what is in view . . . is God's faithfulness" (*Pastoral Epistles*, 406), but on the next page he says that "ἐκεῖνος is Christ here [v. 13a] as in v. 12b. It is he who 'remains faithful'" (p. 407). Hultgren says the reference is to Christ's faithfulness (*I-II Timothy*, 124); Dibelius and Conzelmann assume it is God's (*Pastoral Epistles,* 109).

[21] See Murray J. Harris, "Titus 2:13 and the Deity of Christ," *Pauline Studies: Essays presented to Prof. F. F. Bruce on his 70th Birthday* (ed. D. A. Hagner and M. J. Harris; Grand Rapids, MI: Eerdmans, 1980) 262–77.

[22] Gealy, "II Timothy," 486.

[23] Merkel, *Pastoralbriefe,* 65.

[24] Dibelius and Conzelmann, *Pastoral Epistles,* 109.

[25] ["The author of the Pastorals certainly affirmed the content of these closing lines even though he may have picked them up only as a result of the constraint of citation. His motive for including the traditional element undoubtedly lay in the fact that its first two

Such conclusions rest, however, on a misconstrual of the shape and direction of the surrounding argument.

2 Tim 2:8–13, with its emphasis on suffering and endurance, is clearly part of an argument that extends back at least as far as 1:8. There is a break in the argument between 2:13 and 2:14 but it is not very strong. In fact, the argument of 2:14–26, though introducing a new set of exhortations, is closely connected with the preceding passages, for it delineates in some detail the situation of adversity and controversy that necessitated the admonitions to hold fast to sound teaching (1:13), guard the good treasure (1:14), and endure suffering (1:8). To be sure, the hymnic fragment in 2:11b–13a stands at a turning point in the argument, separating the Pauline model of endurance (2:8–10) from the warnings against faithless opponents (2:14–26). It functions, however, not simply as the theological warrant for what precedes it but also as a bridge to what follows.[26] Read in this light, the relevance of v. 13a can be readily seen.

III

The first point that emerges from a consideration of v. 13a within the wider argument of 2 Timothy 2 is that it contributes to a pervasive interest in faithfulness in this portion of the letter. The message is to be entrusted to faithful ministers (2:2);[27] the saying or word that is quoted is pronounced faithful (πιστὸς ὁ λόγος; 2:11a); and, in the fourth line of the hymn, Christ's faithfulness is proclaimed (2:13a). Elsewhere in these letters other sayings are introduced as faithful (1 Tim 1:15; 3:1; 4:9; Titus 3:8); the gospel is called the "faithful word" (Titus 1:9); "Paul" says he has been judged faithful (1 Tim 1:12; cf. 2 Tim 3:10); Christians are referred to as "faithful ones" (οἱ πιστοί; see 1 Tim 4:3, 10, 12; 6:2; also 1 Tim 5:16; Titus 1:6);[28] and the entire letter of 2 Timothy urges

---

lines allowed him to complete the Christological saying of v. 8 according to his plan and to introduce it into the context."] Roloff, "Der Weg Jesu," 166.

[26] Houlden makes the same point, but without drawing out the implications for v. 13a (*Pastoral Epistles*, 119). Several passages in this letter serve a bridge function in the argument; see, e.g., 3:10–13, which serves as a "foil" for both 3:1–9 and 3:14–17; and 4:6–8, which concludes 4:1–5 and motivates the exhortations in 4:9–15.

[27] The text speaks simply of entrusting the message to "faithful people" (πιστοῖς ἀνθρώποις), but the focus here and throughout this letter is on church leadership (see 1:6; 2:24; 3:17; 4:1–5).

[28] Paul, in the undisputed letters, always uses the participle of πιστεύειν, and not the adjective πιστός, to describe the same group (see, e.g., Rom 1:16; 3:22; 4:11; 1 Cor 1:21; and especially 1 Cor 14:22, where the participle οἱ πιστεύοντες is paired with the adjective ἄπιστοι).

Timothy to continued faithfulness to his office, to the gospel, and to Paul (see, e.g., 1:13; 2:15; 3:14; 4:1–5).

The author of these letters has thus defined a network of faithfulness that stands in sharpest possible contrast to his depiction of the opposing teachers and their message.[29] They are deceitful (2 Tim 3:13); their faith is counterfeit (2 Tim 3:8); they are unfaithful to the apostle (2 Tim 1:15) and to the truth of the gospel (2 Tim 2:8; 3:8; see also 1 Tim 6:3).[30] Their message consists of profane chatter (2 Tim 2:16) and myths (2 Tim 4:4); and they are not servants of the Lord (2 Tim 2:24), but slaves of the devil (2 Tim 2:26), whose nature it is to accuse, slander, and ensnare. They are, in short, faithless. They have undermined the structure of the church by their unauthorized teaching and they have "swerved from the truth" of the gospel.

The reference to faithfulness in the hymn is thus a significant piece of the author's rhetorical strategy. It affirms the principle of divine faithfulness, which provides both the model for the faithfulness demanded of church leaders and the basis for the claims concerning the reliability of the church's message of salvation.[31] In what sort of actions, though, does this divine faithfulness manifest itself? Specifically, what does this author understand to be the relationship between human faithlessness and divine faithfulness? The author has used this hymnic fragment as a bridge from a passage that exhorts Timothy to faithful endurance to one that warns of certain people whose actions and words clearly constitute faithless behavior (2:17–18, 23–26; 3:1–9). His description of God's response to these faithless people should therefore clarify his understanding of the nature and significance of the divine faithfulness mentioned in v. 13a.

---

[29] The precise identity of the opponents is the subject of some debate. It is generally agreed, however, that though they posed a real threat to the church, they are described in stereotypical language deriving largely from disputes between philosophers and sophists. The function of references to them in these letters is often to create a negative example that can serve as a foil for the exhortations. See Robert J. Karris, "The Background and Significance of the Polemic of the Pastoral Epistles," *JBL* 92 (1973) 549–64; Luke T. Johnson, "II Timothy and the Polemic Against False Teachers: A Re-examination," *JRelSt* 6/7 (1978/79) 1–26; Benjamin Fiore, *The Function of Personal Example in the Socratic and Pastoral Epistles* (AnBib 105; Rome: Biblical Institute Press, 1986).

[30] The description of the opponents could be greatly expanded by using material from 1 Timothy and Titus. I have chosen here, however, to focus on the description in 2 Timothy.

[31] See Donelson, *Pseudepigraphy and Ethical Argument,* 150–51.

IV

"Remind them of this" (v. 14a; literally, "mention these things again and again"). With these words the author turns to the situation of the church leaders,[32] who are warned to avoid certain people who have forsaken the truth and whose talk is spreading (literally, "has pasture") like gangrene (v. 17). The image of gangrene devouring the flesh suggests the insidious and dangerous spread of the opponents' influence to "healthy" members of the church; that is, it indicates the opponents' success in attracting people to their views (see also 3:1–5; 4:3–4). Juxtaposed to the description of these people and their actions stands a scriptural quotation: "The Lord knows those who are his" (v. 19a).

These words repeat almost verbatim the words of Num 16:5 (an original reference to God is replaced by "the Lord"). The original context of this promise was a rebellion by Korah and his followers against Moses and Aaron, and the nature of God's response—destruction of Korah and confirmation of Moses' leadership—defines God's knowledge of "those who are his" in terms of God's active support for them. The situation described in Numbers 16 and that envisioned in the Pastorals are so similar (the emergence of opposing claims to leadership) that the citation of the Old Testament text probably draws with it these other aspects of the story as well.[33] It seems, then, that one important implication the author reads out of v. 13a is that the faithlessness of some will not jeopardize God's faithfulness to the elect, especially to faithful church leaders. The apparent success of those who are faithless does not imply that God's firm foundation of support for the faithful has crumbled.

The second quotation, "Let everyone who calls on the name of the Lord turn away from wickedness" (v. 19b), suggests another level of meaning to the phrase "he remains faithful." This quotation is a composite one, echoing the sentiment of Num 16:26 (where Moses urges the Israelites to "turn away from the tents of those wicked men") and the language of Sir 17:26; Isa 26:13; Joel 3:5.[34] In this letter, though, those who call on the name of the Lord and yet have fallen into wickedness can only be those—both church leaders and ordinary Christians—who have embraced the message of the opposing teachers (2:14, 16; 4:3–4; see also 1 Tim 4:1–2).[35] This, too, constitutes faithless-

---

[32] See note 27.

[33] On this concept of "intertextuality," see Richard B. Hays, *Echoes of Scripture in the Letters of Paul* (New Haven and London: Yale University Press, 1989).

[34] See Knight, *Pastoral Epistles*, 416.

[35] See, e.g., Hanson, *Pastoral Epistles*, 138; Fee, *1 and 2 Timothy*, 258; Knight, *Pastoral Epistles*, 416–17.

ness, but it does not bring immediate condemnation. Throughout these letters, God is described and defined as "Savior," [36] underscoring God's characteristic will to save all (see, e.g., 1 Tim 2:3–4; 4:10; Titus 2:11). God remains faithful to this saving nature and thus does not abandon the elect even when they have been swayed by the message of the opposing teachers and have fallen into impiety. To them is extended the invitation to "turn away from wickedness." The image of the house with two kinds of utensils reinforces this point with a promise: "All who cleanse themselves of the things I have mentioned will become special utensils, dedicated and useful to the owner of the house" (2:21).

The tension between the third and fourth lines of the hymn is reflected when the author addresses the fate of the opponents in 2:24–26:

> And the Lord's servant must not be quarrelsome but kindly to everyone, an apt teacher, patient, correcting opponents with gentleness. God may perhaps grant that they will repent and come to know the truth, and that they may escape from the snare of the devil, having been held captive by him to do his will.

Here the author leaves open the possibility that God's faithfulness to God's saving nature could mean that salvation extends even to the opponents. With μήποτε ("perhaps") and the subjunctive mood, however, he signals that this is far from certain. The harsh dictum of line three could prevail: "if we deny him, he will also deny us" (see also 4:14–15).

Other passages in these letters show the same ambivalence. Hymenaeus and Alexander, two opponents named in 1 Timothy, are to be "turned over to Satan"—a clear sign of rejection—but for the purpose of edification—a note of hope (see 1 Tim 1:10). Opponents on Crete are described as "detestable, disobedient, unfit for any good work" (Titus 1:16)—clear grounds for rejection—yet they are to be rebuked "sharply, so that they may become sound in the faith" (Titus 1:13)—a sign of God's continued commitment to them.

V

Attempts to explain 2 Tim 2:13a through pious generalizations or through appeal to the Pauline *Hauptbriefe* do not do justice to its significance within the argument of the letter. Indeed, appeals to God's

---

[36] On the significance of this epithet, see, e.g., Dieter Lührmann, "Epiphaneia: Zur Bedeutungsgeschichte eines griechischen Wortes," *Tradition und Glaube: Das frühe Christentum in seiner Umwelt: Festschrift für K. G. Kuhn* (eds. G. Jeremias, H.-W. Kuhn, H. Stegemann; Göttingen: Vandenhoeck & Ruprecht, 1971) 185–99; Dibelius and Conzelmann, *Pastoral Epistles*, 100–104.

covenant or promises grossly misrepresent the letter's theology, for this author shows no trace of interest in *Heilsgeschichte*. Most especially, such an approach does not adequately define how this author's understanding of God's faithfulness has shaped the letter's ethical exhortations. Far from being "without much point in the context," the enigmatic line, "If we are faithless, he remains faithful," serves as a theological rubric for the exhortations and explications that follow in 2 Timothy. The opponents—former members of the church—have proven faithless, but God remains faithful to the elect. God also remains faithful to those to whom the gangrene of false teaching has spread, and extends to them the invitation to "turn away from wickedness." Even the tension between lines three and four of the hymn reflects a characteristic of these letters. The conflicting demands of divine justice (line 3) and divine faithfulness (line 4) are focused quite specifically by this author on the problem of the enemy within. This leads him to predict the downfall of his opponents, but also to hold out hope for their ultimate redemption.

The concept of divine faithfulness in 2 Timothy is thus not related to the promises or covenants of old. The point of reference is God's saving nature, which has been revealed through the appearance of Jesus (2 Tim 1:9–10). And divine faithfulness is an active concept for this author, not a theological abstraction. It is the warrant for eschatological hope: "The Lord knows those who are his." It is also the grounds for ethical appeal: "Turn away from wickedness." It even dictates the stance the author takes toward opponents, for God "may perhaps grant that they will repent."

Christ Crucified in Paul and in Mark: Reflections on an Intracanonical Conversation

C. Clifton Black

The suitability of an essay involving Mark in a volume devoted to Paul and his interpreters is hardly self-evident.[1] Mark's most salient characteristic, its narrative of Jesus, is evidently lacking in Paul's letters, which offer only the thinnest droplets of information about "the Lord" (e.g., 1 Cor 9:5, 14; 11:23–25; 15:3–7; Gal 1:19; 4:4).[2] Conversely, those letters' most distinctive aspect—their author's creative engagement with the vicissitudes of early Christian communities—is, if extant in the Second Gospel, for the most part cloaked. For centuries Paul has been elevated alongside John as earliest Christianity's seminal thinker, the New Testament's theological titan. Mark, by contrast, has been stereotyped as little more than an unsophisticated storyteller whose interests were more historical, or historicist, than theological. Unlike Ignatius, Mark acknowledges no direct Pauline influence (cf. Ign. *Eph.* 12.2; *Rom.* 4.3); nor does that Gospel articulate many of the apostle's preeminent theological concerns, such as the justification of sinful humanity by grace through faith (Rom 1:17; 3:21–26) and Jesus' post-Easter enthronement as Lord and Son of God (Rom 1:4; Phil 2:9–11).[3]

I. Clearing the Table

But this distance between Paul the apostle and Mark the evangelist has not always been felt. In Christian tradition links between them have

---

[1] I am indebted to Ellen T. Charry, Beverly R. Gaventa, Paul W. Meyer, and D. Moody Smith for their acute responses to earlier drafts of this essay. I am honored to be included in this volume's tribute to Victor Paul Furnish, an esteemed colleague and cherished friend.

[2] See Victor Paul Furnish, *Jesus According to Paul* (Understanding Jesus Today; Cambridge: Cambridge University Press, 1993) esp. 19–65.

[3] The traditional, though surely secondary, ending of Mark (16:9–20, A C D K X Δ Θ Π *f*[13] vg syr[c, p, h, pal] cop[sa, bo, fay] *et al.*) appears inclined towards these Pauline *theologoumena* (N.B. vv. 16, 19).

long been forged and persist in some sectors, despite their loosening by historical criticism.[4] Within critical scholarship by the mid-nineteenth century, at least two rapprochements between the Pauline epistles and the Markan Gospel were possible: one, theological; the other, historical; both, with the benefit of hindsight, problem-fraught. An irreversible torrent has washed over the exegetical dam in the one hundred and forty years since Gustav Volkmar proposed that Mark was an allegorization of Pauline teaching, that Gospel a life not of Jesus but of Paul.[5] Such a position now appears eccentric on its face. Indeed, Volkmar's assumptions concerning traces of Paulinism in Mark were weighed and found wanting seven decades ago by Martin Werner, who found within that Gospel an indebtedness, shared with Paul, to early Christian beliefs but virtually nothing of that apostle's distinctive interests.[6] Werner's assessment has since been refined but not overturned.[7]

A more oblique yet seemingly more propitious strategy for relating Paul and Mark was to regard that Gospel and the other Synoptics as later exemplars of a Jesus tradition to which, it was assumed, Paul occasionally alluded (cf., e.g., Mark 9:42 and parr./Rom 14:13; Mark 10:11–12 parr./1 Cor 7:10–11; Mark 14:22–24 parr./1 Cor 11:23–26). Rumbling not far beneath the search for parallel passages in the Pauline letters and the Gospels is, of course, the heavily disputed question of Paul's relation to Jesus. Victor Furnish's landmark survey of that controversy arrived at this conclusion: "the Jesus-Paul debate has not ever been significantly advanced, nor will a solution of the Jesus-Paul problem ever be finally achieved, by locating parallel passages in Paul and the Gospels."[8] Viewed in the light of subsequent research, Furnish's appraisal remains apt, and for precisely those reasons that he underscored: the subjectivity of criteria for ascertaining Pauline allusions to Jesus' teachings and the problem of establishing linear develop-

---

[4] Consult C. Clifton Black, *Mark: Images of an Apostolic Interpreter* (Studies on Personalities of the New Testament; Columbia, SC: University of South Carolina Press, 1994) esp. 50–60, 149–56, 165–71, 183–91.

[5] Gustav Volkmar, *Die Religion Jesu* (Leipzig: Brockhaus, 1857).

[6] Martin Werner, *Der Einfluß paulinischer Theologie im Markusevangelium: Eine Studie zur neutestamentlichen Theologie* (BZNW 1; Gießen: Töpelmann, 1923).

[7] See, among others, Vincent Taylor, *The Gospel according to St. Mark: The Greek Text with Introduction, Notes, and Indexes* (London: Macmillan, 1952) 125–29; K. Romaniuk, "Le Problème des Paulinismes dans l'Évangile de Marc," *NTS* 23 (1977) 266–74; Andreas Lindemann, *Paulus im ältesten Christentum: Das Bild des Apostels und die Rezeption der paulinischen Theologie in der frühchristlichen Literatur bis Marcion* (BHT 58; Tübingen: Mohr-Siebeck, 1979) 151–54.

[8] Victor Paul Furnish, "The Jesus-Paul Debate: From Baur to Bultmann," *BJRL* 47 (1964–65) 342–81, rev. repr. in *Paul and Jesus: Collected Essays* (ed. A. J. M. Wedderburn; JSNTSup 37; Sheffield: JSOT Press, 1989) 17–50 (quotation, 44).

ment from even demonstrable parallels. So far as I can tell, the nature and degree of continuity between Jesus and Paul appears at present as problematic as ever, throwing the related question—whether any traditions link the letters and the Gospels—into a veritable stalemate.[9]

In short, if some conjunction of Paul and Mark once appeared to open up a *Hauptstrasse* [highway] for exegetical traffic, now more than ever their intersection looks like a *Sackgasse* [dead end]. Why bother to reopen it? There are, I think, at least three reasons for doing so.

First, and most basically, Pauline theology needs location, not only in the variegated worlds of Judaism and Hellenism, but also within the narrower swath of primitive Christianity. Written probably less than twenty years after Paul's extant letters, Mark's Gospel should offer some help, even though of a general sort, in "putting Paul in his place."[10] And those letters can surely return the favor for Markan interpretation. The impulse to situate the Second Gospel within one or another of the religious exigencies of Paul's letters, which in this century may have reached its apex with the work of Theodore Weeden, has not been wrongheaded, though at times it has been allowed to proceed to an improbable extreme.[11] Working as responsible historians with due sense of chronology, Pauline exegetes have been understandably chary of reaching beyond Paul's letters to later Christian documents for interpretive help. The price they have paid for that scrupulous self-confinement, however, has typically been exacted in one or another

---

[9] Among the participants in this ongoing debate, see especially F. Neirynck, "Paul and the Sayings of Jesus," in *L'Apôtre Paul: Personalité, style et conception du ministère* (ed. A. Vanhoye; BETL 73; Leuven: Leuven University Press/Uitgeverij Peeters, 1986) 265–321; James D. G. Dunn, "Jesus Tradition in Paul," in *Studying the Historical Jesus: Evaluations of the State of Current Research* (ed. Bruce Chilton and Craig A. Evans; NTTS 19; Leiden: Brill, 1994) 155–78; David Wenham, *Paul: Follower of Jesus or Founder of Christianity?* (Grand Rapids, MI: Eerdmans, 1995); and the essays in Wedderburn (ed.), *Jesus and Paul.* Although the present essay has nothing material to add to this discussion, it seems to me that the question of Paul's knowledge and use of Jesus-traditions parallels, in some interesting ways, the debate concerning John's knowledge and use of the Synoptics. In both cases the evidence is ambiguous and admits of varying, plausible interpretations; in both cases the way forward may lie in thinking afresh about, and perhaps reframing, the kinds of questions that may be most fruitfully addressed to the limited primary data at our disposal.

[10] Victor Paul Furnish, "On Putting Paul in His Place," *JBL* 113 (1994) 3–17.

[11] Weeden's construction of the Markan community (in *Mark—Traditions in Conflict* [Philadelphia: Fortress, 1971]) draws heavily from Dieter Georgi, *Die Gegner des Paulus im 2. Korintherbrief* (WMANT 11; Neukirchener-Vluyn: Neukirchener, 1964). For a critique of Georgi's method and proposal, consult Jerry L. Sumney, *Identifying Paul's Opponents: The Question of Method in 2 Corinthians* (JSNTSup 40; Sheffield: JSOT Press, 1990) 49–61; on Weeden, see C. Clifton Black, *The Disciples According to Mark: Markan Redaction in Current Debate* (JSNTSup 27; Sheffield: JSOT Press, 1989) 127–57.

"mirror-reading": conjectural inversions of Paul's surface concerns, pressed (with varying degrees of plausibility) into foils for his letters' interpretation.[12] As C. K. Barrett has observed, "There is all too little evidence to inform us about the Christian tradition, oral and written, in the first Christian century, and we cannot afford to neglect any of it."[13] Comparative study of Pauline and Markan theologies should prove instructive, even if the result be little more than a demonstration of broad bands of similarity amidst great variety.

Another reason for renewing this investigative lease involves some angles of vision on Mark and Paul adopted by their modern interpreters. On one side, the Second Evangelist's stock as a creative interpreter of Jesus-traditions was given a powerful boost by William Wrede's classic study of the messianic secret in the Gospels.[14] Reinforced by the pioneering redaction criticism of R. H. Lightfoot[15] and Willi Marxsen,[16] Mark's theological achievement has since been corroborated by a number of literary critics who recognize in that Gospel's convoluted narrative religious insights that unintentionally comment on our own disjointed age.[17] To dust off an old metaphor: if Mark wielded scissors and paste on the tradition at his disposal, it was with the artistry of a collagist, not the drudgery of a printer's devil.[18] While Mark's way of doing theology is very different from Paul's, for most exegetes it now

---

[12] On the disputed purpose of Romans, consult *The Romans Debate* (ed. Karl P. Donfried; rev. and expanded ed.; Peabody, MA: Hendrickson, 1991). On the perils of "mirror-reading" in Galatians and 1 Thessalonians, see George Lyons, *Pauline Autobiography: Toward a New Understanding* (SBLDS 73; Atlanta, GA: Scholars Press, 1985) esp. 75–121, 176–227.

[13] C. K. Barrett, "The Parallels between Acts and John," in *Exploring the Gospel of John in Honor of D. Moody Smith* (ed. R. Alan Culpepper and C. Clifton Black; Louisville, KY: Westminster John Knox, 1996) 163–78 (here, 163).

[14] William Wrede, *The Messianic Secret* (Library of Theological Translations; Cambridge: James Clarke, 1971 [German original, 1901]).

[15] R. H. Lightfoot, *History and Interpretation in the Gospels* (New York: Harper & Brothers, 1934).

[16] Willi Marxsen, *Mark the Evangelist: Studies on the Redaction History of the Gospel* (Nashville, TN: Abingdon, 1969 [German original, 1956]).

[17] For example, Robert C. Tannehill, "The Disciples in Mark: The Function of a Narrative Role," *JR* 57 (1977) 386–405, repr. in *The Interpretation of Mark* (ed. William Telford; IRT 7; Philadelphia: Fortress; London: SPCK, 1985) 134–57; Frank Kermode, *The Genesis of Secrecy: On the Interpretation of Narrative* (Cambridge, MA: Harvard University Press, 1979); Donald H. Juel, *A Master of Surprise: Mark Interpreted* (Minneapolis, MN: Fortress, 1994).

[18] The comparison of the Second Gospel with a collage has been drawn by Ernest Best, "Mark's Preservation of the Tradition," in *L'Évangile selon Marc: Tradition et rédaction* (ed. M. Sabbe; BETL 34; Leuven: Leuven University Press, 1974) 21–34, repr. in *The Interpretation of Mark*, 119–33.

appears beyond doubt that theology, among other things, is what Mark is doing.[19] Interestingly, on the Pauline side of the critical ledger, a story of Jesus, or a story of Israel for which Jesus is climactic, is currently being viewed by some as an infrastructure for Paul's nonnarrative, theological formulations.[20] Whether scholars will attain the same level of comfort in speaking of "Pauline narrative" as in referring to "Markan theology" remains to be seen. In any event, recent considerations of Mark's Gospel or Paul's letters tend to locate their theologies in a common solar system, for all of the undeniable variance in their orbital paths.

A third reason for revisiting the rapport between Paul and Mark lies in our heightened awareness of their inclusion within Christian scripture and our sensitivity to the hermeneutical consequences of their canonization. Although historical critics of the Bible have rightly disciplined themselves to filter out the voices of all save that of a particular text under examination, throughout history the church has heard the voices within its scripture as mutually confirmatory and corrective, with the canon functioning as a theologically trustworthy resonating chamber. Furthermore, through the peculiar "canon-logic" by which segments of the New Testament came to be compiled (Gospels, Acts, Epistles, Apocalypse), the church has tended to hear Paul's letters—which antedate the canonical Gospels by twenty to fifty years—as theological and ethical commentary on a foundational story of Jesus Christ, differently inflected by Mark, Matthew, Luke, and John.[21] If I correctly understand the interpretive project attempted by

---

[19] The intelligibility of this claim depends considerably on what is meant by "theology." Arguably, Mark would not qualify as a theologian if, as Victor Furnish has suggested, theology is appropriately understood as "critical reflection on the beliefs, rites, and social structures in which an experience of ultimate reality has found expression" ("Paul the Theologian," in *The Conversation Continues: Studies in Paul & John in Honor of J. Louis Martyn* [ed. Robert T. Fortna and Beverly R. Gaventa; Nashville, TN: Abingdon, 1990] 19–34 [quotation, 25, originally italicized]). If I rightly understand Furnish's view, theology is a second-order consideration of the gospel's proclamation, which is a first-order religious activity. Yet one wonders if this sharp differentiation between kerygmatic and theological discourse is either necessary or warranted as regards Paul, Mark, or other Christian authors of the first century. Further, would not the demonstration of such a finely honed distinction in Paul's thought and practice stand in tension with Furnish's prudent observation that Paul is not a systematic theologian in the medieval or modern sense?

[20] Richard B. Hays, *The Faith of Jesus Christ: An Investigation of the Narrative Substructure of Galatians 3:1–4:11* (SBLDS 56; Chico, CA: Scholars Press, 1983); N. Thomas Wright, *The Climax of the Covenant: Christ and the Law in Pauline Theology* (Minneapolis, MN: Fortress, 1992). Such reassessments may be viewed as exegetical tributaries of some broader currents in theology, for an appraisal of which see George W. Stroup, *The Promise of Narrative Theology: Recovering the Gospel in the Church* (Atlanta: John Knox, 1981).

[21] See Albert C. Outler, "The 'Logic' of Canon-making and the Tasks of Canon-

Brevard S. Childs and others, this historically anomalous but theologically intelligible tendency is not so much to be lamented, scorned, or throttled as it should be clarified, refined, and deepened. [22] For this process Robert W. Wall suggests an attractive metaphor:

> A canonical approach to the New Testament's pluriform subject matter envisages a conversation that is more complementary than adversarial. In one sense, the *intercanonical* [*sic*] conversation is very much like an intramural debate over the precise meaning of things generally agreed to be true and substantial. The purpose or outcome of debate is not to resolve firmly fixed disagreements among members of the same community or panel as though a normative synthesis were possible; rather, more often it is the sort of debate that clarifies the contested content of their common ground. [23]

There are four aspects of this analogy that I find appealing. First, it does not evade but presumptively welcomes temperate historical exegesis of those points of view expressed by "members of the biblical panel"—without which, be it noted, the pluriformity of the New Testament's witness could not be adequately recognized. [24] Methodologically, this seals off the Volkmar option: we are no more licensed to read Mark as an allegorization of Pauline life and thought than to construe Romans as an epistolary bedecking of the Olivet Address in Mark 13. Second, Wall's approach (like that of Childs) resists shackling the texts' *Sachen* [concerns] to the particular circumstances of their historical origin or the accidents of their evolution. A real theological exchange can occur between Paul and Mark, in their canonical distillates, without smuggling into the affair dubious assumptions of Mark's genetic dependence on the letters or labored arguments for

---

criticism," in *Texts and Testaments: Critical Essays on the Bible and Early Church Fathers* (ed. W. Eugene March; San Antonio: Trinity University Press, 1980) 263–76.

[22] Thus, Gerald T. Sheppard: "Just as the semantic force of words is not secured solely by appeal to their etymologies but gains specific import within the context of a particular sentence, so the context of scripture inevitably influences how earlier traditions come to make sense as a part of scripture" ("Canonical Criticism," *ABD* 1 [1992] 861–66 [here, 862]). See also Brevard S. Childs, *Introduction to the Old Testament as Scripture* (Philadelphia: Fortress, 1979); idem, *The New Testament as Canon: An Introduction* (Philadelphia: Fortress, 1985).

[23] Robert W. Wall, "Reading the New Testament in Canonical Context," in *Hearing the New Testament: Strategies for Interpretation* (ed. Joel B. Green; Grand Rapids, MI: Eerdmans; Carlisle, Cumbria: Paternoster, 1995) 370–93 (quotation, 382). Similarly, see James D. G. Dunn and James P. Mackey, *New Testament Theology in Dialogue: Christology and Ministry* (Philadelphia: Westminster, 1987).

[24] On the tension between historical and theological considerations in Childs's own canonical approach, see D. Moody Smith, "Why Approaching the New Testament as Canon Matters," *Int* 40 (1986) 407–11.

Paul's knowledge of that Gospel's preliterary traditions. (The Jesus-Paul debate is well worth convening, but not in every time and place; nor is it the only intracanonical show in town.) According to this model, third, a carefully structured exercise in "mutual criticism" (Wall) of the positions adopted by Paul and Mark is, for now, an end that is good and sufficient in itself. Areas of common ground can be identified without collapsing their views into a specious homogeneity that well serves neither; points of dispute between them can be sharpened apart from strategies calculated to pronounce the one as theologically superior to the other. Fourth, by conceiving the exercise as a conversation of complements, instead of an adversarial contest, this interpretive paradigm reminds us of a more general quality essential to both the church and its canon: each remains in dynamic conversation within itself and with each other.[25]

Enough of prolegomena; it is time to turn to some interlocutory texts. But which ones? To compare the whole of Mark's presentation with Pauline theology in its entirety, or even the theology within a particular Pauline letter, is, in a single essay, manifestly out of the question.[26] We must narrow the scope. For our purposes two passages of reasonable length may be invited into mutual conversation: 1 Cor 1:18–2:16 and Mark 15:16–41. Needless to say, these passages have not been selected willy-nilly; they are peculiarly promising for the task at hand. There is, to begin with, an intuitive sense of fit between them, borne out by exegetes who draw both texts into a common interpretive arena, often as jointly exemplary of a theology of the cross.[27] For the documents in which they occur, both passages are recognized by most

---

[25] Throughout this essay I use the metaphor of an "intracanonical conversation" heuristically. Viewed historically, the authors of 1 Corinthians and the Second Gospel were not literally in dialogue with each other. To speak strictly, it is the church that has conversed with Paul's letter and Mark's Gospel, both prior and subsequent to their canonization. As a consequence of that canonical process, however, the church has not regarded the apostle's and evangelist's witnesses as detached from each other or as amenable to comparison by mere happenstance. Rather, these and other canonical "voices" have been heard by the church as to some degree theologically interpenetrative and in some sense mutually interpretive (hence, the exegetical principle of antiquity, "Scripture interprets scripture"). The figure of a conversation—between two or more of the Bible's varied constituents, as well as between the church and the Bible as a whole— seems to me, therefore, a reasonable characterization of some religiously important relationships, so long as that trope not be asked to support more weight than any metaphor can bear.

[26] This more ambitious feat has been attempted, with debatable results, by J. C. Fenton, "Paul and Mark," in *Studies in the Gospels: Essays in Memory of R. H. Lightfoot* (ed. D. E. Nineham; Oxford: Blackwell, 1955) 89–112.

[27] See, for instance, Ulrich Luz, "Theologia crucis als Mitte der Theologie im Neuen Testament," *EvT* 34 (1974) 116–41.

commentators as *cruces interpretum* in more ways than one. Structurally, 1 Corinthians 1–2 is Paul's introductory point of orientation for the balance of that letter, while Mark 15 is the climax toward which the whole of Mark's narrative builds. Substantively, the crucifixion of Jesus is central in both passages. Not only does the cross constitute the chief point of material correspondence between these texts; in no other Markan or Pauline passages do these authors concentrate at such length and with such intensity on the cross, as such, as they do here. Prior to the passion narrative there are, of course, general references throughout Mark to Jesus' death (e.g., 3:6; 8:31; 9:9, 31; 10:33–34, 45; 12:7–8); nevertheless, almost all of Mark's references to Jesus' cross or crucifixion occur in 15:16–41 (vv. 20, 21, 24, 25, 27, 30, 32; cf. 15:13–15; 16:6). In Paul's letters only Gal 6:12–15 approaches 1 Cor 1:18–2:16 as a sustained, though more cursory, reflection on the theological significance of "the cross of Christ"; elsewhere in Galatians (2:19; 3:1, 13; 5:11, 24) or in the other undisputed letters (Rom 6:6; 2 Cor 13:4; Phil 2:8; 3:18), Paul's references to crucifixion or the cross are surprisingly rare, in comparison with his more widespread mention of Jesus' death and its significance.[28] Finally, 1 Cor 1:18–2:16 has been subjected to close analysis in two recent essays by Victor Furnish.[29] Our selection of this passage and Mark 15:16–41 thus allows us to converse with that doyen of Pauline interpreters, as he illumines one of Paul's most profound expositions of "the word of the cross."

II. Hearing the Panelists

1 Corinthians 1:18–2:16: Primary Claims of Paul's Argument

Paul's comments in 1 Cor 1:18–2:16 are prompted by partisan strife within the Corinthian church (1:10–11; 3:3), each clique aligning itself with one apostolic leader to the denigration of others (1:12; 3:4, 21; 4:6). Within this context "1:18–2:16 stands as a kind of excursus" (Furnish), which, as Peter Lampe notes, "at first glance, has *nothing* to do with the Corinthian parties."[30] On further reflection, however, this

---

[28] For a careful sifting of the relevant evidence, consult Charles B. Cousar, *A Theology of the Cross: The Death of Jesus in the Pauline Letters* (OBT; Minneapolis, MN: Fortress, 1990), N.B. 21–24.

[29] Victor Paul Furnish, "Theology in 1 Corinthians: Initial Soundings," in *Society of Biblical Literature 1989 Seminar Papers* (ed. David J. Lull; Atlanta: Scholars Press, 1989) 246–64 (hereafter, "Initial Soundings"); idem, "Theology in 1 Corinthians," in *Pauline Theology, Volume II: 1 & 2 Corinthians* (ed. David M. Hay; Minneapolis, MN: Fortress, 1993) 59–89 (hereafter, "Theology in 1 Corinthians").

[30] Peter Lampe, "Theological Wisdom and the 'Word About the Cross': The Rhetorical Scheme in 1 Corinthians 1–4," *Int* 44 (1990) 117–31 (quotation, 118); cf. Furnish,

passage is only apparently digressive, having *everything* to do with the Corinthians' factiousness; for, as Paul understands it, a misconstruing of the gospel lies at the heart of their dysfunctional religiosity. A confusion whose root is *theological* must first be addressed before its social aberrations can be put right. Until then, any counsel that Paul could possibly offer would be misapprehended by the Corinthians as a self-interested move on his part (cf. 1:13–15), which would only exacerbate the problem by playing into the hands of both his detractors and his supporters.

While the structure of Paul's theological response, centered on "the word of the cross" (1:18),[31] is susceptible to different analyses, Furnish's most recent suggestion of a bipartite structure is sensible.[32] First, in 1:18–2:5 Paul considers God's ostensibly foolish but soteriologically purposeful wisdom (1:18–25), confirmed by the Corinthians' own circumstances (1:26–31) and by the substance and style of Paul's preaching (2:1–5). Since a critical aim of the apostle's response is to foreclose the possibility that human beings can reason their way to God's wisdom (1:21), in 2:6–16 Paul unfolds the epistemological consequences: that wisdom, which remains hidden (2:7) and incomprehensible by the standards of an age that is passing away (2:6, 8, 14), is revealed by God through the Spirit (2:9–10, 12–13).[33]

From this framework, some "pivotal theological conceptions" arise, only a few of which may be identified here.[34] To begin with, 1 Cor 1:18–2:16 is nothing if not testimony to the stupefying power and salvific purpose of God. Throughout this passage God is the sole seat of wisdom (1:21; 2:7) and the active, predestining agent (2:7; 2:9b), whether for empowerment (1:18; 2:5) or abrogation (1:28). God is the thwarter of human cleverness (1:19b; cf. Isa 29:14; Ps 33:10), the transmuter of this world's wisdom into foolishness and of this world's

---

"Theology in 1 Corinthians," 64.

[31] All translations are my own, except where otherwise indicated.

[32] Furnish, "Theology in 1 Corinthians," 64–67. In "Initial Soundings" (250–53), a quinquepartite analysis is proposed (1:18–25; 1:26–31; 2:1–5; 2:6–16; 3:1–4).

[33] Furnish's summary of this second movement in Paul's argument—"the hiddenness of God's wisdom"—seems to put the accent on a topic that is minimally developed (only at 2:7 and 9a [the latter citing Isa 64:4]). The flow of Paul's thinking may be better captured by Robin S. Barbour's proposal that 1:18–2:5 is centered on the hidden power of God, 2:6–16 on the knowledge of God's hidden purpose ("Wisdom and the Cross in 1 Corinthians 1 and 2," in *Theologia Crucis—Siglum Crucis: Festschrift für Erich Dinkler zum 70. Geburtstag* [ed. Carl Andresen and Günter Klein; Tübingen: Mohr-Siebeck, 1979] 57–71 [here, 66]). Pressing the point, I prefer to describe 2:6–16 as Paul's pneumatological reflections on "*how* God's hidden purpose is known."

[34] The category is Furnish's ("Theology in 1 Corinthians," 67–69); my comments here are informed by but not restricted to his analysis.

strength into weakness (1 Cor 1:20b, 25; cf. 1:19a), the elector of the foolish, the weak, and even "things that are nothing" to the tasks of shaming and nullifying the wise, the strong, and "things that are" (1:27–28). It is God who saves believers by means of the foolishness of apostolic preaching (1:21) and bestows on them the Spirit, by which God's thoughts and gifts may be known (2:10–12). It is God who is the source of believers' life, who has made Christ their wisdom, rectification, sanctification, redemption, and glorification (1:30–31; 2:7). It is hard to imagine a more uncompromising, tightly focused understanding of God's freedom, sovereignty, and restorative power than what Paul offers here. From these conceptions, grounded in θεός [God], correlative aspects of Paul's anthropology and soteriology are articulated in 1:18–2:16.

Next we may note the presentation of human beings in 1 Cor 1:18–2:16—not because anthropology is central to Paul's argument, but because, in this particular case, its dimensions inevitably emerge in sharp contrast to his depiction of God's sovereign activity. In this passage the emphasis falls both on a perishing humanity's blindness and folly, predicated on any norm of wisdom other than the radically contradictory standard revealed by God through the cross; and on the restoration of those who have entrusted themselves to the strange power of God, to whom the preached word of the cross bears testimony (1:18, 21–23; 2:5, 8–10; also 2 Cor 4:3). Viewed in context, "Jews [who] demand signs and Greeks [who] seek wisdom" (1 Cor 1:22) [35] are typical instances, not of noble but inadequate human attempts to trace God's designs in this world, but rather of the flat incapability of all, whether Jew or Gentile, "[to know] the mind of the Lord so as to instruct him" (2:16a; cf. Isa 40:13; Wis 9:13); of that centripetal human egoism which projects its own self-interest onto the sovereign God, whose thoughts and ways are not our own (1 Cor 1:20, 27–29, 31; cf. Rom 1:22–25; Isa 55:8–9; Jer 9:23–24); of their presumptuous faithlessness in demanding that God produce authenticating warrants before any mortal bar of judgment (1 Cor 1:23). Because the distance between God and humanity is not a matter of degree, Paul does not belabor the

---

[35] In Jewish and pagan writings of Paul's day, there is no single or uniform meaning for "signs" (σημεῖα) or "wisdom" (σοφία). Plausible foils for his critique of the demand for signs might include such connotations of σημεῖα as we find in Philo, as argumentative proof (*Fug.* 204; *Vit. Mos.* 2.263), and in Josephus and at Qumran, as confirmation by sight or other sensory perception (*J.W.* 6.68; *Ant.* 10.28–29; 1QMyst 1:5 [הזאות]). Among the Stoics σοφία was defined as "knowledge of things both divine and human" (ἐπιστήμη θείων τε καὶ ἀνθρωπείων πραγμάτων, Aetius *Placita* 1.2). See Karl H. Rengstorf, "σημεῖον, κ.τ.λ.," *TDNT* 7:200–69, and Ulrich Wilckens and Georg Fohrer, "σοφία, σοφός, σοφίζω," *TDNT* 7:465–528.

superiority of God's wisdom or strength to our own. Rather, by clashing the wisdom of God's *foolishness* and the strength of God's *weakness* (1:25), Paul's proclamation of "the mystery of God" (2:1) effectively anticipates a Barthian "infinite qualitative difference" between the divine and human norms by which wisdom and folly, strength and weakness, are properly construed (thus, 1:20).[36] The fact that such construing is closed to our sophisticated efforts is further and altogether consistently underlined by the fittingness of human nadir—expressed preeminently in the cross of Christ (1:24; 2:2) but also in the foolishness of preaching (1:21), the church's mean status (1:26), and the apostle's weakness (2:1, 3–5; also 1:17; 2 Cor 10:10)—as the medium through which God's alien yet authentic wisdom and power are revealed. For the same reason Paul stresses the unqualified dependence of human beings upon God for their calling to faith (1:24, 26; also 1:2; Rom 8:28), for their progressively restored life in Christ (1 Cor 1:18, 21, 30) and its consummation (2:7; cf. Rom 8:18–21; 2 Cor 3:18); upon "the Spirit that is from God" for discernment and interpretation of the gifts of God's bestowal (1 Cor 2:11b–16; also 4:7). For those who love him, everything is prepared *by God* and is categorically inaccessible to the spiritually unendowed eye, ear, or heart (2:9; cf. Isa 64:4; 52:15).

At the nexus of these reflections on the saving God and a hubristic humanity is the soteriological value of, or transvaluation indicated by, "Jesus Christ and him crucified" (1 Cor 2:2). In 1:30, to be sure, Paul brushes over what later would become the classical vocabulary of atonement, which elsewhere he also adopts though does not explain: "righteousness" (6:11; Rom 3:21–26; 5:17–21 *et passim*; Phil 3:9), "sanctification" (1 Cor 1:2; 6:11; Rom 6:19, 22; 1 Thess 4:3; 5:23; cf. Lev 22:32), "redemption" (1 Cor 6:19–20; 7:23; Rom 3:4; 8:23; Gal 3:13; 4:5). Examined within the context of 1 Cor 1:18–2:16, however, these metaphors in 1:30 constitute a chord whose keynote is surely σοφία [wisdom]: "It is due to him [God] that you are in Christ Jesus, who was made wisdom for us by God." To Job's question, "Where shall wisdom be found?" (28:12),[37] Paul's tacit reply is that σοφία—the core of reality, the essential framework of meaning and value implanted by God in creation—is disclosed with restorative power only in the proclamation of Christ crucified (cf. 1 Cor 1:18–25). Accordingly, for Paul Jesus is not the purveyor of wise teaching *par excellence*, but *wisdom itself*. As Leander

---

[36] Karl Barth, *The Epistle to the Romans* (London: Oxford University Press, 1933; German original, 1919) 10. As Barth notes, the phrase is traceable to Kierkegaard.

[37] Here I am obviously indebted to Furnish's intriguing suggestion that 1:18–2:16 (–3:4) is in a sense propelled by the meditations in Job 28 and other sapiential texts ("Initial Soundings," 254–55). See also Barbour, "Wisdom and the Cross in 1 Corinthians 1 and 2," 62–64.

Keck comments, "In making Christ our wisdom, God made Christ the framework for our understanding of God."[38] Such understanding, which Paul describes here as "the mind of Christ" (1 Cor 2:16; cf. Rom 12:2), is itself a critical dimension of the salvation accomplished by God for believers through the foolishness of preaching (1 Cor 1:21).

The implications of this cruciform epistemology are both profound and far-reaching. First, for Paul it means that the cross of Christ is not a discrete historical datum but *a transformative eruption within the fabric of history*: an occurrence that has recast the character of the divine-human relationship, the way in which we can know and are known by God (cf. 1 Cor 8:3; 13:12). Second, from his description of that event—in terms of mysterious wisdom imparted (2:6–7), a turning of the aeons (1:20; 2:6–8), Christ's death and resurrection (1:23; 2:2; 15:3–28), God's judgment of every human claim and healing of every human aspiration (1:18–31)—it is clear that Paul conceives it altogether *apocalyptically*.[39] Third, Paul's understanding of the cross is *radically eschatological* in the sense of a once-for-all, divine invasion whose impact pulses without surcease into God's present and future with us. As Furnish has suggested,[40] this conviction is subtly yet vividly captured in 1 Cor 1:18– 2:16 by Paul's careful use of Greek verbs in perfect tenses to characterize certain punctiliar events in the past whose effects are related to the present: thus, "we speak of God's *wisdom that remains hidden in mystery*" (σοφίαν ἐν μυστηρίῳ τὴν ἀποκεκρυμμένην; 2:7); "to know nothing among you except Jesus Christ, *who indeed continues to be the one crucified*" (καὶ τοῦτον ἐσταυρωμένον; 2:2; also 1:23). "The Risen and Exalted One remains the Crucified One."[41] Because "Christ has been raised from the dead" (again the perfect tense, ἐγήγερται; 15:20; also 15:4, 12, 15), he continues by God's vivification to be *the Christ*; but because God's raising of Jesus has not eradicated his crucifixion but has vindicated this one and no other, "Christ *crucified*" remains the unremitting focus of Paul's preaching (2:2), the ineluctable scandal for human pretensions to power and wisdom (1:23), the indispensable criterion for human knowledge of God's still hidden power and mysterious wisdom (1:24; cf. 2 Cor 13:4a).[42]

---

[38] Leander E. Keck, "Biblical Preaching as Divine Wisdom," in *A New Look at Preaching* (GNS 7; ed. John Burke, O.P.; Wilmington, DE: Glazier, 1983) 137–56 (quotation, 153).

[39] On the importance of an apocalyptic worldview in Paul's thought, see J. Christiaan Beker, *Paul the Apostle: The Triumph of God in Life and Thought* (Philadelphia: Fortress, 1980) esp. 16–19, 135–81, 351–76.

[40] Furnish, "Theology in 1 Corinthians," 68, 81.

[41] Ernst Käsemann, *Jesus Means Freedom* (London: SCM, 1969 [German orig., 1968]) 67.

[42] See the judicious assessment by Cousar, *A Theology of the Cross*, 103–8.

Mark 15:16–41: Primary Themes of Mark's Narrative

Mark's account of Jesus' mockery, crucifixion, and death comes near the conclusion of a narrative that has been expressly hurtling towards precisely this moment. From its beginning the reader has been privileged with three critical pieces of information that are either unknown, unappreciated, or disregarded by all of the story's figures save Jesus (and God). The first: Jesus is the Christ and Son of God (1:1, 9–11; 8:29–30; 9:2–8, 41; 13:32; 14:36–37, 61–65; cf. 3:21; 4:41; 5:17; 6:1–6a; 12:6; 15:2–11), the Son of Man who must suffer many things (8:31–33; 9:12, 31–32; 10:33–34; 14:21; cf. 12:7–8, 12; 14:62–65). Second: much as they have already arrested and murdered John the Baptist (1:14a; 6:14–29; 9:11–13; 11:30–33a), the religious and political forces of Israel and Rome are busily scheming to snare and to destroy Jesus (3:6, 22; 7:5; 8:11, 15, 31; 10:2, 33; 11:18, 27–28; 12:6–8, 12–13; 14:1–2, 10–11, 53–65; 15:1, 10–15), in paradoxical fulfillment of God's foreordination (1:15; 8:31; 9:12, 31; 10:33–34; 12:10–11; 14:21, 27, 36, 49b). The reader of this intricately entwined plot has also received a third puzzle-piece, equally critical though less emphatically recurrent: once the divinely accredited Son of Man has suffered the full extent of universal contempt, he will arise from the dead after three days (8:31; 9:9, 31; 10:33–34; 14:28). So deeply pervasive of the Second Gospel are these ideas that Martin Kähler's famous characterization of Mark and the other Gospels as "passion narratives with extended introductions" is an exaggeration that nevertheless contains a considerable measure of truth.[43] At the heart of the passion proper is Mark 15:16–41, whose structure consists simply of (a) the Roman guard's scornful abuse of the condemned Jesus (15:16–20), (b) the humiliating crucifixion of Jesus (15:21–32), and (c) the death of Jesus (15:33–41).

What pivotal theological conceptions might be inferred from this narrative? Perhaps the most striking dimension of this text is its portrayal of a human depravity that flouts the mysterious sovereignty of God (ἡ βασιλεία τοῦ θεοῦ) to which Jesus has rendered testimony (Mark 1:15; 4:11, 26, 30; 9:1, 47; 10:14–15, 23–25; 12:34; 14:25). While 15:19 mentions Jesus' physical abuse by the Roman guard, none of the torture of crucifixion itself is detailed in 15:21–41. The ultimate punishment is captured by Mark with stark concision: "And they crucified him" (καὶ σταυροῦσιν αὐτόν [15:24a], the verb in the historical present).[44] Even Jesus' anguish goes unmentioned until the

---

[43] Martin Kähler, *The So-Called Historical Jesus and the Historic Biblical Christ* (Philadelphia: Fortress, 1964 [German original, 1892]) 80 n. 11.

[44] Of Gavius of Messana, "as he hung on his cross," Cicero declares that "he hung there, [to] suffer the worst extreme of the tortures inflicted upon slaves. To bind a

very end (15:34; cf. 15:37). The account dwells, instead, on the heinous conduct of that execution's agents and audience, including even Jesus' fellow victims (15:32b; cf. Luke 23:39–43): their cruelty (15:15–20, 24, 29–32a)[45] and derision (ἐβλασφήμουν; cf. 2:7; 3:28–29; 7:22; 14:64), their garbling of what Jesus has said (15:29 [cf. 11:15–17; 13:1–2; 15:58]); 15:34–36[46]), their blindness to the ironically placarded charge that he is "the King of the Jews" (15:26; cf. Mark 4:10–12; 8:18a), their deafness to the truth that is veiled in their own taunts—"Hail, King of the Jews" (15:18 [also 15:2, 9, 12]; cf. 1:11/Ps 2:7), "The Christ, the King of Israel" (15:32; cf. 1:1, 11; 8:29; 9:41; 14:61–62), "Others he saved; himself he cannot save" (15:31; cf. 8:35; 10:45). In Mark the crucifixion of Jesus exposes a bankrupt presumptuousness that feeds on gross demonstrations of power and self-aggrandizement: "Let him now come down from the cross, so that we may see and believe" (15:32).[47] This grim anthropological landscape is relieved by but few rays of light. One is the centurion, "who stood facing him [and] saw that in this way he breathed his last" and, on that basis, confesses Jesus to be truly God's Son (15:39).[48] Looking on from a distance (cf. Ps 38:11), from among

---

Roman citizen is a crime, to flog him is an abomination, to slay him is almost an act of murder: to crucify him is—what? There is no fitting word that can possibly describe so horrible a deed" (*In Verrem* 2.5.66 [LCL 293:654–57]; see also Cicero, *Pro Rabirio* 3.10; 5.16).

[45] In Mark the mockery of Jesus is not only public but outrageously excessive: "the whole [military] cohort" (ὅλην τὴν σπεῖραν, 15:16) was a battalion of two hundred to six hundred soldiers.

[46] In so dark a context, the offer of sour wine (ὄξος) to the dying Jesus is probably not to be read as a merciful act. Rather, it is humanity's last attempt, uncomprehending of what Jesus has said (Ελωι, not Ἠλία), to force a sign from heaven (see also 8:11; for later instances of the legend that Elijah would return to rescue the righteous, see *b. Ber.* 58a; *b. B. Qam.* 60b; *b. ʿAbod. Zar.* 17b, 18b). That gambit is, of course, utterly futile, since already "Elijah has come, and they did to him whatever they pleased" (9:13).

[47] The final clause, ἵνα ἴδωμεν καὶ πιστεύσωμεν, is without verbal parallel in the other Gospels' crucifixion accounts. As Christopher D. Marshall notes, this phraseology "reverses the pattern established throughout [Mark's] entire story where faith is the presupposition of miracle, not its inevitable consequence" (*Faith as a Theme in Mark's Narrative* [SNTSMS 64; Cambridge: Cambridge University Press, 1989] 205). In support of Marshall's assessment, see Mark 1:15; 2:5; 5:34, 36; 9:23–24; 10:52; 11:22–24.

[48] Some learned commentaries contend that the centurion was convinced of Jesus' identity by the rending of the sanctuary veil, whether by God (Raymond E. Brown, *The Death of the Messiah: From Gethsemane to the Grave: A Commentary on the Passion Narratives in the Four Gospels* [2 vols.; Anchor Bible Reference Library; New York: Doubleday, 1994] 2.1144–46) or by the power of Jesus' superhuman shout (Robert H. Gundry, *Mark: A Commentary on His Apology for the Cross* [Grand Rapids, MI: Eerdmans, 1993] 943–79). At least two difficulties attend this interpretation. First, it leaves unexplained why, under equally miraculous circumstances on the Mount of Transfiguration (Mark 9:2–8), only the voice from heaven—and not Jesus' three close confederates—had acclaimed him

many other women, are Mary Magdalene, Mary the mother of James and Joses, and Salome, disciples who had followed (ἠκολούθουν; see 1:18; 2:14; 6:1; 8:34; 10:21, 28) and served (διηκόνουν; see 1:31; 9:35; 10:43) Jesus while in Galilee (15:40–41).[49] Though neither is exonerated as such, from the Markan standpoint these women and the Gentile commander—minor characters at best—appear to be not far from "the mystery of the kingdom of God" (4:11; 12:34; 15:43). The ultimate outsider, evincing the last full measure of devotion, is the dying Jesus, who submitted himself entirely to his Father's will (14:36, 39; 15:23[50]), whose last words—a prayer addressed to "my God" (15:34)—implicitly maintained a bond with the One who had seemingly left him in the lurch.[51]

Of the presentation of God in this passage, what indeed may we say? If 1 Cor 1:18–2:16 appears to have been animated by Job 28:12, Mark 15:16–41 almost registers as an oblique meditation on Isa 45:15: "Truly, you are a God who hides himself, O God of Israel, the Savior." The word θεός [God] occurs only three times in this Markan section: twice, in the last cry of Jesus (15:34); once, in the centurion's acknowledgment of whose Son Jesus was (15:39). The earlier occurrence is especially significant, as it is a clear echo of the biblical lament, Psalm 22. Gripped by the despondency of Mark's tableau, exegetes have wondered whether, upon hearing that psalm's opening plea (v. 1) on the lips of the dying Jesus, the reader is invited to inject hope within Mark 15 by advancing fast-forward to the concluding praise for the psalmist's vindication in Ps 22:22–31.[52] This question distracts us from

"[God's] Son." (On the relation of faith and miracles in Mark, see the preceding note.) Second, at 15:39 the centurion is clearly positioned as ὁ παρεστηκὼς ἐξ ἐναντίας αὐτοῦ, "the one who stood facing him"—not the temple. In Mark what the centurion saw, explicitly and emphatically, was "that [Jesus] *thus expired*"—unlike either Matthew (27:54) or Luke (23:47), who in different ways ease the Markan paradox that revelation is mediated through *concealment* (4:11–12, 21–25).

[49] *Pace* Brown, *The Death of the Messiah*, 2.1155–57, these women's role as disciples is further suggested by their association with Jesus' burial (15:47; 16:1–2), a task performed by John's disciples for their slain leader (6:29). In Mark, as Brown acknowledges (2.1156), the disciples of Jesus are not coterminous with the Twelve (2:15; 3:7, 9, 13–14; 4:10, 34; 8:34; 9:35).

[50] If the wine mixed with myrrh had analgesic properties (see Prov 31:6–7), its refusal by Jesus might suggest his acceptance of undiminished pain.

[51] For Mary Ann Tolbert, "Jesus [in Mark 15:34] is forsaken by God, and at the same time God is available to be called upon" (*Sowing the Gospel: Mark's World in Literary-Historical Perspective* [Minneapolis, MN: Fortress, 1989], 283). Surely this inverts Mark's point: God is not "available" to the crucified Jesus, but neither is Jesus abandoned by God (15:38; 16:6; cf. 8:31; 9:31; 10:33–34).

[52] This possibility, among others, for softening the cry of dereliction is considered and rejected by Brown, *The Death of the Messiah* 2.1044–51.

Mark's verifiable appropriation of scripture, not only in 15:34, but throughout this passage: it is *allusive*, not explicit. Unlike its Johannine parallel (19:24b, 28, 36–37) and Mark's occasional technique elsewhere (1:2–3; 7:6–7[LXX], 10; 10:5–8a, 19; 11:17; 12:10–11, 26, 36; 14:27; cf. 9:12–13; 14:21, 49), Mark 15:16–41 is riddled with details, drawn particularly from Psalm 22 (vv. 6–7/Mark 15:29; v. 18/Mark 15:24) but also from Psalms 38 (v. 11/Mark 15:40–41) and 69 (v. 21/Mark 15:23, 36), which suggest without directly demonstrating that, in precisely this manner of Jesus' dying, God's will is being fulfilled.[53] Such a pattern of scriptural intimation tallies, not only with Mark's earlier use of passive verbs implying divine agency in the Son of Man's destiny (8:31 [δεῖ, "must"]; 9:31 [παραδίδοται, "is to be handed over"]; 10:33 [παραδοθήσεται, "will be handed over"]), but also with the apocalyptic trappings of the present text (15:33/Ezek 32:7–8, Amos 8:9; 15:38/Isa 64:1, Ezek 1:1) and the paradoxical warrant for the centurion's acknowledgment of Jesus' identity as "God's Son" (υἱὸς θεοῦ [15:39], an anarthrous construction itself patient of connotations both mundane and exalted). Throughout the crucifixion of Jesus—even in 15:38, whose blatancy Mark leaves ambiguous (cf. Matt 27:51–54; Luke 23:44–48)[54]—the outskirts of God's ways are traceable, but only with the fingers of faith (cf. Job 26:14).

Lastly, the christology of this passage invites comment. The classical approaches to this topic, with their monocular concentration on the functions or titles ascribed to Jesus, may mislead us in analyzing Mark 15:16–41, since (a) Jesus seems to perform here no function other than to die in ignominy,[55] and (b) his acclamation as "God's Son" is neither

---

[53] Missing from the earliest and best manuscripts of both the Alexandrian and Western families (ℵ A B C D X Ψ *Lect* it[d, k] syr[s] cop[sa, bo][mss], fay[vid] Eusebian Canon[s][mss]), Mark 15:28 is regarded by most exegetes as a later scribal interpolation, prompted by Isaiah 53:12 (and perhaps also Luke 22:37). By contrast, indirect biblical corroboration is typical of Mark (e.g., Mk 1:6/2 Kgs 1:8; Mk 1:11/Ps 2:7, Isa 42:1; Mk 4:12/Isa 6:9–10; Mk 4:35–41/Ps 107:23–30; Mk 7:37/Isa 35:5–6; Mk 8:18/Jer 5:21; Mk 11:9/Ps 118:25–26; Mk 12:1/Isa 5:1–2; Mk 13:14, 19, 24–26/Dan 9:27, 12:1, Isa 13:10; Mk 14:18/Ps 41:9). On Mark's scriptural interpretation in general, see Joel Marcus, *The Way of the Lord: Christological Exegesis of the Old Testament in the Gospel of Mark* (Louisville, KY: Westminster/John Knox, 1992).

[54] Timothy J. Geddert summarizes no less than thirty-five different interpretations of Mark 15:38 in the scholarly literature (*Watchwords: Mark 13 in Markan Eschatology* [JSNTSup 26; Sheffield: JSOT Press, 1989] 141–43). Within the Markan context (see esp. 11:12–18; 13:1–2, 14) the veil's rending probably suggests a divine judgment on the temple that amounts to nothing less than the rupture of its holiness (cf. Ezek 10:1–22; 11:22–25; *2 Apoc. Bar.* 6:7; 8:2). This suggestion, however, is only intimated by the evangelist, not explained.

[55] The clearest expressions of "functional christology" in Mark appear at 10:45 and 14:24, which, respectively, draw on the analogies of redemption (cf. Lev 25:47–52; Num

self-defining nor, for that matter, unprecedented in Mark (see 1:11; 3:11; 5:7; 9:7; 14:61; cf. 12:6; 13:32). If, taking Keck's advice,[56] we inquire into the pattern of correlations expressed or implied in this text between (on the one side) Jesus and (on the other) God and the human condition, the results, though provisional, are more promising. With respect to the world, what Jesus does in Mark's account of the crucifixion is to subject himself completely to the misery, degradation, and abandonment that he has previously alleviated in others (see, e.g., 1:21–28; 5:1–43; 9:14–29). Jesus' self-subjugation is at the same time an act of supreme obedience to the divine will (14:36): an expression, within the heart of faithless darkness, of that kind of faith in a hidden God which finds salvation to issue most strangely yet assuredly from loss of life for the sake of the gospel (8:35). Dying in this way (οὕτως, 15:39), Jesus' resemblance ("sonship") to God (his *Abba*, Father) can be acknowledged by a sinfully implicated human being—for the first and only time (within Mark), publicly and in truth (ἀληθῶς). Of all the equally accurate acknowledgments of Jesus' affinity with God, throughout the Gospel, here and only here can humanity *truly* recognize and proclaim Jesus as God's Son: because only at his crucifixion do the antinomies around which Mark pivots—the authority and vulnerability of Jesus (10:42–45), his life and his death (8:34–9:1), the cross of the unexpected Christ and the germination of God's mysterious kingdom (4:10–12, 26–32)—converge without simple resolution, yet with the tensive integrity of narrative paradox.[57] The most apt commentary on 15:16–41 may be that of the Markan Jesus, courtesy of the psalmist: "A stone that the builders rejected—this has become the main cornerstone: this was the Lord's doing, and it is amazing in our eyes" (Mark 12:10–11/Ps 118:22–23 [LXX]).

3:45–51) and covenant-ratification (cf. Exod 24:6–8; Jer 31:31) as interpretations of Jesus' death (both activities said to be "for many" [ἀντὶ/ὑπὲρ πολλῶν]). Neither of these is explicitly coordinated with the other, however, and both metaphors are absent from Mark 15:16–41.

[56] Leander E. Keck, "Toward the Renewal of New Testament Christology," *NTS* 32 (1986) 362–77, esp. 370–74.

[57] The soundness of Keck's approach (see above) is illuminated by a passage such as Mark 15:39. With its ambient connotations of political legitimation (2 Sam 7:13–14; Ps 89:26–27; 4QFlor 1:7–12; Dio Chrysostomus, *Orationes* 4.21), righteousness (Sir 4:10; Wis 2:18; *Jub.* 1:24–25), and kinship with all humankind (Epictetus, *Disc.* 3.24.14–16), the title "Son of God" does not so much define Jesus in Mark's Gospel as Jesus redefines what "God's sonship" truly (ἀληθῶς) means. On the generative tensions within Mark's narrative theology, see M. Eugene Boring, "The Christology of Mark: Hermeneutical Issues for Systematic Theology," *Semeia* 30 (1984) 125–53.

III. Talking Points

Aspects of Convergence

For all of their ineffaceable differences, both formal and material, 1 Cor 1:18–2:16 and Mark 15:16–41 intersect, with impressive frequency and depth, on at least four theological issues of fundamental importance.

1. *Both Mark and Paul situate the cross of Jesus within a larger apocalyptic outlook.* Though the language of 1 Corinthians 1–2 and the imagery of Mark 15 are not identical, both draw from a deep reservoir of apocalyptic metaphor (e.g., "this age" [1 Cor 1:20; 2:6, 8]; "in mystery" [2:7]; "that which has been hidden" [2:7] and "revealed" [2:10]; "darkness upon the whole of the earth" [Mark 15:33]; the rending of the temple-curtain [15:38]). Further examples can be multiplied across the pages of 1 Corinthians (esp. 15:3–58) and Mark (esp. 4:1–34; 13:3–37). To be sure, the theological syntax by which such concepts are differently coordinated in Mark and in Paul, their theologies' approach to and divergence from the apocalypticism of their era, and even a satisfying definition for the phenomenon of "apocalyptic" itself are all notoriously complicated questions that cannot be pursued here.[58] In any case, for both Mark and Paul, the cross of Jesus is a historical event of transhistorical significance, which exposes a radical split—quite literally so, in Mark 15:38—between "the rulers of this age" (1 Cor 2:8) and "the reign of God" (Mark 1:15).

2. *Both Paul and Mark concur that the actual though recondite agent behind the cross of Jesus is God.* Of the two, Paul is far more explicit on this point: "the word of the cross . . . is the power of God" (1 Cor 1:18; 2:1–5), however incognizant of this secret and hidden wisdom "the rulers of this age" have proved to be (2:7–8). The cross is the ineradicable stamp of God's radical freedom and sovereignty to judge and to save in a way that overthrows all human expectation and common sense (1:19–21, 27–31). For Paul, the cross is not God's *ex post facto* retrofit of human perversity; such an interpretation would make of the cross nothing more than a fantastic instantiation of the cloying cliché, "making lemonade out of life's lemons." Quite the contrary: for Paul, "Christ crucified" is God's hidden wisdom, shrouded in mystery and foreordained before the ages, for the consternation of this world's wisdom and the salvation of those who are called to believe and who love him (1:18–25; 2:2, 7–9). Similarly, in Mark Jesus avers, "The Son of Man

---

[58] The secondary literature on these topics is vast. For this essay's concerns, Leander E. Keck, "Paul and Apocalyptic Theology," *Int* 38 (1984) 229–41, and Joel Marcus, "Mark 4:10–12 and Marcan Epistemology," *JBL* 103 (1984) 557–74, are useful places to start.

goes as it is written about him" (14:21; cf. 8:31; 9:31; 10:33–34), and the circumstances of his crucifixion are, by their tacit fulfillment of scripture (15:23, 24, 29, 34, 36, 40–41), disguised indicators of God's purpose. Nowhere does the evangelist approximate Paul's nuanced reflections on God's cruciform wisdom, which transcend Mark even in their degree of scriptural explicitness (γέγραπται γάρ/ἀλλὰ καθὼς γέγραπται [for/but as it is written], 1 Cor 1:19; 2:9). Yet, precisely by leaving such matters allusive and undiscussed, Mark strangely captures if not surpasses the apostle's emphasis on the secrecy and concealment of God's activity in the cross.[59]

3. *Both Mark and Paul agree that at the cross of Jesus humankind not only knows but is known by God.* Paul epitomizes Christ crucified as scandalous to Jews and moronic to Greeks (1 Cor 1:23); Mark dramatizes that insight to a harrowing degree (15:16–20, 28–32, 35–36; see also 14:53–72; 15:1–15). Evangelist and apostle concur that all of humanity falls under the judgment of the cross, at the very moment when it fatuously considers itself judge of the crucified Jesus (cf. Mark 14:27; 1 Cor 1:26–29). Such presumption is embedded in a misunderstanding and abuse of power that, measured κατὰ σάρκα (according to the flesh; 1 Cor 1:26), mistakes life-giving self-sacrifice for fatal impotence (Mark 15:29–31; also 8:35–36; 10:42–45). And that cognitive/volitive confusion stems from starvation of faith, manifested in an appetite for signs (1 Cor 1:22): precisely the demand hurled at the crucified Jesus by onlookers (Mark 15:32, 36) who cannot comprehend that mighty acts are an evangelical outcome of trust in God (2:5; 5:34; 10:52; 11:22–24; cf. Rom 15:18–19; 2 Cor 12:9b–12), not magic-tricks that in themselves could ever compel belief (Mark 6:1–6a). By contrast, the faith of which Paul speaks (1 Cor 1:21; 2:5) is implicitly and ironically articulated in Mark by one who wields power κατὰ σάρκα, yet—with patent foolishness that transcends human wisdom—truly acknowledges God's Son on seeing Jesus' weakness *in extremis* (15:39; cf. 1 Cor 1:25; 2:3; 2 Cor 4:7–12; 12:5–10; 13:4). Such faith is no function of human potential, which would ultimately amount to misplaced faith in oneself. Explicitly in 1 Corinthians 1–2 and implicitly in Mark 15, it is faith *in God*, who empowers faith among those called to exert it (1 Cor 1:24, 26–28; 2:5, 7, 10; cf. Mark 4:11, 25; 11:22–24; 13:11, 20, 22, 27; 15:34).

4. *Both Paul and Mark concur that at the cross Jesus is the peculiar pointer to the ineffable character of God.* Although Mark and Paul adumbrate some later developments (Mark 10:45; 14:24; 1 Cor 1:30; also 5:7; 11:25;

---

[59] On the theistic ground of Jesus' teaching throughout Mark, and its emphasis on God's mystery and transcendence, see John R. Donahue, "A Neglected Factor in the Theology of Mark," *JBL* 101 (1982) 563–94.

15:3), neither Mark 15 nor 1 Corinthians 1–2 elaborates medieval theories of atonement concerning the cross. These texts' preoccupation is more obviously christological, and of a distinctive kind. Unlike Luke's presentation of the crucified Jesus as a valorous martyr (23:13–16, 27–31, 34, 40–43, 46–48) or John's understanding of Jesus' death as consummately revelatory of God's glory (12:16, 23–25, 32–33; 13:31–32; 17:1, 4–5), Mark's portrait of Jesus' suffering fidelity to God's will is, without trace of heroism or triumph, "nothing . . . but Christ and him crucified" (1 Cor 2:2; see also 2 Cor 13:4; Phil 2:8).[60] Jesus' identity within the community as the one both crucified and raised, which we observed in 1 Corinthians (1:23; 2:2; 15:4, 12, 15), is also suggested in Mark's description of Jesus' crucifixion and post-resurrection activity with verbs in the present or perfect tense (σταυροῦσιν αὐτόν [they crucify him], 15:24; τὸν ἐσταυρωμένον [the one who has been crucified], 16:6; Προάγει [I am going ahead], 16:7). Indeed, Mark's entire narrative is "the beginning of the good news of Jesus Christ, the Son of God" (1:1), whose theological center of gravity is the Son of Man slain and vindicated (8:31; 9:31; 10:33–34). Although the evangelist does not identify Christ as God's power and wisdom (cf. 1 Cor 1:24), in Mark (15:39) the crucified Jesus is the prism through which humanity truly recognizes, not only Jesus, but also the God whose Son Jesus is. In that sense Charles Cousar's comment about 1 Corinthians 1–2 could be made as well of Mark 15: "The crucified one becomes the foundation for epistemology."[61] And because human understanding is subject to restoration by God at the cross as nowhere else, Mark's account at least implies a soteriological claim, which Paul makes more explicit in 1 Cor 1:18, 21.[62]

Areas of Complementarity

No single text, not even one so rich as 1 Cor 1:18–2:16 or Mark 15:16–41, can comprehend the significance of the crucified Christ for

---

[60] On Paul's and Mark's critiques of heroism, see, respectively, Keck, "Biblical Preaching as Divine Wisdom," 138–49; and Adela Yarbro Collins, "From Noble Death to Crucified Messiah," *NTS* 40 (1994) 481–503. Among the canonical Gospels Matthew's account is closest to Mark's, although Matthew contains unique elements that parallel Luke's accent on Jesus' righteousness (Matt 27:19) and John's realized eschatology (Matt 27:51b–53).

[61] Cousar, *A Theology of the Cross,* 35. Also pertinent is J. Louis Martyn's observation: "The cross is *the* epistemological crisis for the simple reason that while it is in one sense followed by the resurrection, it is not replaced by the resurrection" ("Epistemology at the Turn of the Ages: 2 Corinthians 5:16," in *Christian History and Interpretation: Studies Presented to John Knox* [ed. W. R. Farmer, C. F. D. Moule, and R. R. Niebuhr; Cambridge: Cambridge University Press, 1970] 269–87; quotation, 286).

[62] I owe this observation to the astute reading of Ellen T. Charry.

Paul, the second evangelist, or subsequent Christian theology. To speak, therefore, of these texts' complementarity is to imply, not only their significant divergences from each other, but also the capacity of each to assist in rounding out the other's point of view. Here I can merely touch on three such areas.

First, *with respect to the cross, the material emphases of Paul and Mark offer important counterweights.* Given the need to extricate the Corinthians from their religious solipsism, Paul in this passage explicates the word of the cross "from above." The flow of 1 Corinthians 1–2 is expressly theocentric, its argument radiating from Paul's core convictions about what God has done and continues to do for humankind through Christ crucified. For this approach—principled, strategic, and entirely understandable—a theological price must be paid: even to speak of "God's wisdom, secret and hidden" (2:7 [NRSV]) is to risk compromising its intrinsic mystery and concealment. Paul's claim to have "the mind of Christ" (2:16) might appear to constitute an even further intruding of this mystery. Any tendency towards hubris in such an argument is firmly counteracted (i) by Paul's treatment of things that are held in the world's scale of values to be base and worthless as the very place where God's wisdom is most patently manifest (1:26–2:5), and (ii) by Paul's explicit acknowledgment that "the mind of the Lord" is permanently inaccessible to human striving and requires for its disclosure God's own gift of the revelatory Spirit (2:10–16). Yet the risk of intrusion into the depths of God arguably remains and may be an unavoidable byproduct of the starting-point of the apostle's analysis. Viewed intracanonically, Mark 15:16–41 effectively offers a response to this theological problem by approaching the cross just as steadily (and, one assumes, just as deliberately) from the other end of the field: "from below," accenting the human grotesqueries of Jesus' trial and execution that are only beginning to yield to the force of the cross in the words of the incipiently perceptive executioner (15:39). Yet the evangelist's approach carries its own cost: so muted is God's presence in Mark 15 (N.B. 15:34) that, even with the passion predictions in Mark 8–10 but lacking Paul's more explicit treatment in 1 Corinthians 1–2, Christian theology would be hard-pressed to discern *God's* wisdom within the centurion's cryptic comment. Paul's appraisal of what has happened at the cross is more profound than Mark's: this world's wisdom has been not merely exposed as folly but *made into foolishness,* "moronized" (ἐμώρανεν) by God (1 Cor 1:20). Mark's contribution here is to point up, with a presentation more anthropologically animated, just how scandalous that claim of the cross really is.[63]

---

[63] I appreciate Paul W. Meyer's help in clarifying some points made in this paragraph.

This leads to a second area of complementarity between these texts. Paul insists (1 Cor 2:2) that among his readers he "decided to know nothing except Jesus Christ and him crucified." If it applies to his discussion in 1 Cor 1:18–2:16 as well as to his earlier preaching (see 2:1), this remark is obviously hyperbolic. Beyond its mere assertion, "nothing but Jesus Christ and him crucified" is, in a way, a more fitting description of what we find in Mark 15, whose interpretation of that event is so embedded within a realistic narrative that generations of Christians (and scholars) have scarcely recognized Mark's account as the theological interpretation that it is. Regarded within the context of 1 Corinthians 1–2, what Paul apparently (and naturally) intends by his comment in 2:2 is that the *significance* of Jesus, the crucified Christ—such as Paul articulates it in these chapters and has expressed it in his own life—is the center of his speech and his proclamation (2:3–4). Just here, as I have suggested, 1 Corinthians offers explicitly *theo*logical guidance to the canonical interpreter of Mark. Yet Paul does more than this. By exploring the work of the Spirit, which discerns spiritual things for the benefit of those who have received the Spirit that is from God (1 Cor 2:10–16), Paul provides an explanation for *why* an observer (like Mark's centurion) is able to recognize "spiritual truths" beyond "the spirit of the world," to judge this one crucified to be God's Son on bases altogether contradictory of "matters taught by human wisdom" (2:12–13). In a word: *where Mark elaborates the empirical opacity through which faith must penetrate, Paul amplifies the epistemological means by which faith "can know the gifts bestowed on us by God."*

Finally, *Paul's and Mark's formal approaches to the cross effectively bolster a canonical counterbalance.* Paul's way of doing theology—discursively, in a pastoral letter to an actual church—appears to offer modern, biblically-informed theologians advantages over Mark's more oblique technique, which obscures the presumably ecclesial audience for whom his narrative was created. Manifesting its author's attempt to illuminate particular facets of "the truth of the gospel" (Gal 2:5, 14), 1 Corinthians unintentionally helps us, not only in tracing the contours of Paul's own thought, but in elucidating some cognate convictions of other early Christian thinkers, like the author of Mark's Gospel. In that sense there emerges a canonical Mark, whose message acquires a clarity, distinctiveness, and fullness when heard in conjunction with Paul's "word of the cross" (1 Cor 1:18). Yet, when read alongside the Second Gospel, the apostle's proclamation enjoys a different kind of perspicuity and resonance. Focusing on the cross as a climactically salvific event with theologically discriminative implications, Paul's analysis in 1 Corinthians 1–2 tends to minimize the very dimension that Mark's cruciform story of Jesus maximizes: the character of the one to and through whom that event occurred.[64] To acknowledge this is not, as Bultmann concluded, tantamount to an existentially anxious, theologically invalid attempt to legitimate the kerygma by appeal to the Jesus of history.[65] To the contrary, if Mark's kerygmatic narrative demonstrates anything, it is the indispensability of faith: the vast majority at Golgotha, historically closer than anyone else to Jesus, were stunningly tone-deaf and bat-blind to what the evangelist believes was really happening.[66] At issue, in fact, is not the credibility of the kerygma but its intelligibility: for without attention to the lifelong passion of *this one* crucified and vindicated, such as Mark provides, "the cross" is liable to shrinkage into a detached cipher of the sort that Paul himself would never have countenanced.[67] The potential for trivialization is perilous on both sides: Cut off from Paul's propositional incisiveness, the affecting story in Mark 15 could be misread as some moralistic news from a Judean Lake Wobegon.[68] Isolated from Mark's narrative texture, the trenchant claims of 1 Corinthians 1–2 could be misconstrued as the chance legacy of a surprisingly lucky Jew who won the Almighty's eschatological jackpot. Put more straightforwardly: If Paul's theological method sharpens the disclosure point of "the one crucified" along the horizon of God's eternity, Mark's deepens its irrefragable "this-worldliness," as defined by Jesus Christ.[69]

---

[64] For thoughtful comments in this vein, see Donald T. Rowlingson, "The Moral Context of the Resurrection Faith," in *Christ and Spirit in the New Testament in Honour of Charles Francis Digby Moule* (ed. Barnabas Lindars and Stephen S. Smalley; Cambridge: Cambridge University Press, 1973) 415–25.

[65] Rudolf Bultmann, "The Primitive Christian Kerygma and the Historical Jesus," in *The Historical Jesus and the Kerygmatic Christ: Essays on the New Quest of the Historical Jesus* (ed. Carl E. Braaten and Roy A. Harrisville; New York and Nashville, TN: Abingdon, 1964) 15–42. As is well known, Paul and John stood, for Bultmann, as the twin peaks of New Testament theology; the Synoptics, as an aspect of doctrinal development toward the ancient church (*Theology of the New Testament* [2 vols.; New York: Charles Scribner's Sons, 1951, 1955] N.B. 2.119–54]).

[66] Thus, Eduard Schweizer: "First, it is beyond all doubt that Mark wants to emphasize that God's revelation happened in the historical life and death of Jesus, that is, in a real man. . . . Second, this does not mean that we could see anything which would really help us in the historical Jesus, without the miracle of God's Spirit who, in the word of the witness, opens our blind eyes to the 'dimension' in which all these events took place" ("Mark's Contribution to the Quest of the Historical Jesus," *NTS* 10 [1963/64] 421–32; here, 431).

[67] See also Luz, "Theologia crucis als Mitte der Theologie," 135–39.

[68] Cf. Garrison Keillor, *Lake Wobegon Days* (New York: Viking, 1985), a compilation of that humorist's popular radio monologues.

[69] Apropos of these reflections, see E. Cyril Blackman, "Is History Irrelevant for the Christian Kerygma?" *Int* 21 (1967) 435–46; Paul W. Meyer, "The This-Worldliness of the New Testament," *Princeton Seminary Bulletin* 2 (1979) 219–31; and William C. Placher, *Narratives of a Vulnerable God: Christ, Theology, and Scripture* (Louisville, KY: Westminster John Knox, 1994) esp. 27–52, 87–108.

The Love Command: John and Paul?

D. Moody Smith

Almost a quarter of a century ago Victor Furnish presented a definitive study of the love command in the New Testament, and about two decades later a helpful summary statement on the question of Paul's relationship to, and knowledge of, Jesus.[1] In the earlier book the Johannine literature figured prominently; in the latter almost not at all (the Gospels' resurrection accounts are cited on p. 79). Certainly the omission of John from the latter work is understandable, for it is difficult enough to trace a relationship between Paul and the Synoptic Jesus tradition, much less the Johannine. The possibility that John knew Paul's letters, once a common premise of the history of early Christian literature, has at least since Rudolf Bultmann stood under a cloud.[2] (It is noteworthy how easily Albert Schweitzer could assume as common wisdom that John knew Paul's letters and theology.[3])

In his treatment of the love commandment in John, Furnish understands it as based upon, derivative from, and integral to, the theological truth of God's love for humanity, for the world, which is manifest in Jesus and is the content of the Johannine version of the gospel.[4] This is certainly true, and precisely this relation of indicative and imperative is germane to the understanding of theology and ethics in Paul.[5] In his presentation of the love commandment in John, Furnish is under-

---

[1] Victor Paul Furnish, *The Love Command in the New Testament* (Nashville, TN: Abingdon, 1972); *Jesus According to Paul* (Understanding Jesus Today; Cambridge: Cambridge University Press, 1993).

[2] Albert E. Barnett, *Paul Becomes a Literary Influence* (Chicago: University of Chicago Press, 1941) 104–42, represents the earlier view that John knew Paul's letters. By contrast, Bultmann recognizes important affinities and substantial similarities, but refuses to interpret John as a development beyond, or on the basis of, Paul (for a succinct account of the relationship, see Rudolf Bultmann, *Theology of the New Testament* [2 vols.; New York: Scribner's, 1955] 2.6–10, 12).

[3] Writing later, John hellenizes the still Jewish apocalyptic mysticism of Paul. See Schweitzer, *The Mysticism of Paul the Apostle* (New York: Henry Holt, 1931) 372: "To all this confusion the recognition that the Johannine mysticism is the Hellenization of the Pauline puts an end. By it the resemblances and differences are alike explained."

[4] Furnish, *Love Command*, 132–58, esp. 138.

[5] See Furnish, *Theology and Ethics in Paul* (Nashville, TN: Abingdon, 1968), esp. his careful definition of the indicative-imperative relationship (224–27).

standably more interested in its place in the total theological and ethical scheme of the Gospel and the Epistles than in its tradition-history. (The same would apply to Furnish's work on Paul, where certainly the theological roots of Paul's ethics are more obvious than his relation to the Jesus tradition or other primitive Christian materials.)

Our purpose here is limited but, it may be hoped, worthwhile and useful. In what follows, we shall look at Jesus' initial promulgation of the love commandment in John (13:34), raising questions about where it stands in the history of tradition as we make some comparisons with its occurrences in Paul (Rom 13:9; Gal 5:14). Quite obviously the Pauline and Johannine versions of the command differ, and we shall consider those differences, perhaps the most obvious of which is that John insists, almost stridently in the First Epistle, that the command-ment comes from Jesus himself (1 John 2:7–11; 3:11), while Paul never explicitly refers the commandment to a word of Jesus (cf. Jas 2:8).

In John 13:34–35, Jesus' love commandment, and his subsequent statement about how it will identify his hearers as disciples, actually interrupts the context. If omitted, the transition from v. 33 to v. 36 is perfectly smooth. But even if 13:34–35 were inserted into its present context later, it is thoroughly Johannine in every respect. In fact, its sudden intrusion lends the commandment a certain emphasis and importance. That Peter then seems to ignore it (vv. 36–38) fits his impetuosity and lack of understanding at this point in the narrative. Jesus reiterates the commandment in 15:12 and relates it to his own self-sacrificial death. Now it is no longer called "new" as it was in 13:34.

It has been observed that the description of the love commandment as new is a bit surprising, inasmuch as it is found in scriptural law (Lev 19:18), as well as early Christian tradition.[6] The best explanation of "new" is doubtless found in 1 John 2:7–8. The commandment from the letter writer's perspective is "old," that is, it goes back to the beginning, to Jesus (3:11; cf. 1:1). Yet it is also "new" eschatologically; the new world that Jesus has brought about is moving in, replacing the old (cf. 1 John 3:14). 1 John shows an awareness of the Fourth Gospel, or something like it; otherwise why should the author, after calling the commandment "old," then immediately reverse himself to say that it is "new"? I see no reason to doubt that 1 John accurately understands what the evangelist means by "new" in the "new commandment," and do not find it necessary to suppose that he believes Jesus is uttering a heretofore unheard-of teaching. It is new eschatologically, but not historically. Of course, the Gospel of John does not relate the

---

[6] See Barnabas Lindars, *The Gospel of John* (NCB; Grand Rapids MI: Eerdmans, 1972) 463.

commandment to Lev 19:18, much less derive it from there; if its ultimate origin were scripture, then how would it be "new"? Also, like Paul, the evangelist does not combine it with Deut 6:5, the first commandment, to love God (cf. Mark 12:29–30 parr.).

But that the double commandment, and the juxtaposition of the two, may be known in the Johannine tradition is suggested by 1 John 4:20–21 (cf. 5:1–3), which Furnish calls "the only New Testament passage outside the Synoptic Gospels where we can be fairly sure of a direct reference to the Great Commandment with equal stress on each of its parts."[7] Is something like Mark 12:29–31 then known to the author? This is a nice instance of the whole question of the relation of John and the Synoptics; although it arises out of the First Epistle rather than the Gospel, it has a similar shape and form, and a similar problematic aspect. Knowledge of Mark, or of the Synoptics, would explain 1 John 4:20–21. But if knowledge of our canonical text is assumed, how does one explain the many differences, or in the case of 1 John the fact that the author passes up many opportunities to refer to the Synoptics?[8] At most it might be suggested that at this relatively late stage of the Johannine tradition, the Synoptics are finally being drawn upon (cf. John 21:25; Brown as well as Bultmann ascribed knowledge of the Synoptics to the final stage of the redaction of the Gospel).

Significantly, John, unlike Paul but like the Synoptics, ascribes the love commandment directly to Jesus, if in rather different form. One might put the difference sharply by saying that whereas Paul does not ascribe the command to Jesus, John ascribes it, and no other ethical instruction, to Jesus. Paul knew that Jesus taught other things (1 Cor 7:10–11; 9:14; 11:23–26), whereas as far as John attests he taught only this, to love one another (13:34; 15:12). How much more John knew of the concrete and specific substance of the Jesus tradition as we know it is a moot question. John's version of the love commandment is often thought to epitomize the teaching of Jesus according to the Synoptics, and so it does. But is it a conscious distillation or summation of the synoptic rendition of Jesus' teaching based on those Gospels? The answer to the broader question remains—and may always remain—a matter of dispute. If we had only the Gospel of John we would have no reason to think that Jesus taught anything other—or more specific— than this as far as human conduct and relations are concerned. At the same time there are differences in the way Jesus focuses or applies the

---

[7] *Love Command*, 151.

[8] See Raymond E. Brown, *The Epistles of John* (AB 30; Garden City, NY: Doubleday, 1983) 98, n. 226.

love commandment in John: Love one another—obviously fellow disciples or believers.[9]

At just this point there is an interesting and significant similarity between John and Paul, in that in both cases the love commandment has at least its primary applicability to the Christian community. This is obvious enough in John, as commentators note, but it is also true of Paul. In Gal 5:13 Paul is plainly addressing the Christian community: "For you were called to freedom, brothers and sisters, only do not use your freedom as an opportunity for the flesh, but through love serve one another, for the entire law is fulfilled in this one word: 'You shall love your neighbor as yourself.'" Then he cites Lev 19:18 as the summation of the law (as it is similarly cited in Matt 22:40; cf. Matt 19:19 and Jas 2:8). One might note parenthetically that Paul hardly knew Matthew, but they may both know a common Christian tradition in which this scriptural word is accorded such a prominent status in relation to the whole law. (Similarly, 1 John 4:20–21 may reflect knowledge of a common Christian tradition of the dual commandment).

Something quite similar happens in Romans (13:8–10), although there the context in which love is to be practiced is broadened. Coming as it does right after 13:1–7, with Paul's concluding admonition, "Love does no wrong to a neighbor," the passage reveals that Paul has more than just the Christian community in view. Yet the command to love applies first and foremost within the community: "You yourselves have been taught by God to love one another" (1 Thess 4:9). Probably "taught by God" is an allusion to Leviticus 19:18. Significantly, both here and in Romans 13:8 (cf. Galatians 5:13), the phrase ἀγαπᾶν ἀλλήλους [to love one another] is used to summarize, or give Paul's interpretation of, the love command. These are, of course, exactly the words used in John 13:34 and 15:12. 1 Peter, which apparently stands

---

9 Furnish, *Love Command*, 148, maintains that "the commandment" to love one another need not be regarded in itself as *excluding* love for "neighbors and enemies." I would certainly agree with Furnish's statement, and indeed with his further elaboration that the Johannine command to love another "is neither a softening nor a repudiation of the command to love the neighbor, but a special and indeed urgent form of it." If I have a difference with Furnish, it would be that I regard the latter statement as certainly true only from the standpoint of a canonical perspective or interpretation. That is, I am not confident that John actually has in view the Synoptic formulations, but rather perhaps the Pauline! On the Johannine limitation of the command, see also Bultmann, *The Gospel of John: A Commentary* (Philadelphia: Westminster) 524–28, esp. 528: "This explains why the command of love seems to undergo a limitation through the ἀλλήλους [one another]. It is no general love of mankind, or love of one's neighbor or enemy that is demanded, but love within the circle of disciples. Naturally this does not mean that the all-embracing love of one's neighbor is to be invalidated; but here it is a question of the very existence of the circle of disciples."

under Pauline influence, speaks more than once of loving one another, obviously within the Christian community (1:22; 4:8). Furnish sums up the role of love within the church, the community of Jesus' disciples, quite aptly: Paul would "surely have identified love as the life-force that circulates within the believing community to sustain and energize it."[10] Paul's great hymn to love (1 Cor 13) is, of course, eloquent testimony to the accuracy of Furnish's observation.

What Furnish has recently said of Paul is true in the same measure for John, as I am sure he would agree. Moreover, Furnish is, I think, justified in tracing the love commandment in some form to Jesus himself,[11] albeit with reservations about the relationship between what Jesus actually said and what is reported in the Synoptic Gospels, and its importance for early Christianity generally is not in doubt. Yet it seems safe to say that love as the basis and form of Christian obedience is more central and more important for Paul and John than for any other New Testament or early Christian writer.

This centrality and importance have not so much to do with the certainty with which the ancient writers, or we, can trace the love command to Jesus as with the way in which both Paul and John, in somewhat different and characteristic ways, understand the life and especially the death of Jesus as the expression of Jesus' or God's love for humanity generally, and particularly for those who believe. For both Paul and John the death of Jesus is the revelation of God's love. This fact scarcely needs to be documented, but classic formulations are, for Paul, Romans 5:8 ("But God proves his love for us in that while we were still sinners Christ died for us"), and for John, John 3:16 ("For God so loved the world that he gave his only son, so that everyone who believes in him may not perish but may have eternal life").

It is noteworthy that Paul considers whether one person would willingly die for another (Rom 5:7) and can barely conceive of one dying for a good person. But that "Christ died for us" (v. 8) is said to be a manifestation of God's love rather than Jesus'. Although for John too the death of Jesus manifests God's love, it is also the case that it manifests Jesus' own love (John 15:12; cf. 13:1) for his disciples. Paul can, of course, speak of the love of Christ (e.g., Rom 8:35, which in v. 39 he seems to equate with the love of God) and even of "the Son of God, who loved me and gave himself for me" (Gal 2:20). But John's statements are more deliberately or programmatically formulated. Moreover, in John this is not only a theological formulation. In the narrative Jesus describes his ministry in the parable or figure of the

---

[10] Furnish, *Jesus*, 89–90.

[11] Furnish, *Love Command*, 61–62.

Good Shepherd in such a way as to say quite explicitly that he will give up his life in protecting his sheep (10:11–15). That this means he will die while they go free is made clear in the arrest scene, where Jesus allows the arresting party to take him, while explicitly telling them to "let these men go" (v. 8). The narrator immediately intervenes to say that an earlier word of Jesus ("I did not lose a single one of those whom you gave me"; v. 9) is being fulfilled. The reader thinks of several sayings, also unique to John, in which Jesus speaks of protecting his own (6:39; 10:28; 17:12). One is inclined to interpret these spiritually, or with reference to the salvific work of the Johannine Christ, and that is apparently justifiable. Yet John clearly knows of the flight of the disciples (16:32), although it plays no role in the narrative of his arrest (cf. Mark 14:50; Matt 26:56; Luke, like John, does not mention the flight of the disciples at the conclusion of the arrest scene). Thus, in John, corresponding to the theological assertion that Jesus gives up his life out of love for his followers there is an arrest scene in which he seems to do exactly that. This is just one of several instances in which what John describes in theologically freighted language makes sense of what the Synoptics also report. Jesus died in place of his followers. We need not pursue this line of thought as a historical possibility or proposal any further at present, although doing so might prove profitable on another occasion.

John thus ties the command to love to Jesus' own conduct, to his laying down of his life for his friends (15:12–13), as we have just seen, and his followers' conduct should recapitulate his own fate. For good reason John portrays Jesus as commanding love, and love is his only command because it is the essence of discipleship understood as following Jesus.

The Johannine Epistles underline what the Gospel reports. Jesus is the source of the one old and new commandment, both in precept and example (precept: 1 John 2:7; 3:11, 23–24; 4:21; 5:2–3; 2 John 5–6; example: 1 John 3:16; 4:9–10). In 1 John the command to love is grounded not only in the action of Jesus, but in the very nature of God, who is love (4:8); yet the love of God, and that God is love, are known from the sending of the Son "to be the expiation for our sins" (4:10). Inasmuch as 1 John emphasizes the beginning of the Christian story and tradition (1:1), it is perhaps not surprising that for the author Jesus' original command to his disciples, the old commandment (2:7), is of such importance. It is interesting, and perhaps paradoxical, that the Gospel of John, which narrates Jesus' ministry, places a premium on its present significance, that is, for his intended Christian readers, while the First Epistle of John, addressed directly to the contemporary needs of churches, stresses the pastness of Jesus, that he was in the beginning, that he promulgated not a new, but an old commandment. For John, whether Gospel or Epistle, it is very important that Jesus commanded— and that his whole message can be summed up under the command— that his followers love one another. There can be little doubt that the Johannine author(s) believed Jesus had commanded this.

Did Paul too think that Jesus himself had commanded love? Furnish is prudently reserved about ascribing to Paul knowledge of Jesus tradition where Paul seems to echo Jesus without explicitly citing him.[12] Even so, in Furnish's view the earliest formulation of Jesus' teaching on loving enemies is probably to be found in Paul: "Bless those who persecute you; bless and do not curse them" (Rom 12:14). This is closely related to Matthew's "Love your enemies, and pray for those who persecute you" (cf. Luke 6:28). Of course, the Pauline version does not contain the love commandment per se.[13]

Although Paul does not explicitly ascribe the command to Jesus, the similarities of Rom 12:14–21 to Jesus' teaching in the Sermon on the Mount/Plain (Matt 5:43–48/Luke 6:27–36) are real, as has often been pointed out. In dealing with Paul's parallels with the Jesus tradition, one is caught between two possibilities: Paul does not cite Jesus because he does not know that the item in question (e.g., Rom 12:14) goes back to Jesus; or Paul knows it goes back to Jesus and assumes everyone who reads his letter will know this as well. Perhaps Paul cites Jesus explicitly on a specific issue like marriage (1 Cor 7:10–11) or wages (1 Cor 9:14), but not on matters that were widely known to embody the viewpoint of Jesus (thus Rom 12:14–21). This seems to me plausible and even probable, but we cannot finally be certain.

Indeed, it is hard enough to isolate or be certain of exactly what Jesus said about love on the basis of the Synoptic Gospels, and Furnish's treatment reflects this difficulty. For example, there are problems in tracing the double commandment (Mark 12:29–31 parr.) to Jesus, however certain one may be that it reflects his attitude. Bultmann, whose *History of the Synoptic Tradition* Furnish cites,[14] doubts that the pericope contains even a historical reminiscence, although it may give "fitting expression to [Jesus'] spiritual attitude." Of course, the fact that Jesus is portrayed as citing scripture may in itself raise doubts for Bultmann, although Furnish understandably reasons that as a rabbi

---

[12] Less so Dale C. Allison, Jr., who ascribes much material that is parallel to Jesus to pre-synoptic Jesus tradition. See his "The Pauline Epistles and the Synoptic Gospels: The Pattern of the Parallels," *NTS* 28 (1982) 1–32.

[13] Furnish, *Love Command*, 61–62.

[14] Ibid., 62. See Bultmann, *The History of the Synoptic Tradition* (New York: Harper & Row, 1963), esp. 54–55.

Jesus "would have been asked occasionally to summarize the law in some appropriate fashion." Even Bultmann agrees that in Jesus' command to love the enemy "if anywhere we can find what is characteristic in the preaching of Jesus."[15] The point is that if tracing the Pauline love command to Jesus presents difficulties, these may diminish, but they do not disappear, in the Synoptic Gospels and tradition.

In conclusion, how does it stand with John? Whether John knows the Synoptics is once again the subject of a debate which seemingly holds endless fascination for New Testament scholars. Yet on this particular point at least, the question of whether John knew Paul—either through his letters or from other sources—may be worth revisiting. Like Paul, John has only the love commandment and does not reflect Deut 6:5 (except perhaps for 1 John 4:20–21). Like Paul, John applies the commandment to the community of disciples, the church, using the identical Greek words (ἀγαπᾶν ἀλλήλους, "love one another"), even though he does not include them in the command itself. Like Paul, John considers love the very essence or lifeblood of relationships among believers within the church. Like Paul, John grounds the imperative in the indicative (John 15:12–13, esp. 1 John 4:11), and for John that indicative includes the love of Jesus for his own (cf. Gal 2:20) as well as the love of God for the world. Perhaps unlike Paul, John also traces the obligation to love to a word of Jesus, the love commandment. But Paul knows the commandment based on Lev 19:18, which John nowhere cites. Because it is Jesus' new commandment (or old, in the sense of going back to Jesus himself) John does not base it on scripture: "Before Abraham was, I am" (8:58). We may at least entertain a couple of possibilities whose premise—John's knowledge of Paul—is unproven. Perhaps John knows that Paul knew the commandment goes back to Jesus; or he may have simply assumed that Paul knew it since, by the time he wrote, Christians generally, and for good reason, believed Jesus so taught. (Note Furnish's argument that the Great Commandment finds a place in the context of the tradition of Jesus' teaching.[16]) Obviously Paul knows specific injunctions of Jesus about various matters, which make contact with the Synoptic tradition. John does not reflect such knowledge as directly, but perhaps this is by intention. Arguably, John goes a step beyond Paul by framing a general command

---

15 Ibid., 62. Cf. Bultmann, *History of the Synoptic Tradition*, 105. On loving one's enemies, see John Piper, *'Love your enemies': Jesus' Love Command in the Synoptic Gospels and in the Early Christian Paraenesis, A History of the Tradition and Interpretation of Its Uses* (SNTSMS 38; Cambridge: Cambridge University Press, 1979). Piper does not, however, treat the double commandment in the Synoptics, nor does he deal with the Pauline or Johannine versions.

16 *Love Command*, 61–62.

of Jesus, free of scriptural reference, that aptly summarizes not only his teaching, but the meaning of his life, ministry, and death.

The Johannine literature—Gospel and Epistles, and to some extent at least the Book of Revelation—seems to represent a discrete branch or community of early Christianity, with many of the basic theological commitments of the Pauline or Synoptic communities, but without the obvious external points of contact we find within the Synoptic corpus or among the Pauline Epistles, Deuteropauline Epistles, and Acts. Yet, although Johannine Christianity is a distinct entity, it is not correct to speak of it as isolated. It may be that its distinctiveness has obscured the nature of the points of contact or connection with other documents and traditions. The case for John's having somehow known Paul is at least as strong as the case for his having known the other canonical Gospels. Perhaps stronger, because Paul predates John by more than a quarter of a century, and if Paul had not become a literary influence by that time, he was sufficiently prominent to have been made the hero of Luke's account of the Gentile mission.[17]

Returning to the love command, one could imagine a history of the tradition along the following lines. Jesus did command his followers to love their enemies (Matt 5:44; Luke 6:27, 35). Moreover, the general thrust of his teaching, as well as the perceived course and outcome of his ministry, command and exemplify love. Paul understands this and his general, if brief summations of Jesus' ministry indicate as much (2 Cor 8:9; Phil 2:5–11; Rom 5:6–8; 15:7–9a). Why should the early Christians, disciples or contemporaries of Jesus, have interpreted Jesus' death as they did unless they also saw in his ministry the expression of his intention as well as God's? If there is not a story of Jesus' ministry underlying Paul's letters and theology, is not Paul finally incomprehensible, in his own time as well as ours?[18]

---

[17] Perhaps there is even a specific geographical connection. Ephesus was obviously an important city and mission base for Paul and, of course, tradition associates John with Ephesus. As is frequently observed, Ignatius, in writing to the Ephesian church (Ign. *Eph.* 12.2) makes much of Paul's residence in that city, but fails to mention John, who according to Irenaeus (*Adv. Haer.* II.22.5) had lived in Ephesus much more recently, until the time of Trajan. This is a significant omission, but while it counts against John the Apostle's having lived in Ephesus, it is less damaging to the possibility that the Johannine circle flourished there. This is particularly true if the identification of that circle with the son of Zebedee is some sort of historical mistake. (I am grateful to my colleague Richard B. Hays for reminding me of the possiblity of such an Ephesian connection.)

[18] See Richard B. Hays, *The Faith of Jesus Christ: An Investigation of the Narrative Substructure of Galatians 3:1–4:11* (SBLDS 56; Chico, CA: Scholars Press, 1983) 248–54. See also Hays's article, "Crucified with Christ: A Synthesis of the Theology of 1 and 2 Thessalonians, Philemon, Philippians, and Galatians," in *Pauline Theology, Vol. I: Thessalonians, Philippians, Galatians, Philemon* (ed. Jouette M. Bassler; Minneapolis, MN:

Be that as it may, Paul's understanding of Jesus' ministry, as well as his death, as the expression of God's love, utilizes Lev 19:18 as a summation of the law, which is at the same time still a valid and significant expression of God's will, whether for believers or all people. That Paul knew the love command from Jesus' specific sayings cannot be explicitly shown, although the affinities between Romans 12:14–21 and Jesus' teaching certainly suggest knowledge of the Jesus tradition, especially Luke 6:27–36.[19] Alternatively, if Paul did not so know it, he might nevertheless have recognized it as a summation of Jesus' ministry and message, which is more or less the function it fulfills in John. Conceivably, John simply did what Paul had not yet done; he formulated the love commandment, which was certainly not strange to scripture or to Judaism, as the essence of Jesus' teaching and put it on his lips, believing that it was an accurate representation.

What exactly would have been the content and source of John's knowledge is a good question. Was it simply inferred theologically or narratologically? Or did John know something about what Jesus actually said, whether directly or indirectly? There are a number of items on which John and the Synoptics disagree, but John's information is, arguably, better than the Synoptics.[20] But this question must be left for another day.

Coming finally back to the Synoptics, specifically to Mark 12:28–34 parr., where does this pronouncement story (Bultmann: scholastic dialogue or *Schulgespräch*) fit into our hypothetical development of the tradition?[21] Bultmann's conclusions may after all be correct, in that we have here a scene and saying that accurately represents Jesus' attitude but does not reproduce a historical reminiscence. In other words, it is an ideal scene. What Paul knew on the basis of scripture (Lev 19:18) and as the obvious implication of Jesus' work, if not as an explicit word

---

Fortress, 1991) 227–46.

[19] See Allison, "The Pauline Epistles and the Synoptic Gospels," esp. 10–15.

[20] See D. Moody Smith, "Historical Issues and the Problem of John and the Synoptics," in *From Jesus to John: Essays on Jesus and New Testament Christology in Honour of Marinus de Jonge* (ed. Martinus C. De Boer; JSNTSup 84; Sheffield: Sheffield Academic Press, 1993) 252–67.

[21] In every case (Mark 12:31 parr.; Rom 13:9; Gal 5:14) the citation of Lev 19:18a matches the LXX, but there are only five words of Greek text. In Mark 12:30 parr. (Deut 6:4–5) the Masoretic Text may show its influence as heart displaces mind as the first organ or instrumentality through which one loves God. Yet, as my research assistant Emerson Powery points out to me, the manuscript witnesses differ on both sides (the LXX of Deuteronomy and Mark); so that, for example, Codex D omits the reference to mind in Mark 12:30 and thus conforms to the MT, although most other mss. include it (albeit in third place); while Codex A of LXX has καρδίας [heart] in conformity with MT, although some other LXX mss. have διανοίας [mind] in first place instead.

of the Lord, John formulated succinctly and attributed directly to Jesus. Without taking the uncertain position that Mark knew Paul, much less John, we might then hypothesize that, on the basis of the use of the Leviticus text to support a commonly held Christian teaching (Paul), and a consensus that Jesus had articulated the love command itself (John), there developed in the synoptic tradition an episode in which the text and the consensus were combined, and the Deut 6:4 text added to ensure balance of the love of God with love of neighbor (interestingly, Jesus cites Lev 19:18 without Deut 6:4 in answer to the question posed to him in Matt 19:16–22, but this is probably Matthew's insertion into the pericope as he found it in Mark).

Such a reconstruction of the tradition-history of the love command may seem to attempt to make water run uphill in the sense that it puts at the end of a development what on first glance would seem to belong at the beginning. On the other hand, it projects an intelligible order in which the command is first articulated from scripture, then presented as a saying of Jesus, and finally formulated into an ideal scene combining scripture and saying in the ministry of Jesus in the Synoptics. One does not, however, need to view the Synoptic pericope and formulation as the last stage of this process; it could have been an independent development.

Paul and the Domestication of Thomas

Harold W. Attridge

The influence of Paul on the theology and literature of the early Church has been the subject of considerable attention in recent decades.[1] Scholars have paid particular attention to the role of Pauline materials in exegetical and theological discussions.[2] At the same time, the role of the image of Paul and of the legends that surrounded his name in the *Acts of Paul and Thecla* and related literature has surfaced with new clarity.[3] This brief essay will explore another dimension of the influence of Paul, but the Paul of scripture not of legend, in the imaginative literature of the third century. This essay is dedicated to a scholar and friend who has done much to make the influence of Paul a reality in contemporary theology and ecclesial life.

The influence of Paul appears in one rather unlikely place, the apocryphal *Acts of Thomas*, where Pauline elements help to reshape the image of the apostle Thomas.[4] This work has nothing directly to do with Paul but relates the adventures of the apostle Judas Thomas as he preaches a highly ascetical or encratite form of Christianity on the way

---

[1] See Ernst Dassmann, *Der Stachel im Fleisch: Paulus in der frühchristlichen Literatur bis Irenäus* (Münster: Aschendorff, 1979); Dennis Ronald MacDonald, *The Legend and the Apostle: The Battle for Paul in Story and Canon* (Philadelphia: Westminster, 1983); Andreas Lindemann, *Paulus im ältesten Christentum: Das Bild des Apostels und die Rezeption der paulinischen Theologie in der frühchristlichen Literatur bis Marcion* (BHTh 58; Tübingen: Mohr-Siebeck, 1979); and the conference volume, *Paul and the Legacies of Paul* (ed. William S. Babcock; Dallas, TX: Southern Methodist University Press, 1990).

[2] See Peter Gorday, *Principles of Patristic Exegesis: Romans 9–11 in Origen, John Chrysostom and Augustine* (Studies in the Bible and Early Christianity, 4; New York and Toronto: Mellen, 1983) and idem, "Paul in Eusebius and Other Early Christian Literature," in *Eusebius, Christianity, and Judaism* (ed. Harold W. Attridge, and Gohei Hata; Leiden: Brill; Detroit: Wayne State University Press, 1992) 139–65.

[3] See Margaret Howe, "Interpretations of Paul in *The Acts of Paul and Thecla*," in *Pauline Studies: Essays Presented to Professor F. F. Bruce on His 70th Birthday* (ed. Donald A. Hagner & Murray J. Harris; Exeter: Paternoster; Grand Rapids, MI: Eerdmans, 1980) 33–49; Robert M. Grant, "The Description of Paul in the Acts of Paul and Thecla," *VC* 36 (1982) 1–4; and particularly the work of Dennis R. MacDonald, *Legend and the Apostle* and idem, "Apocryphal and Canonical Narratives about Paul," in *Paul and the Legacies of Paul*, 55–70.

[4] Neither Dassmann nor Lindemann finds any relevant data for their surveys of the influence of Paul in the *Acts of Thomas*.

to and in India. Like other apocryphal acts combining popular legend and religious propaganda, the work serves various didactic purposes while offering edifying entertainment for a Christian audience. The *Acts of Thomas* was most probably composed in third-century Syria,[5] probably in Syriac[6] although it soon circulated in Greek as well. Both traditions exhibit secondary expansions, although, in general, the Syriac has gone further in making the work conform to standards of "orthodox" (i.e., Nicene, with an Antiochene flavor) Christology. The work achieved wide circulation in the two linguistic spheres, both in its full form, and in various abbreviated or excerpted forms.[7]

The first six acts are loosely connected episodes highlighting Thomas's miraculous powers, and some episodes may have circulated independently.[8] The second half of the *Acts* is a more integrated composition with a climactically arranged development of plot and characterization through several episodes. In this portion, the *Acts of Thomas* displays a typical Christian transformation of erotic motifs at home in the romantic novels of the Hellenistic and Roman period. The dramatic tension increases as Thomas's ascetic gospel is accepted by two upper-class women, to the consternation of their powerful husbands. The ladies' love for Thomas and for the God he represents upsets the social order in favor of a new, celibate "family." This portion of the work ends, and the tension finally is resolved, with the apostle's martyrdom.

In addition to narratives of Thomas's adventures, the *Acts* contains distinctive poetic and liturgical elements. The "Hymn of the Bride"

---

[5] In general see H. J. W. Drijvers, "The Acts of Thomas," in *New Testament Apocrypha: Revised Edition of the Collection initiated by Edgar Hennecke* (ed. Wilhelm Schneemelcher; 2 vols.; Louisville, KY: Westminster-John Knox, 1992) 2.322–39.

[6] H. W. Attridge, "The Original Language of the Acts of Thomas," in *Of Scribes and Scrolls: Studies on the Hebrew Bible, Intertestamental Judaism and Christian Origins* (ed. H. W. Attridge et al.; College Theology Society Resources in Religion, 5; Lanham, MD: University Press of America, 1990) 241–5.

[7] For a review of the textual evidence, see R. A. Lipsius & M. Bonnet, *Acta Apostolorum Apocrypha* 2,2: *Acta Philippi et Acta Thomae accedunt Acta Barnabae* (Leipzig: Teubner, 1903; repr., Hildesheim: Olms, 1972) xv–xxvii, and A. F. J. Klijn, *The Acts of Thomas: Introduction-Text-Commentary* (NovTSup 5; Leiden: Brill, 1962) 4–7. In brief, the most complete versions of the work are the tenth-century Greek MS Romanus Vallicellanus B 35 and the tenth-century Syriac MS, British Museum add. 14,645, dated to 936. The earliest witness is the Syriac MS Sinai 30, dating to the fifth century. Bonnet's edition of the Greek utilized twenty other MSS, only one of which, the tenth-century Parisinus graecus 881, is anywhere near complete, lacking only the Hymn of the Pearl.

[8] Yves Tissot ("Les Actes de Thomas, Exemple de recueil composite," in *Les actes apocryphes des Apôtres: Christianisme et monde païen* [Publication de la faculté de théologie de l'Université de Genève 4; Geneva: Labor et Fides, 1981] 223–32) emphasizes the composite character of the text, but on the basis of an examination of a few selected pericopes.

(chaps. 6–7) and the "Hymn of the Pearl" (chaps. 108–113) may have been independent poems adapted to the *Acts*, and their elusive symbolism has elicited a multiplicity of readings.[9] Many episodes culminate in ritual actions. Hence, the work is replete with descriptions of liturgies, especially initiations (chaps. 25–27, 49, 121, 132, 157) and eucharistic celebrations (chaps. 27, 29, 49–50, 121, 133, 158).[10]

The apostle celebrated in this complex novel is familiar from other early Christian sources of probable Syrian provenance, particularly the *Gospel of Thomas* and the *Book of Thomas the Athlete*. The Christianity represented in those works is distinctive for its emphasis on world-renouncing ascetical practice or "encratism."[11] In addition to their radical tendencies these works also contain elements that sit ill at ease with canons of later orthodoxy. The *Gospel of Thomas*, for instance, shows little interest in the death and resurrection of Jesus and apparently attributes life-giving power to his words alone.[12] Perhaps the most problematic affirmation of the Syrian tradition about Thomas is that he was Judas *Didymus Thomas*, the "twin" of Jesus.[13]

---

[9] For the Hymn of the Pearl, see Paul-Hubert Poirier, *L'hymne de la perle des Actes de Thomas: introduction, texte-traduction, commentaire* (Homo Religiosus, 8; Louvain-La Neuve: P. Pierier, 1981).

[10] For some of the distinctive characteristics of these sections, see Sebastian P. Brock, *The Holy Spirit in the Syrian Baptismal Tradition* (The Syrian Churches Series, 9; Poona: Anita, 1979); Gabriele Winkler, "The Original Meaning of the Prebaptismal Anointing and its Implications," *Worship* 52 (1978) 24–45; and idem, *Das armenische Initiationsrituale: entwicklungsgeschichtliche und liturgievergleichende Untersuchung der Quellen des 3. bis 10. Jahrhunderts* (Orientalia Christiana Analecta, 217; Rome: Pontificium Institutum Studiorum Orientalium, 1982); Ruth A. Meyers, "The Structure of the Syrian Baptismal Rite," in *Essays in Early Eastern Initiation* (ed. Paul Bradshaw; Alcuin/GROW Liturgical Study, 8; Bramcote, Nottinghamshire, UK: Grove, 1988) 31–43.

[11] On asceticism generally see Peter Brown, *The Body and Society: Men, Women, and Sexual Renunciation in Early Christianity* (New York: Columbia University Press, 1988). On encratism or sexual self-control, see Arthur Vööbus, *Celibacy: A Requirement for Admission to Baptism in the Early Syrian Church* (Stockholm: Almqvist, 1954), and idem, *History of Asceticism in the Syrian Orient* (CSCO 184; Louvain: Secrétariat CSCO, 1958); Yves Tissot, "Encratisme et actes apocryphes," in *Les actes apocryphes des Apôtres* [see n. 8 above] 109–19, and, for more comprehensive views, Giulia Sfameni Gasparro, *Enkrateia e anthropologia: le motivazioni protologiche della continenza e della verginità nel cristianismo dei primi secoli e nello gnosticismo* (Rome: Augustinianum, 1984), and idem, "Atti apocrifi e tradizione encratita: Discussione di una recente formula interpretativa," *Augustinianum* 23 (1983) 287–307; Virginia Burrus, *Chastity as Autonomy: Women in the Stories of the Apocryphal Acts* (Studies in Women and Religion, 23; Lewiston, NY: Mellen, 1987). On the *Gospel of Thomas*, see the useful treatment by Stephen J. Patterson, *The Gospel of Thomas and Jesus* (Sonoma, CA: Polebridge, 1992).

[12] For a comparison of Thomas and other early Christian traditions on this point, see Gregory Riley, *Resurrection Reconsidered* (Minneapolis, MN: Fortress, 1995).

[13] Cf. *GosThom* 1.

The Thomas encountered in the pages of his *Acts*, while still the "twin" of Jesus, who can easily be mistaken for his brother,[14] and while still rabidly ascetical,[15] has been to some extent domesticated and harmonized with emergent orthodoxy. The domestication of the radical Syrian apostle appears in his citations of scripture, his concern with church order, evidenced in his appointment of ecclesiastical officials,[16] and in his use of an elaborate sacramental system. This treatment of Thomas is a progressive affair whose workings begin with the composition of the *Acts* but then can be traced through the elaborate manuscript tradition of these *Acts*. To follow that story in the compass of this essay is impossible, and other scholars have noted aspects of the accommodation of the Thomas tradition to developing canons of orthodoxy in both Greek and Syriac communities.[17] What I would like to pursue here is the role of Pauline literature in that domestication.

The role of Paul is not immediately obvious, since neither the narrator nor the character Thomas ever explicitly cites a Pauline text, while the apostle frequently cites sayings of Jesus in forms probably dependent on Gospel texts current in Syria.[18] Nonetheless, allusions to Pauline materials play a substantial role in the *Acts* in two ways. First, such allusions help in weaving the biblical fabric that ties the discourse of Thomas, his speeches, homilies and liturgies, to a scriptural base. Secondly, a key Pauline motif plays a role in the construction of the character of the apostle as one "sent to do the Father's will."

Pauline Language in the Christology of the Acts

The first body of evidence consists of allusions to Pauline texts in the discourses of Thomas. The *Acts* introduces Pauline language in two sensitive connections: to express fundamental Christological affirmations and to undergird the text's promulgation of a particular ethic.

The Acts presents its doctrinal position in various prayers and hymns. At *AcThom* 27 Thomas prays over the oil to be used in the first anointing scene, "Come, holy name of Christ, **which is above every name**." The opening of the epiclesis recalls Phil 2:9. Little else in the prayer, with the possible exception of a concluding Trinitarian formula, recalls

---

14 Cf. *AcThom* 11.

15 Note, for instance, the denunciation of marriage and procreation at *AcThom* 12, on the lips of Jesus himself, but he and his twin maintain the same attitude throughout the work.

16 See *AcThom* 169.

17 See especially Klijn, *The Acts of Thomas*.

18 The citations were discussed by H. W. Attridge in "Intertextuality in the Acts of Thomas," a paper presented at the Society of Biblical Literature Annual Meeting, 1995.

canonical scripture. The language may have come to the Acts through liturgical traditions, but, if so, those traditions have been shaped by the Pauline text. The connection with Philippians 2 may be significant in light of the construction of the character of Paul to be explored below.

At *AcThom* 80 the Pauline allusions are more clear. Thomas offers a prayer replete with biblical phrases, at least two of which are Pauline:

> I don't have any way to think of your beauty, Jesus, or anything to say about you. Rather, I am unable. For I don't have the capacity to tell of them, O Christ, you who have achieved rest and who alone are wise, who know what is in the heart,[19] and who understand the workings of the mind. Glory be to your divinity, which appeared on our account **in the likeness of human beings**.[20] Glory and praise to your ascent into the heavens, for through it **you have shown us the way on high**,[21] promising us to be seated at your right hand and to judge the twelve tribes of Israel.[22] You are the heavenly word of the Father. You are the hidden light of reason, that reveals the way of truth, dispels darkness, and obliterates error.[23]

The text illustrates the appropriate way to address Christ with scriptural allusions. It praises the Savior for his incarnation and exaltation, events seen to be paradigmatic for humankind. Pauline language of Christ being in the "likeness" of human beings expresses the moment of incarnation. Further Pauline language about ascent on high expresses the other decisive moment of the Christ event.

It may be of interest that not all witnesses to the *Acts* display both Pauline allusions. The Syriac includes the reference to the way on high, being seated at the right hand, and the triad of word, light, and way. It lacks the reference to Jesus knowing what is in the heart, probably from John, and the Pauline phrase about the "likeness" of human beings. The latter could have been omitted on doctrinal grounds, since the phrase could support a docetic Christology that would be have been objectionable to the later Syriac tradents.

---

[19] Cf. John 2:25.

[20] Cf. Rom 1:13; Phil 2:7.

[21] Cf. Heb 2:10; 9:24; 10:19–22; 12:2. For the purposes of this paper Hebrews will count as Pauline, since it was generally accepted as such in the east. Cf. also Eph 4:8, although the motif of "showing the way" more closely echoes Hebrews.

[22] Cf. Matt 19:28 and parr.

[23] Cf. John 1:1, etc. Translations of the *Acts of Thomas* are my own, from the Greek (Lipsius-Bonnet ed.; see n. 7 above), unless otherwise indicated.

Pauline Motifs in the Paraenesis of the Acts

While Christological doctrine is a concern of the *Acts*, it is much more interested in the portrayal and cultivation of an ascetical lifestyle. Pauline materials also come into play toward these ends. A possible allusion, embedded within a context of other evocations of scripture, appears at *AcThom* 94. Here Thomas responds to the initial conversion of the heroine of the story, the noble lady Mygdonia, with a series of beatitudes:

> Blessed are the chaste saints whose souls never condemn them. Having won them, they are never separated from themselves.
>
> Blessed are the spirits of the chaste saints that have received the perfect heavenly crown from the heavenly sphere assigned to them.[24]
>
> Blessed are the bodies of the chaste saints because they have been deemed worthy to become **temples of God**, so that Christ might dwell in them.

Paul first uses the image of the temple of God in connection with the factionalism of the Corinthian community at 1 Cor 3:16–17. The image there forms part of a warning not to defile the temple of the spirit in view of the impending eschatological judgment. At that point the image is not connected to the body of the individual believer which stands in danger of defilement. Paul's remark at 1 Cor 6:19, concluding his attempt to deal with issues of sexual behavior, applies the metaphor to the individual believer's body. The image in that context buttresses the warning to avoid πορνεία [fornication; sexual immorality generally]. In the *Acts of Thomas*, the second application of the Pauline image becomes dominant and the warning extends to any sexual activity.

Another use of the image appears in the admonition to avoid idolatry at 2 Cor 6:16. While the passage may originally have been non-Pauline,[25] it would be part of the scriptural repertoire available to our Christian novelist. The resonance of the image as used in 2 Corinthians may be felt at *AcThom* 87 where the Mygdonia responds to a homily of Thomas. Here she longs to become a convert to the life of holiness that he preaches:

> I beg of you, take thought for me and pray for me, that I might obtain mercy from the God whom you proclaim, become his habitation, be

---

[24] For another set of beatitudes modeled on those of the Synoptic Gospels, but exalting sexual asceticism, cf. *AcPaulThec* 5–6. The passage represents a tradition of expression but not a literary play.

[25] For discussion of the issue, see Victor Paul Furnish, *2 Corinthians* (AB 32A; Garden City, NY: Doubleday, 1984) 371–83.

transformed by prayer, hope, and faith in him, receive the seal, and become a **holy temple** where he might dwell.

Whether there is a specific Pauline allusion involved, it is clear that the Pauline image is familiar to the author of the *Acts*.

The use of Pauline language in the context of an appeal to sexual purity is particularly clear at *AcThom* 12. Here Jesus, looking like Thomas, appears to a bridal couple on their wedding night and preaches to them the doctrine of celibacy:

> Remember, my children, what my brother told you and to whom he commended you. Know that if you abandon this sordid intercourse, you will become holy temples, pure, freed from afflictions and pains, both manifest and hidden, and you will not assume cares for a livelihood or for children, **the final result of which is destruction**.

The final phrase, reminiscent of Phil 3:19, may derive from homiletic tradition, but it conforms to the ascetical appropriation of Paul noted above. The opposite of becoming temples of celibate sanctity is to be destroyed.

The condemnation of sexual immorality of all sorts recurs constantly in the text. At one point the apostle revives a woman who reports on her visit to Hell. [26] In *AcThom* 55 the woman tells of one of the sights that she saw in the underworld. She describes the particularly gruesome torment of some sinners and remarks: "These are the souls who have **exchanged the intercourse of men and women**." Her phrase clearly echoes Paul's description of homoerotic behavior at Rom 1:26–27. Whether the author of the *Acts* worried about the exegesis of 1 Cor 7:9 is not clear, but for him to be celibate and chaste is clearly better than to burn.

Pauline language is of use not only to describe sins but also to suggest the forgiveness available in the Christian community. At *AcThom* 38 a penitent crowd appeals to Thomas:

> But if he has mercy on us, pities, and saves us, **overlooking our former activities**, frees us from the evils that we have done in our error, and does not make a careful accounting with us, nor remembers our former sins, we shall become his servants and shall do his will to the end.

The hope that God would overlook former sins evokes passages such as Rom 3:25 and Acts 17:30.

---

[26] For discussion of the genre of the episode, see Martha Himmelfarb, *Tours of Hell* (Philadelphia: University of Pennsylvania Press, 1983).

Yet perhaps not all sins, particularly sins committed within the Christian community, will find forgiveness. *AcThom* 51 records a case of punishment for sacramental transgression:

> There was a young man who had committed an unspeakable deed. When he approached and took the eucharist to his mouth his two hands shriveled up, so that they were no longer able to reach his mouth.

Paul recognized that there would be punishment for unworthy reception of the sacrament (see 1 Cor 11:30). While there is no specific allusion here, the Pauline warning may be the ultimate inspiration of the text in the *Acts*.

The eschatological horizon within which Paul worked remained a part of the consciousness of the early Church, although in most circles expectations of the imminent eschaton became muted. At *AcThom* 137 Tertia, the royal friend of Lady Mygdonia, records her response to the apostle's preaching, using at least one Pauline phrase:

> Tertia replied, "I must thank you for sending me to Mygdonia. For I went and heard about a new life and I saw the new apostle of the God who gives life to those who believe in him and fulfill his commands. So I ought to pay you back for this favor and give you good advice in exchange for yours. For you will be a great king in heaven if you listen to me and fear the God who is proclaimed by the stranger and keep yourself in holy chastity for the living God. For **this kingdom is passing away** and your life of ease will turn into tribulation. But go to that man, believe him, and you will live forever."

Tertia's remark recalls 1 Cor 7:31 but has a different focus. For Paul the whole order of things created was about to undergo radical transformation. The basic contrast governing Tertia's thinking is the divide between the temporal world of change and decay and the immortal realm to which she aspires. [27] Secondarily perhaps her remark alludes to the expectation that the political regime under which she lives will pass away in favor of the celibate community that Paul represents. Although the conceptual frameworks may differ, the heroes and heroines of the Acts, like Paul, draw an ascetical conclusion from their conviction that the current shape of things is passing away.

The Characterization of Thomas

The *Acts of Thomas* is literature that seeks to instruct and inculcate values while it entertains. To function effectively it needs to present an image of its hero, the apostle Thomas, that will not be narrowly

---

[27] For other examples of this contrast, cf. *AcThom* 36, 78, 88, 120, 135, 139.

sectarian but broadly acceptable within the Christian world of the third century. To that end the text uses motifs drawn from scriptural depictions of leading apostles. The *Acts of Thomas* organizes its construction of the character of Thomas around the motif of the one who does the will of the Father. This motif evokes two sets of scriptural materials, the Lord's Prayer and the Johannine image of Jesus who also was "sent to do his Father's will." Through those motifs the text defines how it is that Thomas is the "twin" of Jesus, thus avoiding any implications that their relationship is primarily, if at all, physical.

At *AcThom* 3 a brief prayer of Thomas evokes the Lord's Prayer:

> Early on the following day the apostle prayed and entreated the Lord, "I'm going where you want, Lord Jesus. **Let your will be done**."

Similar phrasing occurs at *AcThom* 30, when Thomas encounters a deadly serpent:

> "Lord, was it for this reason that you made me come out here, to see this **trial**? Therefore, **let your will be done**."

The reference to the "trial" recalls Matt 6:13, the petition in the Lord's Prayer to avoid πειρασμός [temptation]. The petition to let the divine will be done certainly evokes the same dominical prayer. This evocation of the prayer forms something of an *inclusio* with *AcThom* 144, the beginning of the final remarks of Thomas, where he prays the Lord's Prayer in its entirety. The use of the petition to let God's will be done serves as a frame for the whole *Acts* and comments on what it is to be an apostle, one utterly devoted to doing the Lord's will.

The Lord's Prayer is an important structural element in the development of the motif. Equally significant is the related motif from the Fourth Gospel, which surfaces in the first major episode of Thomas's journey to India (*AcThom* 4–16). His initial destination is the city of Andrapolis, where he and the Indian merchant who is now his master come upon a royal wedding. Brought to the banquet, Thomas refuses to eat or drink, behavior that leads other guests to ask why he has come. He responds (*AcThom* 5):

> "I've come here," he answered, "for something more important than food or drink, that is, **to do the will** of the king."

The comment evokes John 4:34 and the assertion of Jesus that his food is to do his father's bidding. The comment is again ironic, since, while Thomas has come to the banquet at the behest of the local potentate, he has really come to the country do the will of a heavenly king. To avoid earthly food and merriment and thereby to do the will of the true King is true food and drink for the apostle. The ironic effect is due in large part to a play on the saying of Jesus in John 4. The theme continues later in the *Acts*, e.g., at *AcThom* 79, where Thomas is described as "the one **who does the will of him who sent him**." Even the demons whom Thomas exorcises recognize his status. At *AcThom* 76 one notes,

> if you don't do the will of the one who sent you, he'll punish you. Likewise in my case, if I don't do the will of the one who sent me, then before the appropriate and ordained time I will be returned to my own nature.

The characterization of the apostle as one who does the will of him who sent him thus runs through the *Acts*. The initial episode (*AcThom* 1–3) gives graphic expression to the notion by portraying Thomas, who is initially reluctant to do the will of God, as first of all a slave to Christ, then, in the service of Christ, a slave of a human master, the Indian merchant, Chaban:

> India's lot fell to Judas Thomas, who is also called Didymus. But he did not want to go, saying that he was unable even to travel because of his weak constitution. He also said, "How can I, a Hebrew, go among the Indians to proclaim the truth?"
>
> While he continued to argue in this way the Savior appeared to him by night and said to him, "Don't be afraid, Thomas. Go to India and proclaim the word there. For my grace is with you."
>
> Thomas did not obey but said, "Send me wherever else you wish. I'm not going to India."
>
> **2** While he was pondering these things, there came along a certain merchant named Chaban,[28] just arrived from India. He had been sent by King Gundafar[29] with a commission to buy and bring back a craftsman. When the Lord saw him walking about at noon in the market he said to him, "Do you wish to buy a carpenter?"
>
> "Yes," he answered.
>
> Then the Lord told him, "I have a slave who is a carpenter and I want to sell him." Then he showed him Thomas some distance away and settled with him on a price of three bars of unstamped silver. He drafted a bill of sale that read, "I, Jesus, son of Joseph the carpenter, agree to sell my slave, Judas by name, to you, Chaban, a merchant of Gundafar, the King of India." With the paperwork complete, the Savior took Judas, called Thomas, and brought him to Chaban the merchant.
>
> When Chaban saw him he said to him, "Is this your master?"
>
> "Yes, he is, my lord," the apostle responded.
>
> Chaban said, "I've purchased you from him." The apostle kept quiet.

---

[28] The name in Greek becomes Abbanes.

[29] So in SyrB. In SyrL the name is Gudnafar; in Greek, Gundaphoros.

3 Early on the following day the apostle prayed and entreated the Lord, "I'm going where you want, Lord Jesus. Let your will be done." He went off to Chaban the merchant bringing nothing at all with him except his purchase price. For the Lord had given it to him and said, "Let your purchase price,[30] with my grace, be with you wherever you go."

The apostle overtook Chaban as he was carrying his baggage onto the boat, so he began to give him a hand. When they had embarked and were settled, Chaban asked the apostle, "What kind of things do you make?"

The apostle answered, "With wood I make plows, yokes, scales, ships, ships' oars, masts, and wheels. With stone I make monuments, shrines, and royal residences."

The merchant Chaban said, "We certainly need such a craftsman." They then set sail with a favorable wind and proceeded rapidly until they reached Andrapolis, a royal city.

The episode is full of ironic touches. The sale is necessitated by Thomas's reluctance to go to India. His owner, who is also his "twin," sells him, but gives him the price of the sale for the journey. The characteristics with which the newly purchased slave describes himself suggest one level of the relationship, since Thomas is a master carpenter able to make "plows, yokes,[31] scales, ships, ships' oars, masts, and wheels," as well as "monuments, shrines, and royal residences." Thomas's skills at building spiritual mansions will become a central concept in a later episode (*AcThom* 17–29), but here they suggest to the reader who knows that Jesus is a carpenter (Mark 6:3), and the son of a carpenter (Matt 13:55), that Judas Thomas is his sibling.

It is tempting to see this episode as a reflection of the Christ hymn of Phil 2:6–11, a text to which the *Acts* makes allusion on at least one other occasion, as noted above. Thus Thomas, though in the "form" of his brother,[32] did not consider equality with him to be something that he should exploit but humbled himself taking the form of a slave. If there is any connection with the famous hymn, it is also laced with irony, given the initial reluctance that Thomas expresses to do the divine will.

The Philippians hymn may provide the basic conceptual structure for the episode, but there are other Pauline allusions closer to the surface of the text. Jesus' command to Thomas not to fear, but to undertake his

---

[30] The comment of Jesus is not found in the Syriac and involves a wordplay difficult to reproduce in English, between "price" (τίμημα) and "value, honor" (τιμή).

[31] The *Infancy Gospel of Thomas* 13.1, a popular tale of the "hidden years" of Jesus, describes Joseph as making such items.

[32] The inverse relation is made explicit at *AcThom* 11, where Jesus appears in the form of Thomas.

apostolic mission recalls the Lord's commands to Paul at Acts 18:9 and 27:24. We shall later consider one other possible allusion to the Paul of Acts.

A final Pauline allusion may be imbedded in the curious remark of Jesus to Thomas that he can take his selling price with him. This note may also be connected with another point on which the text is silent. For the narrative does not disclose how it is that Thomas came to be a slave of Jesus. His ready acquiescence in his resale to Chaban is quite unmotivated. It is possible that the text simply assumes unreflectively that Jesus can relate to his apostles as master to slaves. Such a presumption could arise from the metaphors at home in the general language of piety, according to which the pious person appears as the slave of God.[33] Alternatively, the image in Thomas could reflect early Christian descriptions of apostles as slaves of Christ.[34] In fact, a specific connection of the slave motif with a Pauline source appears at *AcThom* 72 where Thomas prays:

> Jesus, you who have taken on (human) form and have come to be as a human being and appeared to all of us so that you might not keep us apart from your love, it is you, Lord who have given yourself for us, **bought us by your blood,** and obtained us as a high-priced possession. What can we give you, Lord, as a recompense for **your life that you have given for us**?

The address to Jesus as one who has "taken on form" may be yet another allusion to Phil 2:7. The reference to purchase by blood, found in both Greek and Syriac traditions, echoes Gal 3:13. The notion that Christ's life has been "given for us" echoes Matt 16:26 and John 16:3. The Pauline references are clearly more than casual scriptural allusions. The reference to purchasing by blood reveals the presuppositions underlying the logic of the first episode of the *Acts*. Thomas's status as a chattel slave is a corollary of the fact that Christ has initially purchased him by his blood. Furthermore, since the apostle's real purchase price is not the silver bullion that Chaban gives Jesus, it is clear that Jesus' remark to his twin that his purchase price is to go with him on his journey has a profound significance. Thomas will most resemble his Twin when he undergoes martyrdom, an event foreshadowed in the anointing that takes place at the banquet scene (*AcThom* 5).

---

[33] Cf., e.g., Matt 20:27; 25:21; Luke 2:29; 12:47.

[34] For Paul: Rom 1:1; Gal 1:10; Phil 1:1; Tit 1:1. For James: Jas 1:1. For Peter: 2 Pet 1:1. For Jude: Jude 1.

Two Narrative Touches

It is clear that the basic elements of the characterization of the apostle Thomas rest on scriptural passages, and that among these passages Pauline texts play a prominent role. Two further episodes suggest other, relatively casual, contacts with Pauline materials.

At *AcThom* 62 General Sifor, seeking aid for his demon-possessed wife, tells Thomas, "I have heard that **you do not accept pay from anyone**, but you provide to those in need whatever you do have." Thomas follows in the footsteps of that other slave of Christ, since Paul, perhaps following the Socratic ideal,[35] refused to accept payment, according to 1 Cor 9:12; 2 Cor 11:7–9.

Finally, while the Paul of the canonical Acts is not prominent in the Acts of Thomas, one episode recalls a portion of Acts. *AcThom* 122 records an escape from prison:

> **22** Afterward the apostle returned to the prison. He found the gates opened and the guards still sleeping. Thomas said, "Who is like you, O God, you who withhold your loving care and concern from no one? Who is merciful like you, who have saved your possession from evils. You are the life that overcame death, the repose that cut off toil. Glory to the only-begotten of the Father. Glory to the merciful one sent from Mercy."
>
> When he had said this, the guards were **awakened** and saw all the **doors opened** and those who had been incarcerated <asleep>.[36] They said among themselves, "Didn't we secure the doors? How is it that they are now open and the prisoners are (still) within?"

The episode recalls the incarceration of Paul and his companions at Philippi, as recounted in Acts 16:23–28. As in that episode, the guards awoke from sleep to find the doors of the prison open but the prisoners within. The motif of miraculous escape from prison is commonplace in ancient narrative and there may not be a direct textual connection.[37] Yet, as in the canonical Acts, the apostle and his companions do not avail themselves of the opportunity for release.[38] Here their restraint is not a device to enable them to shame their jailers, as in Acts 16; it

---

[35] On the influence of the socratic ideal, see Hans Dieter Betz, *Der Apostel Paulus und die sokratische Tradition; eine exegetische Untersuchung zu seiner Apologie 2 Korinther 10–13* (BHT 45; Tübingen, Mohr-Siebeck, 1972).

[36] "Asleep" added with the Syriac.

[37] See Hans Conzelmann, *Acts of the Apostles* (Hermeneia; Philadelphia: Fortress, 1987) 132. He notes that "the miracle is spiritualized in the apocryphal acts of the apostles," and cites Erik Peterson, *Frühkirche, Judentum und Gnosis: Studien und Untersuchungen* (Freiburg: Herder, 1959) 183–208.

[38] Peter, of course, had a different attitude in Acts 5.

rather shows their willingness to accept their fate, to do the will of the One who sent them.

Conclusion

Much of the *Acts of Thomas* involves intricate and allusive play with scriptural materials. In that intertextual operation, the words and deeds of Jesus, as remembered both in the Synoptics and in John, play a role in defining the character of Thomas and the content of his message. Yet along with those materials the letters of Paul and portions of the narrative about him in Acts help to domesticate the Twin of Jesus.

The "Haustafeln" and American Slavery: A Hermeneutical Challenge

Wayne A. Meeks

Most Christians believe that the Bible ought somehow to play a central role in moral formation and ethical decisions. A significant part of Victor Furnish's research and writing has explored ways in which modern critical study of the New Testament may clarify its ethical application. Yet what are we to make of those cases in which an honest and historically sensitive reading of the New Testament appears to support practices or institutions that Christians now find morally abominable? The proslavery arguments of eighteenth- and nineteenth-century America present one of those hard cases.

The Biblical Case for Slavery

In 1844 Patrick Hues Mell, "a Baptist minister," anonymously published a tract designed to show that "slavery is not a moral evil."[1] "I recognize no code of morals," wrote Mell, "but that contained in the sacred Scriptures" (9). Citing texts from both Old and New Testaments, he declared that slavery "is *directly* sanctioned by the letter of the Scriptures" (10). Mell's conviction and his arguments were quite typical of proslavery writing and preaching over the better part of two centuries. The eminent historians of American slavery, Elizabeth Fox-Genovese and Eugene D. Genovese, observe that the abolitionists "increasingly retreated to the swampy terrain of individual conscience," while "Southerners, by contrast, took great comfort in the Bible's demonstrable justification of slavery, which led them to attend carefully to the Bible's pronouncements on other matters as well, for the Word of God referred directly, not abstractly, to their society."[2]

---

[1] Anon. [Patrick Hues Mell], *Slavery: A Treatise, Showing that Slavery is Neither a Moral, Political nor Social Evil* (Penfield, GA: Benj. Brantly, 1844).

[2] Elizabeth Fox-Genovese and Eugene D. Genovese, "The Divine Sanction of Social Order: Religious Foundations of the Southern Slaveholders' World View," *JAAR* 55 (1987) 215. See also the same authors' "The Religious Ideals of Southern Slave Society," *Georgia Historical Quarterly* 70 (1986) 1–16, and Larry E. Tise, *Proslavery: A History of the Defense of Slavery in America 1701–1840* (Athens, GA, and London: University of Georgia Press, 1987). Tise has analyzed the content of formal treatises, tracts, and sermons of 275

Most embarrassing for professional students of the Bible, the proslavery spokesmen were generally better exegetes than their opponents. There were exceptions, of course. For example, Frederick Augustus Ross, addressing the New School Presbyterian General Assembly in 1856, ridicules "the anti-slavery man [who] ran away into the fog of *his* Hebrew or Greek." Ross will have none of it; he upholds "this good old translation," the King James Version, and warns against "teaching the people to doubt its true rendering from the original word of God."[3] And some of the arguments seem silly to us now, especially the pseudoethnology of Ham, Shem, and Japheth constructed from Gen 8:20–27.[4] If we leave aside such specifically racist elements in the slavery apologetic, however, we find that many of slavery's advocates were more careful and detailed in their exegesis and frequently founded their cases on stronger philological and historical grounds than the abolitionists. Even the Rev. Mr. Ross's bluster against Hebrew or Greek was aimed at the embarrassingly wrong-headed attempt by some abolitionists to show that עבד and δοῦλος did not refer to "slave" in the common sense, but to more benign forms of service.

As biblical studies began to emerge as a distinct discipline, in the early to middle nineteenth century, some of its leaders, particularly in the Reformed tradition, found themselves in a troubling dilemma. Drawn morally toward the abolitionist position, they yet could not blink the fact that slavery was taken for granted in the Bible and, indeed, the Bible contained divine commands regulating the institution. How could slavery be "evil in itself," as the abolitionists in the 1830s increasingly insisted, if the Bible approved it? Bruce Mullin has shown in an important article how the conservative hermeneutics that prevailed in the leading Reformed seminaries, Andover and Princeton, led the pioneer biblical scholars Moses Stuart and Charles Hodge into a blind alley in the national debate on slavery.

While the Unitarians had welcomed the approach of the Latitudinarians in England and the Neologians in Germany—"elevating the

---

proslavery clergymen from colonial times through the Civil War. "Scripture," he concludes, "proved the most important source for establishing the morality of slavery" (116). On the abolitionists' failure to formulate a coherent antislavery interpretation of the Bible, see James Brewer Stewart, "Abolitionists, the Bible, and the Challenge of Slavery," in *The Bible and Social Reform* (ed. Ernest Sandeen; Philadelphia: Fortress, 1982) 31–57. Further ironies in Mark A. Noll, "The Image of the United States as a Biblical Nation, 1776–1865," in *The Bible in America* (ed. Nathan Hatch and Mark A. Noll; New York: Oxford University Press, 1982) 39–58.

[3] Fred. A. Ross, *Slavery Ordained of God* (Philadelphia: J. B. Lippincott & Co., 1857); quotations from 59, 60.

[4] A commonplace in the later proslavery literature, which became progressively more explicitly racist. Ross, 25f., offers an unusually florid elaboration of the scheme.

moral kernel of faith over the written record itself"—the Reformed theologians resisted these new trends. Andover followed Ernesti's "grammatico-historical" approach, while Princeton followed the even more conservative line of Turretin of Geneva. Linking Francis Bacon's empiricism with the anti-Hume epistemology of the Scottish "Common Sense" philosophy, the Princeton scholars produced a hyperbiblicism: "Scriptural evidence had the solidity and certainty of empirically verifiable evidence." Both they and their Andover colleages neglected the other, equally strong side of Scottish Common Sense philosophy, recognition of the role that moral sense must play in judgments—the side developed by their abolitionist colleagues like Samuel Hopkins of Andover. "Unable to accept the solutions of either the Unitarians or the evangelical abolitionists, both Andover and Princeton wrestled with the slavery question for three decades caught between a loyalty to their exegetical method and a personal dislike for the institution of slavery."[5]

Clergy trained in the biblicist exegesis brought it enthusiastically to the proslavery barricades, as we can see from the countless sermons and tracts they produced.[6] Typical of the biblically-centered proslavery tracts is one by Thornton Stringfellow published in 1841. Stringfellow summarizes his own argument as showing that:

Slavery has received
First, The sanction of the Almighty in the Patriarchal age.
Second, That it was incorporated into the only national constitution which ever emanated from God.
Third, That its legality was recognized, and its relative duties regulated by Jesus Christ in his kingdom, and
Fourthly, That it is full of mercy.

The Golden Rule is not impeded by the master-slave relation, says Stringfellow, any more than by the husband-wife relation. Especially important, under Stringfellow's third heading, are Paul's admonitions to slaves in 1 Cor 7:17, 20, 24, his order to obey the "powers . . . ordained by God" in Rom 13:1–7, and the household duty codes in 1

---

[5] Robert Bruce Mullin, "Biblical Critics and the Battle over Slavery," *Journal of Presbyterian History* 61 (1983) 210–26; quotations from 211, 217, 214.

[6] It was not only Andover and Princeton that turned out proslavery ministers. Tise has tabulated educational and other biographical features of the 275 clergy whose writings he analyzed, in his chap. 6. Yale heads the list of "colleges most frequently graduating proslavery clergymen" for the entire period from the beginning of the nineteenth century through the Civil War, though over time the weight shifts toward southern schools (Table 6.6). Among seminaries, Princeton leads, with Andover second; in time Columbia and Union (Virginia) Presbyterian seminaries become important (Table 6.10).

Peter, Titus, and 1 Timothy. The directives addressed to the master prove, says Stringfellow, that "the control of the master was unlimited."[7]

Household Order and the Good Society

Among the biblical texts that were adduced to support slavery, those passages in the Pauline corpus and in 1 Peter that modern scholars call "household codes" or, following Luther, *Haustafeln* are peculiarly important. It was all very well to observe that the Patriarchs of Israel owned slaves and that the Torah provided some rules for regulating slavery. Even the most ardent biblicists were not going to follow the Old Testament worthies in every practice: polygamy, for example, had clearly been superseded by Christ's saying on divorce and by apostolic precepts that assumed monogamy. Beyond the fact that Christ did not forbid slavery, therefore, the positive admonitions to slaves to "obey your masters" were a clinching piece of evidence that the rules of morality in this area had not changed. It would not do, then, to set New Testament Gospel against Old Testament Law, insisted the Rev. Alexander McCaine when he rose to rebut an anti-slavery report by a committee of the Methodist General Conference meeting in Baltimore in 1842. "There is but one standard of morals," McCaine declared, "and that standard is one and indivisible—it is uniform and perpetual." As proof that "the Holy Spirit recognizes slavery in the New Testament, and gives directions for the conduct both of masters and slaves," he cited 1 Cor 7:21; Eph 6:5, Col 3:2; 1 Tim 6:1; Tit 2:9; as well as Philemon.[8]

The Presbyterian Mr. Ross, mentioned above, would not agree that morality was "uniform and perpetual." He confesses a radically theocentric ethic in which "right and wrong are results brought into being, mere contingencies, means to good, made to exist solely by the will of God, expressed through his word; or, when his will is not thus known, he shows it in the human reason by which he rules the natural heart."[9] All the more important, then, that the apostolic testimony showed slavery to be enduringly in accord with God's will.[10]

---

[7] Thornton Stringfellow, *A Brief Examination of Scripture Testimony on the Institution of Slavery, in an Essay, First Published in the "Religious Herald"* (Richmond: Religious Herald, 1841); quotations from pp. 5–6, 20.

[8] Alexander McCaine, *Slavery Defended Against the Attacks of the Abolitionists in a Speech Delivered Before the General Conference of the Methodist Protestant Church, in Baltimore, 1842* (Baltimore: Wm. Wooddy, 1842); quotations from 19, 22.

[9] Ross, *Slavery Ordained*, 41.

[10] Ross had apparently hardened his position on this point. Three years earlier he had foreseen a day when "the evil of slavery" would be ended and all Africans returned to the natural home of Ham (ibid., 25–31).

Most of these writers and preachers seem to have held a simple divine-command ethics. The point in quoting the apostolic paraenesis was to show that God, speaking through God's chosen vessels, had acknowledged slavery by regulating it. If slavery were "evil in itself," God would have forbidden it, not given rules for its practice.

Some of the more thoughtful slavery apologists, however, went further to provide a more holistic and historical reading of the household tables. These were people who knew their classics; the world of Aristotle and of Cicero seemed quite real and contemporary to them. For example, John Henry Hopkins, Episcopal Bishop of Vermont, in 1864 reprinted a pamphlet he had issued in 1861, with a long rejoinder to an attack on the pamphlet that had been signed by the Bishop of Pennsylvania, Alonzo Potter, and 161 of his clergy. Hopkins begins with the usual citations, including an extended discussion of the *Haustafeln* with excerpts from standard commentaries. At first he takes these admonitions as simple rules. Then, however, launching a frontal attack on the language of the Declaration of Independence, he expounds a thoroughly hierarchical vision of "the order of creation":

> The Deity seems to take pleasure in exhibiting a marvelous wealth of power through the rich variety of all his works, so that no two individuals of any species can be found in all respects alike. And hence we behold a grand system of ORDER and GRADATION, from the thrones, dominions, principalities, and powers in heavenly places, rank below rank, to man. And then we see the same system throughout our earth displayed in the variety of races, some higher, some lower in the scale—in the variety of governments, from pure despotism to pure democracy—in the variety of privilege and power among the subjects of each government, some being born to commanding authority and influence, while others are destined to submit and obey.[11]

Frederick Augustus Ross also thought the language of created equality and "inalienable rights" an expression of "atheism" and found in the household codes a key to the kind of social order God had willed. The subordination of wife to husband was fundamental: "And, first, God said to the woman, 'Thy desire shall be to thy husband, and he shall rule over thee.' *There*, in that law, is *the beginning of government ordained of God. There* is the beginning of the rule of the superior over the inferior, bound to obey." The *Haustafeln* sealed the argument: "The precepts in Colossians iv.18, 23, 1 Tim. vi.1–6, and other places, show,

---

[11] John Henry Hopkins, *Scriptural, Ecclesiastical, and Historical View of Slavery, from the Days of the Patriarch Abraham to the Nineteenth Century. Addressed to the Right Rev. Alonzo Potter, D.D., Bishop of the Prot. Episcopal Church, in the Diocese of Pennsylvania* (New York: W. I. Pooley, 1864) 21.

unanswerably, that God has really sanctioned the relation of master and slave as those of husband and wife, and parent and child; and that all the obligations of the moral law, and Christ's law of love, might and must be as truly fulfilled in the one relation as in the other."[12]

The Rev. Iveson L. Brookes of South Carolina was explicit in appealing to the historical case of "Grecian and Roman antiquities," for "this institution of God, slavery, so much abhorred by blind and invidious Northern Abolitionists, was the basement of their republican system of government, and the sustaining pillar of their social and political greatness." And the Apostle adopted what was good about that culture:

> When the Apostle Paul, under his special appointment by Christ to preach the gospel to the Gentiles, proceeded with his gracious message to the Greek and Roman States, highly enlightened in literature and the arts, but deeply sunk in the darkness of idolatry and spiritual wickedness in high places, that inspired man, while leveling the shafts of eternal truth at every unholy practice, though at his personal risk, he was careful to guard the authority of civil institutions, saying, "let every soul be subject to the higher powers. For there is no power but of God: the powers that be are ordained of God." He was especially circumspect in watching over the safety and sacredness of the institution of slavery, which every where prevailed . . . . [There follows a citation of Ephesians 6.][13]

These appeals to an organic and hierarchical society, exemplified in Greece and Rome and certified by Christ's apostles, were part of a powerful reaction to the organized abolitionist movement of the 1830s. More than that, they represent what Larry Tise has called "the nation's conservative counterrevolution."[14] Tise and the Genoveses have demonstrated that the proslavery forces were joining in a more widespread reaction to the bourgeois values of modern capitalism. With enthusiastic dependence on Edmund Burke, the new conservatives attacked the individualism of the Enlightenment, enshrined in the language of the Declaration of Independence. They contrasted the familial context of chattel slavery with the "wage slavery" of factory workers.[15]

---

[12] Ross, *Slavery Ordained*, 47, 64; italics original.

[13] Iveson L. Brookes, *A Defence of the South Against the Reproaches and Incroachments of the North: In Which Slavery is Shown to be an Institution of God Intended to Form the Basis of the Best Social State and the Only Safeguard to the Permanence of a Republican Government* (Hamburg, SC: at the Republican Office, 1850) 28.

[14] Tise, *Proslavery*, 348. For his account of this movement, leading to "a form of proslavery distinctively American" (ibid.), see his chap. 14.

[15] See Fox-Genovese and Genovese, "Religious Ideals," and by the same authors, "Divine Sanction."

As James Henley Thornwell, one of the most eloquent of the proslavery intellectuals, said in 1850, "It is not the narrow question of abolitionism or of slavery—not simply whether we shall emancipate our negroes or not; the real question is the relations of man to society—of States to the individual, and of the individual to States; a question as broad as the interests of the human race." He went on to describe the conflict in dramatic terms:

> These are the mighty questions which are shaking thrones to their centres—upheaving the masses like an earthquake, and rocking the solid pillars of this Union. The parties in this conflict are not merely abolitionists and slaveholders—they are atheists, socialists, communists, red republicans, jacobins, on the one side, and the friends of order and regulated freedom on the other. In one word, the world is the battle ground—Christianity and Atheism the combatants; and the progress of humanity the stake.[16]

These words are from a sermon that Thornwell preached on 26 May 1850, at the dedication of a church erected by the Second Presbyterian Church of Charleston for the purpose of "religious instruction of the Negroes." He takes as his text Col 4:1 and appeals also to the parallel in Ephesians 6. The sermon, despite some intemperate defensiveness for the South against "the insane fury of philanthropy," is on the whole a reasoned and fairly systematic statement of the way the best of the Southern intellectuals (and indeed some of the Reformed leaders of the Northern schools of theology) understood the apostolic paraenesis to undergird an ordered, organic society of which slavery was—in the present fallen world—an indispensable factor. Thornwell appeals to reason over sentiment. The reason has a distinctly Stoic flavor—he cites Cicero and Seneca extensively—but it is warranted by the Apostolic directive to masters and slaves. Thus its relevance for our inquiry may justify a fairly extended summary.

Thornwell will have none of the more egregious form of racism that in his day was increasingly being expressed by slavery's defenders: "It is a publick testimony to [sic; read "of"?] our faith, that the Negro is of one blood with ourselves—that he has sinned as we have, and that he has an equal interest with us in the great redemption. . . . We are not ashamed to call him our brother" (11). The leitmotif of the sermon is the question what is really "just and equal" (Col 4:1; see, e.g., p. 12). That issue, he says, is now at the center of a great struggle of principles. "What disasters it will be necessary to pass through before the nations

---

[16] James Henley Thornwell, *The Rights and the Duties of Masters: A Sermon Preached at the Dedication of a Church Erected in Charleston, South Carolina, for the Benefit and Instruction of a Coloured Population* (Charleston: Walker & James, 1850) 14.

can be taught the lessons of Providence—what lights shall be extinguished, and what horrors experienced, no human sagacity can foresee" (13). Then follows his apocalyptic description of the culture war already quoted.

Central to the argument is Thornwell's demonstration that slavery does not deprive the slaves of their essential humanity—it does not reduce them to things, as the Unitarians Channing (the bête noire of the proslavery writers) and Whewell insist it must. For that purpose the Haustafeln are important, buttressed by the Stoic doctrine of inner freedom. Thornwell insists that "the ideas of personal rights and personal responsibility pervade the whole system. It is a relation of man to man—a form of civil society" (19). Warrant for this claim is that "Paul treats the services of slaves as *duties*—not like the toil of the ox or the ass—a labor extracted by the stringency of discipline—but a moral debt, in the payment of which they were rendering a homage to God" (20, citing Eph 4:5–9). "[Paul] considered slavery as a social and political economy, in which relations subsisted betwixt moral, intelligent, responsible beings, involving reciprocal rights and reciprocal obligations" (21). Hence one may properly discuss whether particular practices of masters and slaves are just, or whether particular laws of slavery are—but these do not affect the institution as such (26).

Slavery is not "involuntary servitude," insists Thornwell, for "If by voluntary be meant . . . that which results from hearty consent, and is accordingly rendered with cheerfulness, it is precisely the service which the law of God enjoins" (27). The only truly moral bondage is that to vice or sin—for which sentiment he quotes John 8:34, Seneca, Pythagoras, Cicero, and Claudian (28), whereas the only true freedom is that which God's truth brings (John 8 again), "and it is precisely the assertion of this freedom—this dominion of rectitude—this supremacy of right, which the Apostle enjoins upon slaves—when he exhorts them to obey their masters in singleness of heart as unto Christ" (29). So "involuntary servitude" is the unwilling "eye-service" that the Apostle condemns (30).

Like Hodge at Princeton, Thornwell believes that slavery is not an ideal relationship, but "a part of the curse which sin has introduced into the world" (31). There "will be no bondage in heaven" (31). "It springs not from the nature of man as man, nor from the nature of society as such, but from the nature of man as sinful, and the nature of society as disordered" (31). Nevertheless, "the Gospel does not propose to make our present state a *perfect* one—to make our earth a heaven" (32). "The distinction of ranks in society, in the same way [as the sterility of the earth—he thinks of Gen 3:17], is an evil; but in our fallen world, an absolute equality would be an absolute stagnation of all enterprise and industry" (32). Only at one point does racism enter overtly into his argument, and that with a tincture of progressivism: "The free citizen of England and America could not endure the condition of African bondage—it would defeat his individual development." "But the governments of Asia may be the only ones consistent with the moral development of their people, and subjection to a master, the state in which the African is most effectually trained to the moral end of his being" (33).

Above all, it is the individualism of the abolitionists' moral philosophy that Thornwell rejects. He quotes a long passage from Channing, to which, he says, "we have no other objection than that it represents the perfection of the individual as the ultimate end of his existence, while the Scripture represent[s] it as a means to a higher and nobler end—the glory of God" (38). In a series of quite Stoic-like statements, Thornwell insists on the interconnectedness of society, within which "the same temper of universal rectitude is equally incumbent upon all, while it must be admitted that the outward forms of its manifestations and expression must be determined by the relations which Providence has actually assigned to our state" (37). "The feet are as indispensable to the head as the head to the feet. The social fabrick is made up of divers ingredients, and the cement which binds them together in durability and unity is the cement of justice" (41–42). The Golden Rule means nothing different: "it is nothing but the inculcation of *justice* from motives of love" (42). And of course the purpose of the church here dedicated is not to change the social condition of the slaves: "Our design in giving them the Gospel, is not to civilize them—not to change their social condition—not to exalt them into citizens or freemen—it is to save them" (48).

Family and household were central to the southern view of society. "The household—the plantation, farm, urban workplace or even townhouse—constituted an organic community as captured in the depiction of it as family."[17] The slaveholders and their intellectual spokesmen were able to sell this vision to the yeoman farmers (until the middle of the War, when the latter became disaffected as more and more of the burden of fighting fell on them) because the ideology extended to the hierarchical structure of the whole household, slave and free. The white farmers' potential to be slaveholders themselves "guaranteed their membership in the company of male individuals who held responsibility for the governance of women, children, and labor."[18]

---

[17] Fox-Genovese and Genovese, "Divine Sanction," 221.

[18] Fox-Genovese and Genovese, "Religious Ideals," 8.

Although the "counterrevolution" in American social thought reached its fullest momentum in the antiabolitionist rhetoric of the three decades prior to the Civil War, it had much earlier precedents. The arguments, as Tise observes, were already well developed in colonial and revolutionary times.[19] They are stated with all clarity in "Two Sermons preached to a Congregation of Black Slaves" in 1749 by Thomas Bacon, rector of St. Peter's Church in Maryland, and in four sermons he addressed to the slaves' owners, published the following year.

The sermons present quite a marvelous combination of close biblical exegesis—centering on the Haustafeln but ranging widely in both Old and New Testaments—with close reasoning informed by familiarity with the classics. Neither reason nor scripture leads Bacon to doubt the rightness of slavery in God's providential care for the world. The providential ordering of things is the backbone of his argument: "For this whole World is but one large Family, of which Almighty God is the Head and Master:—He takes Care of all, by causing the Sun to shine, the Rains to fall, [etc.]." Using the New Testament Haustafeln, he describes the structure of that Providence, in terms an Aristotle or an Epictetus would have found familiar: "Now, for carrying on these great and wonderful Ends, God hath appointed several *Offices* and *Degrees* in his Family . . . . Some he hath made *Judges* and *Rulers*, for giving Laws, and keeping the rest in Order:—Some he hath made *Masters* and *Mistresses*, for taking Care of their Children, and others that belong to them:—Some he hath made *Merchants* and *Seafaring Men*, for supplying distant Countries with what they want from other Places:—Some he hath made *Tradesmen* and *Husbandmen, Planters* and *Labouring-Men*, to work for their own Living, and help to supply others with the Produce of their Trades and Crops:—Some he hath made *Servants* and *Slaves*, to assist and work for the *Masters* and *Mistresses* that provide for them:— and others he hath made *Ministers* and *Teachers*, to instruct the rest, to shew them what they ought to do, and put them in mind of their several Duties." Second, Bacon's concept of "justice and equity," which he draws from Col 4:1, τὸ δίκαιον καὶ τὴν ἰσότητα, is Aristotelian in its sense of proportion, compounded with Christian eschatology. What is due from each person depends upon their estate: from the slave, an all-but-absolute obedience to the master or mistress (an exception, the obligation to refuse commands to commit grave sins, is mentioned in the first of the sermons to slaves, 33–34). In return, the faithful slave is rewarded in heaven.[20]

---

[19] Tise, *Proslavery*, 10.

[20] Thomas Bacon, *Two Sermons Preached to a Congregation of Black Slaves at the Parish*

Reading the Haustafeln Today

The New Testament epistles' tables of admonitions to paired members of a household, which were so central to the American ideology of a slave-based society, have been the subject of intensive historical research in recent decades. At first, following hints by Martin Dibelius in his 1913 commentary on Colossians and Ephesians that were developed in a dissertation by his student Karl Weidinger in 1928, scholars thought the form was a specifically Stoic product, borrowed and only lightly "Christianized" by the New Testament writers. Subsequent researchers pointed to significant parallels in some Hellenistic Jewish writers. Eventually it became clear, in work in the 1970s by Dieter Lührmann, David Balch, and Klaus Thraede, that this way of thinking about social location and obligation was much older and broader than had previously been suspected. The pattern appears already in Plato. Its classical formulation is in Aristotle's *Politics* and *Nicomachaean Ethics*. The Roman Stoics adopted it as their own; so did Jewish apologetic writers aiming to show that the laws and customs of Moses supported rather than subverted the social ideals of Greco-Roman culture. Philosophers of the most diverse schools, from Middle Platonists to Epicureans to Neopythagoreans, and rhetoricians of all kinds used this pattern when they wanted to talk about the proper ordering of a household and about the household as microcosm of a properly ordered city, empire, and universe. When the fourth-century compiler Stobaeus collected texts of this sort for his encyclopaedia of *topoi*, 'commonplaces,' he called this chapter "Concerning Household Management." He knew that περὶ οἰκονομίας named a very ancient and honored tradition.[21]

The household management topos persisted for so long in the standard repertoire of moralizing teachers and orators in antiquity, we may suppose, because it summed up a bit of the practical wisdom of the

---

Church of S[aint] P[eter] in the Province of Maryland by an American Pastor (London: John Oliver, 1749) and *Four Sermons, upon the Great and Indispensible Duty of All Christian Masters and Mistresses to Bring Up their Negro Slaves in the Knowledge and Fear of God, Preached at the Parish Church of St Peter in Talbot County, in the Province of Maryland* (London: John Oliver, 1750). Quotations are from the former, pp. 13 and 14–15. For a brief description of Bacon's historical context, see Tise, *Proslavery*, 20–21 and, for the history of publication and republication of his sermons, 375f., n. 15. I am endebted to Prof. Jon Butler for bringing Bacon's sermons to my attention and giving me access to copies of them.

[21] Twentieth-century research is conveniently summarized in David L. Balch, "Household Codes," in *Greco-Roman Literature and the New Testament: Selected Forms and Genres* (ed. David E. Aune; SBLSBS 21; Atlanta: Scholars Press, 1988) 25–50. Balch includes an annotated bibliography and a translation of an important first-century CE representative of the topos, an excerpt from the Augustan court philosopher Arius Didymus.

age. The commonplace retains its power and coherence because it articulates a widely-sensed and comprehensive notion of the way the world in fact works. The duties prescribed for children and parents, wives and husbands, slaves and masters were not ad hoc rules but the necessary corollaries of the structured nature of things. The universal "city of the gods and men" (as the Old Stoics called it) was so constructed that some must lead and others follow, some must govern and others obey. Equity obtains when reciprocal exchange at all levels yields to each party that measure of value or honor that is *proportional* to the status to which Providence has assigned each one.

When some Christian writers of the first two centuries cast their admonitions in this familiar pattern, then, they were not "borrowing" a page from this or that philosophical school. They were thinking with the moral tools their culture had given them, whether they were Jews or of some other ethnic group in the Greek and Roman cities. As the household was the matrix within which the early Christian congregation began its life and took its shape, so the congregation's leaders must concern themselves with a household's good order—"for God is a God not of disorder but of peace."[22]

This century's historical and form-critical investigation of the Haustafeln has thus demonstrated that these early Christian patterns of moral discourse belong to a comprehensive vision of society. That vision significantly resembles the social ideal that the more learned defenders of slavery found reflected in those texts. It was of a patriarchal society, which its elites believed to be an organic whole, with an agrarian base and a household-centered, slave-supported, urban apex.

To be sure, the historical critic today will make some observations about the epistolary paraenesis and its context that would be less congenial to the proslavery apologists. First, slavery in the first-century Roman Empire was different in some significant ways from American slavery in the eighteenth and nineteenth centuries—though not necessarily in the ways many abolitionists suggested. Roman slavery was not racially based. Many if not most slaves could look forward to manumission at a relatively early age. And the legally recognized status

---

[22] The centrality of the household in the formation of the urban Christian groups has been the focus of considerable research in recent years. Suffice it here to mention Abraham J. Malherbe, *Social Aspects of Early Christianity* (2d ed. rev.; Philadelphia: Fortress, 1983); Hans-Josef Klauck, *Hausgemeinde und Hauskirche im frühen Christentum* (Stuttgart: Katholisches Bibelwerk, 1981); Wayne A. Meeks, *The First Urban Christians: The Social World of the Apostle Paul* (New Haven: Yale University Press, 1983); and David C. Verner, *The Household of God: The Social World of the Pastoral Epistles* (SBLDS 71; Chico, CA: Scholars Press, 1981).

and the patronal connection of freedpersons had no counterpart in the American South.

Second, most, though not all, critical scholars regard the New Testament epistles in which the Haustafeln occur as pseudonymous, so that it is possible to see a certain development or even a reaction in early Christianity's assimilation of cultural modes of moral discourse. How much time passed before the writing of the deuteroapostolic letters and how sharp the differences in fact were remain debated points, however. How these facts, if they could be firmly established, would affect the authority of the passages in question depends, of course, on one's understanding of the canon.

Third, historians detect certain tensions among different groups and individuals and points of view in the early Christian groups. The "baptismal reunification formula" that Paul quotes in Gal 3:27–28 and 1 Cor 12:13, and which appears also in Col 3:11 and echoes in Eph 4:24, bespeaks a unity given to those who "put on Christ" in which the polarities Jew and Greek, slave and free, and even male and female are done away. Paul's use of the formula in Galatians to argue against circumcision of Gentile converts shows that he, at least, did not construe this unity to be merely "ideal" or "spiritual" or future, but took it to be an eschatological gift to be realized in the actual life of the congregation.[23] The active engagement of women as leaders, prophets, and patrons of the early Christian communities sometimes seemed to threaten the household-centered patriarchal order—some of these women were themselves heads of households—and brought reactions of various degrees of vehemence that are apparent in New Testament texts.[24] The charismatic style of leadership in the household ekklesia must often have clashed with traditional expectations of the householder's own power and authority, and such clashes are probably a major ingredient in the controversies we see already in Paul's Corinthian correspondence.[25]

The proslavery clergy of the nineteenth century would probably not have been much impressed by these discoveries by our century's historical critics. They had been taught by theologians and biblical scholars who were firmly resisting the disturbing critical voices that were beginning to be heard from Germany and Scotland.[26] Yet, even if they

---

[23] Wayne A. Meeks, "The Image of the Androgyne: Some Uses of a Symbol in Earliest Christianity," *History of Religions* 13 (1974) 165–208; idem, *Urban Christians*, 155.

[24] See above all Elisabeth Schüssler Fiorenza, *In Memory of Her: A Feminist Theological Reconstruction of Christian Origins* (New York: Crossroad, 1983).

[25] Meeks, *Urban Christians*, 117–25.

[26] See Mullin, "Biblical Critics," 219.

had known what we think we know now, would it have made any difference in their argument? After all, critical study appears to confirm their most fundamental position: the New Testament contains passages that do not merely recommend subjection by wives, children, and slaves to their husbands, parents, and masters. In addition those passages signal acceptance of an organic construction of society for which such subjection is essential. Historical criticism may have the potential to undermine the biblicist project in ethics as a whole, and it may discover particular historical facts that lend assistance to revisionist readers, but it appears to provide no knock-down argument against such uses of scripture as the apologists for slavery made.

The Hermeneutical Challenge

It is not easy to state clearly why the proslavery readers of the Bible were wrong. It is even more difficult to enunciate interpretive rules that might help us to avoid making equally disastrous mistakes if we claim the Bible as norm in the ethical issues we face today, especially if we believe (as I have incautiously asserted elsewhere) that we must endeavor to discover a "hermeneutics of social embodiment."[27] If the attempt is feasible at all, it will require more space and time than the closing paragraphs of a short article afford. Nevertheless, it may be useful to outline a few of the possible strategies and some of their shortcomings.

Immutable principles. The commonest response to arguments like those defending slavery cited above is to say that the apologists have failed to acknowledge the historical conditionedness of the biblical rules and admonitions. The biblical writers naturally spoke in the idiom of their time, and their moral view was limited by the shared assumptions that circumscribed their social and intellectual world. It would be a serious theological mistake to identify as the eternal word of God those elements in their teachings that were simply the common coin of their cultural realm, and it would be absurd to apply simple-mindedly to modern situations rules formulated in a culture so vastly different from our own.

Well and good, but where in the Bible is one to find norms that are *not* conditioned by the social arrangements and cultural assumptions of a particular age and people? The classic answer of Protestant Liberalism, which was enunciated already by the abolitionists in the 1830s, was that one must discover the kernel of universal truths and principles that

---

[27] Wayne A. Meeks, "A Hermeneutics of Social Embodiment," in *Christians among Jews and Gentiles: Essays in Honor of Krister Stendahl on his Sixty-fifth Birthday* (ed. George W. E. Nickelsburg and George W. MacRae; Philadelphia: Fortress, 1986) 176–86.

were hidden in the accidental husk of historically conditioned beliefs and world views. A thoughtful evangelical scholar, troubled by the issues raised here, has recently restated this approach with eloquence: "There are within Scripture great principles laid down clearly, for those with eyes to see, which point beyond the advice given to particular people at particular times on these matters."[28] Unfortunately there are grave difficulties with this position, as anyone must know who recalls Karl Barth's critique of "culture-Protestantism" early in this century. When Rudolf Bultmann objected that Barth's commentary on Romans did not adequately distinguish between the Spirit of Christ and "other spirits" of this world in the voice of scripture, Barth retorted that all the words of scripture are "voices of those other spirits"—the Word of God must be discerned in, through, *and against* them.[29]

The issue of discernment—how one gets "eyes to see"—is formidable. In hindsight it is easy enough for us to judge that the defenders of slavery were wrong—because we know slavery to be wrong. Their error, however, was not for want of reason or of exegetical perspicacity, nor for lack of attention to "great principles." Their works are replete with arguments from love, justice, order, and reciprocal obligation, and from the fundamental loci of Christian theology, creation, redemption, and eschatology. "Ideological critics" can without difficulty point out that their reasoning was blinded by their self-interest—but which of ours is not?[30]

The Golden Age. We noted above that recent historical scholarship has reached some probable conclusions about the early Christian commu-

---

[28] Kevin Giles, "The Biblical Argument for Slavery: Can the Bible Mislead? A Case Study in Hermeneutics," *Evangelical Quarterly* 66 (1994) 16. Giles lays out the issues, particularly for evangelical Christians, starkly and clearly. The main point of his article, and it is powerfully persuasive, is that evangelical proponents of the subordination of women are making exactly the same mistake today as the proslavery evangelicals of last century.

[29] Karl Barth, *The Epistle to the Romans* (Oxford: Oxford University Press, 1968) 16–17.

[30] There is much to ponder in David Brion Davis's classic work on the history of western culture's paradoxical perception of slavery (*The Problem of Slavery in Western Culture* [New York: Oxford University Press, 1988]). Davis is concerned to understand how an institution taken for granted for millennia could come to be seen, within a relatively short time, as utterly wrong. Tracing the concept of slavery and attitudes toward it in western thought from classical antiquity to America of the 1770s, he seeks "to demonstrate that slavery has always been a source of social and psychological tension, but that in Western culture it was associated with certain religious and philosophical doctrines that gave it the highest sanction" (ix). The paradox often seen in commentators on American life, between the ideals of freedom expressed in its founding documents and ethos of revolution and the fact of slavery in all thirteen of the original states corresponds with a paradox that runs through the history of Western thought on the subject.

nities and the nature and context of the New Testament documents that would at least discomfit the defenders of slavery. In particular, the diversity of the New Testament statements and of the early Christian communities' ways of thinking and acting has become one of the focal points of critical scholarship. Can we detect in the conflicts among the early Christians signs of some revolutionary *novum* that upset the conventions of the age and promised liberation to the oppressed?

The Haustafeln seem to constitute one of the most opportune cracks into which to insert the revisionist wedge. The New Testament examples are all found in epistles that are thought by most critical scholars to be pseudepigraphical; they can plausibly be understood as a second-generation reaction to the more egalitarian impulses of the earliest Jesus movement and of Paul's own missionary praxis.[31] The "baptismal reunification formula" adapted in Gal 3:27–28 and elsewhere (see above) is often taken as the banner of the original egalitarian impulse. Feminist scholars have found this reconstruction of early Christian history especially congenial, and none has developed it so thoroughly, consistently, with such close attention to exegetical detail, or with so great rhetorical power as Elisabeth Schüssler Fiorenza. She writes of the Colossians domestic code, for example:

> In taking over the Greco-Roman ethic of the patriarchal household code, Colossians not only "spiritualizes" and moralizes the baptismal community understanding expressed in Gal 3:28 but also makes this Greco-Roman household ethic a part of "Christian" social ethic. However, it is important to keep in mind that such a reinterpretation of the Christian baptismal vision is late—it did not happen before the last third of the first century. Moreover, it is found only in one segment of early Christianity, the post-Pauline tradition, and had no impact on the Jesus traditions.[32]

It is thus possible to engage in a kind of *Sachkritik* that does not, like Bultmann's, seek its *discrimen* in the subjectively and individually perceived *Anrede* of the existentialist *kerygma*, but in a countercultural, liberating community formation: the "ekklesia of women" or (for other liberationist interpreters) one or another form of "base community." Like Bultmann, however, this interpretive strategy does set one element or dimension of the biblical testimony against another: the Jesus tradition against the Pauline tradition, Paul against the deuteropauline

---

[31] One has to be wary of a too-simple scheme of dialectical evolution. Even if both Ephesians and Colossians are pseudepigraphic, as I am convinced, there is no clear evidence that they are significantly later than Paul's authentic letters. They could easily have been produced by Pauline disciples immediately after his death or even before.

[32] Elisabeth Schüssler Fiorenza, *In Memory of Her*, 253–54.

development in his own school, and especially the earlier against the later. Ironically—for Schüssler Fiorenza and many of the liberationist critics are Roman Catholic—this strategy also emulates a familiar move in Protestant polemical ecclesiology: "early catholicism" represents the "fall" from the purity of the Gospel into compromise with the worldly orders.

There are at least two problems with the Golden Age argument. First, like all arguments based on a historical reconstruction, it is probabilistic. It therefore runs the risk of falling into Lessing's Ditch: "accidental truths of history can never become the proof of necessary truths of reason."[33] Much of the evidence upon which the reconstruction depends is subject to alternative interpretations; many of the "facts" are to a larger or smaller degree hypothetical. In such a situation, we are tempted to exaggerate the goodness of the earliest. Further, even if we could agree more completely on what the earliest stages of Christian history looked like, what grounds have we for believing that the earliest is necessarily the best?

Moreover, all of our reconstructions are liable to deformation by our own conscious or (more often) unconscious interests. Schüssler Fiorenza and some other feminists see this very clearly, and they are quite candid in advocating an honest and overt adoption of an ideological position against the perceived patriarchy in many of the texts as well as in the tradition that interprets them. An ideology favoring the oppressed may justly displace the regnant ideology of the oppressors. The trouble is that, if all is ideology, then it is hard to see how the oppressor is to be persuaded by any moral compunction that might be shared with the revisionists. The pessimist might conclude that finally only power counts. The abolitionists did not persuade the slaveowners; slavery ceased to have an ethical claim in American society because a war was won and lost.

The second problem with Golden Age reconstructions is that they either ignore or directly challenge traditional conceptions of the biblical canon. This is a pragmatic shortcoming, for the arguments are

---

[33] G. E. Lessing, "On the Proof of the Spirit and of Power," in *Lessing's Theological Writings* (ed. Henry Chadwick; Stanford: Stanford University Press, 1957) 53. For the paradigmatic place of Lessing in modern Protestant biblical inquiry, see Peter C. Hodgson, *The Formation of Historical Theology: A Study of Ferdinand Christian Baur* (New York: Harper and Row, 1966) 271 and Hans W. Frei, *The Eclipse of Biblical Narrative: A Study in Eighteenth and Nineteenth Century Hermeneutics* (New Haven: Yale University Press, 1974) passim. For an argument that Lessing's *garstiger, breiter Graben* [nasty, broad ditch] must be addressed as seriously by modern ethical theory as it has been by two centuries of theological inquiry, and that Kierkegaard may help the ethical leaper as well as the theological, see Samuel Fleischacker, *The Ethics of Culture* (Ithaca, NY, and London: Cornell University Press, 1994).

not likely to persuade just those supporters of the status quo who need most to be convinced and who are most susceptible to an argument from the authority of scripture. More fundamentally, this kind of argument risks obscuring the nature of the authority that grounds it. If, as seems the case, the immediate norm is not the text of scripture but the practice of a certain number (not all and probably not the majority) of the early Christians, which happens to be attested (or can be detected by careful analysis) in some of the biblical texts, then would it not be more straightforward to say that the effective norm is not "biblical" at all, but whatever other principle it is that enables the interpreter to know that just *those* practices (and not the later and more dominant ones) were *good*? To be sure, this is a problem that is by no means limited to the arguments of feminist and liberationist interpreters; it may in fact be endemic to all "biblical theology" that bases itself on modern historical-critical exegesis. Moreover, many of the interpreters in question would doubtless want to say, "Yes, the norm or discrimen by which I choose which particular texts of scripture are in turn to yield norms for behavior is extrinsic to any particular texts, yet it expresses the will of God to which the scripture *taken as a whole* somehow bears witness." In that case the "somehow" cries out for specification.

The seed growing secretly. A second form of historicizing reply to the defenders of slavery and its analogues is like the Golden Age scheme in finding the operative norm hidden beneath the text of scripture, but it holds a notion of historical development that is nearly the opposite of the Golden Age view. Here the egalitarian implications of the gospel are planted like a mustard seed in the soil of the early Christian communities. Very gradually these implications sprout and grow through the history of western civilization until at last they burst into full flower in the emancipationist movements of modernity.

Richard Hays, in his new book on New Testament ethics, provides a particularly elegant example of this strategy. Discussing Ephesians as representative of developments in the Pauline school, he writes:

> Four distinctive features of the household code in Ephesians are noteworthy. First, the particular admonitions are subsumed under a general exhortation to the whole church to "be subject to one another out of reverence for Christ" (5:21); thus, the hierarchical structure of the relations described is tempered by a comprehensive vision of the church as a people living in humility and mutual submission. The conventional authority structures of the ancient household are thereby subverted even while they are left in place. Second, the formal structure of the code is unusual in its pattern of addressing the

subordinate persons in the social order (wives, children, slaves) as moral agents who must *choose* to "be subject." . . . . Third, the Ephesians household code is notable for its reciprocity. It does not merely call upon the less powerful to submit (as, e.g., Tit 2:9–10); it equally charges the more powerful (husbands, fathers, and masters) to act with gentleness and with concern for those over whom they exercise authority. Finally, most importantly, the commandments laid down in this code are given an explicitly theological elaboration that seeks to show how these norms are warranted by the gospel. This is most evident in the author's reading of marriage as a symbol of the relationship between Christ and the church. . . .

[Granting this vision is not egalitarian, but aptly described as "love patriarchalism," nevertheless:] The love patriarchalism of Ephesians is not . . . closed and static in character. When masters are told to stop threatening their slaves because "you have the same Master in heaven, and with him there is no partiality" (6:9), a theological image is set in motion that unsettles the conventional patterns of master-slave relations. Similarly, if marriage is a metaphor for the relationship between Christ and the church, the exalted ecclesiology of Ephesians must deconstruct static patriarchal notions of marriage.[34]

This is an appealing vision, a variant of one that has figured large in the history of Christian apologetics (and the churches' self-congratulation), but there are palpable difficulties with it. What can it mean for "conventional authority structures" to be "subverted even while they are left in place"? Either they are authoritative or they are not. The appeal to the reciprocity of the household codes and to their direct address to the subordinates is one that, as we have seen, the supporters of slavery also made. For them it showed that in the hands of Christian masters slavery is not dehumanizing. Hays apparently sees no irony or double entendre in observing that as "moral agents" the women, slaves, and children "*must* choose to 'be subject'" (my italics). Finally, the most obvious problem with all seed-growing-secretly constructions is the unwanted implication that, if the effects of the egalitarian gospel were invisible for so very many centuries, it cannot have had much force to begin with.

Moral intuition. At this point we may feel some of the frustration experienced by the abolitionists, for whom the evil of slavery was self-evident, but who were again and again defeated when they tried to use the Bible to prove what seemed to them so obvious. Some continued to insist with William Lloyd Garrison that "slavery is prohibited by the

---

[34] Richard B. Hays, *Community, Cross, New Creation: New Testament Ethics* (San Francisco: HarperCollins, forthcoming) [ms. 91–92].

Book of Inspiration," that "slavery at a single blow annihilates THE WHOLE DECALOGUE."[35] Others surrendered the Bible to their opponents, denouncing it as "the Devil's Book." "The Bible," wrote Henry C. Wright, "if Opposed to Self-Evident Truth, Is Self-Evident Falsehood."[36]

Looking back, most of us will agree that the abolitionists' intuitive reading of scripture was more nearly "correct" in the moral sense than the more systematic exegesis of the proslavery clergy and their scholarly teachers, whose method has more in common with our own scientific exegesis despite the distance the latter has traveled in the past century and a half. Some of us will venture to say the same of some issues that are presently dividing our communities, notably the subordination of women and the condemnation of same-sex unions—arguments for which are often strikingly analogous to those used by the proslavery apologists, and for which indeed the biblical basis is very much smaller. Can we find ways to speak responsibly of an intuition formed (in part) by scripture that may at singular moments in the life of the Christian community look squarely at the particulars of the historical record and say, nevertheless, at this moment God wills something quite different from the beliefs and practices of the biblical age?

To introduce the notion of intuition into the discussion obviously risks even further obfuscation. "Intuitionism" has earned general disdain in modern ethical theory.[37] That disdain is due, at least in part, to the common view that intuition is something deeply non-inferential, private, spontaneous, and mysterious. Mysterious it doubtless is, but the other adjectives need not apply. Intuition as I understand it has been formed by the same process that formed the self, and that means that it emerges from experience that is simultaneously personal and social. The process is embedded in a particular culture, which has its unique history. A tradition—or a potpourri of mingling and conflicting traditions—is its life blood. To ask about a critically intuitive reading of the Bible for ethical illumination is therefore to ask about the nexus of public discussion and private conscience in which the Christian tradition may at crucial moments gather its many historic resources into a new constellation.

Pursuit of that question must await another occasion. A first step might be to analyze some exemplary judgments that, in retrospect, seem appropriately to appeal to the Bible's teaching, but which do so in

---

[35] Stewart, "Abolitionists, the Bible, and the Challenge of Slavery" [see n. 2], 38–39, quoting *The Liberator*, July 28, 1836.

[36] *Liberator*, May 11, 1848, quoted by Stewart, "Abolitionists," 49.

[37] See, e.g., Alan Donagan, *The Theory of Morality* (Chicago: University of Chicago Press, 1977) 17–25.

some holistic fashion not easily specifiable either by systematic exegesis or by inferential logic. A clear example appears in the petition of a group of eighteen Scots living in Darien, Georgia, to the Trustees of the colony in 1739, urging rejection of slavery. Among their supports for this position is this statement: "It's shocking to human Nature, that any Race of Mankind, and their Posterity, should be sentenced to perpetual Slavery; nor in Justice can we think otherwise of it, than they are thrown amongst us to be our Scourge one Day or another for our Sins; and *as Freedom to them must be as dear as to us*, what a Scene of Horror must it bring about!"[38] The italicized phrase reveals what is wanting from the textually superior arguments of the slavery apologists, who regularly interpreted the Golden Rule as requiring only that we do unto the slave what we *ought* to desire *if we were slaves* according to the duty imposed by the purported order of creation. The crucial element is that "fellow feeling" of which George Eliot writes: "There is no general doctrine which is not capable of eating out our morality if not accompanied by the daily habit of direct fellow feeling with individual human beings."[39]

Conclusion

There are no magical rules of historical method or of hermeneutics that will assure that a scripture-based moral judgment will be right and just. Moral argument is a matter of persuasion and consensus, always grounded in a particular historical situation. The job of hermeneutics is to set the rules for a fair argument.[40] One job of Christian moral formation is to create practices and occasions that will nurture "the daily habit of direct fellow feeling" so as to shape a moral intuition appropriate to the gospel.

One basic element in such communal practices would surely be the habit of listening to the weaker partner in every relationship of power. A fair moral argument about slavery must at the least entail listening to the slaves. A great many people were prepared in the eighteenth and nineteenth centuries to say what slaves ought to hear the Bible saying to them, but very few were prepared to hear what the slaves in fact were hearing or what they had to say.[41] At least one rule of thumb then

---

[38] Quoted from *Colonial Records of Georgia* 3:427–31 by Davis, *Slavery and Western Culture*, 148. Italics mine.

[39] George Eliot, *Middlemarch*, quoted by Hilary Putnam, "Is There a Fact of the Matter about Fiction?" in idem, *Realism with a Human Face* (ed. James Conant; Cambridge, MA: Harvard University Press, 1992) 212.

[40] I owe this formulation to David L. Bartlett. I am grateful to him, Gene Outka, Jon Butler, and Martha F. Meeks for carefully reading a draft of this essay and offering valuable comments.

[41] Recently we have learned a lot about the religion of the slaves. See, e.g., Albert J.

emerges for ethical use of the Bible: whenever the Christian community seeks to reform itself, it must take steps to make sure that among the voices interpreting the tradition are those of the ones who have experienced harm from that tradition.[42] "The love command in the New Testament" requires no less,[43] and if the love of neighbor is thus understood, it will not so easily be reduced to the cold and narrow "justice" imposed by the possessors of power.

Raboteau, *Slave Religion: The "Invisible Institution" in the Antebellum South* (New York: Oxford University Press, 1978), and Eugene D. Genovese, *Roll, Jordan, Roll: The World the Slaves Made* (New York: Pantheon Books, 1974).

[42] Cf. Wayne A. Meeks, "The Polyphonic Ethics of the Apostle Paul," *Annual of the Society of Christian Ethics* (1988) 17–29.

[43] Victor Paul Furnish, *The Love Command in the New Testament* (Nashville, TN: Abingdon, 1972).

The Fate of Paul in Nineteenth-Century Liberalism: Ritschl and Harnack

William Baird

Among the many admirable features of the scholarship of Victor Furnish is his recognition of the significance of the history of New Testament research. His essay, "The Jesus-Paul Debate: From Baur to Bultmann,"[1] provides a notable example. In this "magisterial survey"[2] Furnish reviews critical opinion about the relation of Paul to Jesus during the last half of the nineteenth and first half of the twentieth centuries. Crucial for the development of the problem is Wrede's assertion that Paul was the "second founder" of Christianity. As Furnish shows, this encouraged some scholars to call for a return to the original source: from Paul, back to Jesus. The stress on Jesus as the founder of Christianity is often identified as a feature of liberal theology. For some, the appreciation of Jesus fostered a depreciation of Paul. Is this true of the founders of classical liberalism? What is the role of Paul in the theologies of Albrecht Ritschl and Adolf von Harnack?

Liberal theology has its roots in Schleiermacher; it was cultivated by Ritschl; it flourished in Harnack.[3] A product of the Enlightenment, liberalism opposes orthodoxy, stresses freedom of inquiry, and is skeptical of the supernatural. Liberal theology has a high doctrine of humanity and a low doctrine of sin. It embraces evolution, heralds human progress, and tends toward universalism. As to the Bible, liberal theology abandons the orthodox doctrine of inspiration and espouses the historical-critical method. Above all, liberal scholars have confidence in the ability of humans to master the data, to solve the historical and exegetical problems.

---

[1] *BJRL* 47 (1965) 342–81; repr., *Paul and Jesus: Collected Essays* (ed. A. J. M. Wedderburn; JSOTSup, 37; Sheffield: JSOT Press, 1989) 17–50.

[2] A. J. M. Wedderburn, "Introduction," *Paul and Jesus*, 11.

[3] See Martin Rumscheidt, ed., *Adolf von Harnack: Liberal Theology at its Height* (London: Collins, 1989).

I

Albrecht Ritschl (1822–1889) was a member of the Prussian establishment. His father was a pastor, later appointed bishop. As a boy, Ritschl met Schleiermacher. Ritschl was educated at Bonn and Halle, with brief stints in Berlin and Heidelberg. In 1845, he transferred to Tübingen and fell under the spell of F. C. Baur. Ritschl began his teaching career at Bonn, where he had the reputation of being a dull lecturer. In 1864, he was called to Göttingen, and there he spent the rest of his career.

The main features of Ritschl's thought are well known. Influenced by Schleiermacher, he stressed religion rather than theology. Following Kant, he eschewed metaphysics and emphasized ethics. Metaphysics, according to Ritschl, was not appropriate to Christian thought, since it focused on objects, not on the transcendent God. God, he believed, was known in history, supremely in Christ. Ritschl's theology is Christo-centric, but it stresses Christ's work, not his nature. Central to the teaching of Jesus is the idea of the kingdom of God. According to Ritschl, the kingdom is the spiritual and ethical rule of God, calling for obedience and love. Ritschl's major theological work, the massive *Die christliche Lehre von der Rechtfertigung und Versöhnung* [*The Christian Doctrine of Justification and Reconciliation*], contends that sin (failure to acknowledge God) is overcome by God's love revealed in Christ, resulting in communion with God and community with believers. According to Ritschl, justification overcomes guilt; reconciliation over-comes alienation.

Although usually viewed as a systematic theologian, Ritschl con-sidered himself a biblical theologian.[4] Indeed, he espoused a high doctrine of biblical authority:

> it stands as the foundation-principle of the Evangelical Church that Christian doctrine is to be obtained from the Bible alone. This prin-ciple has direct reference to the original documents of Christianity gathered together in the New Testament, for the understanding of which the original documents of the Hebrew religion gathered toge-ther in the Old Testament serve as an indispensable aid. These books are the foundation of a right understanding of the Christian religion from the point of view of the community, for the reason that the Gospels set forth in the work of its Founder the immediate cause and final end of the common religion, and the Epistles make known the original state of the common faith in the community, and moreover in

---

[4] See: Clive Marsh, *Albrecht Ritschl and the Problem of the Historical Jesus* (San Francisco: Mellen Research University Press, 1992); Otto Ritschl, *Albrecht Ritschls Leben*, Vol 2: *1864–1889* (Freiburg i.B. and Leipzig: Mohr, 1896) 168–78.

a form not yet affected by the influences which as early as the second century had stamped Christianity as Catholic.[5]

In general, Ritschl rejected the orthodox view of revelation and denied biblical infallibility. He adopted the historical critical method, but considered mere objectivity or secular understanding to be inadequate. He believed the New Testament ought to be interpreted in relation to the Old Testament, and he embraced a Christocentric hermeneutic, reminiscent of Luther.

Ritschl's earliest work on the New Testament was under the shadow of Baur. However, with the publication of the second edition of his *Die Entstehung der altkatholischen Kirche,*[6] he broke with Baur. A few years later, Ritschl published, "Über geschichtliche Methode in der Erforschung des Urchristenthums"[7] in which he attacked both Baur's method and his results. Although Baur had sworn allegiance to the historical critical method, Ritschl argues that Baur's historical research is dominated by his philosophical presuppositions. For example, in interpreting New Testament miracles, Baur dismisses their historicity on the basis of his prior notion that miracles are philosophically impossible. Similarly, Ritschl finds Baur's reconstruction of early Christianity to be flawed both historically and philosophically. Baur's claim that early Christianity constitutes a synthesis of Jewish and Hellenistic thought is historically wrong, since if Jesus is its founder (as Baur acknowledges), then Christianity's origin is without Hellenistic influence. Baur's claim that the origin of Christianity is historical (without supernatural intervention) is philosophically wrong, since if history is the unfolding of the Absolute Spirit (as Baur insists), then history is open to the action of God. Ritschl believes Baur's Hegelianism is in conflict with his naturalism. Ritschl also thinks that Baur's assessment of the sources is not sufficiently critical. Rather than thoroughly investigating questions of the date and authenticity of New Testament documents, Baur has reached premature judgments on the basis of his tendency criticism. For example, Baur considers Colossians and Ephesians to be inauthentic and late because they reflect second century Gnosticism, but he uses them uncritically in his fabrication of the character of second century Christianity—a circular argument.

---

[5] Albrecht Ritschl, "Instruction in the Christian Religion," in *The Theology of Albrecht Ritschl* (ed. Albert Temple Swing; New York: Longman's Green, and Co., 1901) 172.

[6] Bonn: Adolph Marcus, 1857.

[7] ["Concerning Historical Method in the Investigation of Early Christianity"] *Jahrbücher für Deutsche Theologie*, 1(1861) 429–59; repr. in Ferdinand Christian Baur, *Ausgewählte Werke in Einzelausgaben*, Vol. 5: *Für und wider die Tübingen Schule* (ed. Klaus Scholder; Stuttgart-Bad Cannstatt: Friedrich Frommann, 1975) 469–99 .

Ritschl's own reconstruction of early Christian history detects a continuity between Jesus and the apostles, but finds an increasing discontinuity between the church and Judaism.[8] He also detects a continuity between the apostles and the post-apostolic church, but finds a discontinuity between the church of the apostles and the ancient catholic church. With the Reformation, according to Ritschl, continuity with apostolic Christianity is restored. Ritschl explicates the details of the early period of this historical development in his *Die Entstehung der altkatholischen Kirche*. In the introduction, he states his thesis: "we insist that catholic Christianity did not arise out of a reconciliation between Jewish and Gentile Christians, but that it is a stage of Gentile Christianity alone."[9]

The first part of the book deals with the development of the basic viewpoint of Christianity, and is important for Ritschl's understanding of the New Testament. After arguing that Jesus, in sharp contrast to the Pharisees, proclaimed a spiritual and ethical righteousness, Ritschl turns to Paul. He contends that the notion of a radical conflict between Paul and the other apostles was concocted by Baur; it represents a misunderstanding of both Paul and the others, not to mention a simplistic view of Jewish Christianity.

> The notion of a contradiction between the doctrine of Paul and the viewpoint of the other apostles has primarily been created by the attention given to the distinctive thought of Paul with the result that the religious ideas and fundamental views common to all the apostles have not been satisfactorily assessed. The proof of this will not impair the originality of Paul, but at the same time will establish his continuity with the early apostles.[10]

In presenting Paul, Ritschl is anxious to demonstrate that the apostle was not diametrically opposed to Judaism and Jewish Christianity. Thus, Ritschl presents a discussion of the "neutral basis" of Pauline doctrine. According to Ritschl, Paul shares with the other apostles many Jewish concepts, and even displays affinity to the sort of eschatology found in the Apocalypse. Anticipating ideas that he will develop later, Ritschl notes Paul's distinctive ideas of sin and justification. Paul, according to Ritschl, affirms both the universality of sin and human responsibility. Interpreting Romans 7 as descriptive of the situation prior to faith, Ritschl stresses the Pauline struggle between sin and the authentic

---

[8] See Philip Hefner, "The Role of Church History in the Theology of Albrecht Ritschl," *CH* 33 (1964) 338–55.

[9] Albrecht Ritschl, *Die Entstehung der altkatholischen Kirche* (2d ed.; Bonn: Adolph Marcus, 1857) 23.

[10] Ibid., 52.

human will. Ritschl believes Paul's doctrine of justification is concerned with the relationship between humans and God. "Accordingly, Paul in his use of the word δικαιοσύνη [righteousness] does not think directly about a state of the human being, but a relationship of the human being to God, which the latter establishes according to a condition fulfilled by the human being."[11] Faith is the condition; faith is inward; faith means trusting obedience.

In Ritschl's opinion, Paul did not understand the sacrifice of Christ as penalty or appeasement, but as the act of divine-human reconciliation.

> The object of reconciliation is not seen as the wrath of God, but as the sin of the human being in its quality as enmity toward God. . . . Since through the death of Christ the guilt of sin is expiated, or its power abolished, so through that death the enmity toward God is also changed into reconciliation.[12]

As ἱλαστήριον [(gift of)expiation], Christ is representative of God; as θυσία [sacrifice] he is representative of humans. Ritschl does not believe Paul understood the death of Christ as a ransom—especially, a ransom paid to the devil. Instead, redemption is inward, resulting in a new relation with God and a new quality of life for believers—a new creation.

> Justification by faith has the following meaning. The obedience of the sinless son of God is on the one hand effective for the expiation of the guilt of the human being represented by him, and on the other, the effective presentation of the divine will to forgive sin and to declare righteous the believers who in their obedient faith in Christ are put into right relation with God.[13]

Along with this reconciliation comes the gift of the Spirit, and the Spirit, in Ritschl's interpretation of Paul, moves the believer to good conduct, the fruit of justification. The main principle of conduct, as in the teaching of Jesus, is love—the law of Christ that fulfills Old Testament law.

Having presented his understanding of Paul, Ritschl turns to Jewish Christianity. As sources for this investigation, Ritschl uses the Epistle of James, 1 Peter, and Revelation—all accepted as authentic. Ritschl minimizes the differences between James, Peter and John, on the one hand, and Paul, on the other. They, too, he thinks, emphasize ethical obedience and freedom from the law. However, Ritschl detects another

---

11 Ibid., 76–77.

12 Ibid., 87.

13 Ibid., 95–96.

group of Jewish Christians distinct from the apostles: the *Judenchristen*. At the Jerusalem conference, the apostles agreed that Gentile converts need not keep the law, but that they should observe the conditions Jews required of "proselytes at the gate," that is, they should follow the prescriptions of the apostolic decree (Acts 15:23–29). The *Judenchristen*, on the other hand, demanded that the Gentiles keep the law, including the rite of circumcision. Ritschl thinks Paul agreed to the conditions of the decree, although he acknowledges that Paul did not take an absolute position on eating meat offered to idols: at Corinth he mediated between the opponents of eating (the Cephas party), and the more permissive (the followers of Apollos). In regard to the differences between Paul and James of Jerusalem, Ritschl believes the Pauline churches, where Gentiles were in the majority, did not maintain a separation between Jewish and Gentile converts—a separation James believed to be necessary. Upon his arrival in Antioch, Peter followed the Pauline practice (Gal 2:11–12). James considered this a violation of the principles of the decree, and in response to his authority, Peter (and Barnabas) withdrew from eating with Gentile Christians.

In all of this, Ritschl is anxious to show the basic harmony between the Jerusalem apostles and Paul, the diversity within Jewish Christianity, and, most of all, the sharp distinction between the apostles and the *Judenchristen* who are the chief opponents of Paul in places like Galatia.

> The early apostles recognize faith in Christ as the only condition for entrance into the new covenant, but maintain the view grounded in the Old Testament, that this whole people have the call first to enter into the fulfillment of the prophecy given to them, and then to continue the maintenance of their national identity through full observance of the law as religious duty. The strict *Judenchristen*, on the other hand, know and want no Christianity except on the ground of membership in the national association into which the Gentiles must gain entrance through the acceptance of circumcision and the whole Mosaic tradition. Therefore, they deny the apostolic call of Paul, which the early apostles explicitly recognize.[14]

In presenting the later development of early Christianity, Ritschl proceeds to trace the variety and demise of Jewish Christianity. In contrast, he depicts the Gentile majority as deviating from the religion of Paul, and, threatened by heresies like Gnosticism, becoming increasingly legalistic. Out of this deviant Gentile Christianity, Ritschl believes the old catholic church arose.

---

[14] Ibid., 147.

Most important for Ritschl's interpretation of Paul is the second volume of his major work.[15] There he presents the biblical basis for his understanding of justification and reconciliation. Again, Ritschl affirms a high doctrine of biblical authority.

> Therefore, the theology which should be so ordered as to present the authentic thought of Christianity in a positive and scientific form has to be derived from the books of the New Testament and from no other source. And indeed, the content of the New Testament will be confirmed as rule and norm of the theological system under consideration in so far as the use of the New Testament is inclusive and exhaustive.[16]

The biblical material, Ritschl says, must be investigated by an exegesis free from dogmatic presuppositions.

After a discussion of the idea of the forgiveness of sins in the teachings of Jesus, Ritschl takes up the question of the relation of the biblical idea of God to the doctrine of reconciliation. He argues that the orthodox doctrine of justification, with its stress on substitution and penalty, is not in harmony with the God of the Bible. The Old Testament, Ritschl believes, emphasizes the holiness of God whereas the New Testament affirms God's love. "In so far as the holiness of God as the theme of the covenantal life defined the content of the Mosaic law, it is replaced in the New Testament by the love of God."[17] However, even in the Old Testament, righteousness includes the idea of God's grace; the prophets, according to Ritschl, understand righteousness as ethical, involving a relationship with God. In Rom 3:3–5, Paul speaks of righteousness as synonymous with faithfulness. In Rom 3:25–26, he does not present righteousness as punishment, but as the realization of God's purpose to save believers.

Ritschl believes the Old Testament expression "wrath of God" does not refer to a feature of God's character, but provides a vivid description of God's sudden reaction toward breach of the covenant—a passion against human hostility to divine holiness. Ritschl thinks Paul uses the phrase primarily to depict the future eschatological judgment. Paul does not say that believers in the present are redeemed from the wrath of God. Ritschl concludes that "the conception of the emotion of wrath (*Zornaffect*) of God has no religious value for Christians."[18]

---

[15] *Die christliche Lehre von der Rechtfertigung und Versöhnung: Zweiter Band: Der biblische Stoff der Lehre* (Bonn: Adolf Marcus, 1874).

[16] Ibid., 2.18.

[17] Ibid., 2.100.

[18] Ibid., 2.154.

In this volume, Ritschl presents in greater exegetical detail his understanding of the meaning of Christ's death for the forgiveness of sin. Ritschl notes that the resurrection, as well as the death of Christ, is important for forgiveness. He believes the references to blood do not affirm the inherent efficacy of blood, but simply describe the death of Christ graphically. The significance of that death is the fulfillment of Jesus' vocation; it sums up the meaning of his whole life. Thus, Ritschl says that "not the necessity of the death, but the voluntary acceptance of it in the course of full obedience to vocation is the value of the death of Christ as saving event." [19] Ritschl argues that the preposition ὑπέρ in such phrases as "one died for all" (2 Cor 5:14) means "for the benefit of," not "in place of." That substitution is not intended is evident, Ritschl argues, from 2 Cor 5:15, where Paul says that "he who died for all" was also "raised for them" (ὑπὲρ αὐτῶν): surely the apostle does not mean raised "in place of them." The expression "Christ died for (ὑπέρ) our sins" (1 Cor 15:3), according to Ritschl, is parallel to Paul's statement that the death of Christ was on account of (διά) "our trespasses" (Rom 4:25).

Ritschl acknowledges that Paul's doctrine of justification is distinctive. [20] He argues, however, that orthodoxy's attempt to build the doctrine of substitutionary, penal sacrifice on texts from the Pauline epistles is groundless. According to Ritschl, Paul's use of the term ἀπολύτρωσις refers to redemption in general, not to the payment of a ransom or punishment. In reconciliation, it is not God, but the enemies of God who are changed: through Christ, God reconciles sinners to God (2 Cor 5:18–19). Ritschl believes Paul's use of ἱλαστήριον (Rom 3:25) refers to the mercy seat, not to propitiation; it expresses the forgiving grace of God. The whole life of Christ is a sacrifice that offers forgiveness and life. "The obedience to the call given by God, realized in ethical freedom, and in all its consequences, qualifies Christ therefore as sacrifice; the characteristic of his person, that he as a human being is the bearer of divine grace, the image of God, guarantees, under the condition of his obedience unto death, the justification of believers." [21] According to Ritschl, Paul's distinctive doctrine of justification results from his polemical situation. In his dispute with Pharisaic Judaism and Christianity, Paul employs the language of his opponents, giving the misleading impression that he is concerned with legal and ritual matters. Actually, Paul, like Jesus and the rest of the New Testament, understands righteousness as the

---

[19] Ibid., 2.163.

[20] See O. Ritschl, *Ritschl's Leben*, 2.172–77.

[21] *Rechtfertigung und Versöhnung*, 2.237.

fulfilling of the law—an ethical righteousness made possible by the new relation with God and empowered by the Spirit. Ritschl concludes that "justification by faith means nothing more and nothing less than a relation of harmony between Christians and God."[22]

II

The mantle of Ritschl fell on Harnack. At the celebration of the one hundredth anniversary of Ritschl's birth, Harnack declared that "no theologian has arisen in the last generation who equals him in significance."[23] Like Ritschl, Harnack was a member of the Prussian establishment. Although his appointment to the faculty at Berlin was opposed by the ecclesiastical hierarchy, it was supported by Bismarck and confirmed by Wilhelm II. Harnack was elected to the Prussian Academy of Science; he was director of the Royal Library; he was elevated to the nobility—the last academic scholar on whom this honor was conferred.

In the development of his theology, Harnack came increasingly under the influence of Ritschl.[24] When Harnack had completed the first volume of his monumental *Dogmengeschichte* (1885), he wrote to Ritschl:

> As I put this volume into your hands, it is necessary for me to express to you once more my thanks for everything I have received from you. With the study of your *Entstehung der altkatholischen Kirche* 17 years ago, I began my theological work, and since then scarcely a quarter year has passed in which I have not learned more from you. The present book is a kind of conclusion of long-standing studies; without the foundation which you laid, it would probably never have been written, as inadequate as it is.[25]

Under the influence of Ritschl, Harnack broke with the orthodox heritage of his father (a professor of theology at Dorpat and later at Erlangen). Harnack abandoned the idea of the pre-existence of Christ, the doctrine of the virgin birth, and belief in the physical resurrection. With Ritschl, Harnack renounced metaphysics and embraced history.

Harnack is essentially an historian.[26] For Harnack, history is a science (*Wissenschaft*) that demands rigorous analysis of the data, but also the

---

22 Ibid., 2.327.

23 Adolf von Harnack, *Albrecht Ritschl, 1846–1864* (Bonn: Ludwig Röhrscheid, 1922).

24 See G. Wayne Glick, "Nineteenth Century Theological and Cultural Influences on Adolf Harnack," *CH* 29 (1959) 157–82.

25 Quoted by Agnes von Zahn-Harnack, *Adolf von Harnack* (2d ed., Berlin: de Gruyter, 1951) 98.

26 See Adolf Harnack, "Über die Sicherheit und die Grenzen geschichtlicher Erkenntnis," *Erforschtes und Erlebtes* (Giessen: Alfred Töpelmann, 1923) 3–23; Wilhelm Pauck, "The

imagination to comprehend the whole. Harnack believes the study of history must attend to important persons and epoch-making events. History, Harnack thinks, is the key to understanding reality, and the motivating force for action.[27] The decisive person for the understanding of history is Jesus Christ. Although Harnack thinks the life and teaching of Jesus can be reconstructed by historical research, he believes that the person of Jesus is not restricted to the past. Jesus continues to live in the lives of his followers, and Jesus can be known by an unsophisticated reading of the records.

> Let the plain Bible-reader continue to read his Gospels as he has hitherto read them; for in the end the critic cannot read them otherwise. What the one regards as their true gist and meaning, the other must acknowledge to be such.[28]

The decisive question for Harnack himself is, "How can I become his disciple."[29]

According to Harnack, the essence of Christianity is to be found in the life and teaching of Jesus. Harnack summarizes the basic principles that Jesus taught and lived: "Firstly, the kingdom of God and its coming. Secondly, God the Father and the infinite value of the human soul. Thirdly, the higher righteousness and the commandment of love."[30] Harnack believes that Jesus was the unique revealer of God. "The peculiar character of the Christian religion," he writes, "is conditioned by the fact that every reference to God is at the same time a reference to Jesus Christ and vice-versa."[31] Harnack, however, is not concerned with the nature of Christ, but with his redemptive work. In describing this work, Harnack, like Ritschl, abandons the doctrine of substitutionary atonement and adopts a moral doctrine of redemption that stresses Jesus as ethical example.[32] The Christianity Jesus founded "in its pure form is not a religion beside others, but it is *the* religion. And it is the religion because Jesus Christ is not one master beside others, but

---

Significance of Adolf von Harnack's Interpretation of Church History," *USQR* 9(Jan., 1954)13–24.

[27] See G. Wayne Glick, *The Reality of Christianity: A Study of Adolf von Harnack as Historian and Theologian* (New York: Harper & Row, 1967) 108.

[28] Adolf Harnack, *Christianity and History* (London: Black, 1896) 58.

[29] Quoted by Glick, *Reality of Christianity*, 321.

[30] *What is Christianity?* (New York: Harper and Brothers, 1957) 51.

[31] Quoted by Glick, *Reality of Christianity*, 145.

[32] See Adolf Harnack, "Christus als Erlöser," *Aus Wissenschaft und Leben* (Giessen: Alfred Töpelmann, 1911) 81–93.

because he is the Master, and because his Gospel corresponds to the innate purpose of humanity as history reveals it."[33]

Although Paul was not the "second founder" of Christianity—Harnack explicitly rejects Wrede's assertion[34]—the apostle played a positive role in the development of early Christianity. Along with the other early followers of Jesus, Paul recognized Jesus as Lord, and understood religion as a vital experience of individuals. Harnack praises Paul for transforming Christianity into a universal religion. Nevertheless, Harnack believes Paul's formulation of Christology ran the risk of reducing the Christian message to propositions. In Harnack's opinion, "it is a perverse proceeding to make Christology the fundamental substance of the Gospel."[35] Harnack claims, "The Gospel, as Jesus proclaimed it, has to do with the Father only and not with the Son."[36] Actually, Harnack detects two understandings of the gospel in the New Testament: (1) the gospel that Jesus preached, that is, the message of the kingdom of God; (2) the gospel that Paul preached, that is, the proclamation of Christ, the Son of God and redeemer. Harnack insists that there is continuity between these two. On the one hand, the teaching of Jesus referred to his own person and work. On the other, Paul's theology was concerned with human life and the new creation—concerns like those of Jesus. According to Harnack, the second gospel has sometimes been degraded into dogma, but the continuing vitality of the first gospel guards against such distortion. "The 'first' gospel contains the truth, the 'second' gospel contains the way, and both together bring the life."[37]

Harnack presents a reconstruction of early Christianity that is closer to Ritschl than to Baur.[38] In this presentation, Harnack affirms the normative significance of historical research. "History certainly does not have the last word, but in the study (*Wissenschaft*) of religions and especially the Christian religion, [it has] the first [word]."[39] Since God

---

[33] Quoted by Glick, *Reality of Christianity*, 210.

[34] Adolf Harnack, "Das Doppelte Evangelium im Neuen Testament," *Aus Wissenschaft und Leben*, 211–24.

[35] *What is Christianity?* 185.

[36] Ibid., 144.

[37] "Doppelte Evangelium," 224.

[38] Harnack's major presentation of the history of early Christianity is found in his massive, *Lehrbuch der Dogmengeschichte* (1886–1890; ET: *History of Dogma* [7 vols; New York: Russell & Russell, 1958]). A shorter version, *Grundriss der Dogmengeschichte* appeared in 1889 (ET: *Outlines of the History of Dogma* [Boston: Beacon, 1957]). Much of the same material is presented in lectures given at Bonn, *Die Entstehung der christlichen Theologie und des kirchlichen Dogmas* (Gotha: Leopold Plotz, 1927).

[39] *Entstehung der chr. Theologie*, Vorwort [Preface].

is known primarily in Jesus Christ, knowledge of historical origins is essential to understanding Christianity. Harnack also thinks the study of history provides the antidote for all that ails the Christian religion.

> The history of dogma, in that it sets forth the process of the origin and development of the dogma, offers the very best means and methods of freeing the Church from dogmatic Christianity, and hastening the inevitable process of emancipation, which began with Augustine. But the history of dogma testifies also to the unity and continuity of the Christian faith in the progress of its history, in so far as it proves that certain fundamental ideas of the Gospel have never been lost and have defied all attacks.[40]

According to Harnack, the early Christians proclaimed Jesus as the messiah who fulfilled Old Testament prophecy. The church's separation from Judaism, however, was decisive for the historical development of Christianity. This separation, Harnack believes, was promoted by Paul's opposition to Jewish legalism. Whereas Ritschl was reluctant to recognize any Hellenistic taint on apostolic Christianity, Harnack acknowledges that Hellenistic Judaism contributed to the development of early Christian theology. He insists, however, that Philo did not directly influence the first generation Christians, including Paul. Although Paul played a leading role in transforming religion into theology, Harnack believes Paul's thought was essentially the expression of his religious experience.

> Paulinism is a religious and Christocentric doctrine, more inward and more powerful than any other which has ever appeared in the Church. It stands in the clearest opposition to all merely natural moralism, all righteousness of works, all religious ceremonialism, all Christianity without Christ. . . . One might write a history of dogma as a history of the Pauline reactions in the Church, and in doing so would touch on all the turning points of the history.[41]

In short, Harnack believes Paul affirms the essence of Christianity.

In the post-apostolic age, emphasis was placed on Christ as the revelation of God. Christ, Harnack thinks, was understood in two main ways: (1) adoptionist, whereby a man was chosen as unique agent of God; (2) pneumatic, whereby a divine being assumed human form. Harnack believes the latter became increasingly important, preparing the way for the Logos theology of the apologists. In the second century, Gnosticism played a decisive role. Harnack contends that "the Gnostic systems represent the acute secularizing or Hellenizing of Christianity,

---

[40] *Outlines,* 7–8.

[41] *History of Dogma,* 1.135–36.

with the rejection of the Old Testament, while the Catholic system, on the other hand, represents a gradual process of the same kind with the conservation of the Old Testament."[42] Gnosticism's greatest threat, according to Harnack, was not the content of its doctrine, but its transformation of the Christian message into philosophy. "The decisive thing is the conversion of the Gospel into a doctrine, into an absolute philosophy of religion, the transforming of the *disciplina Evangelii* into an asceticism based on a dualistic conception, and into a practice of mysteries."[43]

Harnack also believes that Marcion played a decisive role in the development of early Christianity. According to his understanding of Paul, Marcion attempted to reform a Christianity that he believed had been corrupted by Judaists. Marcion thought the God of Jesus and Paul was not the judging God of the Old Testament, but the loving Father of Jesus, the merciful God of forgiveness. To support his position, Marcion formulated a canon composed of a collection of Pauline epistles and a gospel (Luke), with what he considered to be Judaist corruptions expurgated. The orthodox church countered with a canon of its own—a canon that included the Old Testament.

> Marcion gave the decisive impetus towards the creation of the old catholic church and provided the pattern for it. Moreover, he deserves the credit for having first grasped and actualized the idea of a canonical collection of Christian writings. Finally, he was the first one in the church after Paul to make soteriology the center of doctrine, while the church's apologists contemporary with him were grounding Christian doctrine in cosmology.[44]

Harnack thinks that "Marcion was the only Gentile Christian who understood Paul, and even he misunderstood him."[45] Nevertheless, Harnack is sympathetic with Marcion's attempt to reform Christianity in terms of Paul—an attempt made by Harnack's two other heroes of the history of dogma, Augustine and Luther. In a sense, Marcion betters them both; he accomplished in the second century what Harnack believes should be done in the nineteenth: the de-canonizing of the Old Testament. Thus, Harnack says that "the rejection of the Old Testament in the second century was a mistake which the great Church rightly avoided; to retain it in the sixteenth century was a fate from which the Reformation was not yet able to escape; but still to preserve it

---

[42] Ibid., 1.226.

[43] Ibid., 1.252.

[44] Adolf von Harnack, *Marcion: The Gospel of the Alien God* (Durham, NC: Labyrinth, 1990) 132.

[45] *History of Dogma*, 1.89.

in Protestantism as a canonical document since the nineteenth century is the consequence of a religious and ecclesiastical crippling."[46]

In response to the Gnostics, Marcion, and the Montanists, the church, Harnack thinks, took decisive steps toward ecclesiastical dogma. The simple baptismal confession was replaced by a dogmatic creed. The episcopal leadership became the apostolic office wherein the bishops were recognized as the successors of the apostles. Although Harnack understands the process of the canonizing of Scripture to constitute a pillar in support of ecclesiastical dogma, he believes the witness of the New Testament to the original, dynamic gospel to be a positive force in the on-going history of Christianity. "Therefore the creation of the New Testament after the apostolic age and until today is the greatest and most beneficial fact of church history."[47] In any event, Harnack believes the fatal step was taken by the apologists. With them, Christianity was distorted into dogma; the gospel was secularized. The apologists believed the universe bore the stamp of the divine Logos, and the Logos was embodied in Christ understood as the divine essence. Thus, according to Harnack, the gospel was transformed into philosophy of religion.

> The establishment of the Logos-Christology within the faith of the Church—and indeed as *articulus fundamentalis*—was accomplished after severe conflicts during the course of a hundred years (till about 300). It signified the transformation of the faith into a system of beliefs with an Hellenic-philosophical cast; it shoved the old eschatological representations aside, and even suppressed them; it put back of the Christ of history a conceivable Christ, a principle, and reduced the historical figure to a mere appearance; it referred the Christian to "natures" and naturalistic magnitudes, instead of to the Person and to the ethical.[48]

Thus, like Ritschl, Harnack understands the history of early Christianity to be a story of decline. For Harnack, essential Christianity was founded by Jesus and continued by Paul who broke with Judaism and promoted Christianity as the universal religion. Paul, however, made Christ the center of his theology, encouraging the formulation of ecclesiastical dogma. Finally, under the influence of Hellenistic thought, the apologists turned Christianity into a philosophy of religion.

Besides his work on the history of early Christianity, Harnack published research related to Paul. Important for his understanding of Paul is Harnack's work on Acts. In three monographs collected into the

---

[46] *Marcion*, 134.

[47] *Entstehung*, 73.

[48] *Outlines*, 167.

series *Beiträge zur Einleitung in das Neue Testament*,[49] he presents increasing conservative critical judgments. Harnack is concerned that this move to the right has encouraged some observers to discredit critical research. "Let me, therefore, express my absolute conviction that historical criticism teaches us ever more clearly that many traditional positions are untenable and must give place to new and startling discoveries."[50] In any case, Harnack vigorously contends that the traditional view of the authorship of Acts is correct. His argument includes a detailed analysis of linguistic data to demonstrate that the author of the "we-sections" of Acts is the author of the whole book. Harnack also attempts to counter arguments against Lucan authorship, for instance, that the Paul of Acts is different from the Paul of the Epistles. Harnack acknowledges that Luke's picture of Paul may have been a bit more Jewish that Paul's self-portrait, yet Luke's failure to bring the Jewish-Gentile conflict into sharper focus is explained by his intent to portray the movement of the gospel from Jerusalem to Rome in broad strokes. Thus, Harnack believes Luke's higher purpose "did not allow him to dwell on disturbing trifles."[51]

Of interest is Harnack's research on the notorious apostolic decree. In 1899, he published a text critical study in which he discusses the variants in Acts 15:29, in particular, the omission of πνικτῶν ("what is strangled") by the Western text.[52] Harnack argues that the Eastern text, adopted by most modern editors, represents the original. Harnack proceeds to discuss the conflict between the decree and Paul's account of the Jerusalem Council in Galatians 2, where Paul insists that no requirement was placed upon him. Harnack thinks the corrector of Acts 15:29 (the editor of the Western text) attempted to harmonize Paul and Luke by removing the reference to "what is strangled," that is, by transforming the decree into a moral admonition rather than a ritual requirement. However, in a later volume of his *Einleitung in das New Testament*,[53] Harnack accepts the omission of πνικτῶν as original, and reads the text as offering only moral instruction, with the result that the tension between the decree and Paul is resolved. Thus, Harnack engages in the same kind of harmonizing he had earlier charged to the

---

[49] Leipzig: J. C. Hinrichs, 1908, 1911 (ET: *New Testament Studies* [London: Williams & Norgate, 1909, 1911]).

[50] Adolf Harnack, *New Testament Studies I: Luke the Physician: The Author of the Third Gospel and the Acts of the Apostles* (London: Williams and Norgate, 1909) vi.

[51] Ibid., 134.

[52] Adolf von Harnack, *Studien zur Geschichte des Neuen Testaments und der alten Kirche, I: Zur neutestamentlichen Textkritik* (Berlin und Leipzig: de Gruyter, 1931) 1–31.

[53] *New Testament Studies III: The Acts of the Apostles* (London: Williams & Norgate, 1909) 250.

editor of the Western text. Also in this volume, Harnack presents a complicated analysis of the sources of Acts, and concludes that Acts "is not only taken as a whole a genuinely historical work, but even in the majority of its details it is trustworthy."[54]

In the last volume of this trilogy on Acts,[55] Harnack returns to the question of the Lucan presentation of Paul. Here he finds nothing incongruous in Paul's participation in a Nazarite vow (Acts 21:22–26) or in the report of the apostle's behavior before the Sanhedrin (Acts 23:1–10).

> Our conclusion, therefore, is that the author of the Acts, in his description of St Paul's relation with Judaism, is in essential agreement with St Paul's own epistles. . . . Both from the Pauline epistles and from the Acts of the Apostles we learn that the Apostle came into direct conflict with Judaism *just because he conceded too much to Judaism.* His Jewish limitations were his ruin![56]

Also in this volume, Harnack advocates an early date for Acts. He had previously argued that the reference to Paul's "two whole years" (Acts 28:30) in Rome implied that Paul left Rome after a first imprisonment to engage in additional ministry.[57] Now he argues that Acts was written shortly after that time, that is, in the early 60s. Among other things, Harnack points to Acts 20:25 where Paul is reported to have said that the Ephesians would never see his face again. However, assuming the hypothesis of a second imprisonment, Harnack detects evidence in 2 Timothy 4 that Paul made a later visit to Asia. Harnack, succumbing to circular argument, says that Luke would not have reported this prediction unless he had (at the earlier time of writing Acts) expected it to come true.

Harnack published monographs on Paul and the Pauline Epistles. Among the most interesting is his work on the collection of the Pauline letters.[58] Harnack believes a collection of ten epistles was made in the last quarter of the first century, and that it was expanded to thirteen (including the Pastorals) by the end of that period. He thinks the collection was probably made first at Corinth and the later expansion in Asia. Harnack is inclined to accept all thirteen letters as authentic, though he is cautious about the Pastorals. "Apart from an arbitrary

---

[54] Ibid., 298.

[55] *New Testament Studies IV: The Date of the Acts and of the Synoptic Gospels* (London: Williams & Norgate, 1911).

[56] Ibid., 88.

[57] *Acts of the Apostles*, 31–48.

[58] *Die Briefsammlung des Apostels Paulus und die anderen vorkonstantinischen christlichen Briefsammlungen* (Leipzig: Hinrichs, 1926).

critical decision, one can therefore assert neither the genuineness or the ingenuineness of these letters as they exist."[59] Harnack believes the first recognition of the Pauline letters as canonical—read along with the Old Testament and the gospels—was by Marcion. This was true of the larger church by 200, when Romans was placed at the beginning, references to Rome were omitted, and a non-Pauline doxology (16:25–27) added. Since the letters address seven churches, the collection was understood to speak to the whole church.

> Wherever in the course of the history of the church the need was recognized for a deeper understanding of the religion of faith in contrast to the religion of law, the religion of the spirit and freedom in contrast to literal and ceremonial religion, the religion of earnestness in contrast to the religion of indolence, there that need was met by the letter-collection of Paul. . . . This collection has become the book of reformation from Marcion to Augustine, to the Carolingian theologians, to Thomas Aquinas, to the so-called pre-reformers, to Luther, Zwingli and Calvin, to Pascal and the Jansenists and beyond them until today.[60]

Also of interest is Harnack's essay on the transfiguration and Paul's account of the resurrection appearances.[61] In this essay, Harnack analyzes the early tradition about the resurrection of Christ recorded in 1 Cor 15:3–8. On the basis of a meticulous investigation of terms and grammatical structure, he concludes that the original tradition had two parts: "Christ died for our sins according to the Scriptures and was buried; Christ was raised according to the Scriptures and was seen by Cephas." To this earliest form, the words "then by the twelve" were added. The developing tradition, Harnack thinks, displayed two parallels: "he appeared to Cephas, then to the twelve; he appeared to James, then to all the Apostles." Harnack thinks "the twelve" and "all the apostles" refer to one and the same group. Thus, he surmises, two separate traditions have been combined: the first, a Galilean tradition followed by Mark and Matthew; the second, a Jerusalem tradition followed by Luke and John.

In an imaginative excursus, Harnack presents what he takes to be a suppression of Peter's role as the first witness of the resurrection. The priority of Peter is confirmed by Paul's account of the tradition, and is implied by Mark. Luke reduces the place of Peter by presenting the appearance to Simon as only a part of the larger resurrection narrative.

---

[59] Ibid., 14–15.

[60] Ibid., 27.

[61] "Die Verklärungsgeschichte Jesu, der Bericht des Paulus (I. Kor. 15,3ff.) und die beiden Christusvisionen des Petrus," SPAW 7 (1922) 62–80.

In Matthew, the particular appearance to Peter is omitted, and in John, Peter sees only the empty tomb. Harnack understands these various traditions to represent conflicts within the early church. Turning to the story of the transfiguration, Harnack contends that it is not a misplaced resurrection narrative, but an earlier vision during the lifetime of Jesus in which Peter was the main human actor. This first vision provided the power to overcome Peter's denial and the inspiration for his later resurrection vision.

Also interesting are Harnack's essays on the address of Ephesians[62] and the authorship of Hebrews.[63] In the former, Harnack argues that Ephesians was originally a letter of Paul to the Laodiceans. And why was the address "to the saints at Laodicea" omitted? Harnack answers, the Laodiceans developed a bad reputation as Rev 3:14–22 indicates. Once their name had been excised, an address was needed, and Ephesus, the capital and locus of the collection of the thirteen letters, seemed appropriate. In regard to Hebrews, Harnack makes a strong case for Prisca as its author. He begins by analyzing hints about authorship detected in the document. For example, the use of "we" indicates that the author was once a teacher of the group addressed (which Harnack takes to be a house-church in Rome). The use of "we" sometimes indicates a plural authorship, but the alternate use of "I" suggests a primary writer. The data also indicate that the author belongs to the circle of Paul, and has been associated with Timothy. Harnack believes Prisca meets all of these qualifications. The reason her authorship was not recognized: Prisca was a woman. "But he who takes offense that a woman wrote an epistle that stands in the 'New Testament,' may also take offense that Paul named her a colleague and said in praising her that 'all churches of the Gentiles' should be obliged to thank her; he may also find it offensive that she as teacher reclaimed Apollos."[64]

III

What issues emerge from the biblical research of the classical liberals? For one, the significance of presuppositions is apparent. Ritschl and Harnack are quick to see the mote in Baur's eye but reluctant to notice the beam in their own. This problem is especially acute for theologians who decry metaphysics and disparage philosophy. Theologians who disavow a metaphysical or ontological base for their

---

[62] "Die Adresse des Epheserbriefs des Paulus," SPAW 37 (1910) 696–709.

[63] "Probabilia über die Adresse und den Verfasser des Hebräerbriefs," ZNW 1 (1900) 16–41.

[64] Ibid., 40–41.

work are inclined to imagine that none exists. This tempts them to suppose that their work is neutral and objective. In this vein, both Ritschl and Harnack believe they are writing unbiased history. Actually, their work reflects the influence of a variety of philosophical assumptions, including Schleiermacher's idea of religious consciousness and Kant's ethics. They assume Baur's understanding of historical development, and they are not untouched by philosophical idealism. They are influenced by Romanticism and their own religious experience. They inhale the atmosphere of nineteenth century European culture. Failure to engage these assumptions directly and to make some sense of them leads to ontological confusion, a lack of theological clarity.

In regard to the reconstruction of early Christianity, a variety of issues appear. How is the historian to assess the contextual background? Both Ritschl and Harnack understand Hellenism to be a negative factor. This is in part due to their anti-philosophical bias, but also to their passion to protect Christian origins from pagan impurity. Of course, honest historians could not deny the Jewishness of Jesus, but the liberals supposed he belonged to a special segment of Judaism, heir of the lofty prophetic tradition. Actually, Harnack and Ritschl were ambivalent about Judaism, affirming it on the one hand as the major background of New Testament thought, but opposing it on the other as the inspiration for the legalism of the ancient catholic church. For both Ritschl and Harnack—reflecting the anti-Catholicism of Bismarck and nineteenth century Prussia—the old orthodox church was a synthesis of the worst of both Judaism and Hellenism.

In regard to sources, both Ritschl and Harnack, although liberal in theology, adopt conservative critical conclusions. This is more readily understandable in the case of Ritschl who felt obliged to counter the radicalism of Baur, and who could find comfort from contemporary conservative critics like H. A. W. Meyer. Harnack, on the other hand, was familiar with the liberal criticism of scholars like Holtzmann and the research of the history of religions school, including the work of Johannes Weiss, Ritschl's son-in-law. Of course, for Harnack to have accepted Weiss's apocalyptic interpretation of the kingdom of God would have been to undermine the understanding of Christianity he had inherited from Ritschl. One can appreciate, therefore, Weiss's decision not to drop his apocalyptic bombshell until after his father-in-law's death. The effect would have been devastating to Ritschl who held a higher doctrine of biblical authority than Harnack. Probably, the critical conservatism of both is to be explained by their historicism— their conviction that Christianity was an historical phenomenon, and that historical understanding needed reliable sources.

In regard to method, both Ritschl and Harnack share the Enlightenment legacy of scientific historical criticism. However, both were convinced that historical research involved more than mere collection of data. They believed the understanding of history required faith and imagination. This is especially evident in the work of Harnack: the more imaginative he is, the more interesting he becomes. What should have given the liberals pause was the fact that other scholars following the same method arrived at totally different conclusions. The unbounded confidence in the human ability to comprehend history was unfounded. This does not mean that historical criticism should be abandoned, but that it should be refined and practiced with greater humility. To be sure, the study of history is no abstract science producing absolute results. Yet, if the events of the past are to be understood, documents must be analyzed critically and data arranged and presented intelligently.

The liberals also remind us of the importance of the hermeneutical question. Ritschl assumes that biblical teaching can be applied directly to the current situation, whereas Harnack seems to presuppose some transcendent, self-evident truth that can be perceived by pious readers in all generations. The question remains, What is the basis of continuity whereby the message of the New Testament can be translated into meaning for today?

In regard to the reconstruction of early Christian history, the liberals are surprisingly pessimistic. Of course, the idea of an original golden age followed by a decline is a popular human notion. Intellectuals who are more at home in Athens than in Jerusalem, of course, are unhappy that Ritschl and Harnack blamed the fall on the Greeks. Historically the liberals are hardly correct: Palestine was no hermetically sealed container, and Greek influence had been present since the time of Alexander. Although the liberals were correct in their conclusion that Judaism and early Christianity were more complex than Baur supposed, their penchant for harmonizing in order to enhance the glory of the apostolic age represents a blindness to the conflicts Baur rightly recognized. But what of the theory of decline—especially in relation to the liberal notion of progress? No doubt the belief in historical revelation, so basic to Christianity, involves a view of the priority of the original events. Beyond this, Harnack believes a faithful remnant can be found in every age. Yet, the problem remains as to how Christianity can maintain in its on-going history the vitality of its origin.

Finally, what of the liberal view of Paul? For both Ritschl and Harnack, Jesus is the founder and Paul is clearly a secondary figure. Moreover, Harnack's idea of two gospels has given some encouragement for the later notion of Jesus versus Paul. Both Ritschl and

273

Harnack, however, posit a continuity between Paul and Jesus. Ritschl faces the issue squarely, addressing the problematic texts. He argues that the seeming discontinuity results from a failure to see Paul in his polemic situation. Harnack, on the other hand, admits that Paul was tainted by things like apocalyptic, but contends that these do not represent the essential Paul. Of course, a Paul who wrote everything from 1 Thessalonians to Titus and who conforms to the portrait of Acts is a clouded figure. Nevertheless, Harnack peers through the mist to find the elusive essence of Paul—a Paul who resembles Ritschl's Paul— the Paul of religious experience, the Paul of freedom, the Paul of universal religion.

It is ironic that the fatal blow to nineteenth century liberalism was dealt by Harnack's most famous student, Karl Barth, in the name of Paul. This only reminds us that variety and conflict have been the pattern in the history of Pauline interpretation. As Harnack affirmed, Paul is a perennial reformer who continues in many and various ways to confront his successors. Paul is a dynamic thinker, impossible to pigeonhole. To quote Victor Furnish, "understanding Paul turns out to be less a matter of trying to put him in his place than of engaging his thought, and considering how it may challenge ours and illumine the place where we are."[65]

---

[65] Victor Paul Furnish, "On Putting Paul in his Place," *JBL* 113 (1994) 17.

Pauline Mission and Religious Pluralism

Andreas Lindemann *

The Christian churches consider themselves to be "missionary churches," and in fact churches always have done and still do missionary
work. However at least since the nineteenth century (or even earlier)
this missionary attitude has sometimes been met with sharp criticism
both from within and without the Christian community. To the critics,
mission is (Western) imperialism disguised in religious form. Mission
seems, in particular, to be inconsistent with a free and "open" dialogue
among the different religions which is necessary in our times. The
uniqueness of revelation in Jesus which the Christian mission proclaims
and Christianity's exclusive "claim to truth," appear to be an act of
asserted superiority of Christian faith over all other religions or
religious ideas. How can the Christian churches answer that criticism?
Should Christians seek to foster constructive dialogue with persons of
different faiths and no longer try to convert them to the Christian
confession? Should inter-religious dialogue replace mission? Does
enabling a process of dialogue among religions itself constitute the
primary and basic Christian mission?

These are but a few of the serious questions raised in the world
Christian community. In 1994, the General Assembly of the almost
ninety European Lutheran, Reformed and United churches partici-
pating in the "Leuenberg Agreement" accepted the document "The
Church of Jesus Christ: The Contribution of the Reformation towards
Ecumenical Dialogue on Church Unity."[1] This document contains a
special paragraph on the dialogue with other religions: "Faced with the
religions and religious communities they encounter, the churches
cannot give up their knowledge of God in favour of a neutral view of
the world"; but "this does not mean rejecting dialogue with other

* I am very much indebted to my doctoral student Rev. Daniel Sadananda from India
with whom I had good discussions on the topic of this article; I am also grateful to him for
his help with the English text of this essay.

[1] *Die Kirche Jesu Christi. Der reformatorische Beitrag zum ökumenischen Dialog über die kirch-
liche Einheit. The Church of Jesus Christ. The Contribution of the Reformation towards Ecumenical
Dialogue on Church Unity.* Im Auftrag des Exekutivausschusses für die Leuenberger
Kirchengemeinschaft herausgegeben von Wilhelm Hüffmeier (Leuenberger Texte 1;
Frankfurt am Main: Otto Lembeck, 1995).

religions. On the contrary, in dialogue the attempt is to be made to understand other religions, to eliminate misunderstandings, to do away with prejudices, to discover genuinely common features, to recognize erroneously assumed common features as such and to widen one's own horizon of perception."[2]

This is the modern view of the problem. In the following article, I shall try briefly to explore the following questions: How did the church and theology in New Testament times view religious dialogue and its relation to mission? How did early Christian theologians, especially the apostle Paul, interpret other religions, either pagan or Jewish? Were they interested in dialogue, or did they only seek the numerical and geographical expansion of Christianity? Has there been any kind of dialogue at all?

I

The Christian church, from its very beginning, has been *per definitionem* a missionary community because no one is born as a Christian person.[3] Christian preachers encounter women and men who hitherto were living in their own religious contexts and ties; they seek to persuade them by their message of the truth and uniqueness of Christian faith. In the first years the Jesus movement was largely confined to the Jewish boundaries; its mission was carried out within Judaism. The adherents of the Jesus movement were Jews who confessed that the God of Israel had raised the crucified Jesus from the dead, and they tried to win over their fellow Jews to this creed. Thus we might say that Christian mission began as an intra-Jewish dialogue over the meaning and significance of the Jesus event. The God of Israel has revealed himself in Jesus of Nazareth; this was the message of the Jewish Jesus movement in Jerusalem and in Galilee. Jesus is the messiah, the Lord. Thus, no Jew needed to be enticed away from his or her synagogue to the church. On the contrary, Jewish Christian missionary preachers such as Peter and Stephen were convinced that the recognition of and the belief in the Jesus event as God's act was an integral part of true Jewish existence.[4]

We really cannot know in which direction the relation of the Jesus movement with the various strands of Judaism would have developed

---

[2] *Kirche Jesu Christi*, 117.

[3] In principle this has not changed, even if in practice the relative emphasis on mission varies widely. A person becomes a Christian by choice—a choice usually associated with baptism—not by birth even into a Christian family.

[4] I have tried to explain my view of the relationship of Judaism and Christianity in the first years of the church in my article, "Der jüdische Jesus als der Christus der Kirche. Historische Beobachtungen am Neuen Testament," *EvTh* 55 (1995) 28–49.

had this movement decided to avoid any contact with Gentiles. Might the Jesus movement have gained acceptance by the majority of Judaism, for example in the manner of Rabbi Gamaliel's argument as reported in Acts 5?[5] Would Judaism as a whole perhaps have incorporated the Jesus tradition? Or what might have been the scenario if efforts to expel the adherents of Jesus and eliminate the Jesus movement from Judaism altogether, as Paul had strived for in his persecution of the followers of the "Way" (Acts 9:2), had been successful?

The members of the circle of Stephen, particularly the evangelist Philip exiled from Jerusalem after Stephen's death, began to preach the gospel of Jesus to Samaritans and then even to Gentiles, probably in the Syrian city of Antioch.[6] At this moment the separation of "church" and synagogue began—or to be more exact, at this point that separation had already taken place. The message about Jesus was also addressed to foreign peoples and foreign religions, with the effect that only a few years later Paul could differentiate "Jews and Greeks and the church of God" (1 Cor 10:32), thus depicting members of the synagogue in a certain way already as "foreigners" to "Christians."[7]

The church's mission in the first century consisted of nothing more than public proclamation of the word of God; that is, the spoken word preached either to Jews or to Gentiles was the only method the church used in the missionary work, though the pure "word" certainly was complemented by "spiritual power" (1 Cor 2:4; Gal 3:5).[8] In later centuries mission history demonstrates the practice of quite different methods of converting others to Christianity, including unfortunately shameless

---

[5] Acts 5:38–39: "So in the present case I tell you, keep away from these men and let them alone; because if this plan or this undertaking is of human origin, it will fail; but if it is of God, you will not be able to overthrow them—in that case, you may even be found fighting against God."

[6] See Wayne A. Meeks and Robert L. Wilken, *Jews and Christians in Antioch in the First Four Centuries of the Common Era* (SBLSBS; Missoula, MT: Scholars Press, 1978) 13–18.

[7] For discussion of that text, see Gordon D. Fee, *The First Epistle to the Corinthians* (NICNT; Grand Rapids, MI: Eerdmans, 1987) 489, and esp. Margaret Y. MacDonald, *The Pauline Churches. A Socio-historical Study of Institutionalization in the Pauline and Deutero-Pauline Writings* (SNTSMS 60; Cambridge University Press, 1988) 32–33. On p. 33, MacDonald writes: "Paul would surely have rejected the conclusion that his thought was moving in the direction of a third entity since he believed that all Israel would be included in the 'true Israel' (cf. Rom 11). Despite the ambiguity in Paul's thought, it is evident that in terms of concrete social reality, the Pauline movement exists as a third entity. Gentile converts could not participate in the life of the church as if it was one of many religions (1 Cor 10:21)."

[8] Cf. Hans Conzelmann, *1 Corinthians: A Commentary on the First Epistle to the Corinthians* (Hermeneia; Philadelphia: Fortress, 1975) 55: In Paul's view, ecstatic phenomena and miracles are workings of the Spirit but "they do not prove the truth of the word of the cross, but are for their own part subject to the criterion of the cross."

acts of violence or even murder which were contrary to the very notion of mission for reconciliation.

We know almost nothing about the particular methods and forms of early missionary preaching; even the Pauline missionary preaching strategy, its content and form as addressed to the Gentile or Jewish hearers is relatively unknown to us. The *persona* whom we confront in Paul's own letters is not the missionary Paul but the apostle as an organizer and pastoral counsellor of the already existing communities of Christian women and men.[9] Without any doubt we can observe in Paul's letters different forms of a "passive dialogue," because the apostle like all other New Testament writers naturally used thoughts and language of his contemporary Jewish and Hellenistic world. But this of course does not mean that Paul deliberately and intentionally adopted "foreign" religious or philosophical ideas in order to demonstrate the mutual tolerance of those thoughts and Christian faith.

II

There are several texts which may give us some idea about Paul's approaches to and points of contacts with "Gentiles" and his interpretation of foreign religions. The first important text is 1 Thessalonians 1:9–10. Paul here reminds the Gentile Christians in Thessalonica of their acceptance of the Christian message: in becoming Christians, the Thessalonians had "turned to God from idols, to serve a living and true God." Paul uses the arguments of the Jewish polemics against pagan religiousness. The heathen gods in fact are nothing more than "idols"; they are just graven images, not real divine beings.[10] Here Paul seems to judge the non-Jewish religions rather indiscriminately. In his argumentation it is unimportant to know which particular "idols" the Thessalonians had, in former times, revered. The addressees probably understood it in a similar way. They now are servants of the only God and are waiting for the parousia of his Son from heaven; the past of their respective religious lives seems to be meaningless and entirely insignificant.

In 1 Thess 4:13, accordingly, Paul portrays the non-Christians as "the rest of men" (οἱ λοιποί), the people "who have no hope." Does this description presume that beyond Christian faith and life there is

---

[9] Sometimes Paul reminds his addressees of the beginnings of their Christian existence (see, e.g., 1 Cor 15:1–3), but we never learn in what way Paul persuaded people (in Corinth or elsewhere) to "convert" to Christianity.

[10] Cf. Karl P. Donfried, "The Theology of 1 Thessalonians," in Karl P. Donfried and I. Howard Marshall, *The Theology of the Shorter Pauline Letters* (New Testament Theology; Cambridge: Cambridge University Press, 1993) 31–3.

allegedly no kind of realistic human hope or "eschatology"? In my opinion, Paul here rather maintains that apart from the belief in Jesus' resurrection from the dead there exists no reasonable human hope.[11]

In Galatians 4:8–9 Paul in a similar context explicitly uses the scheme "formerly-now" ("Einst und Jetzt").[12] Pagan life simply means that women and men do not have any knowledge of God but are slaves to "gods" which in their nature are not gods at all.[13] When Paul writes to the Galatians "that you were enslaved to beings that by nature are not gods" he argues that those beings which the pagans formerly revered in fact may exist but in their true nature (φύσει) are no "gods".[14] To Paul it evidently does not occur that the "gods" of Gal 4:8 could in any way be identical with God (4:9) or could be more or less the same 'god,' only under different names. So, in Paul's view, there exists a sharp conflict between the φύσει μὴ ὄντες θεοί on one hand and God on the other hand. It is striking that in Galatians 4:8–11 Paul draws a parallel between the Christian Torah-obedience now propagated by Jewish-Christian missionaries in Galatia and the former Galatian pagan religiousness. Equating Christian Torah-obedience with pagan idolatry, Paul assumes that there is no connection between God and Torah—

---

[11] The theme of 1 Thess 4:13–18, in my opinion, is not the question of parousia (Naherwartung) but the hope for future resurrection (*pace* Donfried, "Theology of 1 Thessalonians," 34). The consolation Paul gives to the Christians in Thessalonica is that the dead will rise "in Christ," and thus the readers need "not grieve as others do who have no hope" (4:13; cf. v. 18: "Therefore encourage one another with these words"). Cf. my article "Paulus und die korinthische Eschatologie. Zur These von einer 'Entwicklung' im paulinischen Denken," *NTS* 37 (1991) 373–399, esp. 376–380.

[12] Cf. Peter Tachau, *"Einst" und "Jetzt" im Neuen Testament. Beobachtungen zu einem urchristlichen Predigtschema in der neutestamentlichen Briefliteratur und zu seiner Vorgeschichte* (FRLANT 105; Göttingen: Vandenhoeck & Ruprecht, 1972).

[13] Hans Dieter Betz, *Galatians. A Commentary on Paul's Letter to the Churches in Galatia* (Hermeneia; Philadelphia: Fortress, 1979) 213: "It is noteworthy that Paul has nothing to say about the religions to which the Galatians adhered in the past. Were they worshippers of the older Celtic Gods? Or did they come from a variety of cults? Differently from his treatment of Judaism, Paul avoids references to details of the former religion of the Galatians. He prefers to lump them all together under the heading of 'the elements of the world' (τὰ στοιχεῖα τοῦ κόσμου)."

[14] Betz, *Galatians*, 215: "Those beings which are worshipped in paganism as gods are 'gods' only 'by convention'. This can mean (1) that they do not exist 'in reality' (φύσει), but only as human projections. In this case, Paul would conform to the atheist interpretation of the Euhemerist theory. Or it can mean (2) that the beings worshipped by the pagans do not exist as 'gods' but are 'in nature' (φύσει) 'demons'. If Paul held this interpretation he would conform to the demonological interpretation, which we find also in Hellenistic Judaism. The identification of the beings which 'in nature are no gods' with the 'elements of the world' (τὰ στοιχεῖα τοῦ κόσμου) speaks in favor of the latter. This interpretation would mean that those beings do have an existence, but only as inferior demonic entities (v. 9)." This interpretation seems to be correct.

certainly a very problematical argument which is never repeated by Paul in his later epistles. [15]

III

Paul's first epistle to the Corinthian community is a special source which can enlighten us on our theme. In 1 Cor 8:4–6, in the context of the debate about eating food sacrificed to idols, Paul maintains that "an idol is nothing at all in the world" (οὐδὲν εἴδωλον ἐν κόσμῳ) [16] and that "there is no God but one" (εἷς). This position of a theoretical monotheism apparently corresponds to the Corinthians' "knowledge" (γνῶσις). [17] But then in 8:5a Paul admits that there are "so-called gods in heaven or on earth"; thus, the apostle reflects the human experiences of everyday life by which in fact the idea of the existence of more than one god is well attested. [18] In 8:5b, Paul even states that "in fact there are many gods and many lords." [19] This is the experience of religious reality; things that bind me actually exist. [20] Finally, in 8:6 Paul confronts his former statements from vv. 4–5 with the confession that "for us there is one God." Paul here is speaking about "God for us" (*deus pro nobis*) who is defined as "the Father." [21]

---

[15] But this is exactly how Paul had argued in Gal 3:19–20.

[16] The NRSV reads "no idol in the world really exists" and "there is no God but one," putting both sentences into quotation marks, thus indicating that Paul is quoting Corinthian statements.

[17] See Leander E. Keck and Victor Paul Furnish, *The Pauline Letters* (Interpreting Biblical Texts; Nashville, TN: Abingdon, 1984) 88–90; here, 90: "Not all members of the house church have sufficiently assimilated monotheism; for them, 'There is no God but one' is still merely 'theoretical'; they have not yet reached the point where they really believe that the gods they had worshiped a few months before really do not exist and that food offered to those gods was offered to nothing." For the question whether for Paul those "gods" are really "nothing" in the sense of non-entities, see below.

[18] Conzelmann, *1 Corinthians*, 143: Paul's "view of the existential character of knowledge has here come into play" - the so-called gods "may very well be existent in the sense of being 'there' in the world and having a certain power - and Paul himself is convinced that they do exist" (cf. Gal 4:8). "They exist in heaven and on earth, i.e., in the cosmos, in the creation, and are therefore themselves creatures."

[19] The RSV puts "gods" and "lords" in quotation marks, thus suggesting that Paul interprets them as being only "so-called 'gods.'" I am not sure whether this is really correct, and interestingly the NRSV drops the quotation marks.

[20] Cf. Conzelmann, *1 Corinthians*, who argues that the gods and lords are "perverted creatures."

[21] Cf. Paul-Gerhard Klumbies, *Die Rede von Gott bei Paulus in ihrem zeitgeschichtlichen Kontext* (FRLANT 155; Göttingen: Vandenhoeck & Ruprecht, 1992) 152: The expression "God for us" shows "daß von Gott nur unter dem Aspekt seiner heilvollen Hinwendung zum Menschen geredet werden kann" ["that one can speak of God only in terms of his

All Pauline discussion about the question of idol sacrifices in 1 Corinthians 8 and 10 is based on the fundamental decision that the existence of gods should not be denied though for the members of God's church the acknowledgement of those gods is completely impossible. To this extent, we can observe that there is a distinct parallel between Paul's position and that of Joshua who said to the people of Israel at Shechem, "Now therefore revere the LORD, and serve him in sincerity and in faithfulness; put away the gods that your ancestors served beyond the River, and in Egypt, and serve the LORD. Now if you are unwilling to serve the LORD, choose this day whom you will serve, whether the gods your ancestors served in the region beyond the River or the gods of the Amorites in whose land you are living; but as for me and my household, we will serve the LORD" (Josh 24:14–15). Paul's confession "for us one God" (ἡμῖν εἷς θεός) excludes all other kinds of religiousness, leaving no space for a "dialogue" or even the observation of possible parallels.

This becomes clearest in the context of the discussion about the Lord's Supper and the pagan sacrifice meals. In 1 Cor 10:19–20 Paul rhetorically asks whether his warning about idolatry means that an idol is anything else but an idol, or food offered to the idol is anything other than food. Paul certainly presumes a negative answer, but we should not ignore the fact that he does not express this answer explicitly.[22] Paul really seems to be uninterested in that "No!" which was a matter of course for him, but he was interested in the statement of 10:20a: "What pagans sacrifice they sacrifice to demons and not to God," the demons really not being non-entities.[23] Gods and demons[24] in pagan worship really exist; and precisely this is the reason why participation in the eucharist and participation in heathen sacrifices are incompatible (10:21). From 10:27–28 we can learn that Paul does not think of a "material," substantial quality of food: only if someone says that this is

---

salvific outreach to humans"]. The question whether or not Paul in 1 Cor 8:1–6 teaches "pure monotheism" does not fit what the apostle says. In Klumbies' words: "Diese Alternative stellt sich ihm nicht. Ihm geht es darum, den deus pro nobis zu verkünden" ("This alternative does not present itself to him; the issue for him is one of proclaiming the deus pro nobis"; p. 153).

[22] The NRSV translates 1 Cor 10:19–20 as follows: "What do I imply then? That food sacrificed to idols is anything, or that an idol is anything? No, I imply that what pagans sacrifice they sacrifice to demons and not to God." But the "No" at the beginning of v. 20 is not present in the Greek text.

[23] Conzelmann, *1 Corinthians*, 173: "For the polemic literature of Hellenistic Judaism, the 'gods' are nonexistent. Paul, on the contrary, regards them as real beings (see on 8:5), namely, demons. To be sure, he denies 'that they are anything,' but this is not to say that they do not exist at all."

[24] Paul writes in 1 Cor 10:19–21 of εἴδωλα or δαιμόνια; but, in my opinion, we can learn from 8:4 that he made no special distinction between "gods" and "demons."

"sacrificed meat" (ἱερόθυτον) does the eating of that food become impossible; I put at risk my own identity if I convey to another person the idea that I accept his or her religious categories as being obligatory also for me.

Paul also uses the customary polemics in 1 Corinthians. This is evident in his argumentation in 12:2: The (Gentile) Christians in Corinth were in their past "led astray to dumb idols," while now by the Spirit of God they are enabled to confess frankly Jesus as the Lord (12:3), with all the consequences which are expounded in vv. 4–11. Paul's statement that the idols, the mere "images," are "dumb" corresponds to the usual Jewish polemics as we read them, e.g., in Psalm 135:15 or Habakkuk 2:18.[25] But even being "dumb," these idols are able to bind women and men and are able "to sweep them away" thus robbing their personal identity, their personality.[26] Once more we may observe that in remarkable dialectics Paul interprets the idols as being more or less "non-existent," while at the same time he recognizes their power, and thus in fact their existence.

IV

In the first chapter of Romans Paul discusses intensively and passionately the phenomenon of pagan religiousness and spirituality. His major argument in this section, as found in Rom 1:18–32, revolves around his claim that pagan life is determined by the principle of refusal to recognize the One God and by their confusion of creator and creature (1:25). Obviously Paul does not see any positive "starting point" or "point of contact" (*Anknüpfungspunkt*) for a dialogue with pagan religions. From 1:23 we certainly must not deduce that Paul rejects only those pagan gods having the image of animal or human beings and that he might, for example, have accepted Stoic monotheism. What Paul writes in Rom 1:21a also includes a Stoic-influenced religiousness or religious philosophy. What Paul, then, describes to be the phenomena of pagan religiousness and spirituality are immediate consequences of their contempt of God.

In the context of Paul's thesis in Romans 2 that possession of the Torah in itself does not produce justification by God, we see glimpses of a different perspective with regard to ethical dialogue with pagan

---

25 Cf. Conzelmann, *1 Corinthians*, 206: The word "dumb" "merely points to the fact that the pagan cult is vain, and indeed surrenders its devotees to the power of the demons."

26 Fee, *First Epistle to the Corinthians*, 578 n. 41 argues that Paul is not thinking "of the frenzied ecstasy and mania of some of the cults (Bacchus, Dionysus, Cybele, etc . . .) since nothing in the text seems to move in that direction." But the phrase ἤγεσθε ἀπαγόμενοι "certainly implies that they were not their own masters" (Conzelmann, *1 Corinthians*, 205).

religions. One should be clear that here Paul is not looking for a positive "starting-point" for any dialogue with pagans but rather wants to show that the doing of what is demanded by the law is possible, even where there is no knowledge of the written Torah. Nevertheless, following Rom 2:14–15, in which the apostle emphatically argues that the Gentiles carry out the precepts of the law "by nature" (φύσει τὰ τοῦ νόμου ποιῶσιν) and to this extent "are a law to themselves," we perhaps may ask whether for Paul ethical issues could have been the "starting point" or at least common subjects for dialogue with pagan religion. Would it not have made sense to discuss τὰ τοῦ νόμου ["what the law requires," lit.: "the (things) of the law"] both with Jews and with pagans? In fact, ethical material in Paul's paraenesis is often taken not only from Jewish tradition but also from Stoic or other contemporary philosophy;[27] and Paul uses these materials without regard for their potential (or potentially absent) religious premises. Although it cannot be proved, we may very well presume that Paul would have considered a dialogue on ethical problems possible—even if it was clear for him that the One God of his gospel and the Stoic deity were not identical.

Paul must have conceded the possibility of a dialogue between Christians and non-Christians. It is most amazing to hear Paul commenting on the question of divorce in marriages between Christians and pagans ("unbelievers") in 1 Cor 7:12–16. Paul does not demand a divorce in that case; on the contrary contextual indications strongly favor the supposition that Paul rejects such a demand, and that he makes a case for and even approves their living together, an option which was perhaps opposed by some Christians in Corinth. Paul argues that the pagan partner does not make his or her Christian counterpart "unclean."[28] We may conclude that the everyday life reality at the homes of married couples belonging to different religious traditions must have been something like a "living interreligious dialogue" in Corinth (and certainly at other places, too).

Later, the opposite position obviously is held by the author of 2 Cor 6:14–7:1.[29] This text forbids any kind of cooperation between Christians

---

[27] See Victor Paul Furnish, *Theology and Ethics in Paul* (Nashville, TN: Abingdon, 1968) 44–51; on Rom 2:14–15, see esp. 48–49.

[28] Cf. Victor Paul Furnish, *The Moral Teaching of Paul. Selected Issues* (rev. ed.; Nashville, TN: Abingdon, 1985) 41–44.

[29] On the scholarly discussion about origin and place of 2 Cor 6:14–7:1 in its present context, see Victor Paul Furnish, *II Corinthians* (AB 32A; Garden City, NY: Doubleday, 1984) 371–83. In my opinion, the passage is best explained by the hypothesis that an originally anti-Pauline text was integrated into the "second" letter to the Corinthians when it was composed from different smaller Pauline letters as a companion to the very long first letter.

and non-Christians ("unbelievers"). The outraged question or rather exclamation "What does a believer share with an unbeliever?" (2 Cor 6:15b) seems to have been written as a direct protest against what Paul had argued in 1 Cor 7:12–16.[30]

V

Did Paul forsee the necessity of a continuing dialogue with Judaism? For the apostle it was crystal clear that God's promises were given to His people Israel (Rom 9:1–5). Therefore Israelites certainly were not "foreigners" to Christians, and Judaism was no "foreign religion." Directly or indirectly Paul sought to find a way to keep open a door for dialogue with Jews who did not believe in Christ; Paul did not interpret Israel's "stubbornness" or hardening (Rom 11:25) as the total breakdown of communication. But Paul expected that by such communication Israel or at least a number of Israelites would become convinced by the truth of the gospel (Rom 11:14). When Paul in Rom 9:1–5 enumerates Israel's advantages he does so to emphasize that Israel's "no" in fact is incomprehensible.[31] From the existence of the Jewish Christians to whom Paul himself belongs he takes the certainty that God has not rejected His people (Rom 11:1).[32] The "holy remnant" gives the evidence that God still sends the message of His salvation to Israel as well as to the Gentiles. Accordingly Paul considers the mission to the Jewish people as an imperative to the Christian community which could not be renounced.[33] In Paul's view Israel's rejection of God's act in

---

[30] The redactor of 2 Corinthians saw the "unbelievers" as identical with the opponents of Paul, and thus thought the passage was the apostle's attack on them, in continuation of the exhortation in 6:11–13.

[31] Often this passage is interpreted as Paul's recommendation of Israel's "special way" ("Sonderweg") to God, without Christ. But from the following paragraphs we learn that Paul tries to understand and explain why the majority of Israel does not accept God's revelation in Christ (see Rom 9:6–23; 9:30–10:4).

[32] It is important to pay attention to the fact that Paul gives an explication of μὴ γένοιτο (Rom 11:1b): "For I am also an Israelite." The conjunction γάρ should not be ignored.

[33] This same perspective on the problem of mission to the Jews is found in Matt 28:19; see Amy-Jill Levine, *The Social and Ethnic Dimensions of Matthean Salvation History. "Go nowhere among the Gentiles . . ." (Matt. 10:5b)* (SBEC 14; Lewiston, NY: Mellen, 1988) 278: "While the phrase πάντα τὰ ἔθνη in Matt 28:19 is best translated 'all the gentiles,' the verse does not imply that the mission to the Jews enjoined in the second discourse [scil. Matt 10] has ended. Rather, the mission to the Jews must continue, since the deity has not rejected the Jews, and since the corporate community of Israel has not rejected either its tradition or its God."

Jesus would never be interpreted as their exclusion from God's redemptive plan.[34]

When in 1 Cor 9:19–23 Paul writes that to Jews he "became as a Jew" this explicitly means that the apostle, being himself a Jew, was willing to engage in specifically Jewish religious practices, especially in Torah-observance (9:20), to find a common "starting point" for his preaching and the Jews' understanding of the gospel. Thus we may read 1 Cor 9:19–23 as indicating Paul's personal readiness for dialogue between Judaism and Christianity—though always under the condition that the Jewish partner in this dialogue finally should be "won" (ἵνα ... κερδήσω).[35]

So, for Paul there is never a dialogue in the sense that both partners are in search for the truth; the apostle is unquestionably convinced that Christ's gospel is the ultimate truth and unique, without any alternative. Were we today to adopt Paul's position without any reservation, we would be labelled "fundamentalists." But fundamentalism is not, in my opinion, wrong because "fundamentalists" demand to know the truth or to preach the truth. The fallacy of fundamentalism is that they usually want the truth to be enforced under conditions of physical or psychical power or threat of violence. Such practices are the opposite of what the gospel teaches. When Paul implores, "be reconciled to God!" (2 Cor 5:20), he does not formulate an imperative claim but invites his readers to accept in gratitude the reconciliation which God also has freely offered to the whole human race in Jesus Christ.[36]

---

[34] Here perhaps is a difference between Romans 11 and 1 Thess 2:14–16, where the apostle had said that God's wrath has come upon the Jews "at last" (the NRSV mentions as possible translation also "completely" or "forever"). But cf. Donfried ("1 Thessalonians," 70), who interprets εἰς τέλος not as "finally" but "until the end" in the same sense as in Mark 13:12–13. On this interpretation, there would be almost no difference between Romans and 1 Thess 2:14–16.

[35] Fee, *First Epistle to the Corinthians*, 427 n. 30: "This seems to be sure evidence that Paul never considered himself released from a mission to the Jews." The document "The Church of Jesus Christ," has a paragraph on "Dialogue with Judaism" (115–17), saying that this dialogue "lives from the fact that both [sc. Jews and Christians] do not suppress the testimony to the truth of their faith as they have experienced it but feed it into the dialogue and listen to each other endeavouring to understand one another" (116). The document does not mention the problem of *mission* to Jews.

[36] Furnish, *II Corinthians*, 350: "The 'word of reconciliation' is both a gift and a summons to receive the gift; the apostles' role is at once to proclaim the good news of God's reconciling love in Christ and to make clear the scope and the character of the claim inherent in that love." Furnish follows Leonhard Goppelt in calling the imperative in 5:20 a "kerygmatic" one.

VI

Let us have a brief look at the image of mission in Luke-Acts. Beginning with Acts 2, Luke describes meetings of Christian missionaries primarily with Jews but also with people from the various pagan religions. In Acts 2–5, the Jewish-Christian preachers try to convince their addressees in Jerusalem of the truth of the gospel (cf. 3:25–26), while on the other side the priests and other members of the High Court make every effort to prevent this.[37] The end of the story of Acts 5:17–42 is significant: "The apostles" are ordered "not to speak in the name of Jesus" (v. 40), but "every day in the temple and at home they did not cease to teach and proclaim Jesus as the Messiah" (v. 42). Reports on discussions about religion are explicitly given by Luke in Acts 6 and 9. Members of several Jerusalem synagogues argue with Stephen, "but they could not withstand the wisdom and the Spirit with which he spoke" (6:10). In a similar way after his own conversion Saul "confounded the Jews who lived in Damascus by proving that Jesus was the Messiah" (9:22). Thus, the aim of these "discussions" is not a common search for a truth which remains "open" or as yet unknown. The Christian preachers are eager to convince their partners of the Christian faith's truth. It should be noted that in the texts just mentioned, the dialogue partners on both sides are Jews.

The "interreligious dialogue" in Acts occurs in the form of "missionary speeches": The preachers—first Peter, then Stephen and Philip, and finally Paul—try to convince their fellow Jews (and, later, Gentiles as well) of God's revelation in Jesus; we never hear anything about a real discussion. There seems to be only one exception, one "dialogue" in the strict sense that is held almost on a partnership basis: Paul's debate with the members of the schools of philosophy in Athens (Acts 17:18–34).[38] Here we listen to a dialogue with both pagan religiosity (17:16, 22–23) and Epicurean and Stoic philosophers (17:18–21, 24–28). Here Paul is at least partly involved in the thinking of his hearers. The Athenians, always eager to talk or to hear about the latest novelty (17:21), ask Paul "what this new teaching is that you are presenting."[39] Once more, Paul

---

[37] See Marion L. Soards, *The Speeches in Acts: Their Content, Context, and Concerns* (Louisville, KY: Westminster/John Knox, 1994) 50–53.

[38] See Hans Conzelmann, "Die Rede des Paulus auf dem Areopag," in idem, *Theologie als Schriftauslegung. Aufsätze zum Neuen Testament* (BEvTh 65; München: Chr. Kaiser, 1974) 91–105.

[39] In my opinion, we have to read the speech within the immediate context of the situation described by Luke in 17:16–20. The speech is the explication of the christological kerygma (v. 18b). Cf. my article "Die Christuspredigt des Paulus in Athen (Act 17,16–33)" in: *Text and Contexts. Biblical Texts in Their Textual and Situational Contexts.*

gives the answer by a speech, not through a discussion.[40] This time, however, he adopts ideas and even quoted statements from his philosophically-minded listeners, and to this extent he initiates a real dialogue with them. First of all he mentions that the women and men in Athens are "extremely religious . . . in every way" (17:22b).[41] As part of this, Paul interprets their worship of the "Unknown God".[42] It is this god whom Paul is now proclaiming. This God, until now really "unknown" to the Athenians,[43] is the creator of the universe and "gives to all mortals life and breath and all things" (17:25). This God himself allotted to the human race the idea "so that they would search for God, and perhaps grope for him and find him—though indeed he is not far from each one of us" (17:27). Paul continues that "even some of your poets have said" (quoting Aratus *Phenomena* 5), "For we too are his offspring." The Lukan Paul thus does not say that the Only God can be found "in" all other deities; he maintains that the "unknown god," who had been worshipped "without knowledge" until now, is in fact the One God—though in the text the formula εἷς θεός does not occur. God now commands everybody everywhere in the world to repent, because he has fixed the day of final judgment, the judge being Jesus Christ who had been raised from the dead by God (17:30–31). When the Athenians heard this proclamation, the audience understandably split into two parties: "Some scoffed; but others said, 'We will hear you again about this' . . . (and) some of them (including at least one woman) joined him and became believers" (17:32–34).[44]

In Acts some pericopes characterize pagan religiousness as being simply despicable or even ridiculous. For example, after Paul's healing

---

Essays in Honor of Lars Hartman (ed. Tord Fornberg and David Hellholm; Oslo: Scandinavian University Press, 1995) 245–55.

[40] For an analysis of this speech, see Soards, *The Speeches in Acts*, 95–100.

[41] Paul—i.e., the Lukan Paul—reports in positive tones his observations of the Athenians' piety (δεισιδαιμονέστεροι) though the reader knows from v. 16 that Paul "was deeply distressed to see that the city was full of idols." Thus the reader learns that the "dialogue" starts with Paul's apparent willingness to accept in the initial stage his partners' religious reality.

[42] It is unclear whether the formula ἀγνώστῳ θεῷ in Luke's view is to be read as determined ("To the Unknown God") or undetermined ("To an unknown god"). The fact that Luke has put the well-known inscriptions of altars "set up in honour even of unknown gods" (Philostratus, *The Life of Apollonius*, VI.3; LCL 17:13) into the singular form, seems to indicate that he wants to suggest a kind of monotheism to be a hidden principle of the Athenians' religiousness.

[43] The text does not think of any Jews living in Athens.

[44] One should not say that Luke describes Paul's missionary speech in Athens as unsuccessful, leaving aside the question of what Luke knew about a mission of Paul in Athens (cf. 1 Thess 3:1).

of the crippled man at Lystra the crowds hail Barnabas and Paul as Zeus and Hermes, and "the priest of Zeus . . . and the crowds wanted to offer sacrifice" (14:12–13). Even after Paul had named the pagan gods "worthless things" (μάταιοι, v. 15), the crowds seem to continue their activities (v. 18). One has to admit that "positive" dialogue between Christianity and paganism in Luke-Acts is exclusively restricted to the particular scene on the Athenian areopagus.

VII

There can be no doubt that in Christianity of New Testament times there existed a kind of "interreligious dialogue" insofar as all missionary work in any case involved talking with women and men who were adherents of a religion different from Christianity. But this dialogue did not have the goal of seeking a common truth or looking for a truth beyond both particular religions. The non-Christian partners were informed that God's truth, revealed in Jesus, was the "good news" for all the human race and thus by the dialogue every woman and every man was invited to accept the gospel for her or his own life.

In our times Christian faith is confronted with religious pluralism to almost the same extent as existed in the first-century Roman Empire. The document "The Church of Jesus Christ" says that "Christian faith must criticize all worship of alien gods and all institution of alien ideologies. . . . Dialogue is no substitute for witness and mission." But Christian faith "enables Christians, in spite of the critique of religion, to perceive the objective and meaning in the rituals and imagery of other religions, even to discern aspects of truth in their worship and understanding of the Divine."[45] Perhaps Paul would have disagreed with that affirmation, while the author of the speech on the Areopagus might have agreed. But the document "The Church of Jesus Christ" continues, "syncretistic harmonizations or the systematization of aspects of truth from other religions into a new super-religion are excluded for Christian faith. The revelation of God in Jesus Christ is for faith a constant reminder of the limits of dialogue between the religions. Christians owe all people, including the representatives of other religions, the clarity of their witness of faith and life."[46] These sentences, it seems to me, could have been subscribed to both by Luke and by Paul.

---

[45] *Kirche Jesu Christi*, 117–18.

[46] *Kirche Jesu Christi*, 118.

Paul in Contemporary Theology and Ethics: Presuppositions of Critically Appropriating Paul's Letters Today

Schubert M. Ogden

I

To agree to discuss "theology and ethics in Paul," or "theology and ethics in Paul's earliest interpreters," is evidently to accept an assignment that is mainly, if not exclusively, historical. And this might also be true if one agreed, as I have, to discuss "Paul in contemporary theology and ethics," since this, too, might be reasonably construed as calling for a mainly historical discussion of ways in which Paul's work is being critically appropriated by theologians and ethicists today. Representative of such ways, so far as my own study goes, is a book like Victor Paul Furnish's own *Moral Teaching of Paul,* or the critical appropriation of "the ethics of Paul" in Willi Marxsen's *"Christliche" und christliche Ethik im Neuen Testament.*[1] In these as well as other books and articles of the same kind, the authentic letters of Paul are not only critically interpreted in the way proper to historical theology and ethics today, but the claim that they make or imply to be adequate to their content and therefore appropriate to Jesus Christ and credible to human existence is also critically validated in the manner proper to contemporary systematic theology and ethics, although, admittedly, Furnish's concern at this point is more with the practical as well as theoretical credibility of Paul's moral teaching, while Marxsen, on the contrary, is single-mindedly concerned with its appropriateness, or with its claim to be "Christian." Consequently, even if one were to restrict oneself to critically interpreting books such as these, giving little or no attention to critically validating their own claims to validity, one might reasonably expect to redeem the promise implied by the title of this essay.

This is not the only way, however, in which one might redeem this promise. For the title may also be construed—and perhaps more

---

[1] Victor Paul Furnish, *The Moral Teaching of Paul* (2d ed.; Nashville, TN: Abingdon, 1985); Willi Marxsen, *"Christliche" und christliche Ethik im Neuen Testament* (Gütersloh: Mohn, 1989).

reasonably—as calling for a properly systematic, rather than a merely historical, discussion of critically appropriating Paul in contemporary theology and ethics. On this construction, what is called for is not only or primarily a *description* of ways in which theologians and ethicists today are critically interpreting Paul's letters and critically validating their claims to validity, but also and first of all a *prescription* of the ways in which such critical interpretation and critical validation have to be carried out if they are to be theologically and ethically adequate in accordance with contemporary standards of adequacy. Of course, one way of providing just such a systematic prescription would be to enter into critical discussion with books and articles of the kind referred to at the point of their own discussion of the presuppositions of critically appropriating Paul today. Thus one could develop a criticism, specifically, of the first chapter of Furnish's book, in which he argues for an understanding of the Bible in general and of Paul's letters in particular as neither a "sacred cow" nor a "white elephant," and of the Prolegomena to Marxsen's book, which sets forth summarily an understanding of theology as such as well as of the particular disciplines of "historical theology," on the one hand, and "systematic theology" (as comprising "dogmatics" and "ethics"), on the other.[2] But any such criticism, like criticisms generally, would need the backing of a constructive understanding of the subject matter itself, which in this case is the presuppositions necessarily implied in critically appropriating Paul in theology and ethics today.

In any event, criticizing the prescriptions of others is not the way I propose to follow here in order to provide the systematic discussion called for by the alternative construction of my title. I propose, instead, to draw upon my own constructive understanding of theology and ethics, for which I have argued at length in other writings, so as to prescribe what theologians and ethicists have to do if they are to appropriate Paul critically today.[3] My basic assumption in this, obviously, is that, although critically appropriating Paul in the way in which theology and ethics are supposed to do must indeed be a special case, it is in no way an exception to the rules otherwise governing their critically interpreting the past and critically validating its claims to validity, but rather is in every way an illustration of these rules. In this sense, I assume that the presuppositions of critically appropriating Paul in theology and ethics today are and must be the same as the presuppositions necessarily implied in any other case of such critical appropriation.

---

[2] Furnish, *Moral Teaching*, 11–27; Marxsen, *"Christliche" Ethik*, 15–33.

[3] See esp. my books, *On Theology* (2d ed.; Dallas, TX: SMU Press, 1992) and *Doing Theology Today* (Valley Forge, PA: Trinity Press International, 1996) 1–91.

Just how these presuppositions are to be understood, however, continues to be one of the genuinely controversial questions of systematic theology and ethics. This is because among the issues on which theologians and ethicists remain more or less sharply divided is how theology and ethics themselves are to be understood—both as such, in their relation to and difference from one another, and in their respective self-differentiations into more particular forms of critical reflection, like historical theology or ethics, on the one hand, and systematic theology or ethics, on the other. In what follows, however, I shall be involved in this controversy only indirectly, because I shall be directly involved in arguing *from* a certain understanding of theology and ethics rather than *for* it—in the hope that I may thereby clarify what theologians and ethicists today have to presuppose if they are to appropriate Paul in a critical way.

II

Up to this point, I have followed the conventions of this book and spoken simply of "theology and ethics" without any further qualifications. In so speaking, however, I have used these terms and will continue to use them, absent express indication to the contrary, exclusively in the specific sense that can be made fully explicit only by speaking of "Christian theology and ethics." This I do, not because I do not recognize other equally legitimate and important uses of the terms that might also inform discussion of our topic, but because of the focus of my own particular interest and competence and of the need, in any event, to limit the present discussion. The other comment on terminology that may be helpful, pending subsequent discussion, is that I use the term "ethics," in the specific sense of "Christian ethics," as strictly equivalent to what I usually call, and prefer to call, "moral theology," again, in the specific sense of "Christian moral theology." This means, for reasons I shall presently explain, that to speak of "ethics," on my usage, is to speak of something not simply alongside theology and somehow conjoined with it, but rather included within theology as an integral part or aspect of it.

But what, exactly, is properly meant by "theology," and by "ethics," understood as thus referring to something included within it? In my understanding, "theology," in the specific sense of "Christian theology," is properly defined as critical reflection on Christian faith and witness, understood as the self-understanding and life-praxis explicitly mediated by the Christian religion. This, of course, is a summary definition that needs to be explained before it can answer our question, and so I shall proceed by briefly unpacking it.

291

I call attention, first of all, to the general distinction that the definition evidently presupposes between "critical reflection," on the one hand, and "self-understanding and life-praxis," as the object of such reflection, on the other. To be human, I hold, is not merely to live but to live understandingly, and that not merely on one level but on two. On the primary level, which is what I mean by "self-understanding and life-praxis," we live only by somehow understanding ourselves in the proximate and ultimate settings of our lives and by believing and acting, and so leading our lives, accordingly. Thus our questions on this level are all the vital questions of life itself—of how to live and to live well, and how to live better; and in answering them as we do, we perforce make or imply certain claims for the validity of our answers. Ordinarily, we can make good on the promises to others implied by such claims simply by appealing, on the same primary level, to what we and they, as members of our particular socio-cultural group, agree in accepting as valid, in the sense of true, good, beautiful, and so on. But whenever appeals on this first level are, for whatever reasons, insufficient to redeem our promises, we have no alternative, if we are to validate our claims so as to remain in communication with others, but to shift to the secondary level that I call "critical reflection." There the questions we have to pursue are no longer the *vital* questions we ask and answer on the primary level of self-understanding and life-praxis, although such questions do and must continue to orient our inquiries, but rather the corresponding *theoretical* questions about the meaning of our answers and about the validity of the claims that we make or imply in answering them as we do.

One point the definition makes, then, is that theology, being a special form of critical reflection in this general sense of the words, belongs on the secondary level of living understandingly, rather than on the primary level of self-understanding and life-praxis, on which Christian faith and witness belong. This means that, although theology is like every other form of critical reflection in being *oriented* by some vital question, it is not *constituted* as such by this vital question, but only by the corresponding way of asking the theoretical question about the meaning and validity of a certain answer to it—namely, as the definition indicates, the answer explicitly mediated by the Christian religion.

If we ask now what the vital question orienting theology is, the only adequate answer, in my judgment, is that it is that most vital of our vital questions that I usually distinguish, following Rudolf Bultmann, Paul Tillich, and others, as "the existential question." By this I mean the question that we human beings seem universally engaged in somehow asking and answering about the meaning of our own existence in its ultimate setting as part of the encompassing whole.

On my analysis, this existential question is a single question having two closely related and yet clearly distinguishable aspects. In one such aspect, it asks about the ultimate reality of our existence with others as parts of the whole encompassing us. And this I distinguish as its *metaphysical* aspect, because, although it is distinct from the proper question of metaphysics in asking about this ultimate reality concretely, in its meaning for us, rather than abstractly, in its structure in itself, the two questions are nonetheless closely related, in that any answer to either of them has definite implications for answering the other. Thus, either ultimate reality in itself has a certain structure rather than some other or else it cannot have the meaning for us that a certain answer to the existential question represents it as having. Conversely, if ultimate reality in itself has a certain structure, the meaning for us that a certain answer represents it as having cannot be inconsistent with its having that structure rather than some other.

In its other aspect, which I distinguish as *moral*, the existential question asks about how we are to understand ourselves authentically, or realistically, in accordance with the ultimate reality of our existence. Thus, while it is distinct from the proper question of morals in asking about our self-understanding, rather than about our action, how we are to act and what we are to do, the two questions, once again, are nonetheless closely related, because the answer we give to one of them sets definite limits to how we have to answer the other if we are to avoid self-contradiction. Either acting in one way rather than another is how we ought to act in relation to others or else ultimate reality cannot implicitly authorize the self-understanding that a certain answer to the existential question explicitly authorizes. Conversely, if acting in a certain way is the way we ought to act, the self-understanding that a certain answer explicitly authorizes as authentic cannot be inconsistent with this rather than some other way's being the right way for us to act.

It is the existential question thus understood that orients theology as a special form of critical reflection. This is true, I maintain, because it is to the same existential question that the Christian religion explicitly mediates a certain answer in thus mediating the specific self-understanding and life-praxis, the Christian faith and witness, on which theology critically reflects. Like religions generally, the Christian religion is a primary form of culture, and thus a particular system of concepts and symbols, through which the existential question that all human beings appear to ask and answer at least implicitly is explicitly asked and answered in a certain way. But, then, theology as critical reflection on the Christian faith and witness explicitly mediated by the Christian religion must be oriented by the same existential question, and thus be, in its own way, or at its own level, "existential." And this is so even though theology, as we have seen, is also precisely "critical"—a special form of critical reflection that is therefore constituted as such, not by the existential question that orients it, but only by the corresponding way of asking the theoretical question about the meaning and validity of Christian faith and witness.

In actuality, of course, it is only through Christian witness that Christian faith is ever given for critical reflection, just as, in general, the only way we can ever reflect critically on the self-understanding of another is through the life-praxis in which it is directly or indirectly expressed. Consequently, one may always define "theology" more simply, if less explicitly, as critical reflection on Christian witness. But on either definition, what is meant by "Christian witness," including the explicit form of such witness that is properly distinguished as "the Christian religion," can mediate its specific answer to the existential question only by making or implying certain claims to validity. Specifically, Christian witness must make or imply two such claims, the first of which may be further analyzed as itself involving two more specific claims.

Thus, being Christian witness at all only because it is the expression of a certain content, it must claim, in the first place, to be adequate to this content. This it can be, however, only by satisfying two more specific conditions—hence its two further claims to be appropriate to Jesus Christ, or to Jesus as Christians experience him, and to be credible to human existence as any woman or man experiences it. But since Christian witness, by its very nature, is not only the more or less adequate expression of a certain content, but also the act of expressing this content more or less fittingly, it must claim, in the second place, to be fitting to its situation.

To make or imply these claims, as Christian witness does, however, is not to settle the question of their validity, but only to raise it. In this sense, Christian witness may be said to anticipate theology as Christian faith's own way of settling this question on the level of critical reflection. But if theology, although anticipated by Christian witness, is constituted as such, as a special form of critical reflection, precisely in order to validate critically the claims of this witness to be valid, this can not be the only thing theology is constituted to do. In this case, as much as in any other, one can ask theoretically whether life-praxis is really valid only if one first asks theoretically what it really means. Consequently, in anticipating the theoretical question about the validity of its claims, Christian witness also anticipates the logically prior theoretical question about its meaning. This is why I have already stated more than once that the theoretical question by which theology as such is constituted is the twofold question about the meaning as well as the validity of Christian witness.

But this means that the constitutive question of theology as such really involves pursuing three theoretical questions: first, about the meaning of Christian witness; second, about its adequacy to its content, and thus its appropriateness to Jesus Christ and its credibility to human existence; and third, about its fittingness to its situation. And this explains, in turn, why the constitution of theology as a special form of critical reflection is its constitution at once as a single field and as divided into the three disciplines of historical, systematic, and practical theology respectively—the first being constituted by the theoretical question about the meaning of Christian witness, the second and third, by the theoretical question about its validity, the second asking about its adequacy, and so its appropriateness and credibility, the third, about its fittingness.

More could be said, obviously, by way of unpacking the definition of "theology" with which we began. But I must now turn to the second part of our question and discuss even more briefly what is properly meant by "ethics," understood as referring to an integral part or aspect of what "theology" has been explained to mean.

Theology, we have learned, is a special form of critical reflection constituted as such by the theoretical question about the meaning and validity of Christian faith and witness—or, simply, Christian witness. In this connection, we have also learned that the existential question orienting theology, although a single question about the meaning of our existence, nonetheless has two distinguishable aspects, moral as well as metaphysical, whereby it is logically related to the other questions proper to both morals and metaphysics. Thus any answer to the existential question, including that explicitly mediated by the Christian religion, at least implicitly answers both of these other questions. This explains why the indirect form of Christian witness properly distinguished as "Christian teaching," in which the implied answers to these other questions are more or less fully explicated, typically includes both properly metaphysical teaching about things that are to be believed (*credenda*) and properly moral teaching about things that are to be done (*agenda*). But, then, theology, at its level, must be as concerned with critically interpreting and critically validating both of these kinds of Christian teaching as it is with critically reflecting on the direct form of Christian witness that is properly distinguished as "Christian proclamation."

Insofar, however, as theology thus concerns itself with Christian moral teaching and, therefore, with things that are to be done, given the self-understanding of Christian faith, it may be distinguished from theology as such, as well as other parts or aspects integral to theology, as "ethics," or, as I would rather say, "moral theology." Thus ethics, in the specific sense in which I am using the term here, is not something other than theology that is somehow conjoined with it, but is itself theology in all the respects previously clarified. At the same time, it is theology, not as such, but in only one of its distinguishable parts or aspects—namely, that oriented not only implicitly but also explicitly by the properly moral question about how we are to act and what we are to do and therefore constituted as such by the corresponding way of asking theoretically about meaning and validity.

This means, among other things, that there is as much reason to distinguish between historical and systematic ethics as to distinguish between historical and systematic theology—with the understanding, naturally, that historical ethics is as much a part or aspect of historical theology as systematic ethics is a part or aspect of systematic theology. Thus, insofar as ethics is concerned with critically interpreting the *meaning* of Christian moral teaching, it may be properly referred to as "historical ethics." Insofar, on the other hand, as ethics has to do with critically validating the *validity* of such teaching, by thus validating its claim to be adequate to its content, and so its further claims to be appropriate to Jesus Christ and credible to human existence, it may be properly distinguished as "systematic ethics."

If the discussion in this section has achieved its purpose, we should now have at least some idea of how theology and ethics are to be understood, both as such, in their relation to and difference from one another, and in their respective self-differentiations into historical as well as systematic forms of critical reflection. But, then, for the same reason, and to the same extent, we should now also understand, not merely historically and descriptively, but rather systematically and prescriptively what it means for Paul to be critically appropriated in theology and ethics today.

There may be some question, to be sure, about just what we are to understand by "Paul." Even if we agree that critically appropriating Paul is, for all practical purposes, equivalent to critically appropriating the authentic Pauline letters, just what these letters express may be characterized in different ways. Thus, to judge from the titles of this book and of its first main part, what they express is "theology and ethics"; and it seems clear enough that what is meant in effect by "Paul" in the title of the third part is the "theology and ethics in Paul" discussed in the first. Far less clear, however, is that "theology" and "ethics," as used in these titles, have the strict senses clarified by the preceding discussion, rather than the broader senses in which they are still more commonly used and in which they are only verbally different from what I have been at pains to distinguish as "Christian witness" and "Christian moral teaching."

But whether Paul's letters are properly said to express theology and ethics or, rather, are more aptly characterized today as expressing Christian witness and moral teaching is a relatively unimportant question. Either way, they and, therefore, Paul can have a place in contemporary theology and ethics only through one and the same process of critical appropriation.

First, they must be critically interpreted, by an interpretation oriented by the existential question and, in the case of ethics, also by explicitly asking the properly moral question; and then, second, and presupposing such interpretation, they must be critically validated, by a validation of the claims that they themselves make or imply to be adequate to their content and fitting to their situation.

III

The purpose of the discussion that follows, in this and the concluding section, is to say a bit more about each of the two steps in this process of critical appropriation. And so we ask in this section: What, more exactly, is properly meant by "critical interpretation," understood as referring to the first step in critically appropriating Paul's letters in contemporary theology and ethics?

The first thing to say in responding to this question underscores something that may or may not have become clear from what has already been said. I refer to an implication of my earlier point that one can ask theoretically whether life-praxis is really valid only if one first asks theoretically what it really means. Necessarily implied by this logical priority of the theoretical question about meaning is that the critical interpretation constituted by asking this question is and must be independent of the critical validation constituted by asking theoretically about validity. In other words, while critical validation necessarily presupposes critical interpretation, the converse statement is false: critical interpretation does not, and cannot, presuppose critical validation.

It is true in general, of course, that interpreting the meaning of what others say and do is simply the first thing we do in somehow appropriating it, or making it our own, by also either accepting it as valid or rejecting it as invalid. And recognizing this, we may think that interpreting things can hardly be completely independent of validating them, since we generally anticipate asking about their validity even as we ask about their meaning, whether we do so on the primary level of self-understanding and life-praxis or on the secondary level of critical reflection. But to *anticipate* something and in this way to be dependent on it is not the same as to *presuppose* something and to be dependent on it in that way. Indeed, the difference is all the difference between being *externally* related to something and being *internally* related to something; and being externally related to something is the precise meaning of being independent of it.

Because it must be independent of critical validation in just this sense, critical interpretation can anticipate the theoretical *question* of validity, but it cannot anticipate and it may not presuppose any *answer* to this question, any more than it may allow its results to be controlled by what anyone accepts as valid or rejects as invalid. But what is thus true of critical interpretation in general is no less true of critically interpreting the letters of Paul in particular, in the way in which theology and ethics and, specifically, historical theology and ethics are supposed to do. As the first step in critically appropriating the letters, it is and must be independent of the second step of critically validating their claims to be adequate to their content and fitting to their situation; and its results, also, must be free from control by anything and anyone other than what the letters themselves say and mean.

This is not to imply, however, that critically interpreting Paul's letters in this way is without presuppositions. Presupposing the results of interpretation is one thing, presupposing what has to be presupposed if there are to be any results, something else.[4] Any interpretation, and so any critical interpretation, has to be oriented by some vital question and therefore is quite properly said to presuppose this question, together with anything the question itself presupposes, such as a vital relation to, and a preunderstanding of, what it asks about and a vital interest in answering it.

To argue, then, as I have, that the critical interpretation proper to theology and ethics is oriented by the existential question and, in the case of ethics, also by explicitly asking the properly moral question, is to allow, in effect, that it presupposes these questions, along with whatever they, in turn, presuppose.

Nor is this all that such critical interpretation of Paul's letters necessarily presupposes. Not only must any critical interpretation presuppose the vital question orienting it, but it must also presuppose that its *interpretandum* is something historical and, wherever what is to be interpreted is a text or texts, also something literary. Consequently, what Paul's letters really mean, given any way of asking about their meaning, including that proper to theology and ethics, cannot be

---

4 Cf. Rudolf Bultmann, *New Testament and Mythology and Other Basic Writings* (ed. Schubert M. Ogden; Philadelphia: Fortress, 1984) 145–153.

critically determined until one first determines critically what they really say. I take it that this is the same point also made sometimes by distinguishing, not between what a text means and what it says, but between what a text means and what it meant. Made either way, however, the point is clear, and so is its implication: theology and ethics can critically interpret Paul's letters only by also presupposing and following essentially the same methods of historical- and literary-critical research that would somehow need to be presupposed and followed by any other way of critically interpreting them.

Of course, what is distinctive about the critical interpretation proper to theology and ethics is that all such historical- and literary-critical methods are there followed in pursuit, not of just any way of asking theoretically about meaning, but only of the specific ways of asking this question constitutive of these forms of critical reflection and, specifically, of historical theology and ethics. But even here the critical interpretation proper to theology and ethics is in every respect but one exactly the same as any other nontheological critical interpretation oriented by the same vital questions. The only respect in which it differs from other such interpretations is that it alone is constituted as such by the constitutive questions of theology and ethics and historical theology and ethics respectively. This means that the Christian witness is not simply one among many objects that it critically interprets, but is rather its *constitutive* object, in the sense of the object, critical interpretation of which constitutes it as such, as the specific form of critical interpretation it is. In all other respects, however, the critical interpretation proper to theology and ethics is exactly the same as any other critical interpretation oriented by the same vital questions.

Thus the critical interpretation proper to theology is otherwise simply what I call "critical existentialist interpretation," meaning by this the way of interpreting oriented by the existential question about the meaning of our existence and therefore constituted by the corresponding way of asking theoretically about meaning. This implies that a properly theological interpretation of Paul's letters asks what they really mean existentially, and so about the possibility of self-understanding, or understanding our existence, that they really represent as our authentic possibility. In a similar way, the critical interpretation proper to ethics is in all other respects nothing other than what could be called "critical ethical interpretation," using "ethical" in another, more general sense than the specific sense in which it is otherwise used in this discussion. In this more general sense, ethical interpretation is simply the way of interpreting oriented by the moral question about how we are to act and what we are to do, and so constituted by the corresponding way of asking theoretically about meaning. Thus a properly ethical interpretation of Paul's letters in this more general sense asks what they really mean morally, and hence about the way of acting toward others that they really recommend as the right way for us to act.

This leads to a final point about the first step of critical interpretation proper to theology and ethics in the specific sense of "Christian theology and ethics." I have argued that such interpretation is the critical existentialist, and, in the case of ethics, also ethical, interpretation constituted by the constitutive questions of theology and ethics and, specifically, of historical theology and ethics. In so arguing, however, I have assumed the analysis of the existential and moral questions that was briefly summarized in the preceding section. I stress this because mine is not the only way of analyzing these questions and, on other analyses, they are sometimes not only rightly distinguished but also wrongly separated—from one another as well as from the proper question of metaphysics, to which they are also closely related even while being distinct. But because my analysis of the questions thus differs from certain others, what I mean by "existentialist interpretation" and "ethical interpretation" is correspondingly different from what others who have used these terms have sometimes meant by them.

Thus, in my view, the properly theological interpretation of Paul's letters that consists in a critical existentialist interpretation of them not only allows for but even requires a properly ethical as well as a properly metaphysical interpretation of their meaning. Because the answer they give to the existential question is like any other such answer in necessarily having both moral and metaphysical implications, what it itself really means can be rightly understood and explicated only by also understanding and explicating both kinds of implications. But it is just as true in my view that any properly ethical or metaphysical interpretation of Paul's letters requires their properly existentialist, if not also theological, interpretation. For neither their particular moral recommendations nor their particular metaphysical proposals can ever be rightly interpreted except as the necessary implications, moral and metaphysical, of a certain possibility of self-understanding that demands existentialist interpretation if it is to be rightly understood and explicated.

IV

In turning now to a comparably brief discussion of the second step in critically appropriating Paul's letters, I deliberately restrict my attention to but one of two tasks involved in taking this step. Here again, both my own interest and competence and the need somehow to limit the discussion lead me to prescind altogether from the critical validation

300

proper to practical theology so as to focus solely on that proper to systematic theology and ethics. Thus, in asking, What, more exactly, is properly meant by "critical validation"? I understand this phrase to refer, not, as it has previously referred, to the whole of the second step in critically appropriating Paul's letters today, but only to the first of its two parts.

That part, as we have seen, is the proper business of systematic theology and ethics and consists in critically validating the first claim of Christian witness to be adequate to its content. We also saw, however, that further analysis of this claim discloses that it itself is complex, in that it involves the two more specific claims that Christian witness is appropriate to Jesus Christ and credible to human existence. Consequently, the critical validation proper to theology and ethics and, specifically, systematic theology and ethics requires critically validating both of these more specific claims.

The first thing to say, then, about the second step in critically appropriating Paul's letters is that it can critically validate their adequacy only by thus validating their credibility as well as their appropriateness. This is in no way to question, however, the assumption widely shared today that the *cura prior* of systematic theology and ethics must be critically validating the claim of Christian witness, and thus also of Paul's witness, to be appropriate to Jesus Christ. On the contrary, I entirely agree that critically validating the appropriateness of Paul's witness, like any other, must indeed be of concern prior to any concern with critically validating its credibility. But to allow, as I do, that concern for its credibility can therefore be only the *cura posterior* of systematic theology and ethics is still to hold that it is their proper concern, and thus to break sharply with views in which it can be of no concern to them at all because their only concern is with the appropriateness of Paul's witness.[5]

A necessary condition of all critical reflection, however, is that it be governed by some criterion or criteria. Thus we saw in the preceding section that the sole criterion governing the critical interpretation of Paul's letters is what they themselves say and mean—what they say being determined in its context by the relevant historical- and literary-critical methods for determining it, and what they mean being determined in its context by methodically pursuing the relevant ways, existentialist and ethical, of asking theoretically about their meaning. But what is the

---

[5] Marxsen expresses such a view in *"Christliche" Ethik* as well as in his other writings. See my argument against it in *"Fundamentum Fidei*: Critical Reflections on Willi Marxsen's Contribution to Systematic Theology," *Modern Theology* 6 (1989) 1–14.

criterion, or what are the criteria, governing the critical validation of Paul's letters, assuming what we have now seen this to involve?

It seems clear enough that one may speak here only in the plural of "criteria," since the appropriateness of Paul's witness and its credibility can be as different as they evidently are only if the criteria for determining them are correspondingly different. It is also clear that neither of these criteria can be merely immanent, like the criterion of critical interpretation, but must lie beyond Paul's letters themselves and, in that sense, be transcendent. But what, exactly, are these transcendent criteria for determining the appropriateness of the letters and their credibility today?

Consider, first, the criterion governing critically validating their claim to be appropriate to Jesus Christ. I maintain that an adequate theological criteriology still confirms the validity of the so-called apostolic principle for determining this criterion. According to this principle, the sole criterion of appropriateness is the witness of the apostles, in the strict sense of the original and originating and, therefore, constitutive Christian witness. Thus, if a given Christian witness is, in fact, appropriate to Jesus Christ, this must be either because it itself simply is (or is part of) this constitutive Christian witness and therefore is formally apostolic and normative for all other witness that claims to be appropriate, or else because it substantially agrees with the constitutive witness and hence is apostolic only in the broad sense of being substantially but not formally apostolic and normative.

Traditionally, of course, Paul's letters have been validated as appropriate for the first of these reasons, being judged, along with all the other writings admitted into the New Testament canon, as themselves formally apostolic and normative. But two centuries and more of following the historical- and literary-critical methods that have to be followed if any text is to be critically interpreted have now established beyond serious question that this traditional judgment is mistaken, in the case of Paul's letters as surely as in that of every other New Testament writing. The sufficient proof of this is that the authors of all these writings, including Paul, clearly make use as sources, oral or written, of expressions of Christian witness still earlier than their own, thereby confirming that theirs could not possibly be constitutive Christian witness. Consequently, if Paul's letters are to be critically validated as appropriate today, this can no longer be for the first reason, but only for the second—because, for all of their differences formally from the constitutive witness of the apostles, they are nonetheless in substantial agreement with this witness in expressing the same possibility of self-understanding and in drawing, more or less explicitly, the same necessary implications, moral as well as metaphysical.

To show that they are thus appropriate, however, obviously involves some real difficulties, if only because our sole access today to the formally normative witness of the apostles is by critically reconstructing it, using the New Testament writings as sources. Not surprisingly, therefore, many, if not most, theologians still try to avoid making the unavoidable decision, preferring a more or less traditional appeal to the canon of scripture to the allegedly more difficult appeal to a canon before the canon in the apostolic witness. But the alleged greater difficulties of the second alternative are so far from obvious as to be quite doubtful.

Compared with any more traditional procedure asserting or implying the formal normativeness of the New Testament writings, the second way of critically validating the appropriateness of Paul's letters is not caught in the dilemma of either abandoning apostolicity as the principle of the canonicity of these writings or else continuing to claim their formal apostolicity in face of overwhelming evidence that they can be nothing of the kind, because, being one and all later interpretations and reformulations of the apostolic witness, they can be at most substantially apostolic.[6] But even more than this, the second alternative is at last unburdened of the anomaly of asserting as the formal norm of all Christian witness what neither was nor could have been thus normative either for Paul's witness or for that of any other New Testament writer, or for any other Christian witness prior to at least the *de facto* closing of the canon, presumably not earlier than sometime in the last half of the second century.

At the same time, appealing to the constitutive witness of the apostles instead of to the canon of the New Testament involves no historical- or literary-critical difficulty that has not always been involved in principle in any attempt to determine what is to count, in fact, as apostolic witness. Even the difficulties, real as they are, of critically reconstructing the history of tradition lying behind our extant sources are obviously continuous with the difficulties all along in determining whether one extant source is earlier or later than another. And so, too, I venture to think, with any other new difficulties that the second alternative may

---

[6] How tortured attempts to escape from this dilemma can be is well illustrated by the argument of Roger Haight, S.J., in *Dynamics of Theology* (New York: Paulist, 1990) 100. Rightly recognizing that "the period of the composition of the New Testament included the work of first, second, third, and possibly even fourth generation Christians," Haight concedes that "it is impossible to say that it is simply the expression of original revelation." Even so, he concludes, "one can say that it is an expression of original revelation in a loose but real sense" (cf. 113). What could it mean to say that the New Testament is an expression of original revelation in "a loose but real sense," except that it is *substantially* but not formally apostolic and normative?

involve in fact, as compared with all more traditional procedures. If such new difficulties are not actually conditioned by, they are very definitely correlated with, the new historical- and literary-critical methods that also enable us to deal with them.

As for the criterion governing critically validating the credibility of Paul's letters today, it can be found in principle, I hold, only in the truth about human existence disclosed, on the primary level, by common human experience and reason and, on the secondary level, by the critical reflection proper to philosophy and the sciences respectively. In other words, whether what Paul says and implies is credible and therefore worthy of belief is to be determined, not in some different way, but in exactly the same way in which we are to determine the credibility of any and all other statements of the same logical type.

This assumes, of course, that there are logically different types of statements and that this must always be reckoned with in reflecting on their credibility and on the criterion or criteria for determining it. That all statements of a certain logical type may and must be validated by the same criterion or criteria—this being part of what is implied in their belonging to the same logical type—in no way implies that all statements of all other logical types must be similarly validated. On the contrary, the only relevant demand is that statements of other logical types must all be validated by the criteria appropriate to *their* respective types, however different these criteria may be from those appropriate to validating other types of statements.

It will be clear for reasons already given why the statements made or implied in Paul's letters, as in Christian witness generally, are and must be of different logical types. If some of them are correctly analyzed as properly existential statements, others are rightly distinguished as properly metaphysical or moral statements. Furthermore, much of the properly moral teaching in the letters consists, not in expounding completely general moral principles, but in issuing quite concrete and specific moral instructions to readers in particular historical situations with their different needs and possibilities. It belongs to any such moral instruction, however, as well as all other less than completely general moral teaching, that it must always beg certain questions about the particular situation and the conditions and consequences of moral action within it. Thus what Paul says, for example, in recommending particular courses of action as morally proper to women in the Corinthian congregation depends upon a background of beliefs and assumptions whose critical validation as credible we today recognize as falling under the competence of the special sciences, natural as well as human. Therefore, whether or not Paul's moral recommendations can be critically validated today as *practically* credible depends, in part, upon whether or not his background beliefs and assumptions can be critically validated as *theoretically* credible by the relevant special sciences.

In the case, however, of the many properly existential statements in his letters, or the other properly metaphysical and moral statements that they necessarily imply, the relevant appeal must be to philosophy rather than the special sciences. This is so, at any rate, if philosophy is conceived classically as comprehensive critical reflection oriented by the existential question about the meaning of our existence and as therefore including both metaphysics and ethics, using "ethics," here again, in a more general sense than the specific sense of "Christian ethics," in which I have otherwise used it. If philosophy is understood in something like this classical sense, its proper business is to disclose, at the secondary level of critical reflection, the same truth about human existence that is always already disclosed at least implicitly on the primary level of self-understanding and life-praxis and that Paul's letters, like Christian witness generally, claim to represent not only explicitly but also decisively. Consequently, critical validation of the claim of the letters to be credible to human existence can only be its philosophical validation.

The conclusion of this essay is not the place to defend this view against the objections usually made to it. Suffice it to say that philosophy is one thing, particular philosophies, something else. This means that to hold, as I do, that Paul's letters can be critically validated as credible only by appealing to philosophy is not at all to hold that they must either be critically validated by this, that, or the other particular philosophy or else rejected as incredible. It is always possible, if not, in fact, likely, that a particular philosophy will be philosophically inadequate and that the truth about human existence that it is supposed to express will be more adequately expressed or implied by Paul's letters, or by the theology and ethics that critically appropriate them, than it is by the particular philosophy itself. Therefore, theologians and ethicists have every reason to proceed cautiously in relation to all particular philosophies in critically validating the claim of the letters to be credible to human existence. They can do so rightly, however, only by fostering the development of an independent philosophy that ever more adequately reflects the truth about human existence that the letters claim to represent. For it is only insofar as they can appeal to just such a philosophy that they can critically validate the credibility of the letters and thus complete the process of critically appropriating them in theology and ethics today.

305

Bibliography:
Pauline Ethics, 1964–1994

Wendell L. Willis

Victor Paul Furnish's *Theology and Ethics in Paul* first appeared just as I was seeking a graduate school to pursue doctoral studies. In those days, biblical ethics was not a prominent area of research (Von Soden's famous article on sacrament and ethics in Paul and Bultmann's classic piece on indicative and imperative in Paul had both been between the World Wars), and Prof. Furnish's work was genuinely ground-breaking. I was so engaged by this work that it led me to study with him.

Theology and Ethics in Paul anticipated a resurgent interest in Pauline ethics and explored key issues which have come to dominate this field of study. Prof. Furnish examined the sources and form of Paul's ethical materials, the motives Paul uses to ground his ethics, and particularly the relationship between Paul's theology and his ethics. As will be seen, these have been the dominant topics of research in the latter half of this century.

In his book, Prof. Furnish included an appendix which surveyed the discussion of Pauline ethics until 1964, so it seems appropriate to honor him on this occasion by continuing that important tradition he so well began. The present essay undertakes to review the literature through 1994, thus sketching the last three decades in Pauline ethics.[1]

Obviously a survey of three decades of *any* topic concerning Paul must necessarily be very selective. This demand is increased by the prominence which ethics has enjoyed as a field in biblical studies since Prof. Furnish's book. Thus in the present survey I have largely restricted myself to works dealing with Pauline ethics broadly, as opposed to studies focused upon one particular ethical topic in Paul (church and state, marriage, etc.) or works on Paul which may have a section on ethics.[2]

Almost contemporaneously with the appearance of *Theology and Ethics*, a major paradigm shift was beginning in NT study with the "Crisis of Biblical Theology."[3] In the last third of this century, the reconstruction of primitive Christianity has emphasized diversity, not unity, and the paradigm has now shifted to "trajec-

---

[1] My organization of material by decades is intended to assist the reader in locating discussions; the divisions do not imply thematic or conceptual unity within each time period.

[2] Valuable extensive bibliographical surveys include O. Merk, "Paulus Forschung 1936–85" *ThR* 53 (1988), 1–81; W. Schrage, "Ethik im Neues Testament," *TRE* X (1982), 435–62 and F. W. Horn, "Ethik des Neuen Testament 1982–92," *ThR* 1995 (32–86).

[3] This title, of course, comes from Brevard Childs, who traced the decline of neo-orthodoxy and its acceptance of a theological core of early Christian doctrine (popularized by Dodd's description of the primitive kerygma).

tories."[4] This revision has impacted studies of both Pauline theology and early Christian ethics.[5]

Perhaps one of the most revolutionary shifts which challenges consensus on Pauline ethics has been the re-assessment of Paul and Pharisaic Judaism presented by E. P. Sanders.[6] Since so many interpretations of Pauline ethics have contrasted Paul's pre-Christian legalism with his Christian agapē-ethics, a change in the picture of Pharisaic Judaism's understanding of the law has major implications for understanding Paul's own views.

The First Decade: 1964–1974

To review Furnish's initial book is unnecessary (and in this context inappropriate). This work received great praise when it appeared and remains a classic treatment on Pauline ethics. I think it is not too much to say that it constitutes one of the most comprehensive and judicious assessments of Pauline ethics in this century.

The same year Furnish's first book appeared, two other significant works on Pauline ethics also were published which share major concerns of Furnish: Anton Grabner-Haider's, *Paraklese und Eschatologie bei Paulus*[7] and Otto Merk's *Handeln aus Glauben*.[8]

Grabner-Haider's short monograph shares two key concepts with Furnish's book. First, it shows the close integration of Paul's ethical teaching with his theology, and second it demonstrates the great importance of Paul's eschatology for his ethical teachings. In both these ways it evidences the revision in studies of Pauline ethics during the last three decades.

Merk is concerned particularly with the question of motivation for ethics in Paul and seeks to show the close relationship between Paul's theological base and his ethical admonitions. He finds the key to Paul's ethics to be the action of God as the presupposition of Christian existence. He emphasizes baptism as the point at which the believer in Christ encounters both redemption and the Spirit who grants and makes possible a new life of service by effecting a change in lordship for believers.

Merk focuses upon the concrete admonitions within Paul's generally acknowledged letters, which he examines one by one. He concludes that Paul's ethical exhortations are not drawn from non-Christian traditions or from Paul's Scripture (=OT), but are grounded in the eschatological salvation in Christ.

---

[4] Walter Bauer's *Orthodoxy and Heresy in Earliest Christianity* (Philadelphia: Fortress, 1971), has exercised great influence in this reconstruction, although it appeared much earlier. Originally published in 1934, it lay virtually unappreciated until the post-Nag Hammadi publications, in which it became important.

[5] For a valuable survey of shifts in biblical interpretation and their involvement with biblical ethics in the last two centuries, see J. I. H. McDonald, *Biblical Interpretation and Christian Ethics* (Cambridge: Cambridge University Press, 1993).

[6] Among his many publications, see *Paul and Palestinian Judaism* (Philadelphia: Fortress, 1977) and *Paul, the Law and the Jewish People* (Philadelphia: Fortress, 1983). While others have also influenced this reassessment, Sanders' work dominated the discussions.

[7] Anton Grabner-Haider, *Paraklese und Eschatologie bei Paulus* (Münster: Aschendorff, 1968).

[8] Otto Merk, *Handeln aus Glauben* (Marburg: N. G. Elwert, 1968). The same year, Leonhard Goppelt published *Christologie und Ethik* (Göttingen: Vandenhoeck and Ruprecht), but the only essays focused upon Paul are on the topic of the state and hermeneutics.

Particularly important is his demonstration of the prominent role played by the Christian community (e.g., in the motivation of οἰκοδομή, "building up").[9] Yet Merk continues the traditional division of Paul's letters into "theological" and "ethical sections" even though his own study shows how the specifics of Paul's ethical arguments are integrated with his theology—and thus undermines the distinction!

Only two years later Heinz-Dietrich Wendland published *Ethik des Neuen Testaments* (1970).[10] Like Merk, he insists that Paul's ethic is grounded primarily in *Heilsgeschichte*, and he focuses upon eschatological existence manifested in Christology, sacraments (esp. baptism) and the Spirit.

Wendland, like Merk, appeals greatly to Romans 6 and 8. He argues that Paul's ethic is substantially an ethic of love in the Spirit but that the apostle is also a realist who knows the tempting power of sin. He resolves the problem of indicative and imperative by saying that the Spirit gives the believer the power to fulfill the commands of God (which include the moral content of the Decalogue as radicalized by Jesus' preaching so that the "law of Christ" means the Sermon on the Mount as it was taught in the Hellenistic church).

A less prominent, but very important, emphasis in Wendland's analysis is the role of the Christian community. In ethics, Wendland says, Paul sees the church in contrast with the world as a whole, a notion of ethical autonomy similar to that commonly taught by the philosophers (Wendland grants that Paul selectively took from the ethical teachings of the society, but Paul greatly changed this content by linking it to the authority of the heavenly Lord and qualified it by his eschatological assumptions).

When these studies appeared, eschatology was only beginning to be recaptured as a positive aspect of early Christian belief, especially with regard to ethics. Ever since Schweitzer's "thoroughgoing eschatology" many had argued that Paul's expectation of Jesus' imminent return really undercut any basis for Christian ethics.[11]

In 1972, Furnish published a second major monograph on biblical ethics, this time focusing on the use made of the love command (Leviticus 19:18) in the whole of the NT.[12] The greater attention is given to Jesus and the Synoptic gospels, but Paul's use of the love command is also considered. Although his approach is more exegetical than systematic, Furnish describes the unity in Paul's teaching as "faith active in love."

Furnish observes that, while Paul quotes Leviticus 19, he does not present the so-called "double commandment" (quoting also Deut 6:4–5). Likewise, Paul characteristically does not speak of the Christian's loving God, but trusting God.[13] The love command in Paul expresses how believers are to relate to others.

---

[9] Both of these points, eschatology and Christian community, are also centerpieces for Furnish's assessment of Paul's theology and ethics.

[10] Heinz-Dietrich Wendland, *Ethik des Neuen Testaments* (Göttingen: Vandenhoeck & Ruprecht, 1970)

[11] Schweitzer, however, thought Paul had a valid ethic, rooted in his "Christ mysticism." See Furnish, *Theology and Ethics,* 258–59. Schweitzer's evaluation of eschatology and ethics is accepted, by others, but as having negative results.

[12] Victor Paul Furnish, *The Love Command in the New Testament* (Nashville: Abingdon, 1972).

[13] Ibid., 94.

Continuing the theme of his earlier work, Furnish insists upon the fundamental unity of Paul's "theology and ethic." Paul stands in contrast to other ethical teachers of his day in insisting that freedom consists of loving obedience. Agreeing with Merk and Wendland, Furnish stresses the eschatological framework of Paul's ethic, especially love as the embodiment of the new age.

Concerning the perennial issues of how Paul's ethic relates to the Mosaic law and the question of the relationship between indicative and imperative, Furnish concludes, "Paul regards the believer as having been *freed from the law* interpreted as a way of salvation, but then also *bound over* in service to the neighbor *by the law* interpreted as the love commandment."[14]

As the first decade after the appearance of Furnish's review came to a close, two major works with similar titles, appeared.[15] Both treatments are brief but examine the whole scope of NT ethics.

Jack T. Sanders' study is perhaps one of the most pessimistic of recent works on biblical ethics. The Foreword leads the reader to anticipate little positive results, in spite of the pathos with which the book is written, and the contents fulfill this expectation.[16] His negative evaluation may be a result of his desire to do more than describe the ethics of the NT. Looking for ethical guidance in contemporary life, he finds little of value in the NT. But even if one were to determine that very little (or nothing) in the NT is helpful for shaping moral life today, that would not prove that there were no significant ethical teachings therein for the writers (or first readers).

In Sanders' brief treatment of Paul, he argues that Paul sets out "tenets of holy law" which are eschatologically based and focused in the love command since love is the eschatological reality already present in the coming age. Sanders examines the problem of the indicative vs. the imperative in Paul and concludes that Paul believed the imperative was grounded in and evoked by the indicative "you are justified." But Sanders adds that this position was possible only "because of his [Paul's] belief in the imminent eschaton" (a connection which he explores in 1 Cor 13; Gal 5 and esp. Rom 12–15).[17]

Previous writers had stressed the eschatological foundation of Pauline ethics, but Sanders uses this eschatological ground to show the impracticality of Paul's ethic. While Sanders thinks that "Paul alone, of all the New Testament writers[18] (and Jesus), . . . offers a possibility for an ethics that is not essentially grounded in an imminent eschatology" (*Ethics*, 63) he nonetheless laments that Paul did not make the shift, but remained committed to an imminent eschatological ethic.[19]

---

[14] Ibid., 111.

[15] Jack Sanders, *Ethics in the New Testament* (Philadelphia: Fortress, 1975) and J. L. Houlden, *Ethics and the New Testament* (Edinburgh: T. & T. Clark, 1975, first ed. 1973).

[16] Sanders compares his own findings about the uselessness of the ethics of the NT with Albert Schweitzer's conclusions about the quest for the historical Jesus. Like Schweitzer, the value Sanders finds in his negative assessment of the NT evidence is that it liberates contemporary people from needing to agree in theory or practice with the early Christian viewpoints.

[17] Ibid., 56. Sanders explores this connection with regard to 1 Cor 13; Gal 5 and Rom 12–15.

[18] He does praise James for its "visceral humane reaction against . . . inhumane ascending Christian theology" (ibid., 129; see pp. 115–28 on the Epistle of James).

[19] Ibid., 66, "If Paul is to be made ethically relevant for today, it would seem to have to be by rejecting this element of his ethics [his eschatology] . . . and by endorsing as accurate the move

Although not as plaintive as Sanders, J. L. Houlden (see above, n. 15) is only slightly more positive. His position is that "strictly speaking there is no such thing as the x [in this case the ethics] of the New Testament" (*Ethics*, 2). By this, he means that the diversity within the NT precludes a unified ethic, although the fourth chapter, on "the Lord," where Houlden seeks to show that all the NT writers (to some degree) have their root in Jesus, seems to suggest a basis for speaking of a "NT ethic."

In his discussion of Paul, Houlden emphasizes the occasional nature of Paul's letters; thus his specific admonitions are rather ad hoc, and some elements are not integrated with the main structures of his thought. [20] The most striking element in Paul's ethic is its Christocentrism, especially the cross, which Paul holds to be the beginning of the new aeon. In many cases, Paul's ethical admonitions are simply inconsistent with his theology of justification because Paul is most interested in the religious questions and only resorts to ethical instructions when compelled by the circumstances of his churches. Thus Houlden finds very limited connection between "theology and ethics" in Paul (which renders the indicative/imperative debate empty).

The Second Decade: 1975–1985

In the next decade, momentum in the study of ethics continued to increase, no doubt partially influenced by the experienced crises of ethics in Western European society and in the U.S. driven by massive cracks in an assumed ethical consensus following the debates over the Vietnam war and civil rights.

Among the works which consider the whole of the NT ethical teachings is R. E. O. White's *Biblical Ethics*. [21] This work presents a radical alternative to both Sanders and Houlden, although it scarcely engages either. Rejecting reconstructions of early Christianity which emphasize such a degree of diversity that the adjective "Christian" can have little concrete referent (p. 9), White insists not only that there is a "Christian" ethic in Scripture, but also that this ethic stands in sufficient agreement with Torah that one is justified in speaking of "biblical ethics."

White deals with Paul in two chapters. The first, "Pauline Moral Theology," is something of a miniature dogmatic theology of Paul. He concludes that Paul's view of salvation necessarily includes ethical dimensions because the one who redeemed also empowers the redeemed to live the new life by the Spirit (he emphasizes the importance of Christ's example and teachings, which Paul knew and passed on to his converts).

The second chapter, "Paul's Ethical Directives," focuses upon the supremacy of love (which White thinks Paul received from Jesus). This "agapē-ethic" is then described in concentric circles as "new life" for the individual, the family and home, daily work, the church and the society, and the state—apparently arranged in order of how the ethical life develops outward from the individual.

Apart from predictable criticisms of White's reconstruction of a very irenic and unified early Christianity, many find White's very flat reading of Pauline ethical

---

Paul makes toward understanding transcendence qualitatively and the ethics of agape implied in that understanding."

[20] Houlden, *Ethics*, 25. This issue is decisive for evaluating various proposals on Pauline ethics.

[21] R. E. O. White, *Biblical Ethics* (Atlanta: John Knox, 1979).

teaching to be problematic. There is little appreciation for the particularity of each letter and the local churches whom Paul instructs. White treats the whole Pauline corpus (including the disputed letters) simply as a source for Paul; therefore, the letters actually interpret each other and, taken in sum, tell the reader about Paul. But as Furnish, among others, has shown, one need not think that Paul's ethical teachings are either ad hoc or theologically unrelated to insist upon the need to understand those teachings situationally.

The same year that White's book appeared, Furnish published a brief work entitled *The Moral Teaching of Paul*.[22] The subtitle, "Selected Issues," is important because the book focuses upon certain topics which are of great contemporary interest and examines passages in Paul which are often discussed in relationship to the themes of marriage and divorce, homosexuality, women in the church, and Christians and the governing authorities. This attention to specific issues is carried out exegetically, and the book does not take up larger concerns necessary for synthesis. [23]

By careful historical study Furnish tries to model how to bridge the gap between the first century and the present time. To what degree he succeeds in building a bridge will be assessed variously by readers, in large part because the topics discussed are controversial. While very brief, his succinct and clear treatment of issues in this work makes a good beginning place for approaching key topics in Pauline ethics.

Yet another book from the same year explored Paul's ethical teachings to show their value to contemporary moral life. That work is Peter Richardson's *Paul's Ethic of Freedom*,[24] in which he examines three topics related to Gal 3:28 and three other topics, mostly taken from 1 Corinthians. The final chapter, "Paul Today," argues that Paul is a theologian of freedom (as is evidenced by word count of ἐλευθερία and cognates in the NT), although Paul's own exposition of that theology is unevenly developed in his letters (pp. 163–68).

However, whether "freedom" is the appropriate center for Pauline ethics remains problematic: (1) It is unclear what basic content or meaning "freedom" has in Paul and whether this meaning is compatible with our contemporary sense of "unrestricted" or "not prohibited." (2) Even the verbal count itself, which shows Paul to be the greatest user of these words, must be carefully nuanced. All the Pauline uses are in four letters (Romans, 1 and 2 Corinthians, and Galatians), and even these refer to different things (e.g., to marriage in 1 Cor 7:39, to social status in 12:13, and to the role of the Mosiac law in Christian life in Rom 7:3 and 8:2 and Gal 5:1). Whether all these shades of meaning can be comprehended in Richardson's understanding of "liberty" is questionable.

Few writers have demonstrated the contextual character of Paul's ethics better than Wolfgang Schrage, whose 1961 monograph[25] made it clear that Paul's ethical

---

[22] Victor Paul Furnish, *The Moral Teaching of Paul: Selected Issues* (Nashville: Abingdon, 1979). This work was slightly revised in 1985, and the present remarks draw upon the revised edition. Furnish notes in the forward that the book's shape was greatly influenced by discussions in clergy conferences and laypersons' studies.

[23] Furnish only sketches some comprehensive themes in Paul's ethic in the first chapter: the Spirit, the love command, and the new age.

[24] Peter Richardson, *Paul's Ethic of Freedom* (Philadelphia: Westminster Press, 1979).

[25] *Die konkreten Einzelgebote in der paulinischen Paränese* (Gütersloh: Mohn, 1961).

instructions were both theologically grounded and situationally specific. His comprehensive interpretation of NT ethics, published in 1982,[26] contains a lengthy section on Paul, entitled "The Christological Ethics of Paul." There, Schrage examines the basis of Pauline ethics, the nature and structure of the new life, and the material criteria before moving on to discuss four examples of "concrete ethics."

Schrage's book is clear, careful, and centrist in exploring Pauline ethics. He works with most of the assumptions of modern biblical scholarship and in typical continental fashion focuses upon Christology as the key to Paul's theology and ethics. His most valuable insight is that Paul's ethics are thoroughly and essentially interwoven with his theology: he questions all intepretations which explain Paul's *paraklēsis* [exhortation] as a peripheral, ad hoc accommodation to practical needs which are unmet by Paul's theology.[27] Similarly, Schrage demonstrates that Paul's eschatology, Christology, pneumatology and ecclesiology are all so integrated that his ethic is grounded in their unity, not in any one of them alone.

If Schrage's book presents a theological approach to Pauline ethics using familiar categories and questions, Gerd Theissen's essays, collected and published as *The Social Setting of Pauline Christianity,*[28] serve as a model for a very different methodology. Theissen approaches Paul's letters from a social-scientific perspective and investigates the communities which Paul addresses (e.g., Corinth) more than Paul himself.[29]

Theissen insists that the Pauline community in Corinth experienced great internal tensions arising from social and economic stratification among the members. Two key issues which he investigates are the divisions at the Lord's Supper and the issue of sacrificial meat. In both cases, Theissen analyzes the conflicts as originating in socio-economic tensions within the church rather than out of theological difficulties.

Paul seeks to surmount these difficulties by transcending them through an ethic of "love patriarchalism" (a term Theissen borrows from Troeltsch). By using the patriarchial family as a model for the Christian community, Paul attempts to integrate the social strata of the church by obligations of love arising from the religious sphere. Since Theissen is really asking limited historical questions, how his reconstruction would impact on a synthetic presentation of Pauline ethics remains unstated. Theissen makes something of an end run around traditional questions about the sources and motives of Paul's ethics and the relationship of indicative and imperative.

Alan Verhey[30] focuses upon the eschatological context for understanding the ethics of the NT. But whereas E. P. Sanders understands "eschatology" as the

---

[26] *Ethik des Neuen Testaments* (Göttingen: Vandenhoeck & Ruprecht, 1982); ET: *The Ethics of the New Testament* (Philadelphia: Fortress, 1988).

[27] *Pace*, e.g., E. P. Sanders and, more strongly, H. Räisänen (see below, n. 35).

[28] Gerd Theissen, *The Social Setting of Pauline Christianity: Essays on Corinth* (Philadelphia: Fortress, 1982). The essays were originally published in 1974 and 1975, but were translated and introduced to a wider audience by John H. Schütz.

[29] This "social history" approach is similar to that of A. J. Malherbe, E. A. Judge and Wayne Meeks (on Meeks, see below), although Theissen represents more of a sociological or "social theory" approach in contrast to the "social history" of the other three.

[30] Alan Verhey, *The Great Reversal* (Grand Rapids: Eerdmans, 1984).

expectation of a soon-coming End (and thus refuted by history), Verhey conceives of eschatology as the new situation inaugurated with the coming of Jesus: "It is the indicative of what has already happened, not so much what is to come, that shapes New Testament ethics."

Verhey both presents an outline of the ethical teachings of the NT and seeks to show the unity they present. He believes that having located certain key themes, it is possible to create a bridge from their teachings to the present world. He has been taken to task for simply assuming a doctrinal (and ethical) unity within the NT that then becomes implicitly the means for his constructive ethics.[31] Nonetheless, Verhey gives a creative reconstruction of Christian ethics shaped by eschatology.

E. P. Sanders' various publications investigating Judaism in the time of Jesus and Paul really focus upon understanding Christology, justification, and soteriology. Sanders locates the center of Paul's theology in "religion," specifically Christology within a framework of eschatology. His reconstruction of how Paul understood the Mosaic law has also impacted Pauline ethical interpretation.

Sanders argues that Paul's controversies over the law arose over what constituted the criteria for admission of Gentiles into the church. In anthropological terms, it was an argument over boundaries. Because Palestinian Judaism stressed circumcision and diet laws as defining the covenant community, some Christians had sought to exclude Gentiles from the Christian community. Paul, being deeply committed to faith in Jesus as the sole ground of acceptance before God, strongly opposed those who saw the law as the basis of community identification.[32]

However, Sanders insists that for those within the justified community, Paul continued to regard the law as offering normative moral guidance, along with other ethical teachings—his phrase is "covenantal nomism."[33] This use of the law is clear, Sanders argues, both because Paul employs the OT as a basis for moral instruction to Gentile Christians and because Paul's ethics stand in line with contemporary Jewish ethics (e.g., on sexual conduct). He concludes that Paul regards the law as both do-able and normative for Christian conduct, even among Gentile believers. "'Good deeds' are a condition for remaining 'in,' but they do not earn salvation."[34]

In summary, Sanders solves the major problem of indicative and imperative in Paul in a unique way by saying that Paul regards the "law" differently depending upon whether the issue is "getting in" or "staying in." He thus allows for a bifurcation in Paul's thought about the law, explaining that Paul is simply inconsistent and apparently never considered his inconsistency.[35]

---

[31] See, e.g., the review by J. L. Houlden, *JTS* 36 (1985) 437–38.

[32] E. P. Sanders, *Paul, the Law and the Jewish People* (Philadelphia: Fortress, 1983).

[33] See the critique by J. I. H. McDonald, *Biblical Interpretation and Christian Ethics* (Cambridge: University Press, 1993) 139–40.

[34] E. P. Sanders, *Paul and Palestinian Judaism* (Philadelphia: Fortress, 1977) 517.

[35] Ibid., 114; see also 144–48: "I have come to the conclusion that there is no single unity which adequately accounts for every statement about the Law. . . . I would urge that Paul held a limited number of basic convictions which, when applied to different problems, led him to say different things about the Law." In this regard, Sanders sees himself as basically in agreement with Heikki Räisänen's view that Paul simply is not coherent in his theology. Among the many critical

Sanders' reconstruction both of Paul's view of the law in comparison with Palestinian Judaism and of Paul's view of Christian justification has certainly not gone unchallenged. Hans Hübner takes him to task for severing the necessary connection between circumcision (which, Sanders thinks, Paul opposes because it has become a community-defining rite among Jewish Christians) and the law (which, according to Sanders, Paul supports as a means of Christian ethical guidance).[36] Since Sanders' reconstruction of Paul's appropriation of the law, and indeed law-keeping, depends upon his distinction between "getting in" and "staying in," his interpretation of Paul's doctrine of justification is fundamental to his Pauline ethics. In fact, because Sanders is willing to allow Paul's theology to be internally incoherent, perhaps contradictory, he avoids the problem of indicative and imperative![37]

The Third Decade: 1984 to 1994

Wayne Meeks took an uncharacteristic approach to Pauline ethics in 1986 when, in contrast to the common preference for either a systematic presentation of Pauline ethical principles or an exegetical investigation of important passages in Paul's letters, he undertook to explore the conduct of early Christians.[38] He thinks it is only possible to understand the practices and the arguments of early Christian ethics if we understand the social world in which they were formed. He is more concerned about "ethos" than "morals."[39] Since it is easier to describe those communities which Paul founded and nurtured than others in early Christianity, Paul's writings are decisive for Meeks's project. Meeks's work is much more descriptive of early Christianity than analytic of Paul's ethics and reflects the interests of communitarian ethicists today.[40]

Meeks has recently published a sequel in which he continues to develop his theme across the broader field of later Christian literature and with a closer focus upon specifics.[41] This book is somewhat more explicit in its treatment of the way morality is shaped by communities and by moral examples. Meeks explains his

---

reviews of this position, one of the most comprehensive rebuttals is that of Peter Tomson, *Paul and the Jewish Law* (Minneapolis: Fortress, 1990). Cf. C. E. B. Cranfield, "Giving a Dog a Bad Name," *JSNT* 38 (1990) 77–85.

[36] Hans Hübner, *Law in Paul's Thought* (Edinburgh: T. & T. Clark, 1984; tr. of *Das Gesetz bei Paulus: Ein Beitrag zum Werden der paulinischen Theologie* [Göttingen: Vandenhoeck & Ruprecht, 1978]).

[37] In a manner of speaking, one could say that Sanders believes that Paul accepts law-keeping for sanctification, but not for justification. However, this is not truly analogous. Paul—in Sanders' view—separates a ritual (circumcision) from the law. Thus it is not really the law that Paul opposes.

[38] *The Moral World of the First Christians* (Philadelphia: Westminster, 1986).

[39] This useful, although narrow, distinction also appears in Leander Keck's evocative article "On the Ethos of Early Christianity" *JAAR* 42 (1974) 435–52. Keck and Meeks (along with Abraham J. Malherbe and other scholars at Yale) have represented something of a common approach to NT study in the last quarter century.

[40] He cites approvingly Verhey's *The Great Reversal*, and Stanley Hauerwas's *The Peaceable Kingdom: A Primer in Christian Ethics* (Notre Dame, IN: University of Notre Dame Press, 1983). The theoretical underpinning of such approaches is the field of the sociology of knowledge, esp. as presented by T. Luckmann and P. Berger.

[41] Wayne Meeks, *The Origins of Christian Morality* (New Haven: Yale University Press, 1993).

preference for describing Christian "morality" rather than "ethics" in that the latter is a consciously reflective, second-order activity, whereas the former is more a dimension of life that encompasses "value-laden dispositions, inclinations, attitudes, and habits" (*Origins*, 4).

Thus at first glance Meeks's project seems to be "softer," less evaluative, and more descriptive than most of the books on Pauline ethics which are examined here. But this appearance is only partly true (as Meeks's final chapter, "History, Pluralism and Christian Morality," shows). The real distinction is in *how* one "does" ethics, and his approach has been both praised and criticized [42] for employing a "community"-based rather than a philosophical or systematic ethic.

In the last decade, two prominent Roman Catholic scholars, Siegfried Schulz and Rudolf Schnackenburg have produced lengthy introductory texts on NT ethics. [43] Schnackenburg reflects the traditional Roman Catholic confessional concern to show the compatibility of natural law ethics and biblical ethics (he especially emphasizes the conscience as a place of agreement between natural reason and faith; *Die sittliche Botschaft*, II.49–58). Schulz, by contrast, stresses the uniqueness of the NT writings and develops his thought more along contemporary historical-critical paths common in Protestant scholarship.

With regard to Pauline ethics, Schnackenburg is more synthetic in approach and less focused upon individual ethical instructions. He treats Romans as if it were the essential Pauline theology; then, grounded in Romans, he argues that the basis of Paul's ethics is Christian gratitude to God for justification (forgiveness and salvation), mediated through baptism (Romans 6). [44] With regard to the law, Schnackenburg believes Paul regards the love command as a summary of the Torah, which can now be fulfilled through the presence of the Spirit in the Christian.

Schulz employs the more exegetical methodology (in this sense, reflecting the approach of Furnish and Schrage), but he distinguishes between two phases. An earlier Pauline ethic (now witnessed only in 1 Thessalonians) valued (although it never expressly cited!) the OT moral teaching as a positive instruction for Christians, especially as that moral teaching was sharpened by Jesus. A later phase, which Schulz says emerged after the Apostolic Council, focused on the idea of justification in a debate with Jewish-Gnostic legalism. In this second phase, Paul greatly reduced the scope and value of the law for Christian ethics (basically the law became the double command to love). [45]

Schulz distinguishes sharply between the later Pauline ethics of gratitude and that of Judaism, which is presented as based on merit and achievement and in which salvation comes from keeping the letter of the law (as if E. P. Sanders' critique of this caricature of Judaism did not exist). But, like Schnackenburg, he thinks Christian ethics share content with natural ethics (taken from the order of creation).

---

[42] See William Countryman's review in *JAAR* 60 (1992) 348–49.

[43] Siegfried Schulz, *Neutestamentliche Ethik* (Zurich: Theologischer Verlag, 1987); Rudolf Schnackenburg, *Die sittliche Botschaft des Neuen Testaments* (2 vols.; Freiburg: Herder, 1986, 1988).

[44] He follows closely Romans as an outline to organize his observations.

[45] Paul, of course, never cites the first of the two commands, a point we noted earlier in connection with Furnish's assessment of the law.

Bishop Eduard Lohse has produced a topical treatment of *Theological Ethics of the New Testament*[46] which presents a broad, fairly traditional, interpretation of early Christian ethics basically from a Protestant perspective and with an eye towards contemporary Christian conduct. Paul, of course, receives extensive consideration, following a review of OT and Hellenistic backgrounds and important themes in the Gospels.

Paul takes over, albeit critically, ethical traditions from Greek philosophy (e.g. "conscience" and vice lists from Stoicism) as well as Judaism (esp. from the Hellenistic synagogues). According to Lohse:

> In Pauline theology, the Christian ethics is developed as the formulation of the new creation in Christ appropriated in baptism. Both the promise of the gospel and the demand of the moral exhortation were always concerned to make clear that the reconciliation grounded in Christ and received on the basis of his act can never be supplemented or improved upon by our own actions done through faith in the gospel.[47]

Paul's ethical approach is shaped within apocalyptic horizons, but fundamentally is oriented to his Christology.

While Lohse presents no new thesis on Pauline ethics, this work will be acknowledged and valued for its positive restatement of fairly traditional Protestant approaches. If clarity and speculative restraint are chiefly desired characteristics, Lohse's book may be among the best of recent works on biblical ethics, and well-suited for its intended audience of pastors.

In the same year as Lohse's original volume, J. M. G. Barclay published a book on Pauline ethics which employs E. P. Sanders' suggestions to critique the traditional Protestant views that Lohse represents.[48] Barclay argues that neither Paul nor Judaism of the day regarded obedience to God's command as a means of "works righteousness." Thus in regard to Galatians the issue is not "grace vs. legal righteousness" but on what *basis* the moral life should be grounded. He thinks the Galatian Gentile believers were persuaded by Paul's opponents to keep the Mosaic law because as Christians they felt that they needed more guidance in shaping the moral life than Paul had provided. In response, Paul sets forth the adequacy and practicality of the Spirit in Christian morality.

In his presentation Barclay agrees with Sanders' description of the positive, decisive character of the law for Jewish theology but he goes beyond Sanders, arguing that Paul's ethical teachings in Galatians are essential for and coherent with his theology.[49] He thinks that Paul saw the law as useful for "staying in" (as opposed to "getting in"), but only because Paul believed that the Spirit really empowers the shaping of Christian character.

---

[46] Eduard Lohse, *Theological Ethics of the New Testament* (Philadelphia: Fortress, 1991; tr. of *Theologische Ethik des Neuen Testaments* [Stuttgart: Kohlhammer, 1988]).

[47] Ibid., 107. Thus the imperative flows out of the indicative, although both are important.

[48] John M. G. Barclay, *Obeying the Truth: A Study of Paul's Ethics in Galatians* (Edinburgh: T. & T. Clark, 1988).

[49] Barclay's study centers on Gal 5: 13–6:10, which he thinks is the real focus of the letter. The issues reflected here arise from concrete situations in Galatia which Paul addresses by pointing to the adequacy of the Spirit to provide concrete moral guidance for believers. He is at pains to point out, however, that the individual ethical instructions need not reflect specifically a concrete ethical failure in Galatia.

Barclay's study serves as a good example of key shifts which have occurred in understanding Pauline ethics since Furnish's first book. There is increased interest in the specificity of Paul's teachings rather than merely in the general principle (nature of love, Christology, etc.) behind them. Likewise, the paraenetic sections of Paul's letters have taken on an increasing importance over against the letters' "theology" (or, more accurately, over against attempts to integrate them into that theology). Still agreement is lacking on whether Paul's imperatives are well-based in his theology or only loosely connected (here Barclay, like Furnish, represents the first view, while both J. T. and E. P. Sanders are more in the latter group).

J. Paul Sampley's brief treatment of Pauline ethics focuses upon the central role that eschatology plays. [50] As the title asserts, he believes that Paul's moral reasoning is fundamentally derived from his belief that Christians live "between the times" of the two defining events: Christ's death/resurrection and his return, what Sampley calls "Paul's Frame of Reference", taken over from the world view of Jewish apocalyptic, greatly revised by Paul's commitment to the way Jesus impacts it. As people living in the "already-not yet," Christians have begun to live out of the future, empowered by the Spirit.

Sampley examines seven aspects of Paul's moral reasoning that are related to this eschatological orientation, beginning with the church and concluding with the matter of final judgment. Particularly strong is his exploration of how the role of the individual interacts with the priority of the community of faith. Still these aspects are basically expository, and frequently overlap, because Sampley thinks that one cannot distill "Pauline ethics" from their concrete presentations.

One way in which Sampley's reconstruction is distinctive is that his focus upon the two boundaries of the eschatological reality provides a clear way of dealing with the indicative-imperative question. Christians, as people between the times, are being reshaped by God into people of the coming kingdom. Thus there is theological room both for progress in the Christian life and for sanctification.

While this book shares much of the concern about social world found in Meeks, it investigates what Paul thought and taught more than how his converts conducted themselves. In this way it is an investigation of Pauline theology of ethics.

One of the most recent comprehensive examinations of NT ethics is that of Willi Marxsen. [51] In a 300+ page book, particularly focused upon *how* one speaks of Christian ethics (and/or theology) in a post-Christian era, Paul receives over a third of the allotted pages. In a way reminiscent of Bonhoeffer, Marxsen is concerned to distinguish between the authentic and the fraudulent, the truly Christian and that which claims to be Christian. Marxsen sets a formidable goal for himself, to investigate the relationships of exegesis, systematic theology and ethics in a holistic way, as his opening claim sets forth: "In our thesis we will maintain that ethics is an integral part of theology. . . . And it is essential, for without ethics theology would no longer be theology" (p. 1).

---

[50] J. Paul Sampley, *Walking Between the Times* (Minneapolis: Augsburg Fortress, 1991).

[51] Willi Marxsen, *New Testament Foundations for Christian Ethics* (Minneapolis: Fortress, 1993; tr. of *"Christliche" und christliche Ethik im Neuen Testament* [Gütersloh: Mohn, 1989]; the English title does not communicate as well what the author has in mind [lit.: *"Christian" and Christian Ethics in the New Testament*]).

Marxsen's prolegomena presents his critical assessment of the key words in the book: "Christian," "ethics" and "theology," and he argues for a Lutheran neo-orthodox understanding that stresses the "I-thou" stance that is necessary for genuine faith (and/or theology). This understanding is important for his task because he wants to establish that Christian ethics is an aspect of Christian theology (both the adjective and noun are decisive). It is not possible in this brief compass to give adequate and fair attention to this larger framework which initiates the study.

Although Marxsen begins with a lengthy (historical-critical) study of "ethics oriented towards Jesus," he gives extensive consideration to Paul as well. And his commitment to Pauline (Lutheran) theology decisively shapes what he finds (and approves!) within the NT.

Brian Rosner's recent study, *Paul, Scripture and Ethics*,[52] focuses upon 1 Corinthians 5–7, but has far-reaching implications for our topic. Rosner builds upon E. P. Sanders' proposed revision of the relationship between Paul and Judaism, but goes beyond this proposal. Whereas Sanders and others have sought to show that Paul fundamentally differed with non-Christian Judaism only on the issue of "boundary rules" for covenantal nomism, Rosner argues that Paul stands firmly within pre-Christian Judaism in his ethics, in his exegesis of biblical texts, and in his understanding of the covenant community.

He is particularly concerned to prove that Paul does not quote from the OT carelessly or only to add decoration to ethical views he acquired elsewhere. On the contrary, Israel's scriptures are a crucial and formative source of Paul's ethics, as is their mediation to Paul through Jewish moral teachings of his own day. Rosner's work calls into question not only the recurring attempt to lionize Paul at the expense of Judaism, but also those proposals which emphasize Paul's basic agreement with Judaism and yet suggest that his ethical teachings are careless or even incoherent.

Conclusion: Shifts in Pauline Ethics

One important issue at the time of Furnish's book which remains prominent today is the issue of the indicative and imperative in Paul. This key issue gathers to itself related questions of Paul's evaluation of Torah and the unity of Paul's theology and ethics. There have been many attempts to show that Paul's ethical imperatives are vitally related to his theology, but especially in recent years there is also a greater willingness to reject this suggestion by denying coherence in Paul's theology and ethics (in E. P. Sanders and H. Räisänen).

Another shift in Pauline ethics in recent works has been in the positive evaluation of his eschatology and ecclesiology in relationship to his ethics. This shift away from individualistic interpretations of Paul's ethics to those grounded in Christian community life was also an emphasis in Furnish's work. It is interesting that as Protestant scholars have given greater place to ecclesiology, Roman Catholic scholars have begun to emphasize Paul's doctrine of grace, and one can see the beginnings of a new consensus about the foundations of Paul's theological ethics.

---

[52] Brian S. Rosner, *Paul, Scripture and Ethics: A Study of 1 Corinthians 5–7* (AGAJU 22; Leiden: Brill, 1994).

Finally, some have begun to explore the impact of social structures on Paul's ethics. Early insightful test holes dug by Theissen have been followed by more comprehensive explorations by Meeks and Rosner. This development had not received much consideration in Furnish's work, although it is not incompatible with it.

Bibliography

In addition to the works discussed above, the following, published since Furnish's book, are valuable sources for the study of Pauline ethics.

Betz, Hans Dieter. *Nachfolge und Nachahmung Jesu Christi im Neuen Testament.* Tübingen: Mohr, 1967.

Bruce, F. F. "The Grace of God and the Law of Christ: A Study in Pauline Ethics." In *God and the Good: Essays in Honor of Henry Stob.* Ed. Clifton Orlebeke and Lewis Smedes. Grand Rapids, MI: Eerdmans, 1975.

Daly, Robert T. *Christian Biblical Ethics.* New York: Paulist, 1984.

Fowl, Stephen E. *The Story of Christ in the Ethics of Paul.* Sheffield: JSOT Press, 1990.

Goppelt, Leonhard. *Christologie und Ethik.* Göttingen: Vandenhoeck & Ruprecht, 1968.

Kertelge, Karl. *Ethik im Neuen Testament.* Freiburg: Herder, 1984

Longenecker, Richard. *New Testament Social Ethics for Today.* Grand Rapids, MI: Eerdmans, 1984.

Longsworth, William. "Ethics in Paul." *Annual of the Society of Christians Ethics* 1981, 229–56.

Merklein, H. *Neues Testament und Ethik.* Freiburg: Herder, 1989.

Merritt, H. W. *In Word and Deed: Moral Integrity in Paul.* Emory Studies in Early Christianity. New York: Peter Lang, 1993.

Moule, C. F. D. "Obligation in the Ethic of Paul." In *Apostolic History and the Gospel,* pp. 389–406. Ed. W. R. Farmer, C. F. D. Moule and R. R. Niebuhr. Cambridge: Cambridge University Press, 1967

Ogletree, Thomas W. *The Use of the Bible in Christian Ethics.* Philadelphia: Fortress, 1982.

Scroggs, Robin. "The New Testament and Ethics: How Do We Get From There to Here?" In *Perspectives on the New Testament.* Ed. Charles H. Talbert. Macon: Mercer University Press, 1985.

Scroggs, Robin. *The Text and the Times.* Minneapolis, MN: Fortress, 1993.

Spohn, William C. *What Are They Saying about Scripture and Ethics?* Mahwah, NJ: Paulist, 1984.

Styler, G. M. "The Basis of Obligation in Paul's Christology and Ethics." In *Christ and Spirit in the New Testament,* pp. 175–87. Ed. Barnabas Lindars and Stephen S. Smalley. Cambridge: Cambridge University Press, 1973.

Tomson, P. J. *Paul and the Jewish Law: Halakah in the Letters of the Apostle to the Gentiles.* Minneapolis: Fortress, 1990.

Westerholm, Stephen. "'Letter' and 'Spirit': The Foundation of Pauline Ethics." *NTS* 30 (1984) 229–48.

Young, Frances. "Paul and the Kingdom of God." In *The Kingdom of God and Human Society.* Ed. Robin Barbour. Edinburgh: T. & T. Clark, 1993.

Index of Biblical References

321

Index of Ancient Authors

Index of Modern Authors